Preaching Prophetic Care

Preaching Prophetic Care

Building Bridges to Justice

Essays in Honor of Dale P. Andrews

Edited by
PHILLIS-ISABELLA SHEPPARD,
DAWN OTTONI-WILHELM,
and RONALD J. ALLEN

Foreword by EMILIE M. TOWNES

◆PICKWICK *Publications* · Eugene, Oregon

PREACHING PROPHETIC CARE
Building Bridges to Justice
Essays in Honor of Dale P. Andrews

Copyright © 2018 Wipf and Stock Publishers. All rights reserved. Except for brief quotations in critical publications or reviews, no part of this book may be reproduced in any manner without prior written permission from the publisher. Write: Permissions, Wipf and Stock Publishers, 199 W. 8th Ave., Suite 3, Eugene, OR 97401.

Pickwick Publications
An Imprint of Wipf and Stock Publishers
199 W. 8th Ave., Suite 3
Eugene, OR 97401

www.wipfandstock.com

PAPERBACK ISBN: 978-1-5326-4337-8
HARDCOVER ISBN: 978-1-5326-4338-5
EBOOK ISBN: 978-1-5326-4339-2

Cataloging-in-Publication data:

Names: Sheppard, Phillis-Isabella, editor. | Ottoni-Wilhelm, Dawn, editor. | Allen, Ronald J., editor. | Townes, Emile M., foreword.

Title: Preaching prophetic care : building bridges to justice : essays in honor of Dale P. Andrews / edited by Phillis Isabella Sheppard, Dawn Ottoni-Wilhelm, and Ronald J. Allen ; foreword by emilie m. townes.

Description: Eugene, OR: Pickwick Publications, 2018. | Includes bibliographical references.

Identifiers: ISBN: 978-1-5326-4337-8 (paperback). | ISBN: 978-1-5326-4338-5 (hardcover). | ISBN: 978-1-5326-4339-2 (epub).

Subjects: LCSH: Preaching. | Andrews, Dale P.

Classification: BV4211.3 P735 2018 (print). | BV4211.3 (epub).

Manufactured in the U.S.A. 06/26/18

Scripture quotations are from Revised Standard Version of the Bible, copyright © 1946, 1952, and 1971 National Council of the Churches of Christ in the United States of America. Used by permission. All rights reserved.

Contents

Contributors | ix

Illustrations | xii

Preface | xiii

Foreword: From a Dean's Perspective | xv
    EMILIE M. TOWNES

Introduction: Brief Biographical Sketch of Dale P. Andrews—A Bridge-Building Life | xix
    AMY E. STEELE

Part 1: Preaching and Practical Theology

1 Bridges: Strong, Purposeful, and Vulnerable | 3
    MARY ELIZABETH MOORE

2 Moral Reflections on the Christian Gospel and the Struggle for Justice | 16
    PETER J. PARIS

3 Understanding the Times and Knowing What to Do | 26
    ROBERT LONDON SMITH

4 Truly More than Just: On the Bridge between the Pastoral and the Prophetic | 35
    TED A. SMITH

Part 2: The Pastoral and Prophetic in Preaching

5 Building Bridges: Pastoral Care for the World in a Prophetic Mode | 47
    RONALD J. ALLEN

6 The Prophet on the Margins | 59
    GENNIFER BENJAMIN BROOKS

7 Getting in the Way: Preacher as Urban Interpreter and Suburban Interrupter | 68
   R. Mark Giuliano

8 In Search of the Beloved Community | 78
   Debra J. Mumford

9 The Application of Moral Chemotherapy in the 21st Century: Prophetic Preaching with a Pastoral Touch | 87
   Frank A. Thomas

10 Unauthorized: Pastoral and Prophetic Utterances on the Ground | 99
   Lisa L. Thompson

Part 3: Prophetic Care, Preaching, and Wider Community

11 Emancipatory Practice: Institutional Maintenance and Prophetic Witness | 113
   Donna E. Allen

12 A Church that Will Survive: Prophetic Proclamation, Community Wellness and Clergy Well Being | 120
   Kenyatta R. Gilbert

13 Prophetic Preaching in a Pastoral Mode: Communities of Solidarity and the White Mainline Church | 129
   David Schnasa Jacobsen

14 In Search of a Prophetic Twenty-first Century Church | 138
   William B. McClain

15 Building Bridges Week by Week | 146
   Mary Alice Mulligan

Part 4: Learning to Preach in the Mode of Prophetic Care

16 Building Bridges: Pedagogical Reflections on a Black Lives Matter Resistance Hermeneutic for Preaching | 161
   L. Susan Bond

17 "That Being Said": A Pastoral Prophetic Transition for Doing Justice | 172
   Teresa L. Fry Brown

18 Encountering the Word: Dale Andrews' Inductive Pedagogy for Prophetic Preaching | 181
   John S. McClure

19 Preaching the Mystery of God's Reign: Encounter, Re-encounter, and
    Pre-encounter | 191
    DAWN OTTONI-WILHELM

20 "The Thursday After:" The Crisis of Formation in the Post-Election
    Theological Classroom | 202
    SHELLY RAMBO

Part 5: Prophetic Care: Particular Topics

21 The Importance of the Pastoral and the Prophetic: For Preaching
    among the Traumatized | 217
    TERESA LOCKHART EISENLOHR

22 Tending the Methodist Roots of Preaching and Pastoral Care | 228
    G. LEE RAMSEY, JR.

23 "The Wrath of God's Love:" Ethical Tension
    in Social Justice Preaching | 240
    AMY E. STEELE

24 Restoration and Resistance: Restorative Justice
    and Black Practical Theology | 247
    SCOTT C. WILLIAMSON

25 A Three-Fold Homiletic Lesson from Dr. King's Pastoral and Prophetic
    Preaching on Violence | 266
    SUNGGU YANG

Part 6: Sermons that Embody Prophetic Care

26 A Biblical Apprenticeship in Bridge-Building Ministry: A Two-Part
    Series | 277
    LUKE A. POWERY

27 The Wall at the Well: A Sermon on John 4:3–30, with Reflection | 290
    ANNA CARTER FLORENCE

Appendix A: New to Whom? | 299
    DALE P. ANDREWS

Appendix B: A Partial Bibliography of the Works of Dale P. Andrews | 302

Bibliography | 305

Contributors

Donna E. Allen, Founder & Senior Pastor New Revelation Community Church, and Visiting Professor of Preaching and New Testament, American Baptist Seminary of the West

Ronald J. Allen, Professor of Preaching, and Gospels and Letters, Christian Theological Seminary

L. Susan Bond, Associate Professor of Religion, Lane College

Gennifer Benjamin Brooks, Ernest and Bernice Styberg Professor of Preaching, Garrett Evangelical Theological Seminary

Teresa Fry Brown, Bandy Professor of Preaching, Candler School of Theology, Emory University

Teresa Lockhart Eisenlohr, Theologian in the Presbyterian Church (USA), Licensed Massage Therapist

Anna Carter Florence, Peter Marshall Professor of Preaching and Worship, Columbia Theological Seminary

Kenyatta R. Gilbert, Associate Professor of Homiletics, The Divinity School, Howard University

R. Mark Giuliano, Senior Minister, Old Stone Church (First Presbyterian Church), Cleveland, Ohio

David Shnasa Jacobsen, Professor of the Practice of Homiletics, and the Director of the Homiletical Theology Project, School of Theology, Boston University

William B. McClain, Mary Elizabeth McGehee Joyce Professor of Preaching, Emeritus, Wesley Theological Seminary

John S. McClure, Charles G. Finney, Professor of Preaching and Worship, The Divinity School, Vanderbilt University

Mary Elizabeth Moore, Dean of the School of Theology, Professor of Theology and Education, Co-Director of the Center for Practical Theology, Boston University

Mary Alice Mulligan, Minister, Westview Christian Church (Disciples of Christ), Indianapolis, Indiana, and Affiliate Professor of Homiletics and Ethics, Christian Theological Seminary

Debra Mumford, Frank H. Caldwell Professor of Homiletics, Director of the Money Matters for Ministry Program, Louisville Presbyterian Theological Seminary

Dawn Ottoni-Wilhelm, Brightbill Professor of Preaching and Worship, Bethany Theological Seminary

Peter J. Paris, Elmer G. Homrighausen Professor, Emeritus, Christian Social Ethics, Princeton Theological Seminary

Luke A. Powery, Dean of the Chapel, Duke University, and Associate Professor of Homiletics, The Divinity School, Duke University

Shelly Rambo, Associate Professor of Theology, School of Theology, Boston University

G. Lee Ramsey, Jr., Marlon and Sheila Foster Professor of Pastoral Theology and Homiletics, Director of the Methodist House of Studies, Memphis Theological Seminary

Phillis Isabella Sheppard, Associate Professor of Religion, Psychology and Culture, The Divinity School, and the Graduate Department of Religion, Vanderbilt University

Robert London Smith, Jr., Minister, Rubislaw Parish Church, Aberdeen, U.K., and Honorary Researcher in Practical Theology, King's College at University of Aberdeen, U.K.

Ted A. Smith, Associate Professor of Preaching and Ethics, Candler School of Theology, Emory University

Amy E. Steele, Assistant Dean for Student Life, The Divinity School, Vanderbilt University

Frank A. Thomas, Nettie Sweeney and Hugh Th. Miller Professor of Homiletics, and Director of the Academy of Preaching and Celebration, Christian Theological Seminary

Lisa Thompson, Assistant Professor of Homiletics, Union Theological Seminary

Emilie M. Townes, Dean, and E. Rhodes and Leona B. Carpenter Professor of Womanist Ethics and Society, The Divinity School, Vanderbilt University

Scott C. Williamson, Robert H. Walkup Professor of Theological Ethics, Louisville Presbyterian Theological Seminary

Sunggu Yang, Assistant Professor of Christian Ministries, College of Christian Studies, George Fox University

Illustrations

Figure 1: Relationship of the Pastoral and the Prophetic | 50
Figure 2: Encounter, Pre-encounter, Re-encounter | 183

Preface

This book is a *Festschrift* in memory of Dale P. Andrews, who was a greatly respected and much-loved figure in the worlds of preaching and practical theology. When he was diagnosed with a serious form of cancer in the winter of 2016–2017, a group of his colleagues resolved to celebrate him and his work by putting together a collection of essays in his honor. Ordinarily, a volume of this kind is at least a year in preparation, usually two years or more. Because of the severity of the illness, and the uncertainty of its timeline, the writers prepared their essays in only a few months. Dale was presented with a rough draft of the collection on Sunday, June 19, 2017. He entered the larger life with God on Friday, June 23, 2017. Seldom is divine providence so evident as in the completion of these essays in time for Professor Andrews to have seen them.

The title of the book, *Prophetic Care,* comes from Professor Andrews himself, who used this expression to describe the underlying purpose of prophetic ministry: the prophet expresses care for the world in moods that range from the confrontative (e.g. Amos) to the consoling (e.g. Deutero-Isaiah).[1] The writers in this volume focus on themes that were central to Professor Andrews' life and work, especially prophetic care through building bridges among communities that often live across chasms. The writers particularly focus on how prophetic preaching and practical theological reflection can serve the larger purpose of bridge building. In a way that befits Dale's conversational spirit, the writers look at these topics from distinctive, even differing, viewpoints.

While the chapters in the book highlight Dale Andrews' particular contributions to preaching and practical theology, they do so in ways that

---

1. See Andrews, "We're Never Done with the Work."

make his work accessible and applicable to preachers and practical theologians in the broader currents of their work. The book does not push a particular ideology of prophetic preaching and practical theology, but seeks to be part of the wider conversation around these topics in the church and academy today.

Some writers in this collection directly interact with Dale's work. Others contribute scholarship in Dale's honor without making reference to Dale's own scholarship. These multiple styles befit one of Dale's central concerns: to honor the diversity of life.

After an appreciation for Dale's spirit by the Dean of The Divinity School, Vanderbilt University, and a brief summary of his life and work, the collection proper begins with four essays that provide overarching perspectives on bridges between prophetic preaching and practical theology. Several authors then offer interpretations with differing nuances on the relationship between the pastoral and the prophetic. Five writers consider practical approaches to pastoral preaching in a prophetic mode in and through the church. After six essays on implications for learning and teaching how to preach prophetically, another six authors focus on prophetic preaching in regard to several particular topics. The book concludes a most fitting way for a volume honoring a professor of preaching and practical theology: with sermons that illustrate the fruit of his perspectives. Within each section, the contributions are printed alphabetically in order of the last names of the contributors.

Finally, this volume includes a representative piece of scholarship from Professor Andrews' own fertile mind (Appendix A) and an abbreviated *curriculum vitae* (Appendix B).

The contributors send this book forth, not with the attitude it contains "the answer" to issues related to prophetic preaching and practical theological analysis but in the hope that it will enrich the ongoing search for how to engage these things adequately in a season of national life when so much is at stake. We pray that Dale's overflowing and reconciling spirit infuses these essays.

All citations from the Bible are from the New Revised Standard Version except as noted.

Foreword
From a Dean's Perspective

EMILIE M. TOWNES

ONE OF THE GREAT pleasures I have had as Dean of the Vanderbilt Divinity School (VDS) was to recommend Dale for one of our new Cornelius Vanderbilt Chairs in the university. At every stage of the process, the response was a resounding yes to this appointment. Dale's contributions to the Divinity School, the university, his professional societies, and his church were outstanding and a model for younger scholars. Indeed, Dale was a strong and valued collegial partner for so many of us who knew him and worked with him over the years.

Many contributors to this volume rehearse his accomplishments as a scholar, teacher, preacher, and son of the African Methodist Episcopal Zion Church. I focus on Dale as a colleague—and a fine one at that. His ability to listen and tease through the many layers that were always present in faculty meetings, committee meetings, and professional society meetings helping bring a sense of humanity to our discussions. He always reminded us that we were not talking about objects but about human beings who are in need of compassion as much as rigorous examination if it was a student we are considering for admission into the graduate program or a junior colleague who was being considered for review or promotion and tenure in the university committees. It is a true testament to Dale's remarkable ability to speak with insight and precision that he could differ with peers, yet maintain his collegial commitments in vigorous faculty debates. And then, regardless of the outcome, Dale worked to implement the decision that was made without rancor or lingering ill-will.

This ability to be present with his peers is the kind of glue that any good faculty needs and his wry sense of humor and infamous one-liners reminded all of us that we need to take life a bit more lightly at times because we will still be able to get the work done that must be done to keep us moving toward the vision we have set for ourselves to teach and research and speak in a global and multi-religious world.

He brought the fullness of who he was as a pastoral theologian into his life with us at Vanderbilt Divinity School. Because Dale was concerned with the application of the study of religion in the context of church ministry, he focused on the pragmatic rather than the speculative in equipping pastors and laity to meet the demands of ministry for our time. He also encouraged us as colleagues to take up this call in our work in the other disciplines present in our theological school. Yes, Dale was fully immersed in the discipline of homiletics; however, his research interests extended beyond the field of homiletics in an interdisciplinary method where he combined it with pastoral care, ethics, and liturgical studies. His writing, teaching, and research were centered around the notion that pastors and churches must balance their pastoral and prophetic roles to be in healthy and nurturing mutual relationships with each other. Thus, he was deliberate in combining social justice and practical theology in his work.

His commitments manifest in how he was always willing to extend the ways in which his Preaching in the Black Church Tradition program that is lodged in our Kelly Miller Smith Institute on Black Church Studies (KMSI) could further the programing for the benefit of students and colleagues in VDS and in other schools and churches. Through this program, he also partnered with Woman Preach! founded by our colleague Dr. Valerie Bridgeman of the Methodist Theological School of Ohio. Dale believed deeply in sharing the resources he had with his colleagues and with his students because for him, generosity was a key biblical message that we must live by. He understood the grace that is found in giving to others and how diminished we are when we hoard our gifts, our knowledge, our joy in God's good creation.

As a colleague, Dale balanced the pastoral and prophetic in who he was and how he was on our faculty. His deep love for people and his astute analysis of institutions lead him to encourage and model healthy and nurturing mutual relationships. As we met over coffee (anyone who knew Dale, knew that his true office was several branches of coffee shops in Nashville) shortly after his cancer diagnosis, I was struck with how much Dale ministered to me and allowed me to minister to him at the same time. He was still stunned by the unexpected diagnosis but he was also building his determination to fight with every ounce of his being to live for his family and for his three young children. I listened as he sorted through when and how to tell folks—not wanting to ruin the Christmas holiday or New Year's celebrations for family, colleagues, and friends. I was struck—and remain so—by the deep care Dale had for all of us. But this was not selfless, for he was worried about himself and what the future might hold for him. He was, once again, modeling the deep richness of humanity as we talked.

I think the best way to describe Dale is that he lived a life of love. True enough, in many ways love is one of the most theologically, ethically, psychologically, and culturally ambiguous concepts we have. We parse notions of love and loving in so many ways—from living it close to the depths of our innards to holding it far away, yet close. I suspect that Dale knew all about the ways we describe love. What I find so heartening about him is that he moved in and out of the ways we reach out to each other with care and compassion with seeming effortlessness. If what is called for is passionate regard or spiritual depth or friendship or compassion or mutuality or self-giving love, Dale was able to be present in those ways with the fullness of his integrity and his profound belief in a God who makes a way out of no way. My experience of Dale's ability to love reminds me that love is one more piece to the fabric of the universe, one more way to signal this restless journey we are on, one more sign that the Emmaus Road is not the end of the journey but its beginning.

A dean cannot ask for anything more from a faculty member! Dale was a colleague who stuck with you and stood beside you, telling you the truths you may or may not want to hear, and listening oh so deeply to our beating hearts, our visions, and the possibilities that were always standing before us.

Introduction: Brief Biographical Sketch of Dale P. Andrews

A Bridge-Building Life

AMY E. STEELE

ON A FLIGHT BACK from Grand Rapids, Michigan, from the Calvin Institute of Christian Worship, a gathering of representatives from divinity schools and seminaries wanting to strengthen preaching, I was fortunate to be seated in the same row as Dale Andrews. We were two-thirds of the delegation from The Divinity School, Vanderbilt University. The usual harmless sarcastic banter in which Dale and I often engaged, peppered with thoughtful reflection, was different this time—more personal. Dale shared a bit of family history, which I found fascinating. His family of origin hails from Cape Verde (now the Republic of Cabo Verde) off the Northwest coast of Africa. These tiny islands in the Atlantic, which served as a European colonial outpost settled by the Portuguese in the 15th century, are home to Dale's ancestors.

Of African and Portuguese blood, mixed slave and free, his people later came to the US and settled in New England. They brought with them religion, song, story, and dreams of a better life. I had known Dale for a short time, just six years, but knowing this particular Diasporic story gave me much more of backdrop for the origins and aims of Dale's work toward justice, transformation, and hope. I could not have been happier to have been given a closer glimpse of someone whom many of us call colleague and friend.

From Dale's story that day I began to understand more of his situatedness, beyond the esteemed appointments and teaching and preaching engagements that have characterized his life. He was a man transcending and yet embedded in complicated histories and complex global networks, who for the time I knew him, was mentor, colleague, and friend. The multiple dimensions of our relationship illustrate a major theme of his life—building bridges from one relationship to another. His was a bridge building life.

His professional *curriculum vitae* is included in this book as Appendix B. However, Dale's CV—lengthy as it is—is not exhaustive. While it does summarize several broad, impressive lines of Dale's work, it does not fully capture the spirit and the nuances of the person that was Dale.

Dale graduated from Wesleyan University in 1983 with an A.B. in sociology and religion. He completed the MDiv at Princeton Theological Seminary in 1991 with a concentration in clinical social work. He completed the MA and the PhD from Vanderbilt University in 1997 and 1998, majoring in homiletics as well as Religion and Personality. Schools in each phase of his academic preparation showered him with honors. Princeton, for instance, awarded him the Graduate Student Fellowship, which sent him to Oxford University for a year. At Vanderbilt, he was a Dorothy Danforth Compton Fellow.

An ordained minister in the African Methodist Episcopal Zion Church, his ministerial identity was central to Dale's sense of his life and calling. Dale served as minister in AME Zion congregations in Connecticut, New Jersey, Kentucky, and Massachusetts. Like many other ministers of that movement, Dale always carried a sermon with him (often on paper, always in mind) so that he could preach at a moment's notice.

His initial teaching appointment was at Louisville Presbyterian Theological Seminary where he was appointed to the Frank H. Caldwell Chair of Homiletics. At Louisville, he began a life-long scholarly partnership with John S. McClure. Few colleagues have enjoyed such remarkable chemistry that showed itself not only in their joint projects but in the ways in which they strengthened each other's distinctive work. Few colleagues have enjoyed such comprehensive life connectedness as their households have become entwined in mutual support.

Dale served as Martin Luther King, Jr. Professor of Homiletics and Pastoral Theology at The School of Theology, Boston University. At Boston, Dale supervised a PhD program in preaching and was, again, the quintessential colleague. In addition to their academic ability, the graduates of the PhD program are noted for their diversity, embodying Dale's passionate commitment to a truly inclusive world. The graduating class of 2007 voted Dale the Teaching Excellence Award.

In 2010 Dale returned to Vanderbilt as a faculty member in the Divinity School and the Graduate Department of Religion of the faculty of

Vanderbilt University. The title of his initial appointment shows the regard with which he came to Vanderbilt. *Distinguished Professor of Homiletics, Social Justice, and Practical Theology.* As Dean emilie townes notes in her Forward to this volume, his scholarly work, his role as a teacher and mentor, his leadership, and his person prompted her to nominate him for the highest faculty appointment at Vanderbilt: a Cornelius Vanderbilt Chair.

In addition to an array of chapters in diverse volumes and journal articles, he authored and edited several pivotal books.[2] His *Practical Theology for Black Churches: Bridging Black Theology and African American Folk Religion* (2002) is a multidimensional foundational work that sets out a methodology for practical theology in African American contexts while simultaneously seeking to bridge a chasm between academic African American liberation theology and the folk theology of many African American congregations. This book represents an essential theme of Dale's work and life: building bridges that bring people together in ways that honor the Otherness of all. With Robert London Smith, he edited *Black Practical Theology* (2015), a comprehensive guide to the interface of traditional academic disciplines and practical theology in African American ecclesial settings. We can see the expansive vision of the editors in a remarkable feature of this book: it brings together not only scholars but also ministers from various expressions of the church, as well as leaders of religious communities beyond traditional ecclesial structures.

Dale's ambassadorial orientation is revealed in the number of books he co-authored and co-edited. He was a leading member of one of the first groups to engage in the empirical study of what happens when people hear sermons: *Listening to Listeners: Homiletical Case Studies* (2004). He helped conceive and edit *Preaching God's Transforming Justice* (2011, 2012, 2013), a commentary on every Bible reading in the Revised Common Lectionary from the perspective of social justice. This innovative series proposes adding 22 new Holy Days for Justice to the lectionary itself, such as Universal Declaration of Human Rights, Martin Luther King Day, Oscar Romero of the Americas Day, Earth Day, Sojourner Truth Day, World AIDS Day, and Children's Sabbath. His contributions to *New Proclamation: Advent through Holy Week, Year A, 2004–2005* (2004) illustrate his exquisite capacity for finding fresh insights in familiar texts. To these volumes must be added about 100 chapters in books and articles in scholarly and pastoral journals.

Dale formerly served as co-editor to the journal *Family Ministry*, and was co-editor, with John McClure, of *Homiletic,* the official scholarly journal

---

2. For a partial bibliography of Professor Andrews' published works, see Appendix B.

of record for the Academy of Homiletics. He was on the editorial boards of too many journals to enumerate here.

At the time of his death, Dale's research projects included a homiletic textbook based in apprenticeship pedagogy, and another textbook addressing challenges facing black prophetic preaching. Dale's bridging spirit shines through both of these projects. He sought to help contemporary theological education learn from the established practice of apprenticeship as pedagogy characteristic of African American church life. He also sought to help preachers speak prophetically in ways that name injustice and call for a transformed society, while seeking patterns of communication that could encourage communities across the racial and ethnic spectrum to become more open and empowered to act in solidarity with justice.

Dale's life included a trail of leadership recognized by the various academic, churchly, and other communities of which he was part. He was President of both the principal academic guilds of his life vocation—the Academy of Homiletics and the Association of Practical Theology. He was on numerous governing and advisory boards ranging from the Fund for Theological Education to WomanPreach! Inc. He was co-founder and co-director of the *David G. Buttrick Homiletics Peer-Coaching Training Program*, a revolutionary collegial approach to improving preaching for established ministers through working together in cohort groups.

Dale was a staple contributor to the lecture circuit, speaking in distinguished series on multiple continents, including the Gardner C. Taylor Lectureship at The Divinity School, Duke University, and the Plenary Lecture, Workshop & Sermon for te Folkekirkens Uddannelses-og Videnscenter Conference in Copenhagen, Denmark.

No interpretive sketch of Dale's life would be complete without reference to his covenantal life partner, Barbara, and their striking family. Here again we see the integrity between Dale's theological orientation on reconciliation in the communities of humankind and nature, and the way he lived. When their son Edwin had reached young adulthood, at the age when most parents are looking forward to an empty nest, Barbara and Dale reached out, and welcomed three more children into their family: Lucas, Mia, and Jonas. Their household is a prolepsis of the eschatological world.

What we know of Dale, his beautiful family, his teaching, writing, committee work, mentoring graduate students, commitments to professional guilds, the church, communities of social protest and transformation, is that Dale's life is a celebration of a loving and just God. His life is a testimony to an unrestricted God whose commitment to create just community is unrelenting and whose mercy knows no end.

Part 1

Preaching and Practical Theology

1

Bridges
Strong, Purposeful, and Vulnerable

Mary Elizabeth Moore

I knew Dale Andrews as a bridge-builder and this volume is dedicated to his passion for creating connections. When Dale was a faculty member at Boston University School of Theology, he was a quintessential connector. He built friendships among people, relationships between the school and churches, and vigorous dialogue across diverse fields of interest, especially attending to his own fields of pastoral care and preaching. Intellectually, Dale was also a connector, linking ideas from church practice and family life to theological and political constructs, and analyzing the connection-breaking practices in social organizations that hurt people who are most vulnerable. He continually sought ways to analyze issues and then to address and transform them into new possibilities. He has been sorely missed since he departed BU School of Theology, but he left a legacy that continues. For this, we are abundantly grateful.

The focus of this chapter is on the practice of bridging, apropos to the legacy of Dale Andrews. I begin, however, with the recognition that bridging is itself a complicated phenomenon. Bridges bring people together and open new possibilities for travel and relationships, but they can also lead into the unknown and affect people and lands in unexpected ways. Thus, I begin with a meditation on bridges and bridging.

> Bridges—pathways between
>> One place and another
>> One people or nation and another
>> One culture, one perspective, one value and another-
>> One and another!
>
> Bridges—strong and beautiful
>> Places to cross as you travel
>> Places to stand as you gaze at the world
>> Places to feel the textures of life—
>> People passing, wind blowing, rain falling, sun shining.
>
> Bridges—structures of purpose for travelers
>> As they journey toward basic life needs
>> As they work, trade, and play
>> As they reach toward others
>> To reshape the clay of a world gone astray.
>
> Bridges—vulnerable to powers of change
>> To the natural elements of wind, sun, and rain
>> To travelers' trodding through eons of time
>> To political maneuvers and competitive forces
>> To changes that erode, destroy, and refine.
>
> Bridges—pathways to hope
>> Hope for human meeting
>> Hope for ecological care
>> Hope for justice and reconciliation
>> In a world longing for life-giving connection!

Bridges come in many forms—land bridges between continents, natural stone bridges across ravines, human-built bridges across waterways, and paths between animals' natural habitats. One could name others. In all of these forms, bridges have *three persisting qualities: they are strong, purposeful, and vulnerable.* In this chapter, I focus particularly on bridges in practical theology—Dale's home field of study and a field that is desperately in need of bridges.

STRONG BRIDGING

Bridges have to be strong to support movement from one place to another and communication across geographical distance or differences in race, culture, gender identity, sexual orientation, ability, age, language, life experience, or worldview. In practical theology, the bridges have to be strong to link people concerned with diverse theological and existential issues, "sub-fields" of practical theology, methodologies, religious traditions, human communities, social patterns, and ecological systems. One major challenge facing practical theology worldwide is to cultivate communication links that enrich the field, encouraging vast diversity while providing common ground for mutual learning and shared work. This is challenging for a newly recovered field in which competition for correctness is wide-spread, complicated by the domination of some intellectual, religious, and cultural traditions over others.

I propose that practical theology—a field of analytic reflection, poetics, and practice—needs strong bridges to foster life-giving relationships in and across religious communities and in the larger society. Practical theology is a field marked by fragmentation—valuing some scholars more than others, some fields (or subfields) more than others, and some regions of the world over others. Our guild has also tilted toward some ethnic scholars and ethnic communities and some genders more than others. I remember sitting with two African American colleagues in 2001 when Fred Smith, also African American, gave a plenary address in the International Academy of Practical Theology. When the address ended, they jumped to their feet with vigorous applause and said to me, "At last, we hear an address that really matters." Dr. Smith had described practical theology that was engaged with the church and with young people in a challenging culture. The incident represents a continuing pattern, leading many Black scholars to find organizations and conferences that are more relevant to them. Bonnie Miller-McLemore tracks similar gendered patterns in the International Academy of Practical Theology.[1]

Dale Andrews was himself a bridge within the field, bridging predominantly European and European-American scholarship with African American scholarship, bridging theoretical developments with African American church life, bridging practical theology with other areas of theology, and bridging homiletics and pastoral theology. Each of these bridging efforts has been significant, building a very strong matrix of bridges that will endure.

Early in Dale's academic career, he was concerned about the disconnection between developments in Black theology and the life of Black churches, describing "the actual situation between the academy of black theology and black churches as a chasm."[2] He described his own work as bridging "the theological axioms of black theology and the faith claims operating in African American folk religion."[3] In excavating the chasm,

---

1. Miller-McLemore, "Tale of Two Cities."
2. Andrews, *Practical Theology* 2.
3. Ibid.

Dale recognized the wisdom that emerged on both sides of the bridge and the urgency to build deeper relationships. He identified a paradigm of "the church as refuge," which could draw upon the wisdom of black churches and scholarship, while holding the deep spiritual traditions and liberative movements of African American peoples.[4] Dale's work also drew from deep biblical veins of tradition, featuring especially covenant and prophecy.[5] His passion for bridging was already born in that first book.

Dale also worked to connect church life and homiletic theory through his specialized work in preaching. One impressive example appears in print. Joining with five colleagues, he produced a collection of homiletical case studies.[6] The purpose was to "listen to listeners" of sermons, interviewing people in congregations to discern their experience of hearing sermons. The interviewees included 260 African American and Caucasian congregants of diverse ages and genders from urban, rural, and suburban churches of many sizes and denominations. The team analyzed listeners' perceptions in Aristotelian rhetorical categories, and presented five representative interviews and one small group interview as case studies. The purpose was to invite preachers and scholars to ponder the wisdom of listeners via cases, then to reflect on insights from the interviews and consider approaches that preachers can use to listen to their congregations. The book reveals many forms of bridging-bridging homileticians with the book's six authors, bridging preachers and listeners, and bridging research with practices of preaching and listening.

Dale's most recent book involved multiple forms of bridging as well. In *Black Practical Theology*, he and Robert London Smith Jr. created a comprehensive hermeneutical conversation that spans many topics: youth, intergenerational relations and ageism; education, class and poverty; gender, sexual orientation and race; and mass incarceration and the justice system. Further, each part includes a conversation with a practical theologian, church leader, and scholar in constructive theological, biblical, and ethical disciplines. Thus, the book is a series of dialogues among people who are diverse in professional roles and yet all concerned with faith in life. Dale often used the term "trialogues" to note the multiple partners in these conversations. The conversations represent "praxiological response criticism," focusing on the experiences and perspectives of people in faith communities in

---

4. Ibid., 34–37.
5. Ibid., 106–28.
6. McClure, et. al. *Listening to Listeners*.

dialogue with theological traditions, which allow all participants to probe complexities and seek guidance for the future.[7]

The kind of bridging work represented by these several publications is testimony to the freshness of Dale Andrews' contributions and his love for complicating dominant assumptions. I recently studied *Black Practical Theology* with a class and I witnessed its generativity for students of many backgrounds—African American, Latinx, Asian, and European American. The specificity of the conversations that focused on the Black church and Black theology touched a chord in readers, as did the conversations themselves. What makes all of Dale's bridging strong is that he built bridge upon bridge for more than 20 years, with publications, lectures, classes, workshops, and interpersonal relationships. With his characteristic vision and persistence, he built bridges of understanding, questioning, and passion on which others will continue to build.

What is needed in practical theology is similar vision and persistence in building bridges. Many have directed themselves to this kind of work in recent years to beneficial effect.[8] The work has only just begun, however, and much more is needed, hopefully led by persons of color and people whose fields and interests have been underrepresented thus far in practical theology. The efforts of many scholars are an important beginning, but scholars such as Courtney Goto remind us of the endemic problems in tokenizing people of color to represent their ethnic communities in a single chapter and not considering white cultures at the same time.[9] What is needed is a reshaping of practical theology with strong bridges for the ongoing work of sharing, listening, questioning and transforming.

PURPOSEFUL BRIDGING

Strong bridges are not sufficient in themselves. What is also needed in practical theology is purposeful bridges that contribute to life. Practical theologians are often preoccupied with definitions and methodologies of the field, paying less attention to the purposes of practical theology in theological and religious studies, religious communities, and the larger society. One can find many exceptions to this, and I name a few here as a sample: Elaine Graham on public theology; John Swinton on disability and ableism; Dale Andrews and colleagues Dawn Ottoni-Wilhelm and Ronald Allen on race, racism,

---

7. Andrews and Smith, eds., *Black Practical Theology*, 11–19, esp. 18–19.

8. Mercer and Miller-McLemore, eds., *Conundrums in Practical Theology*; Cahalan and Mikoski, eds., *Opening the Field*; Miller-McLemore, *Wiley-Blackwell Companion*.

9. Goto, "Writing in Compliance," 110–33.

and social justice; Elizabeth Conde-Frazier on immigrant experience and justice; Katherine Turpin on youth and consumerism; Jeffery Tribble on transformative leadership and congregations; Christian Scharen on church, leadership, and culture; Pamela Couture on peacebuilding; Evelyn Parker on youth and gender, race, and class; Jaco Dreyer, Yolanda Dreyer, Edward Foley, and Malan Nel on human dignity and injustice; Claire Wolfteich on spirituality, women, and public life; Bonnie Miller-McLemore on parenting and childhood; my work with Almeda Wright on youth, justice, and spirituality; and Phillis Sheppard on gender, race, culture and embodiment.[10] These are a few examples of practical theological scholars who address issues of the church and world, and the list is incomplete, even in the publications of the scholars named. In addition, some scholars have begun to address religious diversity as a practical theological focus.[11] This list is partial, but it reveals the vitality and diversity of purposes in practical theology. Many authors have contributed mightily to strong bridging and purposive scholarship.

What then is the problem? Practical theology often lacks bridges that foster dialogue across the diverse issues and areas of research that concern practical theologians; thus, discourses across the matrix of shared purposes are thin. People tend to read and quote the work that focuses on purposes similar to their own interests, but not entertain the vast range of purposes that fuel practical theology. This is a normal and time-efficient approach in light of the vast diversity of concerns; however, it limits the discourse. Further, the silo approach obviates against purposes themselves being significant subjects for discussion. This is an issue that Dale Andrews understood, even as he tried to bring people together-preachers and listeners, and theological scholars and church leaders. He wanted people to hear one another and to consider seriously the diverse passions and concerns that diverse people bring to the table.

To appreciate the challenge of purposeful practical theology and purposeful bridging, consider the global contexts that pull people and ecosystems apart. These contexts form practical theology, and are potentially transformed by it; thus, practical theology functions and sometimes malfunctions within them. The universe itself is relational through and

---

10. Graham, *Between a Rock and a Hard Place*; Swinton, *Becoming Friends*; Andrews and Smith, eds., *Black Practical Theology*; Allen, et. al. *Preaching God's Transforming Justice*. 3 vols.; Conde-Frazier, *Listen to the Children*; Turpin, *Branded*; Tribble, *Transformative Pastoral Leadership*; Scharen, *Fieldwork in Theology*; Couture, *We Are Not All Victims*; Parker, *Sacred Selves*; Dreyer et al. *Practicing Ubuntu*; Wolfteich, *Mothering*; Miller-McLemore, *In the Midst of Chaos*; Moore and Wright, *Children, Youth, and Spirituality*; Sheppard, *Self, Culture and Others*.

11. Cahalan and Schuurman, *Calling*; Greider, "Religiously Plural Persons."

through, but many relationships are destructive and, because the universe is relational, the destruction runs deep and stretches wide. Injurious relationships pit one person, social group, or nation against another. The relations persist, but are poisonous.

The forms of destruction are myriad. Some relationships *abuse* people and ecosystems, creating perpetual wars, cycles of poverty, human rights violations, violence against immigrant or LGBTQ people, violence against racial or religious groups, and abuse in families. Some relationships *perpetuate fear and insecurity*, such as threats against immigrants, fear of violation by powerful people and political factions, or fear of criminal justice systems that reinforce discriminatory practices against racial and ethnic minorities. Further, some relationships *perpetuate stereotypes, discrimination, and scapegoating*. Stereotyping extends in all directions, but some obvious ones are disproportional blaming of some racial-ethnic communities for street violence and blaming pre-selected religious communities for terrorist acts. Stereotyping is used to justify discrimination and scapegoating, thus reinforcing fear and unjust systems. Racial stereotyping is a global phenomenon, but the United States has a long history of stereotyping and scapegoating Native American, African American, pan-African, Latino, and Asian communities. Such practices incite abuse and the destruction of peoples and cultures. Stereotyping of Jews in early twentieth century Germany and elsewhere in Europe led to the annihilation of 6 million Jews in the Holocaust. Today Muslims are stereotyped and scapegoated with terrorist labels, stirring violence against them. The relations across stereotyping, scapegoating, and abuse are frightening.

These examples reveal the dangers that lurk in relationships and the urgent need for strong bridges toward understanding, acceptance, and shared action for good. Mai-An Le Tran describes dangerous relationships as "communicable diseases" that fuel a "virus of fear."[12] She implies that relationships are not actually broken, but diseased. Thus, we do *not* need bridges that link people in ways that perpetuate abuse, fear and insecurity, and stereotypes, discrimination, and scapegoating. We need bridges that link people in relationships that contribute to more compassionate and just futures. Le Tran defines communicability as "the capability of impactful transference through contact," recognizing that human contact may transfer impactful destruction as well as impactful hope.[13] She argues for a "communicable Christian community" that cultivates life-protecting and life-giving

---

12. Mai-Anh Le Tran, *Reset*, 78.
13. Ibid., 79.

relationships (my language) and minimizes those that destroy life.¹⁴ I suggest that the same is true for other religious communities and that concerns for disease include not only human communities but also the whole ecosystem. Relationships within an ecosystem have potential to maximize destruction or to enhance life. A communicable Christian community, or communicable Jewish or Muslim or Buddhist community, has potential to support and enhance life across the human family and ecosystem.

Purposeful bridging has potential to bring practical theologians together around existential and meta-cultural issues such as abuse, fear, and the interplay of stereotyping and scapegoating. *Such bridging also has potential to inspire mutual learning among people with diverse purposes.* For example, the work of John Swinton on disability and ableism has important contributions to make to people who work on issues of cultural diversity, human rights, and dignity. Similarly, the work of Dale Andrews and several others focused on the African American community informs people who work on issues of immigration, congregational complexity, pastoral leadership, and religious diversity. When these various issues are placed into silos, the possibilities of mutual learning across diverse purposes is seriously stunted. Consider the alternative possibilities. Elizabeth Conde-Frazier's work on listening to immigrant children interplays with Bonnie Miller-McLemore's work on parenting and children, and it also has potential to inform the work of Chris Scharen or Jeffery Tribble when they study congregations and pastoral leadership ethnographically.

Two primary issues emerge if we do not attend to purposeful bridging. First, we *fail to listen and learn from one another* and, second, we *fail to join our collective wisdom and action to address issues of suffering in the world*. I have made the first point above, but I will amplify the second with an example from the International Academy of Practical Theology (IAPT). During the period 1999–2001, I served as President. In the 1999 business meeting, the African members offered to host the 2001 conference and they proposed that the conference theme focus on HIV/AIDs because of the tragic physical and social consequences of the disease across their continent. Many non-African members raised concerns about the specificity of the theme. A compromise was struck and the theme was set to be suffering, with a sub-focus on HIV/AIDs. In the same 1999 business meeting, a motion passed to increase the number of women members. Sentiments were simultaneously expressed to increase the number of members from underrepresented ethnicities and countries. Because these actions were at the beginning of my Presidential term, I joyfully threw myself into making these

---

14. Ibid., 80–81.

things happen; however, I received many emails and phone calls regarding the limiting nature of our conference theme and the problematics of diversifying our membership. Some people did not attend the next conference.

I share this example without rancor toward people who raised the issues, but to point to a deeper issue. The case reveals a pattern of resistance to intellectual interactions across lines of ethnicity, nationality, and issues of concern. While the example is now almost 20 years old, the pattern continues in far-reaching, often subtle ways: sometimes small groups with similar interests request a major session to share their work without showing interest or attending sessions on others' work; sometimes groups form their own post-conference edited volumes, inviting only those persons who share their particular interests or travel in familiar circles; and sometimes people express open hostility to a presenter or panel whose work is quite different from their own. The acts of forming groups and issuing specialized volumes are not problems in themselves, but they feed a social system of silos in which people with diverse concerns are not engaging and learning from one another. To do that requires purposeful bridging.

The second issue named above is the failure to join our collective wisdom and action to address issues of suffering in the world. Practical theologians need not utilize the same methods or pursue the same exact concerns to have a collective influence on the well-being of the world. Unfortunately, the field's tendency to focus on definitions and methods rather than shared concerns is a long-lasting pattern and is increasingly problematic. In the 1990s, Gerben Heitink analyzed practical theology in relation to social questions and the purposes of the discipline, especially in relation to poverty and social suffering.[15] He identified nineteenth century practical theologians who sought to relate practical theology to issues and actions of social concern. These included Hofstede de Groot, Abraham Kuyper, and W. van den Bergh in the late nineteenth century and an even older legacy in Philipp Konrad Marheineke (1780–1846). This legacy and the people who led it are largely forgotten.

Practical theologians do still carry this impulse to contribute to a better world; however, the impulse is often dimmed by definitional and methodological debates and sharp judgments by one group against others whose concerns and approaches are different from their own. Practical theologians could be more effective in knowledge-building, religious-deepening, and world-changing if we were willing to listen more deeply and appreciatively to the purposes of one another and to find ways at critical moments to collaborate on shared purposes. To do this requires more purposeful bridging.

15. Heitink, *Practical Theology*, 51–65.

VULNERABLE BRIDGING

To speak of strong and purposeful bridging is to speak of ideals and visions. Yet visions can become tangible realities, and many scholars and religious leaders already contribute to those realities. Unfortunately, the movement from vision to reality is fraught with risk—traveling into social and intellectual unknowns and experimenting with ideas and approaches that are counter-cultural for the academy, public discourse, and faith communities. Academia has become accustomed to dividing and subdividing disciplines and keeping some distance among them, often with claims that one is superior to others. Faith communities are accustomed to critiquing the academy for being irrelevant while asking the same academy to serve their needs: to teach in ways useful for religious professionals, to research questions that directly concern religious communities, and to offer strong formation. These values and others, such as acquiring and contributing to knowledge, are sometimes bifurcated as if they were antagonistic, thus reducing conversations about significant issues to *supposedly* unresolvable dualisms.

People and institutions talk past one another, as do religious communities and religious scholars, as do religious leaders and the larger public. Bridging is urgent in this context, but bridges are only the visible forms of relationships, creating opportunities for encounters that reveal deeper relationships beneath the surface. As I wrote many years ago, the bridge metaphor has limits.[16] It suggests that the only real relationships are visible bridges that link one phenomenon with others, presuming that they are unrelated without these constructed bridges. In reality, the phenomena are already bound in subterranean relationships that can be uncovered by historical, socio-cultural, philosophical, and psychoanalytic analysis. To demonstrate how easily people ignore or remain ignorant of these connections, consider the commonplace language of linking faith and life, or belief and behavior, or theory and practice. Such expressions belie the common assumption that the world can be divided into dyads, and the dyads are only connected when we create intentional and self-conscious linkages. I argue that intentional linkages are most profound when they help people see the deep connections that already exist.

If everything is already connected, the work of African American scholars is already affecting and being affected by cultures and scholarship of Africans, Native Americans, Asians and Asian Americans, Latinx Americans, and many others. The practices of congregations and religious leaders is already affected by practical theological scholarship, and vice versa.

---

16. Moore, *Teaching from the Heart*, 5, 16.

Cultural patterns of justice and injustice, environmental destruction, and violence are already affected by practical theology and religious practices, and vice versa. Sometimes these influences are marked by neglect or unconscious blocking (as an individual might block the memory of childhood abuse), and sometimes the influences are purposefully named and analyzed for the sake of deeper knowing. When people settle for uncritical surface awareness of relationships, the quality of relationships suffers, which perpetuates destruction and suffering. When a church's care for its buildings is not seen in relation to social and ecological justice, the results are often damaging; the buildings may be tended in ways that perpetuate injustice. At the same time, people marching for justice may not consider the significance of their own daily practices in their home spaces.

Bridges connect people and issues in visible ways so they can become more aware of the deep, invisible connections that already exist. Some of these hidden connections are quite positive and can be enhanced with strong and purposeful bridges, and some are destructive and can only be transformed if people are conscious and intentional in analyzing and responding to them. Most relationships are a combination of life-sustaining and life-destroying forces, so tending them requires extensive relationship building and repair over time—the kind of work that people do when they cross bridges. Viewed from this angle, bridges are not structures to connect unrelated realities; rather, they are visible structures that consciously and intentionally connect phenomena that are already connected beneath the surface.

This issue of connectivity becomes particularly evident when one views examples in daily life. Relationships of hostility can lie mostly dormant for many years, even decades. Then, new outbreaks of racist talk and action, renewed policies that deny opportunities to people living in poverty, violence against Muslim and other religious groups, and discrimination against LGBTQ communities explode, revealing deep hostilities to the public eye. People are often not aware of their deeply held stereotypes and hatreds, and a bridge (e.g., a bridge of mutual sharing, angry tweets, public hate talk, or critical analysis) can bring the deep connections into public consciousness and scrutiny. This paves the way for real transformation.

This analysis reveals how vulnerable bridges are. If bridging practices uncover deeply held animosities or prejudices, people need to remain on the bridges long enough to ponder the ugliness that is uncovered, as well as the beauty. The narrations of Holocaust survivors are bridges that uncover the violent history of Nazi violence against Jews, and of other people who chose to be unknowing and silent. The study of Jewish history further reveals centuries of discrimination against Jewish people in many lands. Similarly, the slave narratives and histories of African American people reveal terrible realities, as do those of immigrant people in almost every global land. Standing on bridges of life narratives and historical-cultural study, people make discoveries that raise new questions, confront them with historical and cultural ugliness, beg for analysis and critique, and open painful self-and cultural awareness. These encounters also reveal beauty and the potential for genuine transformation; they reveal narratives and histories of resisters, rescuers and loyal friends. Thus, bridging unfolds a panorama of danger and transformative possibility, alongside the possibility of closing one's senses and moving on.

Bridge encounters bear potential to transform attitudes and behavior in the present moment, but the encounters can be terrifying, even dangerous; they can lead to denial and defensive violence, or to transformative learning and determined action. Vulnerability emerges when people are grasped by realities that challenge self, community, and culture. Such vulnerability can weaken defenses and help people see ugly realities and seek paths toward greater human and ecological well-being People on bridges are inevitably vulnerable: they see potential for danger and potential for good, and they have to find spiritual, psychic, and cultural resources to stay on the bridge for the sake of understanding and stepping toward goodness.

Bridging is also a vulnerable practice in itself. People who build bridges are in a liminal space of moving from familiar places with familiar people into the less familiar and secure. They do not know what they will discover; they have no map and no guarantees that their bridging efforts will bring more goodness than hurt. Robert Quinn describes the fear that people experience when they move into "deep change" and are challenged to courage and growth. He describes this phenomenon of traveling into the unknown as "building the bridge as you walk on it."[17] Bridges are always vulnerable in Quinn's sense; they are often inadequate, so people build as they travel. Even sturdy bridges may be sites for distressing encounters. The very act of bridging is an act of courageous travel into the unknown. This image underscores Dale Andrews' courage in building one bridge after another and encouraging others to do the same.

Another vulnerability of bridging is personal, often requiring self-sacrifice and endangerment, especially when people or cultural communities with less social power are expected to be the bridge builders or to *be*

---

17. Quinn, *Building the Bridge*, 3–13.

the bridges. This idea was articulated boldly in Cherríe Moraga and Gloria Anzaldúa's *The Bridge Called My Back*.[18] The title tells the story. Some people are expected to *be* bridges. Some people, like privileged white people, expect others to bear the burden of bridging. Kate Rushin described the pattern well: "I've had enough . . . Sick of being the damn bridge for everybody."[19] Moraga raised another vulnerability when bridges that serve one group increase the isolation and vulnerability of others. She described the dilemma of traveling, both literally and metaphorically: "Take Boston alone, I think to myself and the feminism my so-called sisters have constructed does nothing to help me make the trip from one end of town to another . . ."[20] These authors name the terrible burden they experience when others expect them to be bridges, or when people offer them bridges that are useless to them. They know their vulnerability.

The authors of *The Bridge* do even more. They name vulnerability alongside the urgency of bridging. The very act of writing a book in four editions was an act of bridging. They were communicating for themselves, including their anger and frustrations. By writing as a collective, they acted as individuals *and* a community to communicate when and how they will build bridges (or not). They will not act as bridges for everyone everywhere every day, but they will produce a book. They assumed authority as people who are wise about bridging and selective about how they will do it. They reveal the power that can emerge out of deep reflection on vulnerability.

If bridges in practical theology are to be strong and purposeful, we have to recognize that they are also vulnerable. We need to face that vulnerability, understand it, and make decisions about how, when, and where to exercise courage and build bridges anyway. We also need to be alert to vulnerability and discern when the journey into vulnerability is worthwhile. That requires wisdom. To be bridge-builders and bridge-travelers, we need to be cognizant of the qualities that make this possible. To be *strong* bridge-builders, we need to be determined and persistent over time. To be *purposeful* bridge-builders, we need to be visionary. To enter the *vulnerability* of bridge-building, we need to be wise and courageous. If we are able to contribute in these ways to bridge-building, we will build upon the powerful legacy of Dale Andrews, our friend.

---

18. Moraga and Anzaldúa, *The Bridge Called My Back*.
19. Rushin, "Bridge Poem," ibid., xxxiii.
20. Moraga, "La Jornada," ibid., xxxvi.

2

Moral Reflections on the Christian Gospel and the Struggle for Justice

PETER J. PARIS

RACE HAS ALWAYS BEEN a principle of division in American social life demarking the life chances of whites and blacks, the former destined for various measures of privilege and the latter for deprivation and misery. Centuries of slavery followed by another century of racial segregation and discrimination virtually normalized the division for whites. In fact, they were oblivious to it as long as blacks "knew their place" and adhered to its restrictions. In those days, the slightest act of noncompliance with the ordinary patterns and routines of daily life would trigger a forceful response from whites who maintained the racial divide either by violence or its threat. As a matter of fact, the racial divide applied to every part of the American society with no exception whatsoever. Though more intense in the southern states, the lack of racial equality was national in scope as black migrants, war veterans, civil rights organizations and churches knew all too well.

The purpose of this essay is to demonstrate that every initiative for structural change in the racial divide has emerged from the discontented souls of blacks who had no way of knowing ahead of time that their endeavors would succeed because they were a seemingly powerless minority intending to oppose an awesome majority comprising the united force of secular and religious powers.

Ironically, most whites interpreted the constitutional separation of religion and the state as the relegation of the Christian faith to the private realm of life. Consequently, the white churches normally embraced the actions of their ruling authorities through their public and private prayers. Evangelical white churches were bent on converting individuals to the Christian faith who in turn would make all things good. Black churches, however, differed because their life and destiny had always been proscribed by the dictates of the white society. Thus, they could never be oblivious to the racial divide. Traditionally, their resistance occurred mostly within the segregated walls of their confinement where their hopes for freedom were expressed in prayers, songs and preaching.

The contrast between the white and black churches was vividly displayed in the middle of the twentieth century by two radically different religious events that soon captured the attention of the public media. The one was led by a white charismatic southern Baptist evangelist whose name, Billy Graham, rapidly became a household term. The other was led by a young charismatic black Baptist preacher whose name, Martin Luther King, Jr., soon gained similar recognition. Both were great orators with rhetoric deeply rooted in Biblical imagery. Yet, their respective emphases differed. On the one hand, Graham's sermons and addresses aimed at proclaiming Jesus Christ as the savior who would deliver all humans from the ravages of sin that divided them from one another and from their God. On the other hand, King's sermons and speeches proclaimed that God's love for humanity implied social justice for all: a perspective that he believed was supported by the Declaration of Independence and the Constitution of the United States. Clearly, the two leaders spoke from different premises with different goals in mind. Graham's message addressed individuals isolated from their social contexts while King's message addressed persons in the context of racial injustice that he believed was perpetrated and sustained by erroneous philosophies of white supremacy and black inferiority.

Graham's massive evangelical crusades were sponsored in various American cities by predominately white interdenominational agencies. They eventually expanded to six continents across many different political boundaries including those of Russia and China. Their main mission was to persuade men, women and children to accept Jesus Christ as their personal savior which countless numbers did by the act of coming forward for prayer as the combined choirs sang Charlotte Elliott's well-known hymn, "Just as I am...."[1]

---

1. Elliott, "Just As I Am," 339.

Born and bred in the Baptist tradition King was altogether familiar with the Christian revivalist tradition. Having preached in similar events in his own church and many others, he was greatly impressed by the success of Graham's campaigns. In fact, he once imagined the possibility of working cooperatively with Graham in a Christian campaign with the aim of redeeming white Americans from their racism. Yet, it soon became apparent that despite his genuine respect for King's leadership, Graham's own theological commitments prevented him from considering any such cooperative alliance. Though he, himself, never ascribed to any form of racism and had often refused to conduct his campaigns in racially segregated arenas ,he believed, nonetheless, that the function proclaiming the Christian gospel should not engage social justice issues because redeemed humans would certainly practice the love of Christ in all their relationships. Thus, he considered King's endeavor to change the nation's laws in pursuit of racial justice as far beyond his own calling to preach the gospel of personal redemption to individuals in order to persuade them to invite Jesus to take command of their lives and thereby solve the nation's moral problems including racism. By contrast, King believed that the Christian gospel does not separate the salvation of persons from the demands for social justice but unites the two. Thus, he viewed God's call to Moses to lead his people out of bondage as united with Jesus' vision of the Realm of God wherein all redeemed persons would strive to redeem the nation as well.

Clearly the different vocational paths that King and Graham chose resulted in radically different life styles for each of them. On the one hand, Graham became a trusted friend and advisor to several presidents (most notably Eisenhower, Johnson, Nixon and Reagan) and appeared on the Gallup list of the nation's most admired men more than sixty times. On the other hand, King had no similar relationship with the nation's presidents and appeared on the Gallup list only twice in the 1960's though much oftener after his assassination. Rather than living a life of stardom, he was imprisoned nineteen times, experienced the bombing of his home twice, was stabbed in the chest once by a crazed woman, received regular death threats, and was assassinated at the age of thirty-nine.

THE MONTGOMERY BUS BOYCOTT AND THE BLACK CHURCH

Unlike Graham, King's public visibility arose from his leadership in the 1955 Montgomery Bus Boycott which marked the beginning of the twentieth century Civil Rights Movement. At that time, with the possible exception of

King, himself, none could have imagined the enormous impact that event was destined to have on the city of Montgomery, the southern states and the nation as a whole. Though the local chapter of the National Association for the Advancement of Colored People (NAACP) and the Women's Political Action Committee had plans to launch a protest against the policy of racial discrimination on the city's buses, the unexpected arrest of the widely respected Mrs. Rosa Parks for refusing to yield her seat to a white man provided the right moment for initiating such an extraordinary event. Most important, it marked the first time in the history of the south that blacks had organized a public protest against the white political and economic power structure. No one, including the organizers themselves could have predicted the black community's universal support for what would become a year-long protest.

In retrospect, the renowned sociologist of religion, C. Eric Lincoln viewed the event as symbolic of the death of the so-called "Negro Church in America" that his senior colleague, E. Franklin Frazier[2] had studied and analyzed so well a few years earlier. Thus, Lincoln concluded that the unified action of the city's black religious leaders in protesting the bus company's policy of racial discrimination marked the birth of "The Black Church in America" with its bold, strident resolve to resist the restrictive conditions of racial segregation and discrimination on the city's buses. Thus, motivated by such a successful venture, the leaders soon expanded their goals to that of dismantling racial proscriptions throughout the south by adopting the method of non-violent resistance that had been employed so successfully by Mohandas Gandhi in India's struggle for independence. In preparation for their ongoing work, the name of the umbrella organization was soon changed from The Montgomery Improvement Association to The Southern Christian Leadership Conference in order to manifest more clearly the biblical basis for their leadership principles. In addition, from that time forward Dr. King viewed Gandhi's method of nonviolent resistance as wholly compatible with Jesus' teaching on love as explicated in his Sermon on the Mount in the fifth chapter of the gospel of Mathew. Most important, he fully realized and taught all who followed him that the method of love in the quest for racial justice in the south would require much suffering that would almost certainly include martyrdom.

Many whites and not a few blacks argued then and later in favor of a gradualist approach toward any meaningful transformation in the nation's racial practices. The NAACP's method of working through the courts

2. See the tribute to E. Franklin Frazier in the foreword of Lincoln, *Black Church*, 101–2.

constituted the prime example of that strategy. King and others desired the coupling of that gradualist approach with the method of non-violent direct confrontation believing that the latter would be more effective in giving public visibility to the hidden reality of racial hatred thereupon moving the consciences of many whites to support their moral appeals for lawful social transformation in race relations.

RACISM AND TERRORISM

Both then and now the vast majority of white Americans did not know what blacks have always namely, namely that life under the conditions of racism is virtually the same as life under the conditions of terrorism. In our day, many investigative reporters and numerous academic researchers are striving to understand the effects of constant life and death threats on the psyches of surviving adults and children who live in regions where their humanity is denied by their enemies who have control over them. Historically, a similar condition has characterized the experience of blacks in America for many centuries. In fact, there is not a living black American, rich or poor, educated or illiterate, light skinned or dark, famous or not, who would deny the truth of this claim. In other words, all African Americans agree that racism is a disease of the human spirit that expresses itself in various hateful activities aimed at maintaining racially proscriptive social customs and policies.

Morris Dees, founder of the Southern Poverty Law Center and its Klanwatch Project has dedicated his life to the lawful destruction of hate groups because their violent actions are motivated by the mere presence of those whom they hate. That is to say, their being alone is sufficient cause for hostile attacks. Accordingly, since the end of the Civil War, clandestine groups like the Ku Klux Klan have thrived on acts of terrorism that have been accompanied by such unmistakable symbols as the burning crosses, hooded men in white sheets covering their bodies and heads, or bands of night-riders speeding by the homes of the vulnerable. Invariably, their threats of violence and actual acts of lynching, burnings, whippings, shootings, and other forms of torture thwart the law and every form of due process. Needless to say perhaps, such hatred produces many horrific effects on the psyches of their prey who have mostly been African Americans even though Jews, Mexicans, Catholics and various immigrant groups have also been subject to their abuse. In short, no amount of accommodation to such terrorism has ever guaranteed safety. More often than not, the Ku Klux Klan in particular has enjoyed the admiration and protection of law enforcement agencies, politicians, newspaper editors and the white churches throughout the south as well as many regions in the north.

REMEMBERING THE MARTYRS

On November 5, 1989, the civil rights icon, Julian Bond, addressed the opening ceremony for the celebration of the Civil Rights Memorial erected near the Southern Poverty Law Center in Montgomery in the plaza across the street from the state capital and round the corner from Dexter Avenue Baptist Church where Martin Luther King Jr. served as pastor at the time of the bus boycott. The flowing waters over the names of the martyrs symbolizes the laments of the survivors for the forty-one men, women and children including Martin Luther King, Jr., who were killed either in or during various Civil Rights campaigns. Suffice it to say that the Ku Klux Klan was found guilty for fourteen of the killings and widely believed to have had a hand in many more. Tragically Bond stated that several of the martyrs were killed not because they were involved in any overt resistance but for no other reason than that of being black. In his speech he called several of their names which included 13-year old Virgil Ware who was riding on the handlebars of his brother's bike when he was killed; two war veterans, Lieutenant Colonel Lemuel Penn and Corporal Roman Ducksworth, Jr. The former was riding home from his day's duty and the latter, a military police officer, was travelling on a bus to Maryland to visit his sick wife when he was ordered off the bus and shot by the police after he refused to comply. The bodies of Charles Eddie Moore and Henry Hezekiah Dee were found when they were searching for three others. It should also be noted that the list of martyrs includes one white woman and three white men which evidences the interracial nature of those who died in the quest for a racially just society. Perhaps the most agonizing sentence in Bond's entire speech is the following; "The state and local government worked in active concern with white terrorism and the movement's people had few allies beyond themselves." Yet, Bond ended his speech with the following conciliatory words: "Let us rededicate ourselves to freedom's fight. Let us gather not in recrimination but in reconciliation and remembrance with renewed resolve."[3]

3. Bond, "Speech."

THE POST CIVIL-RIGHTS ERA

Clearly, under the conditions of racial oppression in the United States life for blacks has always been a matter of life and death. Attacks on their persons, homes, churches and other institutions have never ceased being real possibilities. Virtually every decade of the twentieth century up to this second decade of the twenty-first century, news media have devoted considerable space to terrorist acts against blacks. During the last several decades the work of politicians to curb street violence has resulted in longer sentences for criminals in both state and federal courts. Consequently, the United States now has over two and one half million of its citizens in prisons serving extraordinarily long sentences for non-violent crimes. Moreover, a disproportionate number of them are African Americans and ethnic minorities. Recently this phenomenon has received widespread national and inter-national attention through the publication of an extraordinary book by Michelle Alexander that is appropriately titled, *The New Jim Crow: Mass Incarceration in the Age of Colorblindness*.[4] The similarity between this legal practice with that of racial segregation in the middle of the twentieth century is astounding. Suffice it to say that the book has sparked a national conversation within the halls of academe, religious organizations, many book reading groups, and numerous local forums around the country concerning the justice of such a system. The exact outcome of this informal public inquiry remains to be seen.

Certainly, the terrorist acts that killed such iconic national figures as the Nobel Peace Laureate Martin Luther King, Jr., Malcolm X, Medgar Evers, Robert F. Kennedy and all the others were inspired by an ethos of racial hatred that inevitably restricts, disables, and annihilates its victims. Tragically, all who aid and abet its victims are ostracized, maimed or killed. Historically, a similar fate awaited those in the nineteenth century who aided the escaped slaves on the under-ground railroad as well as the following five twentieth century white Americans: Viola Liuzzo, Andrew Goodman, James Reeb, Jonathan Daniels and Michael Schwerner who knowingly risked their lives and lost them in the twentieth century struggle for racial justice.

Hate groups can be quantified but their hatred cannot be measured by any particular scale because hate focusses its attention on the being of the other. Nothing the other does can mitigate its traumatic effect. Thus, it is altogether erroneous for anyone to suppose as many have done that acts of submission, adaptation, accommodation, or compliance guarantee safety.

---

4. Alexander, *New Jim Crow*.

Consequently, those who refused to join Martin Luther King, Jr. in his mass demonstrations of non-violent protest wrongly believed that those protests would lead to the polarization of the races which in turn would result in violence. Clearly, like ostriches with their heads in the sand those people failed to see that the races were already polarized and racial violence was widespread. Moreover, in spite of their contrary perceptions, they themselves were caught in a web of societal restrictions. This was certainly the case with the Reverend J. H. Jackson, the senior minister of the prestigious Olivet Baptist Church in Chicago, and President of the National Baptist Convention, U.S.A. Inc. who unrelentingly excoriated King for his mass demonstrations in the city of Chicago and elsewhere.

Neither King's method of non-violent direct confrontation nor Jackson's method of moral suasion was effective in dismantling the slums of Chicago as the primary symbols of that city's racist policies effectively maintained by the political machine that was controlled at the time by Mayor Richard Daly. By contrast, King's approach had brought the issue of urban racism to public attention while Jackson's method kept it hidden from public view. Those whites who did not want to live in racially mixed neighborhoods certainly preferred Jackson's method to King's because it posed no immediate threat to the city's *status quo*.

OUR UNFINISHED AGENDA

Admittedly, many changes in race relations have been experienced during this post-civil rights era which we date from the death of Jim Crow in the Civil Rights Act of 1964 and the Voters' Rights Act of 1965. While those actions constituted the lawful end of overt forms of racial discrimination and segregation in public places, they did not end the hatred that racism produced. The assassination of Dr. King and Senator Bobby Kennedy three years later along with the public policies of mass incarceration from the 1980's onwards attest to that fact. Racial hatred was also vividly displayed in the many and varied attempts to delay the enforcement of the law to integrate public schools as evidenced in the faces of mobs of white parents angrily confronting school buses transporting black children to white schools in compliance with court orders. The psychological effects of such threats on countless black children remains unknown. Ironically, most of the public schools in the United States today are not racially integrated in any significant way due to *de facto* residential segregation. Thus, the failure of such schools to achieve their educational goals remains unchanged.

Soon after Dr. King's assassination, the rise of the black consciousness movement rapidly gained ascendancy among African Americans throughout the nation. Its effects were seen in the formation of numerous caucuses in predominantly white denominations and virtually all professional and academic associations soon followed suit. Demands for black studies programs in universities, colleges, and seminaries occurred everywhere. Also, the nation witnessed the death of such nomenclature as "Negro" and "Colored" in favor of "Black" and eventually "African American." The Congressional Black Caucus was organized in 1971 with thirteen founding members. James H. Cone published his first book entitled, *Black Theology and Black Power* in 1969[5] which launched courses in Black Church studies in many seminaries and the Society for the Study of Black Religion was organized in 1970. In short, a phenomenal growth in the black professional class occurred alongside a corresponding growth of those who lacked the resources for upward mobility. These latter ones now constitute what some have called a permanent underclass isolated in urban slums with high concentrations of poverty, violence, drug addiction and, since the 1980's, mass incarceration.

But let none suppose that all is well with African Americans who entered the middle class during this era because large numbers of them suffered record losses of income during the 2008—2009 down-turn in the economy. Further, though many seemingly achieved a measure of economic progress during this era, it was short-lived. Most have experienced either a loss of their jobs due to the impact of globalization on the auto industry or victimized by the sub-prime rate mortgage loan schemes that caused many to lose their homes. Further still, the experience of a glass ceiling for blacks in corporate America and elsewhere continues to mark the limits of black progress in upward social mobility. How that ceiling will be broken remains a mystery.

Perhaps the most surprising event of this post-civil rights era was the election of Barack Hussein Obama as the nation's first African American president in 2008 and who succeeded in winning a second term in 2012. Though he was able to appoint two women to the Supreme Court and to pass the Affordable Health Care Bill, he was stalled in his second term by a Republican Congress that refused to co-operate with him which effectively prevented him from realizing much of his agenda. Tragically, many believe that a vicious white backlash against him paved the way for the successful rise of Donald J. Trump to the presidency whose campaign rhetoric and

---

5. Cone, *Black Theology*.

proposals greatly offended African Americans, progressive women, Muslims, Mexicans and immigrants.

Much work is needed to renew the struggle for racial justice in the nation. Though professionals in all fields are concerned about this subject, they alone lack the necessary resources for success. Black scholars in theology, pastoral care, homiletics, ethics, Bible, etc. have much to contribute to the task of critical analysis as the work of Professor Dale Andrews in *Practical Theology for Black Churches* illustrates so well.[6] But they must find ways to combine their actions with a coalition of like-minded citizens striving for moral transformation in our societal structures and practices. Needless to say, the recent election of Donald J. Trump as the 45th President of the United States does not bode well for progress in racial justice.

In recent years the nation has seen the rise of the Black Lives Matter Movement that took shape as a response to the tragic killings of Trayvon Martin, Michael Brown and many other unarmed young black men and women by the police seemingly with impunity. Unlike the earlier Civil Rights Movement, this one was founded by two lesbian women, Opal Temeti and Alicia Garza, and a coalition comprising disabled and undocumented folk, ex-convicts and others who have been victimized by the prevailing social system. Like their predecessors this movement also seeks to liberate and empower all oppressed peoples. Unlike them however, religion is not its guiding force even though many of its participants are religious devotees.

Those same killings of young black men coupled with the hateful slaughter of nine members of the Emmanuel African Methodist Church in Charleston, S.C. and the political gerrymandering of voting districts in North Carolina and elsewhere have been contributing factors in the rise of another movement called Moral Mondays inspired by the leadership of the Reverend William Jr. Barber II pastor of Greenleaf Christian Church (Disciples of Christ) in Goldsboro, NC and President of the state chapter of the NAACP. He calls for a moral revolution of values which he considers a virtual Third Reconstruction[7] following the first two that occurred respectively after the Civil War and the Civil Rights Acts of the 1960's. Both of the latter ended tragically with renewed and more expansive forms of racial injustice. It remains to be seen whether this new venture will meet a similar end.

---

6. Andrews and Smith, eds., *Black Practical Theology*.
7. Barber, *Third Reconstruction*.

3

Understanding the Times and Knowing What to Do

ROBERT LONDON SMITH

It is always an honour to recognise and express appreciation for the life work of a colleague. While there are many who ply their trade within the academy, far fewer have lasting and valuable impact in the way that Dale Andrews has. I write first of all to recognize Dale Andrews; his scholarship; his contributions to knowledge in the field of black theology and practical theology and his passion for the life of the black church. I am recognizing, not just the work of a gifted colleague and practical theologian, but a good friend. Dale Andrews' contributions as a minister and theologian have certainly helped shaped my own ministry and theological work even before we first met in 2007. His impact on me—professionally and personally—has been meaningful and valuable.

Dale's scholarship has been shaped by and for black theology and black churches. Therefore, issues of justice, violence, racism and poverty are some of the issues that are the grist for his theological mill. This is the case because Dale has always found that "the actual struggle to find theology practical wrestles with the meaning of life and the daily experiences of living."[1] Black church praxis, meaning-making and prophetic preaching are central to the intellectual focus of his work. These issues, objects and foci are prominent in my own thinking as well; indeed, they are what brought Dale's and my

---

1. Andrews, *Practical Theology* 1.

theological trajectories—distinct, yet similar—together. To wrestle with such weighty and complex matters within the academy and for the black church is what makes Dale tick. And he takes on the task of wrestling with those issues and others, in order to point to ways that lead to the creation of transformative forms of black church praxis.

BRIDGE BUILDING: A CENTRAL PLANK

A central plank and key concern in Dale's work has been bridge building. Identifying what he has described as the chasm between black theology and black folk,[2] Dale has sought to develop practical theology methodologies with which to bridge that chasm. He does this understanding that that gulf compromises any collective reform in the black community and white society, thus hindering possibilities to transform situations of injustice, poverty and oppression. As theologians, our work—our raison d'être—is to unpack the meaning of our faith in order to apply it to the myriad experiences, issues and events that shape our consciousness such that we might live faithfully in light of God's narrative.

This task or calling of theology is not new. God's people have always been challenged to bring about change in the world. This is done most effectively when we are able to connect knowledge of where we are—our context historically and culturally—with a clear understanding of who we are—our identity and calling as Christians—so, that, ultimately, we might know how to be and what to do in this world. In the Old Testament Book 1 Chronicles, we find an example of this. God's people were facing a situation that had great significance for them as people of God. Surrounded by enemies, hobbled by Saul, who had turned away from God, and needing to act to bring together God's people, the tribes gathered to turn Saul's rule over to David.

In the 12th chapter, we find a long list of the tribes of Israel and the men who had gathered to support David, to pledge their loyalty to him and to fight for him. These men were described by their readiness for battle and their skill in handling swords and spears; their ability to fight in military formation and to command warriors and defeat enemies. To a man, they were brave, fierce and experienced in matters of warfare. Almost in the middle of this impressive list of fighting men of valour, the writer included the Sons of Issachar. Interestingly, the Sons of Issachar were not military men who were skilful in warfare; they were not brave warriors; and they did not carry shield and spear. This is how the writer described them:

2. Ibid., 6.

"[F]rom Issachar, men who understood the times and knew what Israel should do—200 chiefs, with all their relatives under their command" (1 Chron. 12:32, NIV). This group of men was vital to the efforts of what they were attempting to accomplish. They understood their context—where they were and they knew their identity—who they were. The writer made a point to communicate this to the reader. It was because the sons of Issachar understood these two things that they were able to know what they should do. It is instructive that as God's people prepared to go into battle, they did not rely exclusively on fighting men, but depended upon men who understood the times in order to know what they ought to do! The sons of Issachar knew where they were (their context and situation) and they knew who they were (the Nation of Israel, called and anointed by God Almighty).

Expressing this theologically, we can say that when critical understanding of context, identity and purpose is facilitated, modes of informed praxis[3] are created. God continues to call men and women to be Sons and Daughters of Issachar; men and women who understand our times and know what to do. To put this in the language and context of Dale's work, this requires bridge building. It requires us to connect a critical understanding of context, identity and purpose such that we might know what to do as Children of God. Reflecting on the life of the black church, we see that often there is a gulf, or chasm, between praxis—actions and practices shaped by the Christian faith—and context, identity and purpose. That chasm militates against the black church's ability to act faithfully when faced with the myriad of challenges life brings. Again, to place this within the context of Dale's work, we might ask, "What should the black church do when faced with issues of poverty, sexism, violence and oppression? How might the black church best fight against injustice, hatred and prejudice?" For Dale, those questions reveal what is the life and breathe of what it means to be the black church. So we set about this theological task with a real sense of purpose and calling.

As previously mentioned, part of Dale's theological work is finding ways to bridge the chasm that separates black theology, or the academy, from black folk religion. He has recognised this disconnect, and, understanding how each needs the other in order to meaningfully address the issues that challenge black people today and enable them to faithfully live, Dale has worked to develop methodologies with which to build bridges that address the chasm between them.

Dale understands that the academy has made incredible discoveries and has established a body of scholarship that privileges the black experience

---

3. Smith, *From Strength*.

which has much to offer black folk religion. He also knows very well the distrust and wariness that black folk religion often has for the academy. Crucially, Dale sees clearly that the work of the academy can be strengthened by the traditions and practices of black folk religion and that black folk religion can benefit tremendously from the theological work and insights of the academy. The challenge then is to develop "bridging methodologies" with which to facilitate such important work.

A METHOD FOR THEOLOGICAL REFLECTION IN BRIDGE-BUILDING

Method has always been central to the theological task; it is dynamic and evolving. Methodology not only enables the theological task; it shapes the theologian even as it is shaped by the theologian. One of the real strengths of Dale's work is how he has developed and brought to bear on the theological task, methodologies with which to bridge the chasm that separates the academy and the church. The places of dissonance, incongruity and rupture that are the objects of Dale's attention arise out his understanding of God, the church and the church's place or work within the world. Therefore, issues such as justice, worship, preaching, poverty, education, racism and discrimination are the grist for his theological mill.

Dale's work is courageous—calling to task both church and academy—and creative, teasing out new ways of envisioning the theological task and calling. His keen insight and dogged determination to pursue the ends and outcomes of the practical theological task are not only instructive but encouraging. Dale's ability to locate his inquiry within the lived experiences of African American life has provided a much-valued corpus of work that will educate, motivate and shape generations of all backgrounds.[4]

His projects reflect his desire to bring to bear on the work of theology a wide range of resources, perspectives and contexts. I was fortunate to have been able to work with Dale on one such project: *Black Practical Theology*.[5] Dale's earlier work sought to bridge the chasm between Black Theology and the black church that brought together our two strands of theological inquiry. The questions which energized and gave focus to our exploration were: "How might one address the chasm between black theology and religious practices in black churches? How are we to understand the evolving historical conditions within which the black church's struggles for meaning-making and justice-making are located? What shapes the things we do in

4. Andrews, *Practical Theology*.
5. Andrews and Smith, eds., *Black Practical Theology*.

our churches? How do we live faithfully in today's society as Christians who are to reflect the message and call of Jesus Christ that we are the salt and the light of the world? These are the kinds of questions that animated our thinking and helped shape our project.

Bridging methodologies recognise the importance of praxis for the faithful living of the gospel by those who are called to be part of it. Ecclesial praxis, in order to be faithful and transformational, or praxiological,[6] must be shaped, or informed, by the context in which faith communities are implicated, Scripture, inherited faith traditions and the issues and events that shape human consciousness. Action or praxis that is not clearly shaped by these things ultimately lack focus, integrity and, crucially, the ability to transform people and situations. It is only through an informed praxis[7] of the church that the reality of the gospel of Jesus Christ can be made known to the world in ways that are transformational and relevant.

Dale's hearer-response criticism recognises this important fact. "Hearer-response criticism capitalises on the reader-response process by pressing us beyond the notion that Biblical revelation is a matter of location and extraction of content or truth . . . the desire is to consider the actions and context, which include time and place that are involved in responding to a text."[8] Dale, seeking redress in light of the chasm between the Black Theology project and the African American Church, utilises this approach to unpack how we understand, internalize and then respond to Scripture; also understanding that we are shaped by historical contexts and received faith traditions that we inhabit.

Therefore, privileging church praxis—what it is, what it does and how it is shaped—is a key consideration of Dale's work. Among other things then, his methodological approach also seeks to address the gulf or space between the received traditions of the faith and actions or praxis of the church. In a similar manner, I have argued that, "much of the praxis of the church is uninformed, in that it is not informed by theology and tradition which is then critiqued through the lens of the contextual realities that shape our consciousness."[9]

Using a mutual critical theological method, Dale's bridge building methodology is concerned with finding ways to connect the work of the academy and the working out of black folk religion. The value of his

---

6. Smith, *From Strength*; for more on the praxiological concept, see Evans, *We Have Been*.

7. Ibid.

8. Andrews, *Practical Theology*, 127.

9. Smith, *From Strength*, 3.

trajectory of theological work could not be more important today. Against the backdrop of recent social and political events that have taken place in the US, Europe and other places in the world, the call for the creation of methodologies with which to build bridges that connect our faith, our beliefs and traditions with those issues and events which shape our consciousness become even more valuable and certainly, timely.

It appears that increasingly today strident, entrenched and caustic voices that seek to marginalize, de-value and separate people on the basis of faith, ethnicity, nationality, gender, and sexual orientation have gained a seat at the table of normality. These voices have been, until relatively recently, largely situated within the periphery of accepted social and political norms. However, this no longer seems to be the case. Binary and oppositional agendas and ideologies, which have previously been subtle and entrenched in character, are now being unashamedly heralded, promoted and defended.

What makes this phenomenon so malicious is the rationale often used to support those extreme positions. The rhetoric is often couched in terms that speak of denied or lost freedoms. Individuals and organisations are now claiming that their unique positions and privileges—understood as their right to certain lifestyles—are being eroded. They are now demanding a return of those positions and privileges. Part of this call to freedom is reflected in the US as a return to historical times when America was great, i.e. "Let's Make America Great Again."

Therefore, the call is to return and restore those freedoms, which have been denied or stolen outright. How were these freedoms lost or stolen? How might they be returned? Who are the culprits? Well, the culprits conveniently, are people who look different, are members of different faiths, come from different countries, speak different languages, and uphold different truths. What is now taking place in our communities, cities and nations around the world is a widening of the chasms between us as people and societies and cultures. We are witnessing the erection of walls that isolate us and the widening of ditches that keep us away from each other. The result is an increase in fear and uncertainty, a loss of a shared sense of humanity; and a growing unease and distrust of our fellows.

Against these messages of darkness and death, we hear the message of the light and life of Jesus Christ who calls us to love our enemies and forgive those who harm us; to feed the poor, clothe the naked and love your neighbour as you love yourself. In a clear and direct repudiation of the messages we hear so much today to marginalise, oppress, deny and de-humanise, the gospel message of Jesus Christ calls us instead to love and forgive, to share and to act with compassion, and to be salt and light. That message teaches us that freedom is not something which only a privileged few—traditionally

Western, white, males—deserve, but, in recognition of the grace we have received through Jesus Christ, compels us to deny ourselves, take up our crosses and follow Him; in other words, to bring freedom to all who are imprisoned, oppressed or marginalized.

QUADRALOGUE: A WAY TO ENGAGE IN BRIDGE-BUILDING

How then does the black church—*any* part of the body of Jesus Christ—bring and live that message in today's contentious, fractious and turbulent world? I suggest that—taking a cue from Dale—it means we must become bridge builders. In the language of 1Chronicles, we must become Sons and Daughters of Issachar; men and women who understand our times and know what to do.

There is a chasm between the freedom we have in Christ Jesus that calls us to live out in the world, and the way many of us live our lives on a daily basis. And, given the things we are experiencing in today's world, that chasm is growing at an alarming rate. Therefore, I want to suggest a way in which we might engage in some much-needed and hopefully, timely bridge-building, drawing on Dale's work. I am speaking of bridge-building whose aim is to narrow the chasm between what we embrace and practice in light of the current context of xenophobia, distrust and fear and what the gospel of Jesus Christ has called us to be and do in such a world. In other words, to begin to move toward modes of praxis that are informed by an understanding of the times in which we live, and who we are as sons and daughters of Jesus Christ called to transformational mission in the world.

Beginning with Western secular notions of freedom which, I argue, shape much present-day rhetoric, we unearth some important, if not chilling, indications of the meanings and values which inhabit this rhetoric. There is the notion of the freedom to have a certain lifestyle. This manifests itself not only in economic terms (i.e. freedom to have the kind of employment and income to fund a certain lifestyle), but also in matters of justice (i.e. because I am white, male, American, etc. and you are not, I alone should enjoy these freedoms and you should not).

This clearly does not reflect the freedom that we, as Christians, know we enjoy through the work of Jesus Christ. Therefore, I want to suggest—drawing on the model that Dale and I developed—a way forward to build bridges between our faith and context which allows us to live out the freedom we have in Christ who is the ultimate bridge builder. In coming to think about and suggest ways to develop a Black Practical Theology, Dale and I presented a methodology which utilises a trialogue to bring together black theologians, scholars within practical theology and its sub-disciplines and black faith practitioners.[10]

Beginning with the events and issues black pastors and practitioners identified that shape black consciousness today, we asked black theologians and scholars within practical theology to engage with those issues and events from within their own disciplinary locations. Finally, their responses were fed back to the black pastors for them to reflect on what they had written. By employing this methodology, these groups were drawn together dialectically, which not only facilitated the teasing out of what a Black Practical Theology might look like, but was also a move toward much-needed bridge building. By bringing together scholars and practitioners who are invested in the future flourishing of black churches and communities in order to facilitate ways forward in developing informed, faithful and transformational modes of praxis for the black church, important bridges were constructed.

I suggest that utilizing this methodology to begin to envision and shape a practical theology of freedom would garner similar, valuable outcomes. In shaping this approach, I suggest that another group be invited to the conversation. This would create a four-pronged dialogue or "quadralogue." I understand that to invite too many interlocutors to such a conversation would be problematic; however, in coming to think about notions of freedom and how those notions are currently shaped, it will be crucial to invite civic leaders and those working within the political processes in local, state and federal government into the conversation. They would be asked to identify key issues and events they feel are shaping our communities such that they can be brought into dialogue with black pastors, black theologians and scholars within practical theology and its sub-disciplines to engage with those issues.

As each group within this four-sided dialogue engages with those issues from their particular disciplinary and theological locations, some interesting insights and understandings might be discovered. A key benefit is that this method allows each group a peek into the thinking, perspective and aims of the others. I suspect what might be discovered is that there are many similarities and points of convergence which can be capitalised upon. As well, points of divergence that should be addressed can be identified. What the process does is draw groups and individuals—togetether who might not otherwise join in such a conversation—together in meaningful, critical and transformative ways; building bridges that can help us construct

10. Andrews and Smith, eds., *Black Practical Theology*, 3–5.

ways of being in the world that heal and reconcile us with one another and that bring the love of Christ into the situations that shape our everyday lives.

This is the kind of new scholarly trajectory that Dale and I hoped for when we began this project many years ago. We never intended to create a model which was a means to a pre-determined and static end, but would be something that hopefully might facilitate the beginning of new paths of theological inquiry. It is in this hope, that, building on Dale's work, new directions that seek to address matters that affect our lives might be teased out and explored. Such a project, like the praxiological response criticism Dale and I proposed, entails a heuristic engagement with supposed foundations of the faith, along with the historical contexts and worldviews at work in the theories and lives of black churches and communities.[11]

One of the privileges of academic scholarship is the ability to shape generations of thinkers and seekers in unimaginable ways and to work with some of the brightest lights of the academy. I certainly have been honoured and blessed to have been able to work with Dale. He is a preeminent practical theologian, gifted scholar and an excellent preacher. But above all, Dale is a committed Christian, loving husband and father and very good friend. His impact on the way we "do" theology, think about our faith and understand the crucial work of shaping black church praxis will certainly continue to have an impact on the academy and the faith community for many, many years. We are all indebted to Dale for his invaluable contributions.

---

11. Andrews and Smith, eds., *Black Practical Theology*, 311.

4

Truly More than Just
On the Bridge Beteween the Pastoral and the Prophetic

TED A. SMITH

We often preach that God is just. However, we all had better pray that God is truly more than just. (Dale P. Andrews)[1]

FOR MORE THAN THIRTY years Dale Andrews has been calling the church and the world to live into the justice demanded by the in-breaking of God's reign. And for more than thirty years Andrews has been calling church and world to respond faithfully to the ways that in-breaking promises something more than justice. The challenge—a challenge that preachers have wrestled with for thousands of years—is how to proclaim that "something more" than justice without ever slipping into a cheap grace that is something less than justice.

Andrews has taken up that challenge in an important variety of ways over the years. He has analyzed what proclaiming something more than justice might involve. He has demonstrated what it would mean to proclaim something more than justice in his own preaching and writing. And he has

---

1. Andrews, "Martin Luther King, Jr. Day," 71.

lived that something more in his everyday relationships as spouse, parent, pastor, scholar, teacher, colleague, and friend. It is my hope that this essay can begin to do justice to one thread of Andrews' rich tapestry of thought. And it is my hope that it can do more than justice. For my purpose is not just to engage in academic dialogue, but also to give thanks.

STARTING FROM THE CHASM

Andrews has repeatedly named a great divide as his starting point. In *Practical Theology for Black Churches*, for instance, he describes a "chasm between black churches and black theology."[2] Language of gap, chasm, and divide runs through almost all of Andrews' major works. But that which the chasm separates can vary. It is not only between black churches and black theology. At other times Andrews points to a gap between meaning-making and justice-making, between the pastoral the prophetic, or between black folk religion and black liberation theology. Each of these pairs of terms is distinct; each one adds a layer of depth to our understanding of the divide that Andrews is naming. The pairs are not simply identical. At the same time, the terms cluster into two distinct constellations. One, institutionally rooted in traditional black churches, focuses on the pastoral work of making meaning and providing a refuge for people who endure abuse from a racist society. The other, rooted in academic institutions, focuses on the prophetic task of proclaiming justice and working for social change.

In some of his most recent work Andrews further divides the cluster of academics to produce a map with three constellations: one composed of "scholars who are working within the constructive, biblical, and ethics disciplines of black theology," another composed of "those scholars who are working in practical theology and its customary subdisciplines," and a third composed of "church and parachurch leaders in black communities."[3] This revised map lets Andrews name the gaps between scholars working in practical theology and those working in other fields. But it retains the defining feature of his earlier maps. It points again to the "persistent chasm between the black theological disciplines and religious practices in black churches."[4]

This persistent chasm leaves both sides impoverished, Andrews writes. There are meaningful differences between pastoral and prophetic approaches. The problems arise when those differences are made absolute. "Unfortunately," Andrews writes, the relation between the two "has at times

---

2. Andrews, *Practical Theologys*, 9.
3. Andrews and Smith, eds., *Black Practical Theology*, 3.
4. Ibid., 5.

turned into a false or regretful bifurcation between pastoral care in ecclesial formation or function within church and the more prophetic claims of liberation social ethics fostered alternatively by some social disciplines."[5] The problem arises not simply with differentiation, but when differentiation becomes absolute division that creates a chasm between two approaches that should be intimately related.

A DIALECTICAL BRIDGE

Andrews has repeatedly insisted on the need for both sides of this chasm to be in relation to one another for the sake of faithful witness to the fullness of the in-breaking of the Reign of God. Both pastoral and prophetic approaches are necessary. Neither can take the place of the other; neither can subsume the other without remainder. Rather, Andrews writes, "Prophetic consciousness does not supersede pastoral nurture as the overriding norm of the in-breaking of the reign of God, not does the latter tolerably supplant the former as the norm of discipleship."[6] Both pastoral nurture and prophetic consciousness are necessary. What matters is that each retains its integrity even as it remains in relation to the other. "A sound bridge," Andrews writes, "will reestablish the necessary reciprocity between personal faith and social justice, rather than a subjugation of one under the other."[7] Right relationship between pastoral and prophetic approaches is marked by dialogue, mutuality, and reciprocity. The best bridge between the two sides of the chasm will facilitate significant flows of traffic in both directions.

In Andrews' vision, such reciprocity does not compromise either side. Reciprocity is not accomplished by being a little less pastoral in order to be more prophetic, nor by being a little less prophetic in order to be more pastoral. On the contrary, Andrews writes, "The prophetic and the pastoral should not be considered mutually exclusive." They do not exist in a zero-sum relation. Rather, "Pastoral events sustain the prophetic. In turn, the prophetic reflects back on the pastoral and religious folk like with correction and direction."[8] Each side of the divide enriches the other even as it is enriched by the bridge between them.

Andrews fills out this argument in relation to both sides of the divide he describes. He has been a strong critic of attempts at pastoral ministry that neglect the concerns of justice. Black theology, he writes, "does well to

---

5. Andrews,"Race and Racism," 408.
6. Andrews and Smith, eds., *Black Practical Theology*, 7.
7. Andrews, *Practical Theology*, 9.
8. Ibid., 11.

speak sharply" to such churches. But, he writes, there is more happening in congregations than scholars sometimes see. Andrews rejects "the blanket charge of escapism in black religious life. Liberation is functioning in black religious folk life."[9] Concern for justice is not alien to the best pastoral ministries. On the contrary, it is always already present. American individualism has distorted some black church practices, Andrews writes. But there are also deep traditions of pastoral practice that are already seeking justice. "[A]mong black churches, ecclesial practices of refuge, survival, and pastoral care for wholeness are as much a part of liberation ethics as black theology's appeals for sociopolitical resistance and justice-making are part of pastoral meaning-making."[10] The best pastoral ministries are already seeking justice. Dialectical exchange with prophetic traditions of liberation theology simply helps pastoral ministries live more deeply into the vocations they are, at their best, already pursuing.

At the same time, pastoral concern has much to contribute to prophetic calls for liberation. Black liberation theologies have gained some important traction in "transforming theological traditions," Andrews writes. "Less effective has been black theology's efforts to transform church practices and black theological worldviews that uncritically perpetuate the theological paradigms sustaining the oppressive traditions, at least theologically, and therefore contribute to the lack of prophetic redress among black churches."[11] If black theology is going to perform the work of transformation, it is going to need to do more to engage congregations, Andrews argues. Without attention to lived practice, he writes, black theology is limited to "judgment oracles and theological apologetics. Reform requires work within the religious folk life of the faith community."[12] If black liberation theology is about making material changes in the real world, then attention to the pastoral will not detract from genuine prophetic purpose, but rather contribute to its realization.

THE DIALECTIC IN PRACTICE

In the dialectic Andrews envisions, neither the prophetic nor the pastoral disappears into the other. And neither approach must compromise its deepest commitments. Rather, dialogue elucidates the prophetic dimensions already present in the best pastoral practice. And dialogue pushes prophetic

---

9. Ibid., 130.
10. Andrews, "Race and Racism," 408.
11. Andrews and Smith, *Black Practical Theology*, 7.
12. Andrews, *Practical Theology*, 129.

theology toward practice in ways that help it fulfill its own telos of making change in the real world. The two approaches remain distinct, even as they require one another for fulfillment.

Andrews insists that this vision of a dialectic between the prophetic and the pastoral is not only an academic ideal. It has taken shape in multiple different lived practices over the years. It can be heard in the testimony of wise elders, Andrews writes. And "perhaps no better modern example of the pastoral-prophetic dialectic in practical theological responses to racism exists than the debates over the nonviolence movement of the twentieth century, led by Martin Luther King, Jr."[13] Note that Andrews does not describe the dialectic as embodied in a single person, no matter how complex and heroic. The dialectic Andrews has in mind comes to full expression in the debates within the movement. The dialectic Andrews envisions is social and dynamic, plural and dialogical. It requires actually existing other people, not just imagined interlocutors or the play of ideas in multidisciplinary work.[14] In Andrews' dialectic, pastors, parachurch leaders, and scholars from many different fields engage one another in conversations about the demands of prophetic justice and pastoral ministry. Andrews' dialectic involves a complex social movement in dialogue about the shape of faithful response to the in-breaking of the Reign of God.

Part of the great gift of Andrews' work is that he not only theorizes such conversations but has helped to make them possible across many different social spaces. Vanderbilt Divinity School's Certificate Program in Homiletic Peer Coaching, which Andrews helped lead, opens up space for some of the kinds of dialogue he calls for. The program brings together pastors and practical theologians in ways that press pastors to make their theologies of preaching explicit and test them in critical conversation even as they press practical theologians to continue to learn from and speak to lived practice. The peer-coaching model democratizes expertise in ways that recognize the significance of pastoral wisdom and become acts of justice in themselves.[15]

Andrews also performs this dialectic in the three-volume set of commentaries that he edited with Dawn Ottoni-Wilhelm and Ronald J. Allen. *Preaching God's Transforming Justice* makes a practical and material connection between church practice and justice-making. It starts with the Revised Common Lectionary, one of the signature products of the twentieth-century liturgical renewal movement. It then connects this icon of pastoral, ecclesial

---

13. Andrews, "Race and Racism," 408.

14. In its emphasis on the need for actual other people in dialogue, not just imagined intersubjectivity, Andrews' work shares much with Benhabib, *Situating the Self*.

15. See "The David G. Buttrick Certificate Program."

preaching with a series of commentaries designed to help readers preach prophetic, justice-seeking sermons on the scheduled texts. The pastoral and the prophetic are blended in the very concept of a justice-focused lectionary commentary. The three volumes of the commentary perform the dialectic on yet another level, too, naming 22 different "Holy Days for Justice." The commentary proposes a revised liturgical calendar in which days like World AIDS Day and Earth Day take their place alongside holy days and seasons like Lent and Trinity Sunday. The result is that the dialectic between the pastoral and the prophetic shapes liturgical time itself. The commentary series runs the risk of letting the prophetic colonize some of the greatest treasures of the pastoral. A project like this could end with talk of justice drowning out all other voices. But the lived performance of the commentary on the pages displays a steady, ecclesial piety that is enhanced rather than diminished by the attention to justice.[16]

Andrews performs this dialectic in yet another way in his most recent book, *Black Practical Theology*, co-edited with Robert London Smith, Jr. The process of writing the book brought together "scholars and practitioners from black theological constructive disciplines, practical theology, and pastor/community ministries in contemporary black life."[17] Teams of authors gathered in dialogue around topics of shared concern like mass incarceration, immigration, and health care. The process was not easy, the editors write. Scholars from different fields struggled with the modes of practical theology. But Andrews and Smith urged the authors to maintain the "praxiological intent" that they take to be a hallmark of practical theology. The point, as Marx wrote in his "Theses on Feuerbach," is not just to interpret the world, but to change it. The book creates a series of "trialogues" with just that purpose in mind. It not only describes a black practical theology, but also shows what black practical theologies can do and be.

Andrews' repeated performances of practical theology give his work an internal consistency that not all practical theology displays. It is necessary, in some moments, to theorize things like the relation between theology and practice or the question of what it means to define practical theology as a discipline. But it is ironic when such talk about the significance of practice is itself almost completely unconscious of its own connection to practice. This results not only in performative contradictions, but also—just as theories of the relation between theory and practice suggest it will—an impoverishment of thought. Andrews, on the other hand, is repeatedly *doing* the practical theology he is trying to describe on the page. And an attentive reader can

16. See Allen, et. al., *Preaching God's Transforming Justice*.
17. Andrews and Smith, eds., *Black Practical Theology*, 13.

see his thinking deepening and expanding as it circulates between theory and practice. Andrews' early work, like *Practical Theology for Black Churches* (2002), assumed a dialogue between scholars and pastors. But the work of engaging in that dialogue led to a more complex and accurate framing for later work like *Black Practical Theology* (2015). As noted above, Andrews' realization of the gaps between practical theologians and other scholars led him to subdivide his set of scholars and describe a conversation between three parties instead of two. And his attention to the lived reality of black religion in the United States led him to move from a tight focus on pastors to a broader sense of the many different kinds of practitioners who might be leading institutions: pastors, certainly, but also activists, directors of NGOs, foundation officers, and other community leaders. In reflecting on his own practice of practical theology, Andrews displays a deep internal consistency. And in reflecting on his own practice of practical theology, Andrews broadens and refines the concepts with which he started his thinking. This is just the kind of work practical theology needs to do, even when it is engaged in the work of offering a theoretical account of itself.

INSTEAD OF UNITY

Stories that feature fissures often begin with a "Once upon a time" wholeness that is then lost and lamented. Talk of the gap between pastoral and prophetic theologies can certainly take this form, recalling great preachers, scholars, or saints of the past who somehow always held the two together. But Andrews takes care to reject that narrative frame for his own discussions of the gaps. "I do not mean to argue for a return to the 'good ole days.'"he writes. "That would be nostalgic! I try, instead, to clarify the critical impediments to mutual resolution of the dissension between black theology and black churches."[18] While Andrews' dialectic works to bridge gaps, it is not seeking to restore an original unity.

I would argue that the dialectic he describes should resist not only the nostalgic pull of a presumed past unity but also the progressive allure of a projected future unity. Such a narrative can be smuggled in through language of dialectic, which can suggest the drive toward some Hegelian whole. That kind of narrative would hold out hope that the conversation between the pastoral and the prophetic might generate some higher term that consumed, transcended, and replaced both terms—and the intellectual traditions and social institutions that give rise to them.

18. Andrews, *Practical Theology*, 129.

Andrews does commend combinations of the pastoral and prophetic that bring out the best in both traditions. Arguments about nonviolence in the civil rights movement are just one example. But I think it is best to see such combinations as tabernacles rather than temples. They are not grand, stable edifices at the end of history, but temporary tents for communion with the divine. These little resolutions of the tensions between the prophetic and the pastoral are set up by particular people in particular places in particular times. Eventually they are taken down as situations change and the people move on. And the people move on with the trust that because God has delivered them and because God has promised to bring them to a new home, they will be able to erect new tents of meeting along the way as they are needed.

This vision of dialectic in which resolutions are temporary and contextual has both intellectual and institutional implications. Intellectually, it calls for less effort to construct grand accounts of practical theological method and more grounded attention to the small, contingent spots of "overlapping consensus" that can be found in and around particular social movements. These moments of consensus require not just theories of practice but careful historical and sociological attention to actually existing situations. They are informed by what Andrews calls "praxiological intent," but they are not mere strategic compromises. They are rather agreements rooted in the deepest values on each side of the gap.[19]

Institutionally, this vision of temporary, contextual bridges between the pastoral and the prophetic resists attempts to combine church and parachurch organizations with academic organizations in ways that form new kinds of institutions that replace the constituent parts. Such drives toward institutional wholes exist, for instance, when mega-churches start theological schools within themselves and when theological schools become congregations unto themselves. Efforts like these erode the institutional base of difference, and so of dialogue. They drive to bring the dialectic to an end.

A better vision attends to Andrews' rejection of nostalgia for past unity and learns how to resist the temptations of future unity. It accepts as part of our condition the basic division between pastoral and prophetic emphases and its contingent institutionalization in the enduring division between church and academy. If it does not rejoice in that division—for that would be to paper over its real cost—this better vision also does not seek to overcome the division once and for all by its own power. This better vision instead seeks to encourage both prophetic and pastoral traditions to extend

---

19. I borrow the concept of "overlapping consensus," and the distinction of this concept from a *modus vivendi*, from Rawls, *Political Liberalism* 134–49.

themselves toward their own distinct teloi. It seeks to sustain the particular institutions in which they can flourish on their own terms. And, crucially, it seeks to create social, liturgical, and intellectual spaces in which theory and practice, the prophetic and the pastoral, the academic and the ecclesial, can engage in dialogue.

This vision does not call us to close the gaps that Andrews has analyzed with such insight. It rather calls us to build bridges across those gaps. Some of those bridges might be great spans that endure for a long time. Others might be more temporary, like rope bridges across a river. Some will support heavy traffic in both directions. Others might be composed of more fragile filaments-and no less precious for that. Some bridges might be created from books or articles. Others might be built up through sermons, songs, or prayers. Some might be built in classrooms or conference halls. Others might be constructed in sanctuaries, hush arbors, or virtual spaces for shared testimony.

Dale Andrews has spent a lifetime building such bridges. If they do not close all the gaps, neither do they let gaps become absolute. Instead they turn the divisions that create differences into resources for responding to a God who is never less than just but always more.

PART 2

The Pastoral and Prophetic in Preaching

5

Building Bridges
Pastoral Care for the World in a Prophetic Mode

RONALD J. ALLEN

POLARIZATION AMONG SOCIAL GROUPS is one of the most distinctive—and disturbing—characteristics of the early twenty-first century. When I think of polarization, the first thing to come to mind is political polarization—red groups and blue groups who act as if their worldviews and projects are imperial and exclusive. But the fact is that polarization occurs in various degrees across the social spectrum today—not only among political parties, but also among social classes, racial and ethnic groups, age cohorts, religious communities, and more. Polarization also takes place within groups—for example, within political parties and within religious communities. Indeed, religious polarization sometimes leads me to think I have more in common with some non-religious communities than with other Christian bodies. Polarized communities often use extreme adversarial rhetoric to justify their own positions and to denigrate others, thereby intensifying polarization.

From the standpoint of my deepest theological convictions such a polarized social world works against God's purposes for human community. This essay contends that an important dimension of the call of prophetic preaching is to encourage the larger human family toward greater relatedness, solidarity, mutual support, and mutual accountability.[1] For reasons

---

1. Prophetic preaching is also called to help the human family recover awareness and embodiment of its covenant with nature. But in a short essay, I focus only on

that will unfold in the following pages, I join Dale Andrews in seeing an important dimension of prophetic preaching as expressing pastoral care in and to the polarized world. In a vivid turn of phrase, Professor Andrews refers to this approach as "prophetic care."[2] Indeed, seeking to care for others, is itself a prophetic act.

This chapter considers (1) prophetic preaching as an expression of pastoral care (prophetic care), (2) polarization as undermining God's pastoral purposes for community, (3) bridge building as an expression of prophetic care, and (4) some possibilities for when a bridge fails.[3] Such a short essay can only be suggestive in these matters.

PROPHETIC PREACHING AS PASTORAL CARE

Preachers sometimes think of the pastoral and the prophetic as different qualities in preaching and in wider dimensions of ministry and ecclesial life. Speaking in caricature, some ministers say that pastoral preaching empathizes, assures, and is tender and solicitous. By contrast, some ministers

---

human community/ies.

2. Andrews, "We're Never Done." Professor Andrews focuses particularly on bridging a chasm characteristic of some African American communities between liberation theology as political movement with formal academic overlay, and the everyday beliefs and practices of believers and congregations. In addition, many of the chasm-crossing concepts that Professor Andrews articulates so well can be adapted to Eurocentric settings. I gather from conversation among scholars of preaching and preachers in Latinx, Asian, and other communities that Professor Andrews' word is informative in those contexts also.

3. I subscribe to a "conversational" view of preaching. This perspective differs from mainstream views of preaching that *assume* that a biblical text contains theological perspective that only needs to be clarified and applied. A conversational approach listens to the voices in an interpretive situation (usually the Bible, church history/tradition, the experiences of the communities involved, scientific and other data) and helps the community consider interpretive options that are consistent with the community's deepest convictions (or challenge those convictions) and possible implications. The preacher helps the community toward an adequate interpretation of God's purposes in the context in which the sermon is preached. On this perspective, a recent statement is Allen and Allen, *Sermon Without End*. I do not believe that the sermon is inherently *the* Word of God. Nor do I believe, as do quite a few exponents of prophetic preaching, that the preacher speaking as prophet categorically speaks for God. In my view, the prophet seeks the most adequate interpretation of God's purposes for a particular situation. The prophet helps the community struggle toward naming and correcting things that frustrate those purposes. I recognize that this "soft" view of prophetic preaching is conditioned, in part, by my comfortable social location as an upper middle class, Eurocentric, heterosexual. If I were in a more threatened social location, I might take a different view.

say that prophetic preaching challenges, confronts, and calls for change, especially with respect to wider social issues. The prophet courageously names sin (especially social injustice), exposes those responsible for it, and demands repentance.[4]

As noted, the preceding pictures of the pastoral and the prophetic are cartoon-like.[5] Nevertheless, they point to a typical distinction in the contemporary scholarship and practice of preaching between the pastoral and the prophetic as if these are two different kinds of preaching. We speak about the pastoral *and* the prophetic, or even of the pastoral *versus* the prophetic. Preachers who seek to soften the dualism of such thinking sometimes propose approaching prophetic preaching in a pastoral mode or bridging the pastoral and the prophetic.

Charles Hartshorne, a philosopher and theologian, offers a more nuanced perspective within which to understand the relationship of prophetic preaching to other modes of preaching. Hartshorne explores the nature of the relationship between two notions that appear to contrast significantly with one another. People often think of such things as opposites or dualities. Hartshorne notices that in many such relationships, one element is really the larger, inclusive element, embracing the other element. The more inclusive member of the pair forms "the given context, the total reality," within which the other element plays an important role in the service of the larger element.[6] The secondary element contributes to the larger, more inclusive dimension. We might picture the relationship as a larger circle within which there is a smaller circle (see below). For instance, from the standpoint of a traditional theological contrast, grace and law are not opposites, but, rather, grace includes law. Indeed, law is an expression of grace in the sense that God provides law (instruction, guidance) to help the community embody the implications of grace in personal life and in social relationships.

When we look more closely at what it means to be "pastoral" in many of the biblical traditions and in many voices in church history, we discover that to be pastoral is to build up the community to strengthen its identity, quality of life, and mission. The word "pastor" is a transliteration of the Latin

---

4. Prophetic preaching often uses tools of social analysis under theological management to expose systems of injustice. Prophetic preaching is sometimes clothed in the emotion of righteous anger.

5. For concise, contemporary, and much more nuanced summaries of the notions of pastoral and prophetic preaching, see "Pastoral Preaching" and "Prophetic Preaching" in McClure, *Preaching Words*, 100–101, 117–18. One one the best guides to the relationship of the pastoral and prophetic operating under the rubrics of pastoral *and* prophetic, especially in Eurocentric circles, is Tisdale, *Prophetic Preaching*.

6. Hartshorne, "Logic of Ultimate Contrasts," 99–100.

pastor which refers to a shepherd (or a herd). In the world of the Bible, the shepherd was responsible for the full range of things necessary to maintain a strong and healthy flock.[7] As Psalm 23 famously indicates, the shepherd recognized many individual sheep, took the flock to green pastures, brought them to life-sustaining water, led them through danger, and protected them from animal and human predators. When the sheep were injured, the shepherd treated them with oil and healing balm. It is crucial to note that the shepherd also took corrective action, disciplining the sheep when necessary. "The rod and the staff occasionally help to keep a sheep from going astray or loitering." Yet, "Even severity in leadership, may become a comfort" when such leadership warns the flock against things that can do the flock harm, including its own misbehavior.[8]

In short, the shepherd must do what is necessary to encourage the flock toward optimum health. Sometimes shepherding leadership involves tender care, at other times guidance and instruction, and at other times discipline.[9]

From this perspective, the pastoral element is the larger, inclusive one in the relationship of the pastoral and the prophetic, while the prophetic serves the larger goal. A simple visual representation depicts the relationship between the pastoral and the prophetic. See Figure 1.

Figure 1

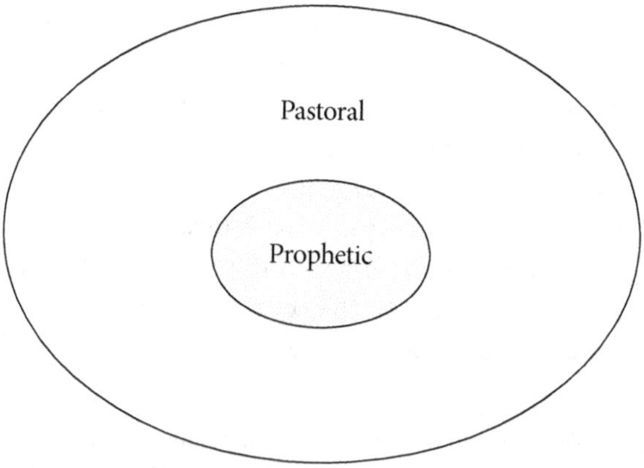

Pastoral

Prophetic

---

7. This data is summarized in Allen, "Relationship of the Pastoral," 173–89.

8. Terrien, *Psalms*, 240.

9. Not surprisingly, biblical writers sometimes refer to God as shepherd (e.g. Ps 23:1; Isa 40:11). Biblical writers sometimes refer to monarchs, priests, and others in positions of authority. Indeed, prophets can call such folk "false shepherds" when they violate the safety and mission of the flock (e.g. Jer 23:1–2; Ezek 34:2–10).

Building Bridges 51

The goal of the pastoral vocation is to encourage the strength and vitality of the community. Biblical materials describe the goal of the common life in multiple ways—e.g. living in covenant, the blessed life, the way of wisdom, salvation, the Realm of God. The different ways of speaking are not simply synonyms, but they do include shared values, such as love, peace, justice, respect, mutual support, security, and abundance for all.[10] Marjorie Suchock summarizes God's purpose as "inclusive well-being."[11]

The prophet arises when the community is on a path away from pastoral goals for the common good and toward diminished quality of life. The prophet seeks to help the community correct its direction so that it will return to the way that leads to blessing (and will turn away from path that leads to collapse). In the early decades of the twenty-first century, we are especially attuned to violations such as injustice, exploitation, fractiousness, and violence, and to concomitant calls for repentance and social transformation. At the same time, we should remember that some of the biblical prophets preached when the great danger to the people was not their complicity in social injustice but was their lack of confidence in God and in the promises of God. During the exile, for instance, the community was in despair and in danger of giving up on God and embracing the gods of Babylon. Deutero-Isaiah sought to correct the people's drift by highlighting the promises of God and the power of God to keep those promises. That message was every bit as prophetic as Amos calling out the cows of Bashan.

As we noted at the outset of this essay, Dale Andrews uses the vivid expression "prophetic care" to describe the prophet's vocation. In the broad sense, prophetic preaching expresses pastoral care for the community as community. The preacher seeks to build up the pastoral qualities of the community's life by urging the community to correct its trajectory. As Dale Andrews points out, "Ultimately, prophetic agency intends reform and reconciliation."[12]

The prophet does not simply denounce injustice or wish to bring down the mighty from their thrones. The prophetic message is intended to help the community make theological sense of its life and to respond appropriately. The community may need to repent of social injustice. But it may also need to recover its confidence in the promises of God. Indeed, the foci, the prophetic modes of expression and the nuances of feeling are as many as there are contexts and preachers. The important thing is that the preacher

---

10. For an eloquent discussion of covenant, see Andrews, *Practical Theology*, 106–28.

11. Suchocki, *Fall*, 66.

12. Andrews, *Practical Theology*, 11.

thinks with the congregation about some aspect of the community's life that needs to take another course if it is to fulfill God's pastoral purpose.

POLARIZATION UNDERMINES GOD'S PASTORAL PURPOSES FOR COMMUNITY

Prophets express prophetic care in specific contexts. As we mentioned at the outset, polarization is a disturbing characteristic of the second decade of the twenty-first century.[13]

To be sure, postmodern consciousness often celebrates difference, diversity, and otherness. This celebration is particularly apt when communities live together in mutual support. At the same time, it can be important for communities to delimit boundaries to maintain identity and to help members recognize attitudes and behaviors that are appropriate and inappropriate.

In polarization, however, people withdraw into gated enclaves of closed perspectives, and regard others with suspicion and even hostility. Polarized groups tend to see the world in binary terms of us and them, right and wrong, and seek to dominate the social world. They seldom take the perspectives of others into account, and typically claim to have *the* answers for the larger world. Indeed, counter-perspectives and resistance to the group often reinforce the commitment of group members to their polarizing ideology. Polarizing groups sometimes reject a proposal from a rival group simply because the proposal originated in that outside source, and with no reference to the strengths and weaknesses of the proposal itself. My impression is that polarizing groups sometimes seek power more for the sake of having power than for the purpose of advancing an agenda.

A billiard table is a good image for the interactions that take place in polarized cultures. Groups bang against one another like solid clay balls trying to knock other balls off the table.

Polarization violates God's pastoral purposes for community as it promotes exclusive well-being. It not only works against solidarity and common vision for the common good, but reinforces artificial, alienating possibilities for relationship in community. Polarizing attitudes and

---

13. To state the obvious, polarization is only one of many things that subvert God's pastoral aim for the community of humankind and nature. Examples of other things that subvert a truly pastoral world include racism, sexism, homophobia, economic injustice, political repression, ecological abuse, and religiophobia. As ethicists are quick to remind us, these things are systemically related. These corrosions feed polarization which reinforces them. For purposes of discussion, we have polarization on the screen while other distortions run in the background.

behaviors undermine prospects for love, peace, justice, respect, mutual support, security, and abundance for all. Indeed, polarizing groups sometimes actively wish ill being on those at other poles. Moreover, polarizing groups, though beset with relativity and finitude, often ascribe ultimacy to their ideologies, leaving polarizing to wallow in idolatry.

BRIDGE BUILDING AS AN EXPRESSION OF PROPHETIC CARE

From the standpoint of preaching as prophetic care, bridge-building is both an identity for the preacher and a strategy for preaching. The prophet's purpose is to encourage pastoral qualities in common life. The prophet should intend for everything in preaching to point toward the possibilities for a world that is pastoral in all its dimensions.[14]

It follows, then, that the prophet would try to use methods of communication that are consistent with pastoral life, that is, methods that are themselves loving, peaceful, just, respectful, mutually supportive, promote security, and have abundance in view for all. Prophetic care calls for the preacher not only to seek to build bridges across the chasms of personal and social separation and alienation, but to do so in ways that are consistent with the pastoral goals of restoration, renewal, or even re-creation. Building bridges to others is indigenous to communities of mutual support.

14. Preachers who seek to express prophetic care through preaching often have two related audiences. The preacher sometimes speaks to these audiences separately, but sometimes members of both audiences are present in the same congregation. The preacher needs to take them both into account.
  In a polarized cultural setting, the obvious audience is those who create and reinforce the community-denying poles. They benefit from polarization because polarization reinforces their social power (and often fiscal and other benefits that come with it). The preacher seeks to cross the bridge to help those individuals and groups to name the possibility of the corrective action of repenting and moving toward more pastoral approaches to life, to recognize its benefits for them and for the larger world, and to join the movement toward re-creating a more pastoral world. Some people associated with this far side of the bridge may be in the congregation, or in a circle where they can receive the invitation and act on it. But many will not be in range of the voice of preacher. In that case, preacher and congregation face the challenge of bringing their voice to expression in a setting in which this first audience may have a chance to hear it.
  The other audience is members of the congregation in which the sermon is preached. Some members will essentially agree with the preacher. The sermon does not so much need to invite them to repent as it seeks to help them toward meaningful interpretations of the polarizing circumstance, help them deepen their hope that transformation is possible, and help them enlarge their commitment to participation in the movement transformation. The preacher's invitation to those on the other side of the bridge is itself a reinforcement to the group on the original side.

I hesitate to say this, but wrapped in the mantle of prophetic preaching, ministers sometimes contribute to polarization by painting the world in stark and unambiguous terms of justice and injustice. Indeed, ministers sometimes contribute to polarization in the very classification of preaching as pastoral or prophetic—as if these are polar approaches—the first caring and nurturing while the second is confrontational and judgmental. Prophetic preachers can use adversarial rhetoric with intensity exceeding that of the most firebrand politician. In the name of the highest ends, some prophetic preachers engage in manipulative, even abusive rhetoric characteristic of other polarizers; preachers can caricature, name-call, invoke a them-and-us mentality, blame, scapegoat, distort, oversimplify, abandon facts altogether, and play to the fears of the audience.

These considerations raise the question of what it means to build a bridge. A bridge enables a person or a group to go from one side of a divide to another, and to be able to return, as needed. When the person or group (call them Group A) is on one side the bridge, they can see quite a bit of what is on the other side (where Group B is located), but Group A can only see what is immediately apparent. They cannot see things that are partially or completed obscured. Group A cannot see fully how it appears to Group B. When Group A crosses to the other side, they can see more of the world of Group B. Group A can see behind or in things that were previously obscured. They have a much clearer and closer perception of the members of Group B. When Group A arrives on the other side, and looks back across the divide to the side from which they started, they can apprehend, at least on a surface level, how their worlds appear to Group B. To be sure, Group A cannot grasp Group B's interpretation of the world simply by coming over the bridge and looking around. Group A must listen to Group B's explanation of the world, raise questions, ask for clarification, and test its perceptions against those of Group B. Such encounters should lead to deeper mutual understanding, which can then open the door to negotiating and renegotiating relationships in ways that can become mutually supportive.

In describing the bridge, I use a lot of language, like "quite a bit" that is intended to signal that our perception is always partial or finite. We can never *fully* cross the bridge of perception into the worlds of others. We can never completely understand the world from the standpoints of others. Nevertheless, human imagination is such that when exposed to others in perception-enhancing ways, we can come the point of perceiving "quite a bit" (if never enough). As the word "imagination" suggests, through disciplined attentiveness to others, we can often imagine enough of how others see the world to have some grasp of why they do so, and, consequently, of why they feel, and act as they do

A bridge typically allows people to cross in safety. For example, a group can walk on planks in safety above a roaring river. But we should not romanticize the idea of crossing the bridge. Some bridges creak and groan and sound as if they might collapse. Some bridges are unsafe, even to the point of collapse. A bridge just wide enough for one person suspended from a single line over a deep canyon can tremble from nothing more than the fact of a person walking on it, and can shake in the wind so as to turn the knuckles white on a person caught in the middle. Every so often, the news pictures interstate highway bridges—seemingly the epitome of sturdy construction—in failure, sometimes with loss of life.[15] In such cases, even something intended to provide safe passage can itself be dangerous. Crossing a bridge can call for the wisdom to check out the possible dangers of the bridge, as well as the courage to cross.

In a polarized setting, the attempt to build or cross a bridge can serve several purposes with respect to the preacher and the sermon. It can give the preacher a better (if partial) understanding of how those on the other side of the bridge see the world as they do, and why they do so. The preacher might then be able find points of identification between the issues at stake and the concerns and values of people locked into their own polar enclaves. The preacher might then be able to approach corrective guidance less from an adversarial position and more from the standpoint of what community members can do together to improve the situation of all. The sermon can have more a tone of invitation than condemnation and threat. The preacher can invite people onto the pathway of blessing for all even while alerting them to the consequences of not following that path.

If the crossing fails, the attempt nevertheless demonstrates to those on the other side care on the part of the preacher and the preacher's community. The preacher maintains covenant with God's purpose for people to live together in solidarity.

This does not mean a prophetic caregiver should never speak strongly or sternly from the pulpit. In order to correct its path from one continuing

---

15. Some bridges do not really serve their purposes. For example, the San Gabriel mountains in southern California contain a "Bridge to Nowhere," a bridge that was largely completed in the late 1930s but never used because climatic events destroyed the roadway on which it is located. This image is a humorous though useful one to explain some sermons—they are bridges to nowhere.

to support polarization to one leading toward blessing, a community needs to know what it is doing wrong and to have an idea of what to do about it. To use a simple analogy, a parent must sometimes warn a child about a danger to the child. In situations in which danger is extreme and immediate, a parent may speak with urgency. When a child is about to touch a hot burner, for instance, a parent will probably cry out a warning and try physically to reach the child's hand to prevent it from touching the hot burner.

Of course, oracles of judgment are a staple of prophetic speech in the biblical traditions. However, prophets do not usually speak such oracles as final words of condemnation. Prophets typically voiced oracles of judgment in the context of calling for repentance. The oracle of judgment named ways in which the ancient community violated covenant. I like to describe the oracle of judgment as pastoral warning or pastoral interpretation. The prophet does not simply rail against injustice or other qualities distracting from pastoral qualities in the community's life, but alerts the community to the consequences of its current path. If repentance is possible, the oracle is a pastoral warning: the community can repent, and avoid the outcome of is misbehavior, If repentance is not possible—that is, if the situation has reached the point that nothing can be done about it—then the oracle is pastoral interpretation intended to help the community make theological sense of why its life is collapsing. Either way, the oracle of judgment even with its hard edge is an expression of care.

WHEN A BRIDGE FAILS

When a group crosses over a bridge from one side of a chasm to the other, those on the far side are sometimes much less welcoming than anticipated. Indeed, they can be hostile and even violent. Bridges themselves sometimes fail. Although approaching prophetic care through bridge building offers optimum opportunities for real communication, it is not a magic formula for success in communication or in building community.

What does a preacher do when trying to bridge a social chasm fails? What seem to be the most promising (and least destructive) possibilities for responding to bridging attempts that have come to unsuccessful ends? How the preacher responds to immediate bridge failures can frustrate the possibility of the situation moving in a pastoral direction.

Speaking autobiographically, when a social bridge fails, I am often beside myself with frustration, and even angry, especially if those to whom I attempting to cross are a combination of smug, dismissive, arrogant, and angry themselves. If preachers allow unfiltered disappointment and anger to shape the expression in the sermon, the preachers have a certain self-righteous satisfaction at telling them off, and colleagues in the ministry may congratulate such a preacher on her or his courage. But my observation is that such anger, blasting at those who frustrated the bridging process, typically only feeds the anger present in the system, and increases the violence of the system. Anger begets anger.

At the same time, anger is powerful, and systems analysis teaches us that anger suppressed in one part of a system will come out elsewhere. When pure, reactive anger, even in the name of righteousness, is injected into the mix, the anger-factor increases the potential of destructiveness in the situation.

A more pastoral approach, it seems to me, is to take a step back from the immediate surge of emotion in the situation, to name and analyze the presence and dynamics of the anger of the preacher and communities associated with that anger. Rather than blast the anger directly at those who continue to maintain and benefit from polarization, the preacher might take the approach of sharing with them why the anger has come about, the destructive effects of the circumstances in the community that prompted the anger, as well as the destructive effects of the anger itself, not only with the community. Instead of eyeball-to-eyeball confrontation, the preacher says, in spirit, to the polarizing bodies. "Let me share with you something that touches my heart, that I think will touch your heart, and that we can change together." This approach does not guarantee a positive outcome, but it attempts to deal with a genuinely prophetic concern in a way that is consistent with pastoral goal itself.

The preacher cannot take responsibility for how people respond to prophetic care expressed in thoughtful and pastoral modes. The recipients of the sermon have the freedom to respond as they will. If they accept the invitation toward a more pastoral world, they may take some tentative steps in that direction and become a part of the transformative process. If they do not accept the invitation born from prophetic care, they may maintain, and even intensify, present manifestations of polarity, in which case the situation could actually be worse than before, as when a powerful group, blood in its eyes, cries out, "We'll show you who's in charge here." The sermon is not solely responsible for such responses. The preacher, however, *is* responsible for framing the sermon in such a way as to minimize unnecessary interference between the speaking and the hearing, and to offer as clearly as possible optimum opportunities for recognizing the value of embracing a pastoral approach to life and for suggesting initial steps on that journey.

In the end, a preacher may need to acknowledge that a particular bridging attempt is not bearing the traffic that the preacher intended. Indeed, the people on the other side may close the bridge, or the structure of the bridge itself may fail. The preacher cannot simply yield to failure. Resignation and despair may offer themselves to the preacher as companions. Indeed, they give the preacher and the congregation a place to hide. Preachers may be tempted to shake the dust from the feet that visited the far side of the bridge and to "leave that house" to the destructive consequences of its own behavior.[16] Of course, it is important for the preacher to acknowledge impulses toward resignation and despair so the preacher can deal appropriately with them, and so they will not interfere inappropriately with the preacher's will toward pastoral community. Moreover, shaking the dust off one's feet and leaving the people in the house to their own devices is inconsistent with the values and practices of a pastoral community.

When the bridge fails, the preacher might take a pastoral pause, a time-out. The preacher can step back to survey the scene of bridge failure, to consider what went wrong, and why, and to ponder next steps. Such steps could include renewed (if different) approaches to preaching. In sports, a time-out gives the team a little time to rehydrate, munch a protein bar, and think about next steps in the game.

From my point of view as a process theologian, God is omnipresent in every bridging attempt (in fact, in every moment of life) offering possibilities for pastoral community. People have the option of choosing, rejecting, partially choosing, or modifying possibilities for the development of a pastoral world that are present in every situation. God never gives up attempting to encourage authentic community. When one bridging attempt fails, other prospects are in the mix, even if they are not obvious to the preacher. A strategic pause gives preacher and congregation an opportunity to think afresh about possibilities.

Preachers do not control the effects of sermons in the genre of prophetic care, nor do preachers know what effects such sermons have over time. On the one hand, a sermon's full effect may end before the preacher has spoken the last word of the sermon. Dead on arrival. Dead before arrival. On the other hand sermons may fall into the heart of a person or a group without their awareness. But like the seeds growing secretly (Mark 4:26–30), the sermons may someday push their way to the surface of personal and social consciousness with a pastoral harvest.

---

16. Per Matt 10:14; Mark 6:11; Luke 9:5; Acts 13:51.

6

The Prophet on the Margins

GENNIFER BENJAMIN BROOKS

HERE ARE TWO COMMONPLACE statements. "The prophet speaks for God." "Prophetic preaching puts the word of God into the mouth of the preacher." These two statements have often been offered in relation to prophetic peaching, but without careful consideration as to their meaning. They have been used especially by preachers who tout the biblical record when a scripture text has been used to offer negative judgement against specific persons. But as we consider the situation in the USA, and in the world, where such a large percentage of people are marginalized by societal, cultural, economic and other factors, it leads to the question: What is God's word to those on the margins? More specifically in relation to the focus on pastoral prophetic preaching, how does the prophet bring a relevant word from God to those on the margins?

The preacher inhabits the space between the good news of the text and the context of the people's lives. The preacher as prophet claims explicitly or by inference to offer a word of justice, a word of hope, a word that offers reconciliation from God to the people. Understandings of prophetic preaching vary across a wide spectrum, but unfortunately, much of what is offered as prophetic rarely follow in the mode of the biblical prophets. A facile explanation of prophetic preaching is that it speaks truth to power;

however, Walter Brueggemann offers a slightly more complex explanation of the prophet's task. He says, "The task of prophetic ministry is to nurture, nourish, and evoke a consciousness and perception alternative to the consciousness and perception of the dominant culture around us."[1] In other words, being truly prophetic requires the one so called to be deliberately and intentionally pastoral. For those who have been shunted to the margins of society, the call to pastoral prophetic preaching demands that the preached word become a bridge that connects those who have been bowed down by the vagaries of life, that earned them a place on the margins, to the uplifting enlivening word of God.

Following Bruggemann's thought, with respect to guiding and encouraging Christians, and particularly the marginalized, to experience an alternative consciousness, the pastoral role is intended to meet the people in the context of their individual and communal lives on the margins, and to offer nurture that is authentic and practical in helping them to find the paths that lead to justice and reconciliation for themselves. Dale Andrews writes,

> Somewhere between the pastoral nature of personal faith and the prophetic demands upon religious communities lie the structures necessary for spanning the chasm between black churches and black theology. *Care must be given to understand the destructive capacity of individualism in religious life that produces a communalism quite content with its own likeness. The corrective, however, must press beyond a simply subjugation of spiritual formation to liberation ethics. A sound bridge will reestablish the necessary reciprocity between personal faith and social justice rather than a subjugation of one under the other.*[2]

His words are particularly appropriate for speaking to the situation of marginalization given the reality that Black people as a group in the USA experience the hegemony of marginalization even at the highest levels of society. Further, the reality is that Africa has the largest percentage and number of poor people in the world and poverty is perhaps the greatest cause of marginalization.

Although the prophet continues to be charged with the responsibility to seek justice in the face of systems and practices that demean, diminish, and deny those on the margins from living into the fullness of their humanity, prophetic preaching, if it intends to continue in the line of the biblical prophets must be a true embodiment of the message of hope in the midst of judgment brought against and for the community. It cannot be simply be a

---

1. Brueggemann, *Prophetic Imagination*, 3.
2. Andrews, *Practical Theology*, 9 (Andrews' emphasis).

message of judgment or challenge to those who seek to prevail against the community, nor can it focus only on encouragement and hope for the community and ignore the community's culpability or collusion with the forces that work against its prosperity and seek its demise.

If the prophet's proclamation is to be the bridge that offers a path to understanding the divine will, it must be representative of the divine call to justice and reconciliation of the whole people of God. Pastoral prophetic preaching is an ongoing call to consistent witness and action. Brueggemann suggests "that prophetic ministry has to do not primarily with addressing specific public crises, but with addressing, in season and out of season, the dominant crisis that is enduring and resilient, of having our alternative vocation co-opted and domesticated."[3] In other words, the ministry of prophetic proclamation is part and parcel of pastoral ministry and requires the one who would claim the appellation of prophet, and who would focus on offering the good news of divine grace to be fully aware of the needs of the context of that proclamation. Prophetic preaching, to live up to its name, must be fully pastoral.

In order for preaching to be authentically prophetic, the preacher must take the time necessary to do an analysis of the context before daring to engage the task of proclamation that offers transformation through the offering of good news. Although there are communities and prophets engaged in work of authentic bridge-building that not only allows but guides both the people and the perpetrators of marginalization into activities of justice and reconciliation, the reality is that the church has been and continues to be in collusion with the culture within which it operates to push individuals and groups to the margins.

One current example of this phenomenon of marginalization can be found in The United Methodist Church within which I hold my ordination status and my membership. I write this chapter within a few days of the announcement by the bishops of my church that there will be a special session of the General Conference, the level at which church law is constructed, within three years of the last conference, instead of the usual four years. The major and perhaps only agenda for spending the multi-thousands or maybe millions of dollars that are required to offset the cost of a General Conference, is the church's, or perhaps the Council of Bishops', inability to build the bridges necessary to resolve the church's stance on homosexuality, particularly with respect to ordained clergy. And this decision came upon the heels, or maybe in tandem with the ruling by the Judicial Council of the UMC offering a decision on a petition brought by the South Central

3. Brueggemann, *Prophetic Imagination*, 3.

Jurisdiction (representing the South Central area of the USA), with respect to the consecration of an openly homosexual bishop. The decision upheld what many in the church believed to be an unjust law and saw the bishop to be in violation of its law that considered homosexuality inconsistent with Christian practice.[4]

Both the Judicial Council ruling and the call for a Special session of the General Conference challenge the notion of justice and run counter to the practice of reconciliation represented in the teaching and example of Jesus Christ. Both actions are representative of the continued marginalization of groups within the church. The United Methodist Church has continued to bewail, for more than two decades the spiraling loss of members and yet there seems to be a disconnect among those who would insist that they speak for God (or at least the Bible) on the position they have taken that denies the identity of homosexuals, or the more inclusive identifier of this marginalized group, LGBTQAI persons, as full persons and participants in the reign of God.

John Wesley, the founder of the Methodism, stressed the need for both personal faith and social holiness, but not as a dualistic model of Christian faith. Rather he believed that personal faith led to the justice and reconciliation of all people, inherent in social holiness. Wesley, following in the footsteps of Christ, reached out to those on the margins with words and actions that inspired personal Christian zeal and moved the adherents to action on behalf of those who were victims of the hegemonic systems of their society and culture. In the same way that the church of Wesley's day had lost its place and its standing in the society, to a large extent, the established church has lost its place and its standing in society, hence the continued membership loss and the increasingly strident "conversation" among many streams of mainline Christianity about dividing. Instead of finding ways to bridge the gap between understanding and misunderstanding of the issues that separate one group from the other (in most cases that of homosexuality), instead of adopting a deeply pastoral mode of engagement of the people on both sides of the spectrum, instead of focusing on justice and striving for reconciliation, the church has walked away from the inclusive teaching of Jesus. In doing so, the church has ignored Christ's outstretched arms that encompass the whole world, and added to its list of marginalized people, who they have pushed outside the boundaries that have been set by those who consider themselves insiders.

Modeling its proclamation on the ancient prophets, the church is being called to commit itself to prophetic witness that moves all people from

---

4. See Paragraph 304.3 of *Book of Discipline 2016*.

the margins of life and makes the church a welcoming, inviting and hospitable place for all people. Leonora Tubbs Tisdale names the challenge that confronts parish pastors because they,

> . . . unlike most Old Testament prophets, are called to be both priests and prophets to their people. Living within that tension is often difficult. How do you speak hard words of judgment from God, often controversial words, to a people you dearly love in a way that does not shut down your relationship with them? And how do you walk that delicate tightrope in ministry between pastorally building up people who have been beaten down in life while prophetically calling them to live responsibly in relation to others who have been beaten down by this world, its peoples and its systems?[5]

All who have responsibility for nurturing the people of God, whether as pastors of local congregations or not, are called to offer words that speak truth not only to systems and purveyors of power, but to the reality of God's care for all people that is the heart of justice and that reconciles all to oneness with God and one another.

Issues of justice and reconciliation have plagued Christians from the beginning. The call for separation between proponents and opponents on the issue of homosexuality is just one more chapter in a saga that has seen the church divide on other issues, the most heinous and yet unfinished being that of the racial divide and the hegemony of racism. I consider racism a sin against God, but so too are sexism and homophobia. Indeed, the defining characteristics represented in sexuality, gender, and orientation are part of our God-given identity. Focusing on the issue of racism, as an issue within which the need for justice and reconciliation are visibly present, within established church structures, Black congregations have adopted an ecclesiological mode of care and faith. With unflinching awareness of their diminished place in a society where whiteness is centralized and worshipped, Dale Andrews notes,

> Black preaching and black worship have established traditions centered in nurturing black wholeness and empowerment for living under oppressive conditions. The preaching task has focused on interpreting black Christianity in the interests of black humanity and faith development in black life.[6]

---

5. Tisdale, *Prophetic Preaching*, xii.
6. Andrews, *Practical Theology*, 23.

In other words, despite the fact that the Black churches have been lauded extensively for their preaching, which has generally been considered prophetic, the nature of most prophetic Black preaching has been pastoral.

Brueggemann's model of exile and hope, representative of the literary traditions of Jeremiah, Ezekiel, and Deutero Isaiah,[7] offers a description of the prophetic preaching that has sustained the Black people in the church, as it has continued to be confronted and marginalized because of their race. He writes,

> The world is perceived under the twin aspects of *relinquishment* and *receiving*. The perception of reality is based on an unshakeable theological conviction: God's powerful governance is displacing the present idolatrous order of public life and is generating a new order that benefits God's will for the world. This theological conviction is not rooted in political observation, economic analysis, or cultural yearning. It is rooted decisively in the notion of who God is and what God wills.[8]

This model spawned the prophetic preaching that is notable in the Black church, that has sustained a people neglected and abused, beaten and brought low from the rejection and injustice perpetrated by society and even the church.

For a people shunted to the margins of both society and culture, such prophetic preaching has bridged the gap between who they are, clearly imbued with the *imago dei,* and who society perceives them to be, as less than human. Where the Israel of 587 BCE was called to relinquish who they were once the temple was destroyed, and to receive a new world ordained by God, Black people in the United States enslaved and reluctantly freed, but not fully liberated from human bondage, were called by pastoral, prophetic preachers in the newly developing Black Church tradition, to relinquish the stigmas of slavery and to press forward in hope and faith to receive the new thing, the new world, the new order that God had ordained for them. However, the audacious hope that once fueled the prophets of the Black church that emerged from the brush arbors seems to have been lost to time.

Marvin McMickle laments that "More than likely our people will hear sermons about the values of patriotism, the paths to peace and prosperity, the appropriate methods for baptism and communion, why God does not approve of women in ministry and why a woman's right to control her reproductive choices is the single greatest evil in the world today."[9] There

---

7. Ibid.
8. Ibid., 4.
9. McMickle, *Where Have All the Prophets Gone?*, 26.

is undeniable truth to what McMickle says. His words speak poignantly to Brueggemann's call to beware of focusing on the issues of the day and neglecting the greater call of the divine "to live in fervent anticipation of the newness that God has promised and will surely give."[10] I am also unconvinced that praise songs and prosperity gospel are the major reasons for the continued marginality and the unreconciled differences between marginalized groups, and the whiteness that is pervasive in the church of Jesus Christ.

By whiteness, I am not referring simply to skin color that is considered white. The term whiteness as used here refers to the embodiment of the dominant white culture that is represented by the white middle or upper middle class heterosexual male. It speaks of a preference for those of the white race, and particularly those within the white race of a particular stratum of society and of a particular gender and sexual identity, who consider that it makes them superior to all others. I submit that whiteness, as described, is hegemonic and operates in the church in a way that demeans, dismisses, and demoralizes those who do not fit those stringent characteristics. Whiteness as normative decries the equality of human beings, made in the image of God. The hegemony of whiteness that operates in the church flourishes in large part because of economics.

Major financial resources are not generally available to marginalized people. Across Christianity, Christ's concern for the poor is an accepted tenet of faith, and in many ways that are commendable, denominations and individual congregations have expressed concern for the poor. Mission and outreach to those in need are widespread across the Christian Church, but too often the church offers them as largesse from rich to poor, and fails to be truly representative of Christ's mandate of love of neighbor and the biblical call for hospitality to all. In too many churches, arms-length mission is not accompanied by pastoral prophetic preaching that would call the community to deep engagement with the divine call to justice for all people. In fact there are those who consider prophetic preaching the purview of the Black Church or pastors that are deemed liberal.

Pastoral prophetic preaching considers all who constitute the church and proclaim the message of Christ that gave attention to the poor and the marginalized. From the background of her own white established church, Leonora Tubbs Tisdale suggests a reason why prophetic preaching does not find favor or application from a pastoral perspective. She notes,

> One challenge we face in claiming a rightful place for prophetic preaching is the marginalization the prophets and the prophetic

10. Brueggemann, *Prophetic Imagination*, 3.

dimensions of the gospel received in the churches of our own upbringings. Because some of us grew up in churches that thought politics had no place in the pulpit, that believed evangelism (not social justice) was at the heart and soul of the gospel of Christ, and that have, through their own biblical interpretation in preaching and teaching, relegated prophetic texts to the periphery of the Scriptures, we too have a tendency (even if a subconscious one) to place them there, too.[11]

I accept Tisdale's reading of the issue, but find that it also does not explain the church's reluctance to engage the pastoral mode of prophetic preaching as the bridge that connects individuals with one another and with the divine.

Preaching is always contextual and defining the context requires pastoral understanding of the people and the situation wherein the message is being delivered. Understanding the people is foundational to developing the message. It is essential as the church continues to be part of the system of marginalization that is so prevalent in the culture of the USA. Jesus listened to the people and responded, as he promised, with good news that liberated them from their oppression. He refused to judge them, even when such judgment seemed warranted according to the mores of society. The most important context in which the people, all people, live, is that of the created order. It speaks of who we are at the most basic level, namely children of God. If God created all people, and Jesus offers salvation for all, it is a betrayal of Christ to push some persons or groups to the margins, away from the gathering that professes to be the body of Christ, and to do so in the name of Christ.

Further, the church's claim to speak in the name of God makes its proclamation prophetic. As Dale Andrews writes, "Prophecy indicates God's communication or revelation. The prophetic experience is God's communication not only to the prophet, but to the life of the intentional faith community."[12] If prophetic, then preaching must call out the entire community to face what it is, and to relinquish that which does not represent the grace of God. Only by doing so can the church claim to speak for God. As preachers, our task is not simply to speak words that sound good to our ears or that support and justify what others say. If we are following in the footsteps of Christ, and if we are maintaining the legacy of the apostles, then as preachers, our responsibility is to preach good news to the poor and freedom to the oppressed. We are called to offer release to those in captivity

---

11. Tisdale, *Prophetic Preaching*, 11.
12. Andrews, *Practical Theology*, 110.

and sight to those blinded by the glare of oppressive world systems. These are the marginalized and obeying the mandate of Jesus brings about justice and reconciles the people of the world to one another and thereby to God.

Every day, more and more people and groups are marginalized. The percentage of the world's poor increases daily and the gap widens exponentially between the haves and have nots. That is the world, or more precisely, it is the world outside our doors in the USA. But within the body of Christ, we are called to reject conforming to the world and to be transformed by the renewal of our minds in Christ. Above all, we are commanded by Christ to be one as he and the Father are one. We are directed to care for the sick and dying, to clothe the naked, to feed the poor, to bring into the fold all the lost and lonely. Our task is not to erect walls or to push others outside of the community because we are displeased with who God made them to be. Justice and reconciliation in the church requires pastoral prophetic preaching that bridges the gaps that exist between people and between groups of people. True pastoral, prophetic preaching brings into consciousness the word of God for the whole people of God. It is the task of the preacher to build those bridges through offering the proclamation of the good news of God's active presence in the lives of people. It is a pastoral task that bridges the divides that separate and disenfranchises some even from their God-given access to the free grace of God.

7

Getting in the Way
Preacher as Urban Interpreter and Suburban Interrupter

R. Mark Giuliano

Great cities are not like towns, only larger. They are not like suburbs, only denser. They differ from towns and suburbs in basic ways, and one of them is that cities are, by definition, full of strangers.[1]

A NOT SO FUNNY thing happened to America on our way to the suburbs. We lost touch with one another. Or should I say, we lost touch with *the other*. And by "the other" I mean those who are disadvantaged in and, more often than not, by America because of class, color, creed, ability, gender or sexual orientation.

 The migration from city to suburb isn't the only reason America fell out of touch with the other, but it is a big one. In our hurry to shake loose from the choking smog and crushing crowds of our growing cities, those who could afford to, hopped the trains of the early twentieth century and headed for the open air and green pastures beyond the urban core. Then, on new roads built by Roosevelt's Works Progress Administration from 1935 to

---

1. Jacobs, *The Death and Life*, 30.

1943, the accessibility of the automobile in the postwar boom, and a plump G.I. Bill that helped fund mortgages for returning soldiers seeking their place in the sun, we drove ourselves toward opportune places far away from the problems of the city: crowding and a shortage of affordable housing, pollution, poverty, crime and, a little later, newer social issues which many white Americans found disagreeable, such as integration, busing, and new immigration.

By the last quarter of the twentieth century, many of America's inner cities had been sliced through the core by thruways and expressways that allowed those with means to drive themselves out of the way. Downtown and near downtown neighborhoods had been decimated-abandoned by those with even modest wealth, robbing them of a base that once supported schools and churches, neighborhood grocery stores and thoughtful, community-based policing where kids and cops, often neighbors, had long established relationships.

At risk of oversimplifying a complex set of issues, one wonders if Cleveland's Tamir Rice, the 12 year old African-American boy gunned down in the park while flashing-about his toy gun, might be alive today if the white officer, Timothy Loehmann, who killed him, had a more substantial relationship with and commitment to the very community he had sworn to protect and serve.[2]

The late Yale scholar and Harlem pastor, Letty Russell, once compared the twentieth century American city to a battered woman.[3] It's an apt metaphor. We take what we want from the city, often abusing her with neglect and outright abandonment, and then when she fails us with her infrastructural hemorrhaging and social lesions, we blame her as if she somehow did this to herself.

Rather than take responsibility for the healing of the city, many chose, instead, to move to neighborhoods where people looked alike, dressed alike, even loved Jesus alike. We founded private "Christian" schools so our kids didn't have to have encounters with the other, while depleting resources for public schools by abandoning old neighborhoods for new. Then, we put the front porch around the back, built man-caves and entertainment rooms down the basement, and rolled-up the sidewalk so we wouldn't accidentally bump into the other, either. We got out of each other's way.

2. One wonders, too, if the Cudell community might have had prior knowledge of Loehmann, an officer with a disreputable professional history that was only fully understood after he had killed Tamir, if he had not come to them as an outsider. For more, see Ferrise, "Cleveland Officer."

3. Russell, "City as Battered Woman," 152–55.

I experienced my first taste of race-driven neighborhood dereliction when I was just 6 years of age. Our neighbor, Mr. Capuzzi (pseudonym), a dark skinned Siciliano, showed-up at our front door one evening cradling a clipboard in his arms like a newborn infant. Having rarely seen, let alone met, Mr. Capuzzi, my brothers and I tucked-in behind dad, curiously peeking-around his towering height to see why our neighbor would be ringing our doorbell this particular evening. It turned out that Mr. Capuzzi was gathering signatures for his petition "to keep black people out" of our neighborhood.

"Capuzzi! Paisano! Have you looked in the mirror lately?" Stunned by our neighbor's ask, my father stood there shaking his head in utter disbelief. Our street was filled with families whose last names ended in vowels: Giuliano, Drago, Capuzzi. There were other immigrants, as well. Apparently, Mr. Capuzzi drew the diversity line at "black."

He never did acquire enough signatures to have an impact, except, perhaps, to turn his neighbors against him. In the end, a black family moved-in across the street and Mr. Capuzzi moved out. He traded our little cosmopolitan street for the most prestigious—read "white"—neighborhoods around. In my adult mind, I like to think that before Mr. Capuzzi was able to purchase his new home, that, perhaps, some of his new neighbors circulated a petition to keep Sicilians out. It probably didn't happen that way, though; after all, Mr. Capuzzi had enough money to buy his way out of the way of any other that didn't quite fit with his worldview.

I must confess, I played into that culture of urban abandonment as a young urban planning student in the 1980s. My first and only neighborhood development project reflected my rather narrow vision of community. Mighty McMansions, squatting on tree-stripped lots, were drawn up and down a schematic of numerous short streets—a series of neatly planned cul de sacs designed to slow down local traffic and dissuade, almost entirely, those who didn't belong. In my plan, there were no sidewalks. No jaunty paths leading to community parks, or neighborhood schools, churches or stores. Everyone would drive, of course, and, in driving, stay out of each other's way-road rage notwithstanding. As a planning student, I learned how to create subdivisions that kept people isolated from the other.

Dietrich Bonhoeffer wrote that, "We must be ready to allow ourselves to be interrupted by God. God will be constantly crossing our paths and canceling our plans by sending us people with claims and petitions."[4] Of course, Bonhoeffer didn't mean petitions like Mr. Capuzzi's. To the contrary, Bonhoeffer was referring to those petitions from the vulnerable, the other.

---

4. Bonhoeffer, *Life Together*, 99.

The suburbs gave us the unique opportunity to manage those claims and godly interruptions, to enjoy a life uninterrupted by people whose needs and experiences differed from our own. The suburbs provided us the means to get out of their way and to keep them out of ours.

To be clear, this is not a down with the "burbs" and up with urban people essay, although I am a proud and active denizen of the city, a citizen who is clearly biased toward the diversity and mobility of urban walking communities. But even people who live in the city can work pretty hard at getting out of the way, too. On days when I'm just too tired for Bonhoeffer and his godly interruptions, for example, I choose to walk on the north side of Euclid Avenue, Cleveland's main drag, where there are fewer panhandlers angling for cash.

I am also very much a product of the suburbs. As a child, for instance, I cannot recall meeting any person of color in our white exurb of Toronto (unless you count Sicilianos) until the fifth grade when an Indian kid joined our hockey team. Diversity wasn't in my vocabulary. If it was, it would be used simply to point to the fact that I had one or two friends who went to the Roman Catholic school rather than the Public School.

From images on the news to tales told by those who spent time downtown, I was taught that the city was a dangerous place. City planner/architect, Jeff Speck has pointed out recently that his generation, and mine, grew-up ogling the homes and lifestyles of suburban television families like the *Brady Bunch* and *Partridge Family* as opposed to the urban-set shows that reflected my children's millennial interests in the city such as *Seinfeld* or *Friends*.[5] While both generations suffered from homogenously white portrayals of American culture, my kids' generation got a much more positive view of the city than my own.

The danger with the suburban version of getting out of the way, or any other kind of isolating practice, however, is that it tends to reduce commitment to place and the diversity of people that defines that place. It also negates opportunities for the kind of holy encounter the city and its diversity offer. Getting out the way neglects people's "deep longing for a spiritual dimension in public life"[6] and, instead, encourages them to "abandon citizenship altogether, or . . . import into politics a narrow, essentially mean-spirited religiosity which in fact only worsens the prevailing gracelessness of public life, thus driving new multitudes into alienation."[7]

---

5. Speck, *Walkable City*, 20.
6. Kemmis, "Living Next to One Another," 10.
7. Ibid.

In a 2006 interview with Colleen O'Conner of *The Denver Post*, David Goetz, author of *Death by Suburb: How to Keep the Suburbs from Killing Your Soul*, named the disconnect from which conservative, suburban Christians suffer. "My tribe will flail me for this," he said. "But conservative Protestants are so disconnected. They're not integrated with the real world."[8]

It's not surprising, then, that an arguably "narrow and essentially mean-spirited" presidential campaign[9] waged by Donald Trump in 2016 was especially appealing to suburban voters. Demographer, Joel Kotkin, warns that the "popular notion of 'city' and 'country,' one progressive and 'vibrant,' the other regressive and dying, misses the basic geographic point: the largest metropolitan constituency in the country, far larger than the celebrated, and deeply class-divided core cities, is the increasingly diverse suburbs.[10] Kotkin points out that Donald Trump won the suburbs handily with a full 5 percent more of the vote than his rival, Hillary Clinton, and made gains in swing-state suburbs of almost 10 percent over of the 2008 presidential election.[11] In other words, it was the likes of Mr. Capuzzi and other suburbanites who sought to "wage an interior war against outsiders"[12] who helped Donald Trump secure his victory.

URBAN INTERPRETER

If the white American church—suburban in particular, but also urban, metropolitan, rural small town, college or other—is going to engage in the work of justice and reconciliation in and for the city in more meaningful ways than, perhaps, it already is, then those preachers who occupy its pulpits must intentionally and thoughtfully "get in the way"[13] by being both urban interpreter and suburban interrupter. Preachers will stand as peacemakers and reconcilers on the battlefield where the interior war against the other is being waged.

8. O'Conner, "Blessed Aren't the Burbs."
9. Thompson. "Who Are Donald Trump's?" Even before the primaries had concluded, Thompson (and others) argued that polling revealed that Donald Trump's attacks on women, people of color, and immigrants, as well as his incitement of violence at his own rallies appealed to voters who wanted "to wage an interior war against outsiders."
10. Kotkin and Cox, "It Wasn't Rural 'Hicks.'"
11. Ibid.
12. Thompson, "Who Are Donald Trump's?"
13. I have borrowed the phrase, "getting in the way" from Christian Peacemaker Teams who, in response to the teachings of Canadian–American social activist, Ron Sider, get in "the Way" (e.g. Acts 9:2) of Jesus by getting in the way of warring factions by standing between them, literally and figuratively.

First, as urban interpreter, preachers hold a unique opportunity to articulate an urban theology that understands and promotes the city as good—a place and a people that matter dearly to God. Preachers are in a position to gentrify an aged urban narrative by naming the city, not as a place to be avoided but, as a part of the very world "God so loved," and not simply as victim or charity recipient, either, but as a place and people through which God may be encountered.

To preach a new urban narrative is to be in awe of and point toward the myriad ways that the God of the city is known. Preachers may point to the faithful aspirations and expressions of the divine within the human spirit easily located in the soaring architecture or dynamic street-scaping of our great cities, or toward orchestral scores or musical performances, dramatic paintings, unnerving films or whimsical tales told by the artists and storytellers among us, or toward the lives of those who dream of and labor for a new realm of justice and peace on earth from within the city, or toward the complexity of human diversity, extraordinary relationships, and the ways that the very sinew of love binds them together in the life and work of the city.

We want to be careful not to romanticize the city, of course; not all is well within the city gates. The God who loves our city is not *in-love* with many characteristics of our city—its fiefdoms, the governmental powers and economic principalities that keep her most vulnerable citizens bent or broken. At the same time, the work of the preacher, as interpreter, is to cry foul when language, abusive cultural myths or dramatic anecdotes that keep the city down are employed within the church and beyond.

The practical rhetoric employed in our pulpits that keep the battered city battered are unacceptable. Referencing Russell's metaphor of the "city as a battered woman," I have stated elsewhere that "one of the best ways to help a battered woman heal is through a kind of love which empowers her. Fear and reproach, or perpetuating misguided myths about her dangerous behavior, only keep her down. Truth-telling, love and generosity of spirit are what will lift her up again."[14]

As the pastor of a city-center congregation, I am often frustrated at the sight of those well-meaning suburban church members who pour into downtown Cleveland on Sunday nights to feed the poor while ignoring the staggering poverty rates in America's suburbs which grew by 65 percent between 2000 and 2012, at twice the rate of poverty in big cities. Certainly, the visible poor are easy to spot in the urban core, although in Cleveland very few actually live nearer than 20 blocks from that core. However, there are

---

14. Giuliano, "Don't Abandon or Blame."

now 3 million more people living in poverty in the suburbs of America than in its cities. Half of voucher households are in the suburbs. Worst of all, suburban communities are often support-impoverished, lacking in non-profits or government agencies to help.[15] In jest, I often remark to my suburban colleagues that maybe it's time for urban and metropolitan churches to load-up their buses and head-out to suburban streets to hand out food to hungry school children, or offer credit counseling and legal advice for single parent and mortgage poor families.

Moreover, cities have been growing more rapidly than their suburban counterparts.[16] The young professionals in suburban congregations who grew-up on a steady diet of those urban television shows (*Seinfeld, Friends*) and who long to live, work and play in the city, if they haven't already moved there, will be confused by messaging from the pulpit that paints the city as an unwelcoming or destitute place.

A number of years ago I was asked to write a regular column called "From the Trenches" about living and working in downtown Cleveland. However, when my first article[17] articulated why "trenches" was an inaccurate term to describe a downtown that was experiencing unprecedented residential growth, 4 billion dollars in economic development, and a complete infrastructure makeover, my first article turned out to be my last. Disclosing cultural myths has prices to pay, large and small.

Preachers must be on watch, though, and ready to name within the church and beyond those places in culture that are antithetical to the God who calls us to work and pray for the wellbeing of the city (Jer 29:7), or to Jesus who told disciples to wait in the city until they were clothed with power from on high (Luke 24:49), or to the fiery Spirit that gave birth to the church in the city (Acts 2:1–21). Through a word fitly spoken from the pulpit on a Sunday morning or one pecked-out on a keyboard for blogs, social media posts or op-eds, the preacher must exercise the authority of the pulpit, even what little of it that may be left in this era of the sideline-church, in faithful attempts to disclose the misinformed and destructive narratives that continue to entrench the city even as it succeeds.

SUBURBAN INTERRUPTER

As preachers do the courageous work of disclosing those cultural myths about the "dangerous city" they must also direct their people toward those

15. Kneebone, "Urban and Suburban Poverty."
16. Frey, *Brookings Institute*, May 23.
17. Giuliano, "From the Trenches."

places of divine encounter with and through the other. If the burden of suburban America is its geographical dislocation and, therefore, disconnection from those who are different, and the resulting social and political heart-hardening toward them, then the efforts of the preacher, in part, will be interruptive and counter-cultural. Whereas the démodé urban narrative focused on the broken city, the new narrative invites us to see the city, and in particular—the other within the city—as a means of divine encounter.

Canada's urban philosopher, Mark Kingwell, recently stated that, "play is the divine element in city life."[18] As opposed to the zero sum transactions of this world in which there are often winners and losers, the city offers "gift games," open-ended design, planning and interactive elements that lead to increased meaning and richer experience. Similarly, my position is that chance meetings with the other offer us open-ended opportunities for divine encounter. Just as the physical design elements of the city can act as a threshold to greater thinking and strategies about the city, so too, the encounter with the other can act as liminal gateway to the divine among us.

I have been living in downtown Cleveland for almost a decade. I choose to see many, though not all, of the interruptions on my daily path as godly interruptions. The outstretched hand of poverty may get in my way, but more often than not, when I respond—even if it is simply to acknowledge the other—I find that I am blessed with an awareness of the divine dwelling within me. Encounter becomes honest encounter when I enter time and space with the other, when I allow for both proximity and openness to the stranger along the road.

It's not that the preacher can create the divine encounter—that's God's doing. And it's not that all encounters are divine. But as interrupter, we can lead our people toward those physical and spiritual places where the encounter with the divine has been known to happen—on the streets of the urban core, in its shelters and ministries, or urban churches and other active congregations where the diversity of the city is reflected in the diversity of the congregation.

Goetz says that among suburbanite Christians, "There's a resistance to really do what Jesus calls us to do, to serve the poor and have friendship with the poor. To me, the gospel is about losing the anxiety of being around people who are different than you are."[19] Whether we worship in the city or in the suburbs, when we engage in the life of the city in spite of our anxiety, encounters with the other often become holy encounters.

18. Kingwell, "Rites of Way."
19. O'Conner, "Blessed Aren't the Burbs."

For me, the blessing may come from Michael, the man who sells the homeless newspaper on East 4th and who almost always greets me with a hug and asks that we might hold hands and pray together on the street. Or from Teddy, the street musician who plays soulful rhythm and blues on an amplified keyboard at East 6th and who, whenever he sees me coming, shouts through his microphone, "Alright everybody! It's the Stone Church!" Teddy knows that "Teddy" is short for Theodore and, because I told him, he now knows that the root of Theodore is "theos," which means God, and *doron,* which means gift, and Teddy knows that I think that he is a gift from God as he blesses our street with his hospitable spirit and his heart-full music.

You don't have to live in the urban core to have a holy encounter through or with the other. To me, the church in all places is at its best when it willingly allows itself to be vulnerable enough to be interrupted by the stranger, or by the humble preacher who attempts to give the stranger voice, when we choose to be in relationship with those whom the world too often passes by, and when we allow for the encounter with the other to impact us, shape us, soften our hearts and fill us with divine compassion.

I saw something in worship recently that moved me so deeply that I felt inclined to take off my shoes; I was on holy ground. One of our members had just been returned to us after months of incarceration. This was a man who had already served over two and a half decades in prison for a much more serious crime when he was first adopted by our church. He is a person who is currently transitioning from male to female. He clearly acts and looks differently than many in our faith community. Though he is not alone in our diverse congregation, for all intents and purposes, he is the other. Yet, on his first Sunday after release, he was back in worship, in his usual pew. What a powerful witness to his persistent faith, to his humility and his sense of needful connectedness to his church. When worshippers were invited to pass the peace, an elderly, suburbanite woman in the congregation walked across the aisle, hugged him and said, "Welcome home! Don't ever leave us again."

Encounter becomes divine encounter when we transcend our anxieties, meet each other in the confidence and freedom of God's grace, on the common ground of godly interruption.

I wonder if Mr. Capuzzi might have experienced something of the divine within himself if he had a gracious preacher emboldened enough to get in his way, a preacher who was both prophetic and pastoral enough to encourage Mr. Capuzzi to look for and welcome the moments of godly interruption in his life as opportunities to encounter the sacred as he encountered the other. Is it too much to imagine that instead of marching from door to door with a petition to keep blacks out of the neighborhood, Mr. Capuzzi might have found enough grace, enough love, enough of the divine within, that he might have organized the community, marched across the street to greet the other, and then thrown a block party to welcome his new neighbor?

8

In Search of the Beloved Community

DEBRA J. MUMFORD

DALE ANDREWS WAS INDEED a bridge builder. He served as a bridge builder for me and other African American graduate students pursuing PhDs in homiletics. He advised us as we navigated our way through our programs, helped us understand the inner workings of the Academy of Homiletics and held us accountable for completing what we started. His time commitment, along with his scholarship, demonstrated that he did not just believe in justice and diversity as ideas, but he believed that in order for them to be realized, real people have to personify them. As a result, to honor Dale's life and work, I believe it is fitting to examine the very practical theology of a man who was a consummate bridge—builder, Martin Luther King, Jr. We will examine his theology and its implications for preaching in particular and Christian life in general.

At the heart of everything King did, said, and worked for so diligently throughout his twelve and a half years of public ministry was his vision of the Realm of God which he called the *beloved community*. The beloved community for King is not some utopian vision in which people continuously gathered to join hands and sing "We Shall Overcome." The beloved community is a state of being in which every person is recognized as being created in the *image of God* by the one and same creator God.[1] The image of God is a biblical term that refers to the inherent dignity and innate worth

---

1. "The King Philosophy," *King Center*.

of all humans. Since all humans are created in the image of God there is "no graded scale of essential worth."[2] No one race has more divine right than any other. The "indelible stamp" of the creator is etched in the personality of every human.[3] This understanding of the image of God undergirded King's preaching, public speaking, and most of all his political activism around issues of racial justice, poverty, and opposition to the Vietnam War.

The ethos of the beloved community further distinguishes itself from secular society for King through its mandate to be guided by love in all things. Since all people are loved by God, they must be respected. It is not a person's intellect, race or social position that determines human worth. Rather, each person is valued simply because they are valued by God.

King's belief in the *imago dei* and his philosophy of being guided by love in all things influenced not only his commitment to seeking justice but also the means by which he believed justice should be sought. He believed the means that one uses to achieve a goal should directly correlate with the goal itself. Since the end goal of resisting injustice is the beloved community, love should be the means through which the goal is accomplished: agape love. King defined agape love as the kind of love that seeks nothing in return. People who have agape love do not love others because they are likeable. They love because the love of God is working inside of them. They love others because God loves them. Agape love enables the people of God to love the person who does evil while abhorring the evil they do.[4] Agape love seeks good for one's neighbor and not just for oneself. Those who have agape love don't discriminate with their love by discerning who is worthy and who is not. Their love is not contingent upon the particular qualities people possess. They make no distinction between friends and enemies.

Therefore, though it would have been easy, and even understandable, for African Americans involved in the civil rights struggle of the 1960s to hate their enemies and retaliate with violence when met with violence, King's interpretation of agape love compelled him to teach protesters to respond with love instead. Though the Bible was King's primary source for his practical theology, it was from a Hindu that he learned the resistance strategy that embodied agape love perfectly.

While at Crozer Theological Seminary, King happened upon the life and teachings of Mahatma Gandhi. Gandhi's form of non—violent resistance, which he deemed *satyagraha*, truth—force or love—force, served as

---

2. King in Washington, ed., *Testament*, 119.
3. Ibid.
4. Ibid., 13.

an effective strategy of resistance in the struggle for freedom.[5] King's rationale for his nonviolent strategy was both theological and practical. Nonviolence reflected the biblical mandate to love one's neighbor as one loved oneself even while resisting the core tenants of unjust laws. In addition, the hard reality was that in an armed conflict, African Americas would have to deal with a fanatical right wing that would willingly exterminate the entire African American population if they felt the survival of white Western materialism was at stake.[6]

Voluntary suffering is the key to successful satyagraha. Gandhi contended, and King concurred, that adversaries can be won over through the voluntary and unearned suffering of resistors.[7] King believed that voluntary and unearned suffering is redemptive because it has the potential to educate and transform. He quoted Gandhi when teaching and preaching about suffering: "Things of fundamental importance to people are not secured by reason alone, but have to be purchased with their suffering."[8] For King, suffering is powerful because it has the potential to shame the opponents into a change of heart.[9] When nonviolent adherents refuse to physically attack their oppressors, they expose the barbarity of the oppressor for the world to see.[10] The act of "self—suffering" or suffering as a voluntary act is the sacrificial offering of a person who sees the misery of others so clearly that she or he is willing to suffer on their behalf in order to bring an end to it.[11] King compared and contrasted suffering resulting from violence and nonviolence itself as social forces for change. War is an example of the implementation of violence to bring about a desired result. However, war often begets more violence. Nonviolence, on the other hand, sows seeds of peace by focusing on the long—term goal of positive and substantive change rather than the short term—goal of retaliation. King believed that godly transformation is only realized nonviolently.[12]

Also at the heart of King's concept of the beloved community is his holistic conception of salvation. We can discern King's understanding of salvation by examining the motto of the Southern Christian Leadership

---

5. Ibid., 38.
6. Ibid., 55.
7. Ibid.
8. Ibid., 18.
9. Ibid., 26.
10. Ibid., 485.
11. Ibid., 57.
12. Ibid., 47.

Conference (SCLC), his concern for victims of racism, and his concern for the souls of white racists.

After the success of the Montgomery bus boycott in which the African American community stopped riding buses for three hundred and eighty—one days to protest the segregated bus system, a group of people got together in 1957 to take the movement nationwide. A young minister named Martin Luther King, Jr. was elected as its president. When the sixty ministers and faith leaders met to establish the SCLC, they decided that their motto needed to be something that not only reflected the purpose of the group, but the state of the nation in which the group would function. They chose as their motto "To save the soul of America."[13] By using faith language of *salvation* and *soul,* the faith leaders of King's day used their lenses of faith and demonstrated that they understood that America did not just have a justice problem. America did not just have a civil—rights problems. America had a deeply spiritual problem. The SCLC founding members believed that all people were fearfully—and wonderfully—made in God's image. Unless America as a nation began to treat all of its people equally, its very soul would be lost.

For King and the founders of the SCLC, America needed to be saved from herself. Their goal was not only securing civil rights for African Americans. They sought to have America live up to the true meaning of her creed that all people are created equal. America had never lived up her own standard. However, SCLC was determined to help this nation become what she was intended to be: a place of equality and equal opportunity for all people.

King's concern for the soul of America was a critique of the systems and structures put in place in this nation that oppressed African Americans simply because of the color of their skin. While the soul of America was in jeopardy because of the sin of racism, the souls of victims of racism could not fully experience the salvation of God because they are victims of sin. For King, salvation was not just about the sins perpetrated by individuals but was also about structural sin that kept people in bondage and kept them from experiencing the fullness of God's love in their daily lives.

King's understanding of salvation can also be discerned through his concern about perpetrators of injustice. King believed that the souls of white people were greatly distorted by segregation and racism. Their souls were at stake when they continuously oppressed people who are created in the image of God. As a result, whites needed African Americans for the

---

13. Ibid., 233.

sake of their own souls. It is the agape love of African Americans that could remove the "tensions, insecurities, and fears" of whites.[14]

In the beloved community, remaining silent in the face of injustice is unacceptable. King said in many of his speeches, "We will have to repent in this generation not merely for the vitriolic words and actions of the bad people, but for the appalling silence of the good people."[15] Some of King's harshest words were aimed at those who sit back, watch injustice happen, and say or do nothing while the rights of others are being trampled underfoot. His words were often aimed at Christian people: saved, sanctified, and filled—with—the—Holy—Ghost people. He criticized both white Christians and African American Christians for their silence. He criticized Christians for being so heavenly focused that they were no earthly good. He criticized those of all races who were so afraid they would lose their status and positions in society and their respectability that they could not bother to become involved in a movement to help other people. King often reminded his listeners that human progress is not inevitable. Rather, progress comes from "the tireless efforts and persistent work" of people who are willing to be co—workers with God.[16] Co—workers of God speak up in the face of injustice.

In the last year of his life, King took every opportunity he had to speak out against the atrocity of the Vietnam War. He had many theological reasons for his objections. First of all he felt the war in Vietnam was one of the most unjust wars ever fought in the history of the world.[17] He felt it was unjust because just wars are fought to free people from oppression rather than take away their freedom. Just wars are fought to secure more bright and hopeful futures for the people rather than bring about their demise. The war in Vietnam was the opposite of a just war. Rather than fighting the war to liberate the Vietnamese from oppression, America was fighting the war to advance its own economic agenda. Rather than siding with a regime that would best meet the needs of the people, the United States had sided with a regime that brutalized and marginalized its people while helping the United States achieve its own economic ends.[18]

Secondly, the war violated the biblical mandate of helping the poor. Billions of dollars were being appropriated by Congress for mass murder in Vietnam that could have been used to address issues of poverty and

---

14. Ibid., 19.
15. Ibid., 296.
16. Ibid.
17. Ibid., 275.
18. Ibid., 235.

unemployment at home. Before the escalation of the war, King had hoped that the nation would begin to concentrate on meeting the needs of the poor through the poverty program. The program would have offered new beginnings for white and black poor people alike. But when the government began to build up troops in Vietnam, King suddenly realized that the nation was more committed to war than to the eradication of poverty.[19]

He was against the war in Vietnam because of the poor who were dying in record numbers. Soldiers who were fortunate enough to return home often did so physically or mentally impaired. After fighting in a war for their country, they were often left worse off (financially, physically, and mentally) than they were before the war began.

He was against the war in Vietnam because even in combat, the government refused to treat all people as those created in the image of God. For example, the same Congress that authorized money to fight the war in Vietnam, refused to allocate funds to include African American Veterans in a fair housing bill. White veterans were provided low interest loans to purchase homes after they returned from war. African Americans were denied those loans.

For King, a nation that was as morally bankrupt as the United States needed to undergo a revolution of values in order to finally become a beloved community. A true revolution of values would cause the United States to shift from a thing-oriented oriented society to a people-oriented society, from a society solely focused on material prosperity to a nation focused on meeting the needs of its people.[20] A nation seeking to become the beloved community will give up the privileges that evolve from tremendous profits in favor of engaging in activities in the best interest of its poor and marginalized members.

A true revolution of values calls into question past and present policies that develop or maintain poverty. King often likened this aspect of the revolution to the Jericho Road in the parable of the Good Samaritan. King believed that the people of God are called to be Samaritans on life's highway by helping their sisters and brothers who are in distress. However, he also believed that the Jericho Road needs to be transformed so that people will not constantly be in danger of being robbed. True compassion is more than giving a beggar a coin. True compassion is restructuring the system that produces beggars in the first place. In like manner, he believed that a

19. Ibid.
20. Ibid., 240.

revolution of values seeks to dismantle structures that give rise to poverty and oppression.[21]

A true revolution of values finds ways of settling conflicts other than always of going to war. Wars create orphans, widows, and people with life—long mental and physical impairments. War siphons off resources that could be used to lift up those who are outcast. Instead of always resorting to arms when conflicts arise, a nation seeking to become the beloved community will try to understand the root causes of the conflicts and develop positive and sustainable solutions.

When speaking of the need for a revolution of values, King invited his listeners to reclaim the revolutionary spirit that is part of the fabric of this nation. Western nations such as the United States have inspired people all over the modern world to fight for justice and equality. However, he also noted that people in our nation must resist their proneness to adjust to injustice.

King's most famous speech, "I Have a Dream," is a stellar articulation of his conception of the beloved community. In the speech, he critiques the injustices of racism, social leprosy and poverty and advocates for agape love, freedom and equality. His belief that all people are created in the image of God is especially conveyed in the latter portion of the refrain "I Have a Dream:"

> I have a dream that one day this nation will rise up, live out the true meaning of its creed: "We hold these truths to be self—evident, that all men are created equal."
>
> I have a dream that one day even the state of Mississippi, a state sweltering with the heat of injustice, sweltering with the heat of oppression, will be transformed into an oasis of freedom and justice.
>
> I have a dream that my four little children will one day live in a nation where they will not be judged by the color of their skin but by the content of their character.
>
> I have a dream that one day in Alabama with its vicious racists, with its governor having his lips dripping with the words of interposition and nullification, one day right there in Alabama little black boys and black girls will be able to join hands with little white boys and white girls as sisters and brothers.[22]

When this speech is examined in tandem with his theology, it can be understood as more than an oratorical masterpiece. It can be appreciated as

21. Ibid., 241.
22. Ibid., 220.

an expression of King's prophetic imagination—an imagination he worked diligently to realize every day of his life as a public theologian, prophet, and preacher. The prophetic imagination refers to the ability to see through the limited possibilities presented by the status quo to the unlimited possibilities of an omnipotent God.[23]

IMPLICATIONS FOR PREACHING

Issues and concerns stemming from King's life and ministry coincide well with the scholarship and ministry of Dale Andrews. One place of overlap is in the importance of vision for all people of God. It was King's vision of the beloved community—his understanding of what this nation and world could be—that compelled him to spend his life fighting for the rights of the poor, oppressed, marginalized and socially disenfranchised. His vision transcended seeking justice. It embraced positive peace and existential possibilities that are made possible by all people being treated as though they are created in the image of God. King's vision stimulated the nation's *prophetic imagination*.[24] Fueled by his prophetic imagination, King's vision of the beloved community served as a catalyst for not only the Civil Rights movement, but for subsequent movements and campaigns of resistance. Vision has the power to motivate the people of God for change.

Dale also had a vision of what the Realm of God could be. In his vision, all people, and especially people of African descent, experience social, personal and spiritual liberation. All of humanity is reconciled to God and to one another.

From King's life and ministry preachers glean the importance of a well—developed, well considered, contextually relevant practical theology. Though King's theology was informed by European theologians whom he studied at Crozer and Boston University, it was also informed by the demands of his lived reality. Preachers should help their congregations think theologically and critically about the world around them. Dale sought throughout his academic career to bring together black scholars and theologians with black pastors and practitioners to think critically about and develop practical approaches to the myriad of issues that face people of African descent in their daily lives. He critiqued the wholesale categorization by some black scholars of black churches as otherworldly in their concerns

---

23. Brueggemann, *Prophetic Imagination*. Kindle Edition.

24. Ibid. The term "prophetic imagination" refers to the ability to see through the limited possibilities presented by the status quo to the unlimited possibilities of an omnipotent God.

and orientation. Simultaneously, while acknowledging the continuing importance and influence of African American churches, he acknowledged that some black churches do ignore social accountability and social ministry. Dale agreed with King that issues such as the image of God, (voluntary) redemptive suffering, salvation, agape love, non—violent response to enemies, and just war are not just academic considerations for systematic theologians. These are topics for Christian living. Preaching doctrine is not always seen as necessary in our contemporary times. However, King's theology of the beloved community, along with his ability to communicate it by thought, word, and deed, proves that when elements of Christian doctrine are understood and lived out by the people of God, they can change lives and change the world.

In King's day, African Americans were social lepers—ostracized because of physical characteristics over which they had no control. Though racial segregation has been rendered illegal in this nation, Dale reminded his readers, colleagues, and students that African Americans are still treated as social lepers in the twenty first century. Though segregation is illegal, many of the social conditions that plagued African American communities in King's day such as poverty, unemployment, education inequities, and lack of instructional opportunities are still present. As Dale espoused, preachers can help their congregations identify and partner with the social lepers of our day including: people of various races and ethnicities, who are differently abled/disabled, severely overweight, lesbian, gay, bisexual, transgendered, or gender nonconforming, economically poor, etc. Since all people are created in the image of God, no one should be marginalized and oppressed because of who they are. Preachers can encourage their congregations to foster environments of love and acceptance and to serve as advocates when needed.

Preachers can remind their congregations of the consequences of silence in the face of injustice. If the people of God remain silent when they witness injustice, victims will suffer and not be able to live the lives they were created to live. Manifestations of injustice happen in all of our lives. We see injustice in our homes, families and communities such as child and elder abuse, domestic violence, racial, sexual or gender discrimination and police brutality. Victims of injustice need witnesses to speak out against injustice whenever they see it and work to eradicate it. Therefore, all people can benefit from Dale's belief that prophetic preaching rooted and grounded in pastoral care and praxis can have a tremendous impact on the lives of the marginalized and oppressed in particular and all people in general.

9

The Application of Moral Chemotherapy in the Twenty-first Century
Prophetic Preaching with a Pastoral Touch

Frank A. Thomas

Influenced heavily by thought leader Dov Sideman, I believe the United States presidential election of 2016 was a protest election.[1] While most elections are usually contested around candidates, ideas, platforms, and vision for the country, this election was based in the belief that the "system was rigged." Sixty per cent of the electorate wanted to disrupt, not just Washington, but "the system," i.e. capitalism, the economy, etc. Many pundits referred to the sixty-percent as "angry" and concluded that the overall electorate was deeply "divided." There have been many exit polls, research projects, and conclusions published since the election to pinpoint the source of the anger and protest.

Sideman argues, and I completely agree with him, that within the communication structures of American media, there operates a substantial "industry of outrage." Huge sums of money are being made by media outlets, cable and otherwise, whipping people up into a frenzy of outrage, with little and slanted consideration of facts, evidence, or truth. Along with these profit-based corporate communication structures is the explosion and ease

1. Seidman, "Great American Divide."

of communication facilitated by the venues and platforms of social media. Twitter, Facebook, internet, etc. allows any person to voice their views, opinions, and biases, and if one is able to garner enough shares and likes, one's outlook can go viral regardless of its veracity. We have seen the implanting of "fake news," not only by individuals and groups, but now governments to influence elections. Far too often fake news goes viral with many people consuming, digesting, believing, and even acting upon murky and spurious truth from deceitful and devious sources. Words are being intentionally used across ubiquitous communication structures and platforms to deceive, manipulate, and shape belief in alternative realities, facts, news, and even history. This is propaganda at a level of dispersion that the world has never seen before.

Sideman argues that technological and communication innovations are helping to create an abundance of "freedom from," a massive casting off of authority, truth, decency, institutions, or anything that attempts to control or define. For example, he mentioned that Uber was casting off the taxi-cab industry and Amazon was casting of the big box stores and malls. The spirit of the age was the casting off of all authority, "freedom from" based in technological innovation and the culture of outrage. In my words, he suggested that we live in a "low sympathy" world, and it leads quickly to moral outrage, and when we are outraged, we are more focused on "freedom from," or casting off, "rather than freedom to." We cast off, without much clarity about what we would be adhering to. In this state of moral arousal, the tendency is to skip conversation and dialogue, and go right to resolution, such as "throw the bums out," "take the name off the building," or "lock her up."

The opposite of moral arousal is moral progress, and where there is moral progress, there is nuance, equanimity, patience, deliberative working through things, multiple conversations and patient dialogue. But, in the culture of outrage, there is little of the nuance of morality. The one who is outraged demands immediate relief. This is not to say that some forms of oppression, racism, misogyny, xenophobia, homophobia, violence, etc. warrant outrage and immediate relief, but from Sideman's perspective, it is always wise to remember that the ultimate truth is always garnered from the domain of nuance and discussion. When we "throw the bums out," we get resolution, but make no moral progress.

With Sideman, I believe that people are "angry" and "divided" but people's anger and outrage is being stoked through these communication structures and platforms. We cannot ignore the fact that people are being intentionally divided, sometimes for profit and other times for nefarious motives such as control and execution of political ideology and agendas.

Given the massive crater of division that is so obvious to us all, the question must be asked if it is even possible to build bridges for a world of justice and reconciliation? Is it possible with prophetic preaching and a pastoral touch to build bridges of justice and reconciliation? And if so, how?

If we would consider these questions, first of all, there must be a defining of terms. It is important to define the words "prophetic" and "pastoral." First, there is such a cauldron of meanings around the word "prophetic" that I would like to be clear about my definition of prophetic. I will explore the term, "prophetic politics" that I first developed in my book, *American Dream 2.0: A Christian Way Out of the Great Recession*.[2] Second, I want to develop an understanding of pastoral with the helpful concept of "chaplains of the common good," as developed by Joseph E. Lowery. With these definitions in tow, I want to explore the practical implications of prophetic and pastoral preaching through Cathleen Kaveny's concept of "moral chemotherapy." Finally, I will highlight the example of William Barber and the Moral Monday movement as an example of building bridges for a world of justice and reconciliation through a pastoral and prophetic touch. I will begin with an understanding of "prophetic politics."

PROPHETIC POLITICS

Paul D. Hanson develops what he calls a Christian political theology and names it "prophetic politics."[3] Hanson lists five political models represented in the Old Testament, the most significant of which is the prophetic political model:

> The prophetic political model embodies the primacy of faith over human agency and temporal institutions . . . the oneness of reality grounded in the oneness of God . . . the prophets entered every political dialogue by stating clearly the necessary grounding of every political strategy in submission to God's universal suzerainty. Complete trust in God was the quality without which prophetic politics was impossible. The inevitable concomitant of the ascription of absolute rule to God alone was the relativization of every human institution.[4]

---

2. Thomas, *American Dream 2.0*.
3. Hanson, "Prophetic and Apocalyptic," 52–53.
4. Ibid., 53.

Hanson then lists the cardinal characteristics of the prophetic model. He does not list them in the manner stated below, but in the attempt to quickly synthesize his thought, I have summarized them.

1. Unqualified Allegiance to God's Domain—while refusing to endorse any political ideology as identical with God's eternal rule, prophetic politics demands of all people of faith, regardless of their host governments, unqualified allegiance to God's universal domain. It is from this perspective of allegiance to God's universal domain that the prophets critique the present order.

2. The Divine Call to Advocate for God's Reign—prophetic politics is for those who have received the divine call to advocate for the standards of God's universal divine reign that transcends all human boundaries. It is impossible to understand a prophet or prophecy until one grasps the prophet's sense of divine reign, and a call to represent that reign on earth.

3. Human Governance Outside of God's Reign—the prophet's task is to remind a nation that its structures of governance are not identical with divine rule. If a government is to survive, it must articulate both domestic and foreign policy consistent with moral principles in line with the will of God that transcend partisan politics and nationalistic self-interest.

4. Prophets are Not Popular—on behalf of the universal and sovereign God, prophets speak with a consistency that rattles earthly Kings, High Priests, Presidents, governments, and electorates. Because their silence cannot be purchased, they expect rebuke, vilification, violence, and even death.

In summation, those who ascribe to prophetic politics "give expression to their patriotism by ascribing to their government limited, penultimate authority, while reserving their ultimate allegiance for the universal sovereign, the Creator God of all nations."[5] I believe that if there would be a world of justice and reconciliation, the preacher must engage in prophetic politics and prophetic politics with a pastoral touch.

---

5. Ibid., 56.

PROPHETIC POLITICS AND A PASTORAL TOUCH: CHAPLAINS FOR THE COMMON GOOD

In defining the word "pastoral," generally we mean spiritual care or nurture of the souls of people or a congregation, and in the broader sense, the care of the soul of a nation. Often in the care of the soul of a nation, the preacher must be prophetic, such as in the case when the nation moves away from moral values and founding principles. As an example, the Southern Christian Leadership Council, (SCLC) placed in their founding documents that they sought to "save the soul of America." One of the early stalwarts of SCLC, and an excellent example of the prophetic with a pastoral touch, is the ministry of Joseph E. Lowery. In his book, *Singing the Lord's Song in a Strange Land*, Lowery published a sermon entitled, "Chaplains for the Common Good."[6] In 1998, after his retirement from SCLC, Lowery joined with other activists and formed the Coalition for the People's Agenda—a coalition of advocacy groups on civil rights, peace, labor, women's issues, justice, youth, human rights, etc. At the end of each meeting, they would together quote this line: "We are Chaplains of the Common Good." He said they meant that while many see the role of chaplain as reading scriptures and praying prayers at hospitals, community, civic, governmental, religious, social, and even organizational meetings before they eat or discuss business, they saw the role as much deeper than that. A chaplain is the conscience of an organization, nation, or church, urging all to do what is right and what is pleasing to God.

> Through Scriptures, prayers, and sometimes a clap of thunder, they jar us to righteous reality. Sometimes it is a flash of lightning making plain the landscape of societal ills; sometimes it is a whisper into our still conscience; sometimes it is an alarm clock saying it is time to rise; sometimes it's a bugle call to engagement; sometimes it is a cool breeze of thankfulness following the glory of triumph or the agony of defeat; but it is always on the side of the Creator, always calling out the best in us for the common good.[7]

When I say building bridges for a world of justice and reconciliation through prophetic preaching with a pastoral touch, I mean chaplains for the common good. Chaplains of the common good pastor the soul of a nation. But even as we seek to be chaplains of the common good, we must recognize the difficulty of the practical preaching of the prophetic

---

6. Lowry, *Singing the Lord's Song*.
7. Ibid., 84.

and pastoral word, what Kaveny calls the administration of moral chemotherapy.

CHAPLAINS OF THE COMMON GOOD AND MORAL CHEMOTHERAPY

Cathleen Kaveny, in her book, *Prophecy Without Contempt: Religious Discourse in the Public Square*, argues that public discourse in the United States consists of two distinct rhetorical forms, moral discourse, which principally seeks to reason its way through dilemmas, and prophetic indictment, where the prophet calls the community back to values and principles of covenant.[8] She argues that prophetic indictment based in the Puritan sermon form of the jeremiad has been woefully misunderstood and neglected and as a result has diminished public discourse in general. Both styles, prophetic indictment and practical deliberation are needed in the religious and public discourse of America. Moral or practical deliberation and reasoning is our normal moral language that provides the framework for countless decisions we make every day. Prophetic rhetoric is, at its heart, an unusual form of moral discourse that seeks not to replace moral deliberation, but to return it to health. Kaveny comments:

> I have suggested that we view the language of prophetic indictment as a type of moral chemotherapy. It takes aim at morally cancerous assumptions or perspectives that threaten to destroy the possibility of reliable practical reasoning . . . Like chemotherapy, prophetic rhetoric is inherently destructive, but in the service of an ultimately constructive purpose: The goal of prophetic rhetoric is the reestablishment of a healthy, functioning political context for moral deliberation and decision. Those considering whether or not to invoke prophetic discourse . . . do well to consider whether the cure will cause more harm than the disease.[9]

In an earlier article, Kaveny argues that "all prophetic rhetoric has the potential to rip the moral fabric of the community to which it is addressed."[10] Prophetic indictment is strong and dangerous medicine for the body politic. When the human body suffers from the ravages of cancer, chemotherapy can be the hope for restoring health. At the same time chemotherapy can

---

8. Kaveny, *Prophecy without Contempt*.
9. Ibid., 315–16.
10. Kaveny, "Prophetic Discourse."

have destructive consequences, and if not administered properly, can do more harm than good and kill the patient.

Kaveny argues that prophetic indictments: 1) demand that wayward citizens make a renewed commitment to the moral basis of their community, and 2) shock wayward members of the community out of the indifference to their own flagrant pattern of sins, and the harm those sins cause to other members of the community. She distinguishes two kinds of prophetic indictments found in the prophetic books of the Bible. First, "oracles against the nations" are prophetic utterances where God punished the nations, excluding Israel and Judah, for their sin, and the punishment often took the form of destruction and obliteration. Oracles against the nations are not designed to heal a political community and cannot be interpreted as constructive. They announce destruction and offer no hope of repentance and renewal. When the Puritans left Europe, they articulated oracles against the nations in Europe. Second, "oracles against Israel and Judah" are different because God chastises God's people frequently in language as harsh as that of oracles against the nations, but God repeatedly forgives. God often uses the nations to punish Israel and Judah, but in the end, God restores the people and the destruction is undone.

Kaveny suggests that a helpful "rhetorical stance" for the moral chemotherapy of prophets to take toward the community that he or she is addressing: 1) prophets should frame their remarks as oracles against Israel and Judah rather than oracles against the nations, 2) prophets should stand with their audience in the trials and tribulations despite their sin, and 3) the prophet's call to repentance are to be heard as constructive chastisement within horizons of hope and possibilities of community renewal. In my estimation, this sounds much like prophetic preaching that is pastoral.

In *Prophecy Without Contempt*, Kaveny argues that the most pressing issue for the use of prophetic indictment in our time is whether it is possible to practice humility within prophetic indictment. The greatest danger to moral character associated with practice of prophetic indictment is arrogance. Too many practitioners of prophetic rhetoric assume they are uniquely in right relationship with God and are therefore fully aware of God's purposes and plans. She raises this powerful question: "Is it possible to condemn evil while still remaining suitably modest about one's knowledge of the divine will and one's own status in the eyes of God?"[11] She offers analysis of the biblical tradition of Jonah as example of ample room for the cultivation of humility and self-criticism in prophetic speech, the Second

---

11. Kaveny, *Prophecy without Contempt*, 9.

Inaugural Address of Abraham Lincoln, and the work and words of Martin Luther King, Jr.

One final word about Kaveny before a contemporary example of constructive prophetic and pastoral rhetoric. William Storrar, in a pre-election article entitled, "In the Hands of an Angry Electorate: Rhetoric in the Presidential Election," argues that though Kaveny ends *Prophecy Without Contempt* with the 2004 presidential election, her essential argument is a primer for the 2016 election.[12] Storror argues that an angry God has been replaced by an angry electorate. The angry and dispossessed of the American Dream flocked to two "unlikely prophets," Donald Trump and Bernie Sanders, while "the most experienced candidate for the presidency in generations, Hillary Clinton, the note of practical reason, talking of hard choices and reasoned decisions." Storrar regards the 2016 campaign season as a choice between anger and administration. Kaveny argues that when utilizing the moral chemotherapy of prophetic indictment, prophets as well as citizens would "do well to consider whether the cure will cause more harm than the disease."[13]

PASTORAL PROPHETIC MORAL CHEMOTHERAPY: MORAL MONDAY

It is important for the last portion of this discussion to locate and celebrate significant pastoral and prophetic ministry that utilizes moral chemotherapy and builds bridges for a world of justice and reconciliation. William Barber II and the Moral Monday movement is one of the most important pastoral and prophetic movements in contemporary America today. The purpose here is not to detail or explain the Moral Monday movement. There is enough already published and any reader who desires more information can find it easily and quickly.[14] I want to connect Barber and Moral Monday with the aforementioned three characteristics of Kaveny's helpful rhetorical stance for the moral chemotherapy so that readers might have benefit of what one model of applying the pastoral and prophetic together in the administering of moral chemotherapy has to offer. Kaveny suggested the following as a helpful "rhetorical stance" for prophets to take toward the community they are addressing: 1) frame their remarks as oracles against Israel and Judah rather than oracles against the nations, 2) stand with their

---

12. Storrar, "In the Hands of an Angry Electorate."
13. Kaveny, *Prophecy without Contempt*, 316.
14. I suggest two articles that are easily accessible and might be helpful: Rab, "Meet the Preacher," and Barber, "Moral Mondays."

audience in the trials and tribulations despite their sin, and 3) the prophet's call to repentance are to be heard as constructive chastisement within horizons of hope and possibilities of community renewal.

First, prophets should reframe their remarks as oracles against Israel and Judah rather than oracles against the nations. One of the ways that Barber and Moral Monday could be framed as oracles against Israel and Judah is the movement's decision and deference to locate itself squarely with American historical movements for freedom and justice. Barber ties Moral Monday to the United State's first Reconstruction, where immediately after the Civil War, newly freed black and whites worked together to elect black leadership, making huge strides to equality and full participation the newly freed slaves in American democracy. Though strides were made, white backlash and racism gutted the movement and retrenched into Jim and Jane Crow. It took almost 100 years for the Second Reconstruction, the Civil Rights Movement of the 1950's and 60's, to overcome segregation and make strides again for the inclusion of black people as American citizens. In both of these movements there was "fusion" politics where people of many backgrounds worked for justice and equality. Consistent with the white racism of American history, again there was retrenchment and white backlash summarized in the form of what Michelle Alexander calls, "the new Jim Crow," mass incarceration to name just aspect of contemporary institutionalized and racialized public policy.

Barber casts the Moral Monday movement as the Third Reconstruction—a third movement of freedom and justice for all people and says:

> You can't understand America's deep need for a Third Reconstruction without studying our history of partial progress, which has been met, time and again, by immoral acts of deconstruction. In North Carolina, we look back to the state Constitutional Convention, where the Rev. Robert Ashley and the Rev. J.W. Hood—one white and one black—worked tirelessly to codify the language of fusion politics in our state's primary legal document. Such cooperation could not have been possible if Frederick Douglass and Harriet Tubman had fought alone for their freedom. They built power throughout the nineteenth century by working with allies such as Levi Coffin, the white Quaker from Greensboro, who helped establish the Underground Railroad.[15]

---

15. Adapted from Barber "New Fusion Politics."

It is the reading and connection of deep movements for freedom with American history that establishes the pastoral and prophetic works as oracles against Judah and Israel.

Second, prophets should stand with the audience in the trials and tribulations despite their sin. While this truth should seem obvious, Kaveny offers a stunning critique of much prophetic indictment in our time:

> True prophets—those who understand themselves as called by God to deliver a message to the people—have no real option. They believe they must do as God commands and condemn the practices God tells them to condemn. Yet most of the people who use prophetic rhetoric in the public square do not understand themselves as actual messengers of God comparable to Isaiah or Jeremiah. They are *making a choice* to use prophetic rhetoric rather than deliberative rhetoric in order to advance their political views.[16]

The goal is the advancement of a political agenda rather than the needs of the people, and as such, the prophetic message is often a put-down either of the people or some other group. Far too often, the result is blaming, scapegoating, demonizing, and condemnation. The goal is often not redemption or reconciliation of all people but the winning of their side of the political argument. Kaveny argues for compassionate and humble truth telling as a corrective on the condemning tendencies of prophetic rhetoric. The prophets stands with the people in their trials and tribulations and does not stand above the people, or feel the need to allow the people to escape by casting their sin on innocent bystanders. What is needed most of all is humility.

William Barber does not use the term moral chemotherapy, but uses a similar analogy, moral defibulators. Barber, standing in the prophetic tradition of Isaiah and Jeremiah, says in his 2016 speech at the Democratic National Convention that religion was being used to "camouflage meanness," because America has a heart problem." Barber comments that there are forces that want to "stop and even harden the heart of democracy." Barber believes that there are moral issues that are beyond Left versus Right, Liberal versus Conservative, but are in fact, "right vs. wrong." Barber mentions Dorothy Day who called for "the revolution of the heart," and Martin Luther King, Jr., who called for a "radical revolution of values." Barber says:

> No, my friends, they tell me that when the heart is in danger, somebody has to call an emergency code. And somebody with a good heart will bring a defibrillator to work on the bad

---

16. Kaveny, *Prophecy without Contempt*, 9.

heart. Because it is possible to shock a bad heart and revived the pulse. In the season, when someone tries to harden and stop the heart of our democracy, we are being called like our foremothers and forefathers to be the moral defibrillator of our time ... We must shock this nation with the power of love. We must shock this nation with the power of mercy. We must shock this nation and fight for justice for all. We can't give up on the heart of our democracy, not now, not ever![17]

Barber's conclusion is that the revolution of the heart and moral defibulation means that we would move past our divisions and labels and treat our issues as issues of the heart, issues of all the people, and realize there is something more than political victory, but right and wrong.

Finally, the prophet's call to repentance should be heard as constructive chastisement within the horizons of hope and community renewal. One of the most powerful aspects of the prophet's ministry is preaching, whether in words, symbols, or deeds, the truth of God's displeasure at the mistreatment of people. The way that the prophet's call is heard as constructive chastisement for hope and community renewal is that the prophet's words illumine and empower the people who are effected by terrible public policy speak to the nation and the issues. The prophet's words chastise the nation and government and activate people at the grassroots level to speak and protest for themselves for their right to redress. For example, the prophet will speak to effects of bad legislation and public policy such as, for example, HB 229, which imposes voting rules that could affect thousands of citizens. Based in fusion politics, which shapes a multiracial, multigenerational coalition with ministers and church folk protesting with business leaders and academics, average and everyday people who suffer the negative consequences of HB229 speak to its deleterious effects in their life and community. It is these stories by grassroots people in the diverse numbers of fusion politics that move the needle and are constructive chastisement for hope and community renewal because it activates citizenship and the willingness of citizens to hold their leaders and government accountable. At its base, the preaching of the prophet inspires civic engagement. It is the words of the prophet in conjunction with the told stories on the ground that produces hope and the empowerment of community renewal in participants. It is the people, and the stories of average people who commonly suffer from bad public policy that connect and unite people to activate and in activation of fusion politics. Empowerment of citizens in this moment is oracle against Judah and Israel that produces hope and community renewal.

17. Barber, "Speech at Democratic National Convention."

While this discussion of William Barber II and Moral Monday is admittedly woefully inadequate given the scope, depth, and power of the movement, the attempt was to clearly demonstrate the possibility and practicality of building bridges for a world of justice and reconciliation. We are called as pastoral chaplains of the common good to engage in prophetic politics to apply moral chemotherapy to heal the nation and restore true moral deliberation.

10

Unauthorized
Pastoral and Prophetic Utterances on the Ground

LISA L. THOMPSON

CONSIDERING THE QUESTION, "WHAT is the nature of prophetic preaching that is pastoral in the pursuit of bringing to fruition a world of justice and reconciliation?" remains a worthy endeavor. In some ways we do not learn more about the possibility of preaching that holds together prophetic and pastoral dimensions by continually revisiting false binaries between prophetic and pastoral alone. The potential to learn more about the texture of faithful utterances in the midst of everyday life is in our willingness to visit the sites that give attention to the care of the soul as it is inextricably connected to bodily existence. These sites involve those that extend well beyond traditional pulpit spaces and their authorized voices. At every juncture these sites are contextual and attend to the particularities of concrete lived experiences; these are the places where we as human beings simultaneously encounter all that is no less than good and all that is no less than evil about the world in which we live. Life is contextual and that which responds to life as we know it is contextual—even theological and religious paradigms.

As for me, I was shaped and formed within black religious traditions of the United States. These traditions were significant for the black women of my youth as they made sense of life and the world in which they lived. This included living in defiance of the ways in which economic, racial, and gendered dynamics, of a complicated history of the southern states in particular and the U.S. in general, landed square and center in their lives and upon their bodies. Faith had its accountability to the world as they knew it. These women were often in traditions that did not affirm them as individuals authorized to preach. And yet, they were undoubtedly mediators of revelatory occasions and experiences.

With or without acknowledgement from the proper structures, the black women of my youth divided wisdom and truth for the community; these occasions often took place around the kitchen table, carpools to textile mills for work, canning vegetables, and crop-gathering.[1] This dispelling of wisdom and truth was grounded in the world they knew, the faith they claimed, and the belief in a right to live. Their declarations were those that possessed the nature of what it meant to care for black life and transform what the existential realities of black life brought with it. The most faithful utterances were not just those declared to them but also those that they themselves uttered—echoing that which they deemed necessary for their own moving about in the world. These were the utterances they offered in the freedom of their own spaces and on their own terms.

Dale P. Andrews and Robert London Smith contend that practical theologies that support black life are those that are useful on the ground and in direct conversation with black life on the ground.[2] If we take this claim seriously, then our next work is to seek out proclaimers on the ground who are in direct conversation with black life on the ground. We ordinarily think of on the ground as preaching on the ground; however, the pulpit is still a step removed from the ground in many cases. The way in which the most minoritized in a community are engaged in facilitating faithful speech is significant because they often exist at the deepest fissures of injustice.[3] Their ability to affirm and mediate right-fitting utterances intonates toward that which is most needed when attending to holistic preaching practices.

---

1. Teresa Fry Brown describes the ways in which spaces outside of the pulpit are significant in the lives of black women as they are sites where spiritual values and wisdom are shared between generations; these are not insignificant sites when considering the ways discriminatory practices within communities of faith have limited the access of black women from pulpit spaces; see Brown, *God Don't Like*.

2. Andrews and Smith, ed., *Black Practical Theology*, 12. Dale P. Andrews describes black preaching itself as an act that holds together dimensions of pastoral care and prophetic aspects while giving attention to personal and communal experiences and needs of care; and to this end personal experiences have the opportunity to expand those experiences of the community and expand the community of faith's understanding as a whole; see Andrews, *Practical Theology*, 24–26.

3. Andrews and Smith contend that the work of practical theology emerges from the adverse sites in life within the contexts of history and contemporary life; Andrews and Smith, *Black Practical Theology*, 12.

And yet, we must contend with the fact that these bodies and voices are often most marginalized from pulpit spaces; the spaces we have deemed authoritative in homiletic discourse.

The rise of the Black Lives Matter (BLM) movement and its subsequent iterations provides a unique convergence of circumstances for considering the demands upon preaching that attends to the work of justice and reconciliation in the 21st century.[4] In conversation with BLM, this essay explores the nature and ends of utterances that are faithful to the theological and ethical aims of proclamation itself, as they exist outside of the pulpit and are carried forth by unauthorized voices. I contend that these unauthorized voices have resonance with the voice and the task of proclamation entrusted to the mere mortal who proclaims in the valley of dry bones (Ezek 37). Here proclamation is considered an occurrence that destabilizes the very entities that make it possible. In other words, proclamation is the hoped for end in preaching but by no means sequestered to the practice of preaching. These sacred intonations are those that provide care for the individual (and her state of existence) in ways that make room for the world to transform into a place that offers nothing less than life more abundant for all the created of God.

DESTABILIZING-UTTERANCES

Sacred utterances cannot be confined to particular containers and tropes, as they bubble up when and how they choose to appear. Truth does not wait its turn. We recognize truth and affirm its presence when we experience it. Here the reference to truth simply refers to that which is discerned as right-fitting by a community and possesses the authority to shape the ways in which we make meaning of life and name belief, as it yields the potential for reshaping the course of life.[5] We often speak of these revelatory occasions thru preaching as God's Word, or Word of God. These encounters with significant utterances are encounters with proclamation.

Proclamation has an effect and makes way for an experience, as it generates and conjures forth something. For instance, authentic proclamation is not a description of inspiration, belief, and empathy; somehow in the presence of authentic proclamation one experiences the elusive intangibility

---

4. For a h(e)rstory of #blacklivesmatter by its founders see: http://blacklivesmatter.com/herstory/.

5. This description of truth is based in part on philosophical hermeneutics and philosophy of the meeting of horizons in the process of interpretation; see: Gadamer, *Truth and Method*.

of that which is meant by the words inspiration, belief, and empathy. That which is familiar is made use of in often imaginative ways to disclose, unveil, or name what eludes being named. The community recognizes or bears witness to the moment of proclamation when it occurs; it functions in a mode of call and response. There is a "calling out" that occurs but the act is only complete when one responds back that something has rung clear.[6] The proclaimer relies on a type of imaginative precision that affords their ability to meet listeners right where they are. This is an act dependent upon community and God.

Preaching is dependent upon God to transform the fragility of human speech into something recognized as viable and true; the Spirit moves where and how she chooses. Just as preaching is dependent upon God so too is every medium that somehow moves beyond the fragility of its working parts and stirs our very being.[7] The medium that affords the presence of proclamation is incidental, as in not the primary concern nor necessary for its appearance; but instead, just that—a medium. To this end, such utterances naturally destabilize our ability to systematically categorize and predict what makes way for their existence in our midst, if we allow them.

When we encounter that which we deem as true it reaches our deepest places of knowing and intuiting. The moment echoes backward and forward to what we have known and know, whether that moment is in a conversation, prayer, or sitting in the midst of a musical performance. And yet, our expectations of proclamation, including its shape and form, have conditioned our expectations of when and how it shows up in our midst, even as our experiences may indicate otherwise. We expect sermon and scriptures to somehow reveal sacred utterances, or what we typically call Word of God. And that expectation often limits our openness to experiencing proclamation in its other sites of appearance, particularly when those sites are nontraditional or have not been necessarily authorized by communities of faith. For instance, one might often seek to discern God's presence in a sermon, but not so readily thru the encounter of a novel.

If we earnestly believe that the spirit cannot be confined nor her utterances, it then seems that we cannot ignore the utterances that spurred

---

6. I have written in other places about the way in which communities of faith name and mark legitimate preaching practices based on experiences of proclamation, while these moments are not disconnected from historical interlocking factors of bodies, power, and permission to occupy pulpit space; see:Thompson, "Now That's Preaching!" and my forthcoming *Ingenuity*.

7. James Nieman describes practices as those that have their own aims in connection with preaching as a particular practice that has its own aims; see "Why The Idea of Practice Matters."

from a movement pioneered by queer black women in the summer of 2013. Theirs are some of the most fringe voices in our faith communities, and yet, they found their resonance in life on the ground. The gestures of this movement managed to find and facilitate alternative pulpits, and talkback to *what* we consider the purposes and shape of faithful speech. These voices push us to reexamine both the presumed sites and nature of proclamation.

THE MORTAL IN THE VALLEY

In Ezekiel 37 we see humanity existing at the fissures of life—or more aptly lingering somewhere between existing and not existing at all.[8] The reader is introduced to a valley of dry bones in Ezekiel 37. The mortal has been transported to the valley to observe, give an account of that observation, and then speak; ultimately, the mortal is called not to speak back to God but into the valley itself. The final conclusion of this vision is that the spoken witness will be both for the bones of the valley and for the observers to know what has occurred; namely, that the promise to the created of God is confirmed as no less than the full life-giving Spirit of God as she moves through these bodies and as they move through the world (Ezek 37:24–28). In this strange passage of a whirlwind vision and slippage between real time and other-worldly time, we see something about the one who proclaims, the state of human existence, and the nature of the utterances the Holy One authorizes in this encounter.

"The mortal" comes face to face with the fragmented experiences between body and spirit; this fragmentation is a desolate valley of dislodged bones absent of breath. After the mortal is given the first directive to speak to the bones, they come together with a "noise, a rattling. . . ." (Ezek37:9–7).[9] As the mortal squints and looks closer he recognizes that even as the bones seem upright and connected they are not alive. They can't breathe. They cannot inhale the full breath that comes from the four corners of the earth. In the valley the mortal, is contending with the presence of the imitation of life, namely that which mimics or intonates toward life and yet is not the fullness

---

8. What follows is not a historical-critical exegetical exploration of Ezekiel 37. While I take into account the historical parameters the text and its study, the hope here is to mirror the practice in preaching traditions of making creative use of scripture in conversation with the lived experiences on the ground for the sake of sustaining and attending to life as we rely on faith practices for such resources. This is not a co-optation of the story of Israel, its exodus, nor exile motifs. And at the same time I am making use of the thematic issues that arise when trying to live out of histories of movement, exile, and contexts that constantly create an alienation from one's traditions and culture.

9. Direct citations from the Bible are from the NRSV.

of life. And again, he is directed to prophesy and call forth life, that which exists outside of the bones, to come and take up habitation; "Prophesy to the breath. . . ." (Ezek 37:10). The utterance teeters at the brink of present existence and the new possibilities of existence. The present existence is the imitation of life; the possibilities of existence are life abundant. Both the bones of the valley and the breath of life respond and affirm the veracity of the call made out to them.[10] This is the give and take exchange in proclamation recognized as true.

The mortal has an encounter that shapes his ways of knowing and intuiting and seems to be transported back to real time and given the task to speak to the house of Israel. The bones are the house of Israel suffering in exile. The created of God are saying "our bones are dried up, and our hope is lost; we are cut off completely."[11] A segment of humanity is in a fractured existence and cut off from the vitality of life and the great source that gives life. Their laments are echoes of what they have once known in part to be, no longer being at all. To say, "We are cut off." implies that the current experience is not as it should or could be.[12]

The opening of chapter 37 might be read as no less than an invitation to participate with the Holy One in responding to the now lived trauma of the house of Israel. The invitation is in the form of a question, "Can these bones live?" (Ezek 37:10). The mortal shrinks back in human finitude and the limitation of knowledge answering, "Only you know Holy One." And then he witnesses what gives experiential-knowledge of not only the answer but also his role in filling the risky-gap of declaration. Ezekiel is confronted with the task of calling forth life in ways that gather-up and attend to the lost pieces. But first the mortal must dare to name the absence of life and the imitation of life. The mere human must name what evades being named and

---

10. There are some assumptions here about performative utterances—those utterances that bring about the action they speak. Though Luke Powery engages this passage as an exploration of preaching, he observes from this passage that the spoken word, the proclaimer, and God all work together and that life is generated through the spoken word. The implication is both a dependency upon God and God's entrusting the act of preaching to the one who proclaims, indicating that God has not given up on creation nor the possibility of "divine transformation" through "pneumatic speech" in what Powery calls "the domain of death;" see Powery, *Dem Dry Bones*, 81.

11. Here once we enter chapter 37 and the valley of dry the emphasis is not given to the sins nor repentance of the house of Israel. I am not ignoring these portions of the book of Ezekiel, while I am attending to the particularities of this vision and prophecy in the book as it is set apart from other messages Ezekiel is directed to carry. See Ezekiel 37:11.

12. Luke Powery describes lament as a type of spirit speech and its significance thru preaching, as it is initiated by the by the Spirit in response to the Spirit; see Powery, *Spirit Speech*.

call forth that which remains elusive. This is an act of discerning between life that still intonates the rattling of death and life that intonates the abundance of Spirit. The proclaimer speaks to both the acute cries of lament that exude from real bodies and the corporate vision of life abundant.[13]

In the valley of dry bones Ezekiel is not called priest or prophet but simply, "mortal." And the one to whose ordinary humanity is constantly referred is entrusted with what is ultimately the work of proclamation. The utterances in the valley name the absence of life, speak to the promise of life, and proclaim nothing less than the fullness of life.[14] This is a large promise in the context of everything that denies life while affirming death; and yet, this is the intonation of sacred-speech as it arises in our midst. These are the utterances that call out and to which we respond.

TWENTY-FIRST CENTURY UNAUTHORIZED ITERATIONS OF PROCLAMATION

The proclamation of the valley has theological and ethical impulses. These utterances have overtures that affirm the sanctity of life as a continuation of God's breath. They simultaneously affirm that trauma, death, and suffering in exile do not reflect the full promise of life's possibilities. The proclaimer affirms the recognition of what should not be even as they co-create the fruition of life in the contradictory locale of death amidst the groans of creation. Furthermore, the utterances of the valley give care for human existence; simultaneously, they are a part of transforming human existence and predicated upon a give and take of call and response. If we attend first to the theological and ethical aspects of proclamation, we might both recover sites of such utterances wherever they show up today, while giving more attention to our modalities of expression, preaching or otherwise, and their continuity with the hopes of proclamation itself.

More specifically, beginning with the nature of proclamation opens up the possibility of understanding those utterances that reach to the edges and depths of black life when and where they break into our lived domain.

---

13. I have written in other places about the characteristics of holistic preaching practices as they particularly attend to this fragmentation in the lives of black women; see: Thompson, "In Search."

14. Luke Powery in *Dem Dry Bones* draws a theological sketch of preaching that has its start in preaching hope from death, and contends that this is the context from which every sermon begins. Here my emphasis is not on the metaphor in Ezekiel 37 as the starting place of preaching itself, but instead on what we learn about the nature of the call and response that occurs in the moment of proclamation and how the valley might symbolize any site where this call and response occurs.

Proclamation that sustains black life considers black life and that which is required for its flourishing as well as that which prevents its flourishing. In a society that is anti-black this itself is what makes such proclamation pastoral-, prophetic-, justice-, and reconciliation-oriented in nature. This includes their presence in forms other than what is perceived as traditional practical theological containers.

In 2013 "#blacklivesmatter" began populating social media threads, t-shirts, conversations, protest signs, and media streams. Alicia Garza, Opal Tameti, and Patrisse Cullors created the phrase and hashtag, as they describe in their own words: "after 17-year-old Trayvon Martin was post-humously placed on trial for his own murder and the killer, George Zimmerman, was not held accountable for the crime he committed. It was a response to the anti-Black racism that permeates our society and also, unfortunately, our movements."[15] The work and protests of #blacklivesmatter is a response to anti-black racism, while affirming the sanctity of all black life across its spectrum of existence decentering the historical attention given to cisgender heterosexual black men even in black liberation movements. At the rise of its inception #blacklivesmatter responded to the brutal deaths of black people, often at the hands of law enforcement officers. These deaths were (and are) often met with sentiments that assumed the disposability of black life, including a lack of criminal convictions, delayed investigations, and a lack of provocation by the victims that matched the outcomes of death.

In contrast to anti-black sentiments, the phrase "Black Lives Matter." is a complete sentence and thought that propels forward a counter narrative to pervasive social narratives and beliefs that black lives do not matter and are insignificant to the point that they are indeed dispensable. These anti-black narratives lump black life into a monolithic story that dismisses the humanity and sanctity of such lives and, instead, replaces sanctity of life and humanity with sentiments that support unjust practices that have the death of black life as their final end. To be sure #blacklivesmatter is a form of calling out to justice and attends to the personal and corporate traumas of black life while trying to build a way forward in a world deplete of justice for black people. To this end, the spurs of protest, be it song, hash tags, anthems, rally cries, or dance in the midst of the valleys of death are all forms of proclamation that demonstrate greater connections with what we have typically codified as prophetic preaching than some aspects of preaching that continue from pulpit spaces. These myriad expressions of the movement, its sister movements, and unaffiliated yet responsive aesthetic works are often led by voices considered "unauthorized" by traditional power structures,

---

15 See "Herstory of Black Lives Matter."

including those of the historical black liberation movement, church, and society. And yet their reverberations are those of proclamation.

Singer and artist Janelle Monáe and writer Ta Nehisi Coates are two windows into both the pastoral and prophetic aspects of utterances far beyond the pulpit space. Janelle Monáe and other artists from her record label Wondaland released an anthem entitled "Hell You Talmbout"[16] in the summer of 2015. The anthem came on the heels of the killing of Mike Brown in Ferguson, Missouri and a wave of others that summer and before. The song is undergirded by the beat of the drum and chants that resemble the practice of hymn-lining; the lyrics are almost non-existent only consisting of the repetitively chanted title as a refrain; the verses are interludes not sung but spoken and shared by two voices. One calls out a name and the other says "say her name" or "say his name"[17]—listing names from Emmett Till in history down to Sandra Bland of the contemporary time. Their cries of persistence are similar to declarations surrounding the time and the determination to place names with faces of black women and men killed; the cries evoke the memory of life and the inability to deny the discernable pattern of death. In a similar trajectory and the same summer as Monáe, but thru a different medium, Ta Nehisi Coates published *Between the World and Me* framed as a letter to his son; the book is brutally intimate account of how systemic anti-black racism functions in the U.S. and eventually finds a place to land upon and break individual bodies.[18] In "Hell You Talmout" the listener could hear the unrelenting cries, anger, terror, defiance, and grief in the artist's voices. In *Between the World and Me*, the reader observed these sentiments as they moved across the page.

Both Coates and Wondaland Artists attested to the threat and reality of disembodiment and erasure of black bodies in North America, as well as the anger, frustration, and sadness of such realities. However, it is the movement of writing, singing, speaking and saying that we need to consider. These are the actions that led and pushed an experience of truth into our domain of existence that at times eludes being named. These movements are movements that lead toward life and freedom in the midst of an unsatisfying and death-dealing world. These movements are similar to those captured as images, such as the one of Ieshia Evans standing alone in a dress and ballerina flats unarmed with quiet fearlessness in the face of an armed

---

16 See Monáe, "Janelle Monáe Releases."

17. "Say her name" and "Say his name" were not trademarks of Monáe and Wondaland; the artists used the expressions as they were currently being used on the ground to insist that names be placed with the faces of black women and men who were killed.

18. See Coates, *Between the World*, and an excerpt titled "Letter to My Son."

police battalion in riot gear.[19] These movements of the voice, pen, and body are confessional.[20] Their work is the action of holding together the tension of the erasure of personhood yet underscoring personhood. These works of inscription counter the act of erasure. Their actions to inscribe names, experiences, and the reality of black lives in the context of North America are not only an inscription of reality but somehow a calling forth or into a new reality thru aesthetic mediums.[21] The new reality is the possibility of life abundant, as opposed to life deficient. These contemporary proclaimer prototypes leverage imaginative precision in their utterances, just as the proclaimers of old, and meet the imaginations of their listeners and observers in ways that preaching has sometimes failed to do.

To be sure death, despair, and trauma are not the only thematics of black life; they are accompanied by joy, hope, and laughter just as any situated human experience. And yet, the history of the black life in the midst of narratives of conquest, colonialism, and enslavement prove a particular tension between hope and despair, grief and joy, and laughter and tears in the "black thematic universe."[22] These protest utterances actually attend to the aspects of the fullness of what it means to be black and move about in the world as bodies under constant threat that need to be reclaimed as human and sacred. These utterances have pastoral dimensions while they also insist upon a different vision for life than the one that we know. In this regard, these utterances of protest are both pastoral and prophetic helping black life both claim its vitality in the midst of the denial of such and claiming black life as such to those who are direct or indirect interlopers.

The quest for faithful responses for the purposes of social engagement is not a new question for faith communities isolated to the 21st century.

19. See Evans, Image.

20. Anna Carter Florence argues that there is link between the process of describing what one has encountered in their engagement with a text for preaching and the pushing forward/outward of belief about what one has witnessed. The emphasis here is on the connection between the questions "What do I see?" and "What do I believe?" Acts of description such as inscription push closer to answering the two questions. Florence, *Preaching as Testimony*, 43–145.

21. Kenyatta R. Gilbert attends to black prophetic preaching in history thru the lens of it being an aesthetic endeavor that held together naming the existential realities of black life in connection with faith and scripture, while these speech–acts often emphasized the relationship between deliverance, judgment, freedom, and hope; such emphasis and naming did not exclude aspects of using dimensions beauty in language, poetry, and sound. Gilbert, *Pursued Justice*, 62–70.

22. Andrews and Smith describe the black thematic universe as "the set of historical and cultural circumstances defining the situations and conditions that shape the experiences of reality for generations of Africans and Pan Africans." See their *Black Practical Theology*, 8.

And yet every era brings with it a unique convergence of circumstances that are connected to that time and its present-day scenarios. The work of prophetic preaching remains both consistent across time and has different textures and shades across it various iterations in time. Our decision to reassess continually what it means to be faithful assumes that the task of preaching, and its hoped for aim of proclamation, remains accountable to contemporary communities and contexts.

The work of preaching that seeks to build bridges between the prophetic and pastoral for the sake of justice and reconciliation has to first begin translating the everyday life world as a matter of faith, not as something tangential or separate from faith. However, in that translation before we can move to language of reconciliation we must first correct injustice by way of justice oriented practices. This correction involves attending to both the ways in which injustice affects us at individual and corporate levels. What is more, proclamation that attends to this correction holds together pastoral and prophetic dimensions—including that which lends to joy and sorrow, hope and despair, laughter and tears, and most importantly, life and death. Proclamation continually stirs our imaginings to the eschatological echoes that breach our walls from time to time. The divine and human exchange in the valley continues to ripple throughout the world today, even in the most unexpected locales such as valleys, the corners of street protest, and the plains of discord.

If we are attentive to the hopes of proclamation, we might be more attentive to where and how it shows up, even those voices that are deemed unauthorized in more traditional understandings of church and religious life. Such openness yields the possibility to explore and place multiple streams of proclamation in conversation with one another, yielding a greater impact on our faith practices as a whole. Spoken word might speak to the harmonies of song; preaching may attend to overtures of protest; protest might be genuine care for the soul. Here we may witness all that is sacred disclosed anew in the most everyday circumstances and utterances. These are the places that build bridges between sometimes divided ideals of how we intonate toward a world established thru justice that then leads to reconciliation. Visiting these sites of disclosure helps us more readily attend to preaching as its hope is nothing less than proclamation and an encounter with sacred in-breaking.

PART 3

Prophetic Care, Preaching, and Wider Community

11

Emancipatory Practice
Institutional Maintenance and Prophetic Witness

Donna E. Allen

In November 2011, Dale P. Andrews gave the Gardner C. Taylor lecturer at Duke University. His lecture was entitled, "Jus' Couldn't Keep It to Myself." Following the lecture he gave an interview to *Faith and Leadership*, a learning resource for Christian leaders and their institutions from Leadership Education at Duke Divinity School that included some of the themes of his lecture. The following is an excerpt from an edited transcript of the interview, beginning with the question proposed by the interviewer.

> Q: What about those leaders in the church who may say, "Well, social justice is a goal, but we are trying to keep our organization together, trying to keep it healthy, trying to keep it alive"? How do those two issues intersect?
>
> R: Institution survival is a reality. It is critically important. There was an age when the development of the black church itself—the institutional development of the black church—was a form of political resistance. When the development of the institutional black church was a form of spiritual nurture; that ... personal salvation or the nurture of the soul was a form of justice-making. To re-dignify—to re-humanize—the personalities who were coming to the church was a form of protest as well as a form of nurture. The development of the black church in

society had that same dual capacity. It was a form of protest, but it was also a form of nurture of black communal life. So the goal of institutional maintenance or the goal of institutional survival is not necessarily a defiled goal. So I support that work. That being said, I do think our churches struggle under extraordinary economic difficulty, particularly black churches or churches with a high constituency dealing with poverty or working poor. At some point, we have to learn how to go about nurturing our resources that does not also—or developing our resources together—that does not buy into some of the cultural aspects of prosperity that are uncritical . Yet, at the same time, we have to take care of the maintenance of the building, the maintenance of the institution, the maintenance of the staff. The staff have to survive, as well. However, that is not the sum total of the work of the church. This is a problem . . . because that work is so difficult to sustain, it ends up being all the church is about, or most of what the church is about. . . . If we're going to die, if we're looking at facing death, then let us go out trying to be the church. We still work at the institutional maintenance, but if we're facing death, let us face death with faith that our death is not the end of our life. And let us go out dying by doing that justice making out in the community, and we will be faithful in doing it and trusting in God's faithfulness to work with us. And if we die while we're being faithful, our death is not the end of life. What happens when the work of the church is about only developing the church? I don't think, in our theological self-awareness, that's our claim. But when we're functioning that way, it becomes an incredible distortion of what it means to face survival or what it means to face ministry.[1]

Dr. Andrews' assessment of what is required to face ministry as a preacher in a financially struggling black church resonates with my experience as a pastor. The balance of the immediate urgent demands of institutional maintenance and pressing demands of the work of the church as an agent of social justice and personal and communal transformation is an ever-illusive and frustrating dance. Dr. Andrews' comments that the particular challenge of a church, with limited resources, that has transitioned from struggling to survive to facing death not being exempted from the work of the church, is difficult. As he noted as a former pastor, his words were not intended as an indictment of the church but rather an empathetic summons or a reminder to be faithful to the justice work of the church even in a season of institutional decline.

1. Andrews, "We're Never Done."

I interpreted Dr. Andrews' words as a prophetic call with implications for preaching. The prophetic call was to "go out by doing that justice making out in the community, and we will be faithful in doing it and trusting in God's faithfulness to work with us. And if we die while we are being faithful, our death is not the end of life."[2] The first time I heard these particular words from Dr. Andrews, and this sentiment expressed in both Dr. Andrews' lecture and the interview, it was a balm to my weary soul and it soothed my hoarse preaching voice. It inspired me to continue to face ministry as a preacher and pastor and to reframe the work of institutional maintenance and social justice ministry. As a womanist preacher, a component of my preaching that received new hope was the way I thought about emancipatory praxis.

In a previous publication I offered a summary of Katie G. Cannon's womanist-critical evaluation of Black preaching, the last item focusing on emancipatory praxis. The following list summarizes the central homiletic concerns of Cannon's womanist analysis of Black preaching. She calls for preachers to do the following.

1. Eliminate "negative and derogatory female" images. She wants preachers to identify and refute the "androcentric, phallocentric stereotypes that are dehumanizing, debilitating, and prejudicial to African-American women."

2. Address the marginalization of women in the biblical text and context. "A Womanist hermeneutic seeks to place sermonic texts in the real-life context of the culture that produced them . . . Images used throughout the sermon can invite the congregation to share in dismantling patriarchy," and create an emancipatory response.

3. Eliminate discriminatory language and the marginalizing of women characters in the sermon that in the biblical text are central figures. To challenge the sermonic retelling of the biblical story in such a manner that women are inferior to men. "What happens to the African-American female children when Black preachers use the Bible to attribute marvelous happenings and unusual circumstances to an all-male cast of characters?"

4. Monitor the impact of images to empower women and create "an ethic of resistance" to oppression. "As Womanist theologians, what can we do to counter the negative real-world consequences of sexist wording that brothers and sisters propagate in the guise of Christian piety and virtue?"

2. Ibid.

5. Consider the socio-cultural context of the preaching event. Examine the words of the preacher and the context of the community. What are the leadership roles of women within the church community? "This practice removes men from the normative center and women from the margins."

6. Manifest praxis of resistance. The faith communities' response to the "proclaimed word" is the emancipatory praxis.[3]

Emancipatory praxis is the action, or praxis, that the sermon demands as a response to the Word of God proclaimed. It is the audience's action in response to the central lesson or revelation of the sermon. It is often the place wherein the preacher makes an appeal for a particular social justice action. Emancipatory praxis often includes denouncement of oppression and injustice, and calls on the church to live out its faith in the world in some particular way.

In my preaching in particular, emancipatory praxis was interpreted almost exclusively as a call to transform the communities in which the church was located through specific social justice work, such as voter registration, voter education, and voter turn out. The call to praxis of almost every sermon included some form of organizing the community around ballot initiatives and legislation that would impact injustices in our education system, criminal justice system, and health care systems. Emancipatory praxis was about action in the streets, protests, rallies, sit-ins, community organizing, and the like.

Dr. Andrews' prophetic call to "face ministry" and resist a distortion of the gospel convicted me to re-fame what it means to do ministry in a church that has limited resources and struggles to maintain the institution. At the same time, the preacher is to consider the social justice work as an emancipatory praxis reflecting the Good News, and to also to consider the work of maintaining the institution as a necessary and important emancipatory praxis that is also part of the Good News part of the work. I was called to be faithful and to be a pastor in such a church. I realized I had distorted the appeal in the sermon. The sermon was almost exclusively toward only one audience response, toward social justice, and the appeal was almost exclusively an appeal to justice without much room for an authentic audience-fashioned response and was void of pastoral care. There was no balance, no harmony I had distorted the Gospel message to mean almost exclusively social justice work, so that, from my point of view, if we as a church failed to engage in social justice work, we had failed to be an authentic church. There

---

3. Allen, *Toward a Womanist*, 114–21.

was a need to re-frame the work of institutional maintenance as no longer an unfortunate evil, but rather as an act of resistance and in preaching. In a womanist homiletic, it was an emancipatory praxis in harmony with social justice work.

As it relates to re-framing the work of institutional survival, we should carry out institutional care with an ethic of care for the human expense of responding to the demands of the daily work (e.g. keeping the lights on, nurturing staff, maintaining the edifice) and an ethic of urgency for being the church as it relates to doing justice work.

In these regards the womanist sermonic call for an emancipatory praxis becomes not only a call to actions regarding systemic injustice in the larger society, but also a call to the work of institutional maintence. Too often, my preaching has ignored the hard work of church preservation as an act of resistance. Re-framing in this way is not intended to draw the gaze of the church to solely upon itself, but is rather to have balance. As Dr. Andrews stated in the interview:

> What happens when the work of the church is about only developing the church? I don't think, in our theological self-awareness, that's our claim. But when we're functioning that way, it becomes an incredible distortion of what it means to face survival or what it means to face ministry. We have to learn to give for the sake of the other and just for their sake, to do that work because of the value that they hold to God and the value that they need to hold to us if we understand the relationship of the divine with creation. Our relationship with God and our relationship with humanity—those spiritual values which for the black church extend all the way back to African spiritual values of being in harmony with the creation, being in harmony with the divine and being in harmony with one another—and how that translates into Christian theology for us is critical. We're never done with that work, and that's the beauty of our faith. It's also the frustration.[4]

Emancipatory praxis in preaching becomes a balanced pastoral and prophetic invitation to make critical connections between the economic state of the church and the community, as well as national and global issues of economic injustice. The perpetual fiscal condition of many churches of making bricks without straw must be linked to economic policies in the society at large. Emancipatory praxis should reflect a more nuanced interpretation of

4. Andrews, "We're Never Done."

how social injustice shows up in our churches in disparity of resources and access to finances for expansion, and a legion of other matters.

Emancipatory praxis needs to be pastoral in honoring the work of those who provide direct service ministries in impoverished communities, such as providing food and clothing and shelter. The emancipatory praxis assessment can be balanced in also acknowledging the ways in which the criminalization of the poor and homeless contributes to the need for such services. The cost of providing such services on the church budget is an act of resistance. The church carries out an act of resistance when the church refuses to allow the many to go hungry because the church only has a few loaves of bread and a few fish. The emancipatory praxis of linking how local churches are on the frontline engaging persons with mental illness, again providing resources on a very limited budget while the national health care policy makers limit federal and state financial support for mental illness education, stigma reduction and medical care. The church carries out an act of resistance when the church does not abandon the frontline to help its bottom line. These are just a few examples of how the emancipatory praxis called for in a sermon can link the direct service ministry of the church with the social justice ministry of the church, and can link he survival of the local church with the survival of the community.

What are some of the pastoral care possibilities? One way to frame it is as reflected in the following passage of scripture which I interpret as being very social justice oriented:

> When he came to Nazareth, where he had been brought up, he went to the synagogue on the sabbath day, as was his custom. He stood up to read, and the scroll of the prophet Isaiah was given to him. He unrolled the scroll and found the place where it was written: "The Spirit of the Lord is upon me, because he has anointed me to bring good news to the poor. He has sent me to proclaim release to the captives and recovery of sight to the blind, to let the oppressed go free, to proclaim the year of the Lord's favor." (Luke 4:16–19)

The pastoral support of acknowledging and celebrating the work of sustaining the church as an emancipatory praxis honors the value in sustaining a vehicle for bringing good news to the poor and encourages and inspires those who do that work to perceive the work of institutional maintenance as providing a platform for the dissemination of the Good News. The investment of resources in underserved communities bears witness that the Lord's favor is at hand and the reign of God is breaking out to meet the needs beyond the resources of the church. The healing and reconciliation that comes from recognizing that the work of sustaining the church positions the church to sustain the oppressed long enough to be set free, while simultaneously working on institutionalized barriers to freedom. The pastoral work of healing, reconciliation, affirmation, meaning making, service, and nurturing an ethic of human connection that comes from keeping the doors of the church open are all balanced pastoral and prophetic emancipatory praxis.

I think what will emerge in my preaching in the future are sermons more centered on the particulars of the lived experiences of the individuals in the congregation living as a congregation, living as ecclesia, a people called out doing the work of justice that includes many acts of resistance even resisting the death of the institution upon which the Spirit of the Lord rests to become and proclaim the Good News.

12

A Church that Will Survive
Prophetic Proclamation, Community Wellness, and Clergy Well-Being

Kenyatta R. Gilbert

I REMEMBER HOW ELATED, though anxious, I felt minutes before walking into the standing room only Hanover Hall conference room at the Hyatt Regency on Peachtree in downtown Atlanta. Respected biblical scholars and homileticians lined the walls and, of course, the ever too eager doctoral students had secured front row seats. I had accepted an invitation to participate on a panel entitled "Preaching and the Personal" with homiletician Anna Carter Florence and the eminent Old Testament scholar Walter Brueggemann at the Society of Biblical Literature and Academy of Homiletics' 2010 annual meeting. Two others had been invited, one withdrew for an undisclosed reason, and the other had to attend to a family emergency. With the meeting scheduled only a month out, I was tapped to stand in as the substitute. Obviously, for a young, green, pre–tenured homiletics professor like myself, only five years into my academic career and a book due out in six months, this event signaled moving to a steeper climb in the guild.

I knew the profitability of accepting invitations to present working papers having attended my fair share of annual meetings in previous years as a doctoral student. In such spaces one earns his or her academic stripes, and perhaps more importantly, have one's academic proposals vetted in a critical context before pursuing publication. I knew to value the moment. I would not squander it. To declare this as the high point of the start of a banner year would be a gross understatement. But in this sea of spectators I knew not to flatter myself; most had come to hear Professor Brueggemann's paper "The Risk of Testimony," based on Isaiah 43. Thankfully, since I had come off a long season of book writing I had a paper polished enough to present. It also happened to be in step with the theme and easy enough to abridge to fit within the fifteen-minute time constraint.

My paper focused on the person of the preacher, namely, what W. E. B. DuBois referred to as the most unique religious personality born out of the Black lived experience in North America—the Black preacher.[1] I sought to challenge on the one hand the uncritical bias of some to romanticize the African American preaching tradition, and on the other to address the wider culture's ill-informed assumptions about African American preachers, which seemed particularly important in the wake of the Jeremiah Wright and President Obama media debacle that gained national attention before the 2008 Presidential election.

Beyond dreadful caricature I had perceived that few scholars had obtained an appropriate interpretation of the Black preacher's complex self-identity. And fewer still had a well-reasoned understanding of the distinct context-functional roles Black preachers assume in light of their congregation's expectations—expectations tied inseparably to the preacher's persona and theological commitments. Given what I knew about doing ministry in African American churches and communities, I could convincingly argue without fear of contradiction that if context-functional roles assumed by African American preachers are aligned with Jesus' norm-setting vision[2] for Christian proclamation, then promising practices that enhance a community's wellness and promote clergy well-being would follow.

THE PREACHER'S CALL AND THE CONGREGATION'S RESPONSE

By all accounts, the foremost venerated and formative practice of the Church is preaching. The assumptive claim upon which such a declaration stands is that in preaching the hope of God speaks. No other speech-act heard in time and space shares equal footing, or better, is equal to the task. Christian preaching bears promises upon which hope is grounded and ethical action is forged. And when this theo-rhetorical discourse is prophetic, it is a means by which God reminds a society of God's concern for justice,

1. DuBois, *Souls*, 116.
2. Luke 4:16–21.

freedom, and human dignity in a less than perfect world. The preacher's words are meaning-making when the concern is the gospel, and never is this concern separable from the preacher and listener's faith identity, core values, and theological commitments. The preacher's powerful way of waging linguistic wars to expose the problem of evil and interpret life's contradictions, whether speaking freely in open air or through the survival tradition of indirection, casts the preacher in the unique role of local theologian and priestly guide in matters spiritual, social, and psychic. Thus, as it pertains to the life of the gathered faithful, central to the preacher's vocation and sacred obligation is going to scripture on the community's behalf in search of a fitting address to engage the specific needs of real people with complex problems and concerns.

Without the preacher's persistent calls for social justice, church reform, spiritual conversion, and moral and ethical responsibility, healing the "village," specifically, the local neighborhoods and communities with predominantly Black populations in the U.S. of which I am most familiar, finding solutions to address multiple crisis points militating against the health and well-being of our communities is practically unachievable. Given the particularly challenging and community corrosive effects of self-deceptive theologies of opulence, vocational quietism among clergy, and the church's slight attention to the mental health needs of Black clergy, preaching that brings good news to the poor, recovery of sight to the spiritual blind and liberty for persons captive to physical, social and spiritual death still matters.

Black churches that remain loyal to their historical identity as critical arenas in the maintenance of community are befittingly labeled sanctuaries—reservoirs of communal care, religious formation, and liberating hope. The preacher's role is crucial to the development of sanctuary, because, as Scottish theologian P. T. Forsyth once expressed, the "one great preacher in history is the Church, and the business of the individual preacher is to enable the Church to preach."[3] Although the deeply urgent task of enabling their congregations to preach persists, Forsyth could have never imagined the tremendous challenges facing the Church in the postmodern era, challenges brought on by a matrix of social forces in an information saturated, market-driven age of intense spiritual and economic crisis.

AME bishop Reverdy C. Ransom's farsighted quadrennial address, "The Church that Shall Survive," which he delivered before his denomination in 1936, posed two critical challenges relative to the Black Church's future viability. A church survives, declared Ransom, when it "strives to find relevance in a rapidly changing atmosphere yielding a slate of new

---

3. Forsyth, *Positive Preaching*, 79.

problems."⁴ That church willingly interrogates their conventional norms of practice and remains "flexible enough to minister to the actual conditions that confront it at a given time."⁵ Ransom's detailing of what is at stake merits an extended quote:

> Few things in the church's history are more pathetic and distressing than the manner in which the church functioned during the world war, unless its in the manner in which it is behaving in the face of social, political, economic, and spiritual crisis that menaces the civilized world today. How may the Negro church survive a thing apart [from English Christianity in India and South Africa, or American Christianity in the United States]? It is already a thing apart in management and control. But there is small hope for its survival if it continues to copy and follow the programs and practices of fellow Christians.⁶

Ecclesiastical survival requires that congregations update their methods of congregational care, reconfigure how the work of evangelism and missions work are carried out, and find their distinctive voice in the culture; and, while in pursuit of accomplishing these tasks, they must give primacy to individual personhood and spiritual well-being.

Ransom's second challenge to the Church is equally important. If the church is to survive, he asserts, it must "furnish its own redeemers and prophets to lead . . . and go forth and walk with a timeless and ageless God," but in doing so acknowledge that there are "just as many formidable foes to progress within the church to contend with as forces without."⁷ This challenge is particularly significant for persons seeking refuge in Black congregations today for two important reasons. On the one hand, it expresses that the preacher plays a vital role in leading the congregation into its unsettled and unsettling future, and on the other, it insists that those whom the church seeks to help often impede progress.

If community wellness is a divine concern, then the church must evolve and rediscover its public witness and ministry to meet the real and complex needs of real people. In order for preaching to matter today within African American congregations the Black church must recover its relevance in a world of radical social change and furnish her pulpit with leaders who walk with the Divine. Answering Ransom's challenge in our time can only mean that preachers refocus their ways of representing themselves as ministers,

4. Ransom, *Making the Gospel Plain*, 102–11.
5. Ibid.
6. Ibid.
7. Ibid.

so that they might more clearly signal an understanding about the complex needs, circumstances, and aspirations of their particular communities.

The listening community's role as aural appraisers of the preacher's message is indispensable to any congregation's forward progress. Part of the genius of the liturgical ritual of "call and response," still preserved in various quarters where some of the best of African American preaching takes place today, is that the preacher's reception of antiphonal "Amen" requires more than what the preacher's charismata alone could conjure. Sermons still matter in Black congregations because hope is sought. Congregants still look for the "buy ins" that speak truth to the actualities of their sorrows and existential crises. The beauty of the African American preacher's conversation with the people is that the community gets a share in helping the preacher see that her or his words have consequence. If the preacher is faithful to the functional task of interpreting scripture and nourishing the church's life in loving, critical, and constructive ways then that preacher profits the people and, morally and ethically, honors his or her vocation.

SABBATH REST AND RESTORATION: CLERGY HEALTH AND SPIRITUAL WELL-BEING

Intrinsic to a congregation's state of well-being is the well-being of the individual who seeks to lead and ensure that the Church remains faithful to her holy calling of equipping people to live a responsible life of faith in pursuit of God's vision. Keeping one's sense of call and vocational responsibilities in proper perspective takes discipline and personal commitment. But answering one's call has never meant sacrificing one's family or physical health and emotional well-being. Sadly, despite supportive resources many preachers fail to see the importance of self-care and spiritual renewal. New York Times journalist Paul Vitello reported that "members of the clergy now suffer from obesity, hypertension and depression at rates higher than most Americans."[8] But not only this, "in the last decade, their use of antidepressants has risen, while their life expectancy has fallen."[9]

One crucial factor for promoting clergy care and wellness is insisting that ministers take sabbaticals—time off for theological reflection, professional counseling, and spiritual renewal. Several thriving African American congregations are becoming alert to the benefits of providing pastors time off to refresh themselves. New Jersey pastor of First Baptist Church of Lincoln Gardens of Somerset, Rev. Dr. DeForest B. Soaries, Jr., with whom I

8. Vitello, "Taking a Break."
9. Ibid.

served while in graduate school, received a Lilly-funded three-month sabbatical grant. He used his time off for travel and devoting stricter attention to family. Because this would typically be a hard sell for any African American congregation, given the high ministerial demands placed upon Black pastors, astutely, this pastor and his leadership team created what they termed *The Great Preacher Series*. Every Sunday over a three-month period a guest preacher filled the pulpit, preaching back-to-back sermons at the church's two worship services. With a competent clerical staff to manage the daily goings on, this unprecedented experiment proved mutually beneficial to both pastor and congregation.

"The Preacher's Sabbath" is a Lilly Foundation funded clergy renewal project, of which I am a program consultant and retreat facilitator, is another positive example. In my consultative role I serve alongside three ordained African American clerics holding Ph.Ds and tenured positions in history, homiletics, and pastoral counseling at different theological institutions. As collaborative thinkers having deep commitments to ecclesial ministry and preparing ministry leaders, in our consultation, we set out to define and outline our work and vision for a three-day summer retreat to take place at a Richmond Hill Christian ecumenical retreat center located in a monastery that sits atop the highest point in Richmond, Virginia. In planning we asked ourselves: "Why is the event necessary? Who will we serve? What will we accomplish? Why should people come? What will we teach? How will they learn? and What will this become?" Thoughtful ideas emerged from each consultant's responses and spawned other generative questions: "Is this a secondary or tertiary intervention? Are we going after working clergy on the edge? Should our programming include vocational coaching and work to identify specific resources for developing systems of accountability?" A gap closure between the academy and church was underway as our group brought focused thought around what we could distinctly provide based on training and interest.

We determined that not only do clergy need strategies for negotiating congregational and organizational systems that suck the energy out of them, but also retreating spaces that work to disrupt the weekly grind. When ministers are led to sit quietly free of distraction, new and creative possibilities emerge and the will to do the work of ministry is strengthened. A close second to the importance of continual self-care, particularly in African American church contexts where a high view of scripture and the authority of preacher is wed to preaching, is continuing education programming. No church community can sustain its viability without encouraging its clerical leaders to seize continuing education opportunities, namely those that help preachers improve their homiletical skills in a constructive, peer-affirming environment. If the church is to survive, and I believe it will, creative strategies that bridge the church and academy must be envisioned, tapped, and implemented on an ongoing basis.

UNMASKING MELANCHOLIA: WHY KING IS PEDAGOGICALLY INSTRUCTIVE

Given the high costs a demanding preaching schedule exacts, Martin Luther King Jr.'s homiletical context and preaching life are particularly instructive for working and aspirant clergy. King's death-warning final sermon *I've Been to the Mountaintop* is emblematic of the notion that preaching in some cases invites death. King's message to poor sanitation workers and sympathizers, at each turn, addressed the fact that God was attuned to human suffering, and just as God had heard the rallying cry of the enslaved Israelites, God had heard the cry of the American Negro to be free. But if we put this sermon into its proper context, historically, it is not difficult to notice that as the sermon progressed the soundscape of King's words shift from melancholic tone toward confident resolve in a matter of minutes. King's disposition of melancholy was palpable and must not be overlooked.[10]

That night in Memphis, to use preacher-speak, "King preached himself out of a storm." The storm metaphor signals that personal suffering and loneliness often accompany the preacher on the homiletical road. Toward the end of King's life his feelings of despair had become especially pronounced. While "no one will ever fully understand the psychodynamics of King's bout with depression," it is well documented that like many other great preachers that preceded him, including famed clerics such as nineteenth-century England's great expository preacher, Alexander Maclaren and Harry Emerson Fosdick of Riverside Church of New York City, he suffered with depression. In fact, Fosdick credits his period of hospitalization for depression as both a critical factor in his preparation for ministry and being the literary wellspring for his autobiography *The Meaning of Prayer*.[11] It was King's sensation of despair that led him to become fixated on his own death. But even if this overstates the matter, King's colleague and friend Rev. Dr. Gardner C. Taylor went on record describing King as "a peculiar man . . . and a deeply troubled person [with] some darkly brooding element

---

10. See an extended analysis of King's "I've Been to the Mountaintop" sermon in my *Pursued Justice*, 105–10.

11. See Dayringer, "Clergy and Depression," 107–26.

in his makeup."¹² Taylor went on to say, "I don't think anybody will ever know the interior torture that Martin King went through."¹³

Unlike other Afican American leaders of his day, King had unrivaled access to the Oval office, having advised Presidents Eisenhower, Kennedy, and Johnson. But after speaking out against the Vietnam War, King no longer occupied the role of central prophet.¹⁴ His near-death protestations earned him another title role: peripheral prophet. Having to struggle with his own feelings of hostility toward Whites and personal experience with a domineering father, one might say that the act of preaching itself was one way King dealt with his interior torture. Richard Lischer maintains that even if a compelling psychohistory about King's mental state could be presented, one would still arrive at unsatisfactory conclusions. However, what is clear in his record of sermons is "how thoroughly he associated the symbol of the crucified Messiah with the mission of his people and his own impending sacrifice."¹⁵ Though uncommonly used by the Divine and thus lionized in our sacred imagination, King was utterly human. I would venture to say that the humbling negatives of depression and anxiety were chief among agents that sandbagged any will toward arrogance he might have had or him falling victim to the political co-optation of the nation's powerbrokers. Of King, Lischer writes:

> King organized the achievements, failures, anger, depression, and indeed his whole sense of private and public identity in the only way he knew how: he adopted a series of biblical personae—masks that captured the several roles he understood himself to be playing in American life . . . King not only wore these masks but spent his life in an effort to live into them. They became the marks of his truest self. The first of these was the prophet.¹⁶

Masking tears and channeling the bygone poets of biblical antiquity, King's preaching life embodied the way of the prophet, and that is why King's preaching life proves instructive for Black clergy today. Through King's private prison of psychic pain and distress, from a metaphorical mountaintop, King, with impassioned speech, cried out and set a beleaguered band of Black exiles on course for entrance into a new world he saw coming into view.

12. Lischer, *Preacher King*, 190–91.
13. Ibid.
14. Ibid., 170.
15. Ibid., 172–73.
16. Ibid., 193.

Ministers play a vital role in securing the church's survival. A church that survives, I have argued in the main, remains flexible enough to minister to the actual conditions that confront it at a given time; furnishes and resources its own prophets and redeemers; and creates a congregational infrastructure that promotes the health and wellness of its clergy. Though preachers carry heavy loads, many are learning that carrying heavy loads need not mean that preachers have to do ministry at their family's expense and to the detriment of their psychological, spiritual, and mental well-being .Churches and leaders who heed this charge form churches that can and will survive.

13

Prophetic Preaching in a Pastoral Mode

Communities of Solidarity and the White Mainline Church

DAVID SCHNASA JACOBSEN

MUCH DISCUSSION OF THE prophetic in Christian preaching has presupposed a substantial gap between preachers as prophets and the communities with whom they engage. In a prior essay, I argued the "lone ranger" model of prophetic preaching played an inordinate role in the way the white mainline church in particular has conceived the prophetic task.[1] While this misconception was built on very individualistic assumptions about prophecy, a review of the shape of prophecy in the Hebrew Bible and Early Christianity brought out the importance of communities in prophetic work and discernment, as well as the place of covenant in the former and ecclesiology in the latter. The prophetic is emphatically not a lone ranger enterprise.

One of the great scholarly contributions of the work of my colleague, Dr. Dale Andrews, has been to flesh out this community character in more profound ways. In this book, *Practical Theology for Black Churches*, Andrews calls specifically for a deep reconciliation between the prophetic and

---

1. Jacobsen, "*Schola Prophetarum*," 12–21.

the pastoral.² His book seeks to find a way forward between the liberationist and prophetic claims of black theology and the refuge-oriented, more individually and spiritually shaped view of African American folk religion. Andrews does not view these two traditions as utterly bifurcated. In fact, he thinks a focus on the praxis of the African American church will yield space where the linkage between the prophetic and the pastoral can be explored and claimed. Overarching this careful discussion is a conviction that the pastoral concern of the refuge view of salvation and the prophetic view of liberation need each other in the same intimate way that the twin sources of covenant theology in the Hebrew Bible do: (1) the Sinaitic covenant, grounded in the sovereign God of exodus who gives a covenantal law of liberation to which the prophetic tradition calls to return and (2) the Davidic covenant which is grounded in God's commitment to institutional presence and dynasty. The two covenants need each other. In the same way, Andrews hopes to have African American religious communities see that the individual call to personal salvation cannot be cut off from the history of liberation in which it finds itself. The most effective form of prophetic preaching therefore finds its strength in just such a covenantal awareness precisely while grounding a powerful sense of personal presence in living commitment to social justice. In this way, the prophetic call is grounded in a gospel of grace, repentance, and reconciliation. Andrews hopes to reconnect the prophetic and pastoral again.

In the same spirit, I wish to explore more deeply what brings the prophetic and the pastoral together and precisely as an instantiation of a more communal sense of prophecy. I do so with some trepidation. The problems around reconciling the prophetic and the pastoral in preaching vary considerably across communities, their privilege, and their positionalities. The reconciliation of the prophetic and the pastoral in the pulpit of white mainline denominations like mine calls forth a different set of acknowledgments, a different kind of reflection, and a different kind of praxis. This chapter honors the work of Professor Andrews by posing a question: how can a new discernment of solidarity, that is, what and who gets noticed, eventuate in a different conception and praxis around the relationship of the prophetic and the pastoral in preaching itself? Can it do so in a way that presses past the obliviousness of those who, enmeshed in privilege, too often fail to notice injustice and struggle to make a deep connection between themselves and others?

---

2. Andrews. *Practical Theology*. What follows is my partial summary of his work.

NOTICING AND OBLIVIOUSNESS IN THE WHITE MAINLINE CHURCH

The way in which "noticing" and "not noticing" complicate the move toward the integration of the prophetic and the pastoral is quite clear at the level of the wider culture. In *Manufacturing Consent*, Edward S. Herman and Noam Chomsky demonstrate that media news crises are used to further policy objectives.[3] They point out that political agendas especially impact the selection or amplification of a given story in the media. It is not uncommon that officials will seize upon an event in order to sway sympathy in order to advance an agenda. This is also true in crisis moments where governments prioritize appropriate victims. Herman and Chomsky write,

> Our hypothesis is that worthy victims will be featured prominently and dramatically, that they will be humanized, and that their victimization will receive the detail and context in story construction that will generate reader interest and sympathetic emotion. In contrast, unworthy victims will merit only slight detail, minimal humanization, and little context that will excite and enrage.[4]

The point is that at the level of public media, we are already being shaped to notice and not to notice.

At the level of community practice in churches, this becomes all the more prominent. In a powerful ethnographic study of a multi-racial church that intentionally includes and engages persons with disabilities, Mary McClintock Fulkerson begins to trace through the thematization of her own habituated, bodily reactions, how white racism shapes interpersonal relations and even sponsors a kind of obliviousness. A priori commitments to "color blindness" and pretending not to notice real bodily differences show that such obliviousness reaches deeply into experience, especially the experience of the privileged. Part of the problem of reconciling the prophetic and the pastoral in white mainline preaching concerns just this gap: noticing and not noticing human beings and the ideologies and habituated values that render some people oblivious and others invisible.

I select this example for a very personal reason. While reading McClintock Fulkerson's work, I became aware of the ways racism had shaped

---

3. Herman and Chomsky, *Manufacturing Consent*, 32. In this section of the book, Herman and Chomsky analyze public crises like the shooting down of the Korean Airliner by the Soviet Union in 1983 as an example of how selectively noticing helps to foreground certain public sympathies.

4. Ibid., 35.

my own perceptions and embodied reactions. Whatever prophetic preaching does, and whatever way in which the prophetic and the pastoral can be related in such an act, will deal ultimately with the impediments to the gospel posed by injustices as they already impact preachers and hearers at the level of perception and practice.

At the same time, and here I also remain on a very personal level, the possibility of noticing is a small first step that can open up different ways of doing prophetic work. After a trip to Denmark, Professor Andrews told a story about how amazed he was to see these words spray painted on a building in Copenhagen, "I can't breathe." The reference is to the words of Eric Garner as he was placed in a life-ending chokehold by police in New York for selling loose cigarettes. I wondered, as I heard Professor Andrews recall this story wistfully, why he had to travel so far to find a European culture that was able publicly to notice, to name the deadly truth, and to show some small modicum of solidarity. The bad news is that US white mainline churches largely failed to notice and demonstrated little solidarity. The good news, albeit small, is that someone in Denmark did.

My contention in this essay is deceivingly simple. If the prophetic and the pastoral are to be reconciled in white mainline prophetic preaching, it must do so recognizing this particular element of privilege: the uncanny ability to escape notice, to be oblivious, and to *fail* to show solidarity across the artificial lines of culturally inscribed power relations. I write this to set an agenda for a pastorally-oriented form of prophetic preaching in the white mainline church: it needs to be in the business of fomenting not only a more communal sense of the prophetic, but of care and solidarity as well.

FOMENTING A COMMUNAL PROPHETIC VISION OPEN TO THE PASTORAL: WALTER BRUEGGEMANN AND ELISABETH SCHÜSSLER FIORENZA

To my mind, Walter Brueggemann contributes to just such a vision with his unique take on the prophetic—and one that acknowledges the importance of the pastoral along the way. In *The Prophetic Imagination* the problem is precisely a crisis of consciousness.[5] The contemporary church, whether left or right, is captive to consumerism. The right reduces prophecy to future predictions about Jesus, the left lives in an eternal present focused on "issues," critiquing but never engaging beyond their thematization in the prophetic pulpit.

---

5. Brueggemann, *Prophetic Imagination*. A summary of Brueggemann's position follows.

For Brueggemann, therefore, the problem is that the church is captive to the dominant imagination and needs to remember its own tradition to see differently. This "seeing" has two elements relative to the dominant consciousness: critiquing and energizing. Critiquing is an act of dismantling the dominant consciousness. Energizing means to articulate a hope toward which people can live, one capable of sustaining an alternative consciousness in the present by pointing to a future. Precisely this critiquing and energizing is the stuff of prophetic ministry. For Brueggemann, it this dialectic which allows hearers to be faithful to God.

For Brueggemann, a Hebrew Bible scholar, Moses is the paradigmatic prophet who sought to evoke just such an "alternative consciousness" in Israel. Pharaoh's religious system is one of static triumphalism built on the politics of oppression and exploitation. It can permit no newness. It is what is, was, and ever shall be. It is a world that cannot be critiqued and also cannot energize, but can merely enslave. For Moses to critique this world is more than just thematizing issues, but to show such status quo gods are in fact no gods. As an alternative, Moses discloses the freedom of God which he crucially joins to a politics of justice and compassion. Exodus's "alternative consciousness" produces then a new social community that corresponds to this vision of divine freedom.

Of course, such consciousness raising is both a prophetic and a pastoral act. Part of the critique is to demonstrate that Egyptian gods cannot deliver on their promises. But part of the critique is also the cry, a word of lament. The people of Israel groan under their bondage . . . and God hears it. Then God remembers God's covenant. Brueggemann says that the real capacity to criticize resides in the ability to grieve. The Empire wants everyone to think it's all OK. The grief, and its public statement, put the lie to that and thus open the possibility of critique. For they are complaints that expect answers—they know something is wrong, because it is not as promised.

I would like to submit that such communal prophetic vision is intertwined with care in different ways. For all the benefit of Brueggemann's understanding of a debilitating royal consciousness which stifles grief, not everyone hearing such a prophetic word suffers in the system in the same way. If the prophetic imagination helps us to see pastoral care as a deepening of the sense of grief in moving from "royal" to "alternative consciousness" of Exodus, some of us need to acknowledge positions of privilege within the pyramidal system of Egypt. The Pharaonic power structure crushes Hebrew slaves, but others stand in differentiated relationships to system of power. This, to my mind, complicates the pastoral work of grief in Brueggemann's communal prophetic vision. And yet part of Brueggemann's vision holds:

"only grief permits newness."[6] But how, given the fact that our connections and relationships to power are not one, but many?

Elizabeth Schüssler Fiorenza offers a more differentiated way of thinking about power that moves beyond the binary of Brueggemann's dialectic. She argues in *Wisdom Ways* for what she calls "kyriarachy" as representing a more differentiated understanding of systems of domination. For her, kyriarchy can function diagnostically in that it "allows us to investigate the multiplicative interdependence of gender, race, and class stratification as well as their discursive inscriptions and ideological reproductions."[7]

The upshot for this communal prophetic vision that includes the pastoral is a way prophetically of naming grief *differently*. Preaching as a prophetic and pastoral work will require an intersectional wisdom and a more differentiated way of naming the very grief that leads to newness by means of the prophetic imagination. These may well be ways of grounding the kind of communal care and solidarity that the prophet needs to name among those who fail to notice and those unduly numbed in obliviousness.

FOMENTING A COMMUNAL PASTORAL VISION OPEN TO THE PROPHETIC: LEE RAMSEY

In his book *Care-full Preaching*, G. Lee Ramsey seeks to move the opposite direction: From a renewed vision of communal pastoral care to the prophetic.[8] How does he get there?

Ramsey notes that much pastoral care is dominated by the "therapeutic." He expresses the concern that the pulpit in particular has been taken over by therapeutic language. Instead of replicating such an individual (and professionalized) orientation to care, the pulpit should actually release the whole people of God to care.

Ramsey wonders just what prevents churches from sharing in such a communal pastoral vision? He notes two problematic theological roadblocks. First is a too narrow theological anthropology. By buying into a therapeutic mindset about care, preachers may just re-inscribe individualistic therapeutic selves in their sermons. In contrast, Ramsey considers that something of our humanity is actually more bound up with each other. Ramsey mentions favorably Ed Farley's interest in "the interhuman" and notes by contrast how individuality in some cultures is actually an

---

6. This quote comes from the name of a section in Brueggemann's subsequent work, *Hopeful Imagination*, 9.

7. Fiorenza, *Wisdom Ways*, 119.

8. Ramsey, *Care-full Preaching*.

abstraction. Second is a woefully inadequate ecclesiology. We are neither merely individuals, nor with a more reified identity rendered as simply apart from the world or over against it. A more adequate vision for a communal vision of care is grounded in an understanding of the church in the world, which still God so loves.

Ultimately, says Ramsey, communal pastoral care is theological. It is emphatically about God's care and its relationship to communities who hear the Word of God. The question is: what to do? Ramsey's program begins by noting that, for good or for ill, the words of preaching form pastoral communities, not just atomized caring individuals, or re-inscribed clergy-focused, professional care. In fact, Ramsey argues that homiletical representation of care in sermons should reflect that the pastor is *not* in charge of caring, but allows the congregation to care.[9]

This, to my mind, actually has prophetic implications. Prophetic preaching in light of Ramsey's vision of communal pastoral care is not limited to clergy professional interventions, nor to culturally bound forms of therapeutic individualism. Ramsey puts it this way:

> Communal care rests on the theological conviction that world and church, individual and society, are united in God's Realm [Kingdom]; all express the fullness of creation that God intends. To heal the world is to heal the individual in the world. To express care within the church is to contribute to the wider environment of care that extends to the end of the earth. This why distinctions between pastoral (inward) and prophetic (outward) are not only incorrect but counterproductive within the caring community of the church.[10]

A communal vision of the pastoral, by virtue of a vision of the pastoral as the life of a caring community, leads naturally to the prophetic.

A COMMUNAL VISION FOR SOLIDARITY: UNITING THE PROPHETIC AND THE PASTORAL WITH SHARON WELCH

The problem, of course, is that the natural is anything but inevitable. The history of the white mainline church, and its own need to unite the prophetic and the pastoral through a more communal vision of both, stumbles precisely at this point and threatens in the midst of its failure to remain

9. Ibid., 56.
10. Ibid., 132–33.

oblivious and to re-inscribe the powers that be. For this reason, we move here toward a deepened communal vision for solidarity as a means for exploring places where the prophetic and the pastoral might intersect concretely. To do this, we turn specifically to the work of Sharon Welch in *Communities of Resistance and Solidarity*.[11]

In her book Welch aims to account for both the reality of liberation and the reality of ecclesial failure that accompanies it in practice. She wishes to see communities as places where resistance and solidarity are born and become both the source and the means of grace by which such communities engage the world. For her, solidarity is not just an add-on to traditional theology, but a starting point in practice, a critical principle for purposes of social critique, and *an "impetus for political action."*[12]

Failure for Welch is real, but not inevitable either. Christians in community need to acknowledge that solidarity has not always been. This, however, is not a matter of theological necessity, but a result of "the fragility and the unpredictability of the historical process itself: the possibility of the failure of a genuinely liberating ideal, or the oppressive impact of an ideal that is ostensibly liberating."[13]

What happens in such communities of solidarity and resistance is a living liberation faith in all of its ambiguous and fragmentary power. It is able to produce an "awareness of a liberating God who evokes solidarity with other people, an affirmation of the significance of human life and thus protest against suffering and oppression," even while "the reality of that God is called into question . . . in light of the barbarities of the twentieth century: the holocaust, Vietnam, Hiroshima-Nagasaki, sexism, racism, the nuclear arms race, the torture of political prisoners."[14] Communities of solidarity bring with them entailments that already begin to open up possibilities of new perception, critical principles for theological work, and the very sustaining empowerment of grace that sponsors liberating faith in the midst of struggle in practice. This reality of communities of solidarity Welch attributes to grace and relatedness:

> The symbolic language of grace is appropriate at this point: the ability to love and to work for justice is something we are given through the power of community. An attempt to bring justice does not make sense as an abstract imperative or judgment outside of this communal context. Within a liberating faith, we find

11. Welch, *Communities of Resistance*.
12. Ibid., 46.
13. Ibid., 85.
14. Ibid., 5.

social structures that mediate the divine and enable solidarity, rather than an abstract call to justice. The imperative of justice is motivated not by guilt or duty, but by love, by the power of relatedness.[15]

Such communities are for many reasons places of struggle. However, a communal vision of the prophetic and the pastoral, in deep connection to communities of solidarity, explore at the level of practice and begin to name possibilities of liberating faith in struggle.

CONCLUSION

For this reason, I aim to emphasize that in taking up prophetic preaching and pastoral care, especially in contexts of privilege, communal visions need to be grounded in an ever-wider arc of solidarity. Two of the key theological principles that guide my course in prophetic preaching read like this:

1. Prophetic preaching is not solely the prerogative of the clergy, but a manifestation of the ministry of proclamation that is given to the whole people of God. The Spirit which is given with the prophetic Word is given to all God's people, not just the clergy. This also means that the prophetic Word should rightly aid God's people in becoming who they are already in Christ.

2. Prophetic preaching emerges not solely from anger, but also from a pastoral articulation of human grief and loss experienced in the presence of God in Christ as disclosed in the cross. Pastoral solidarity is its common ground, a solidarity which joins together hearers by means of their shared pain, visible and invisible, connecting them to each other and the world God loves so much.

These principles for prophetic preaching in the white mainline church are modest. Still, a move toward a deeper sense of relationship between the prophetic and the pastoral can help foment a more radically communal vision of both, grounded graciously in communities of solidarity for whom that solidarity is a practice, a fund for critique, and the gracious means of prophetic care. Such a move holds the promise of breaking through obliviousness and bearing witness, even if in fragmentary ways, of God's intentions for humanity and creation in just relation.

15. Ibid., 67.

14

In Search of a Prophtic Twenty-first Century Church

WILLIAM B. MCCLAIN

FIRST, I WANT TO state a basic philosophy of education in reference to teaching homiletics and worship and preparing persons for excellence in ministry, a basic pedagogy, if you will. I believe my colleague and friend, Dale Andrews, not only embraced it, he was a prime example—a living, teaching exhortation of this philosophy without apology and without shame. It takes the whole of the theological school faculty to develop excellent preachers and leaders of worship, and not simply the faculty who teach in these specialized areas.

A PREACHER MUST BE INTERDISCIPLINARY TO FACE THE QUESTION, "IS THERE ANY WORD FROM THE LORD?"

I believe that excellence in preaching, and Christian preaching in particular—we need to be aware that there are other kinds of preaching—involves being able to be interdisciplinary and to integrate knowledge and resources from various fields of theological study into a message proclaimed with preparation and passion which calls the people of God who gather around the Word and the Sacrament to decide for or against Jesus Christ. This is what distinguishes this form of communication from speeches given at a

PTA meeting, or after-dinner addresses at the Annual NAACP gathering, or lectures presented in the classroom or the lecture hall. Sermons are not essays to be read or research papers to be mere documentation of certain information. Preaching involves bringing the entire sweep of the Gospel and "the whole counsel of God" to bear on human needs.

My good friend and colleague in the ministry, the late Gardner Calvin Taylor who was a pastor and long-time teacher of preaching, occasionally for Harvard Divinity School (where he and I first met as adjunct faculty many years ago), and a prince of the pulpit by any standard of reckoning, once put it this way: "Mac, the preacher is a guilty one, telling guilty ones, of the just call and the judgment of God upon their lives and society, but a mercy wider than the justice, and a grace kinder than judgment, and therefore more devastating."

D. T. Niles, the great preacher-theologian of another era, often said about preaching: "Evangelism is just one begger telling another beggar where to find bread."[1] I used to often quote to my students and re-enforce Karl Barth's famous advice (perhaps apocryphal in this formulation, but nevertheless good advice): "We preach with the Bible in one hand and the newspaper in the other."[2] With modern technology and the advances made in new forms of communication, perhaps we may need to say it a little differently, but the point is the same: to be aware of the ambiguities of our time, the currents of history as they churn into rapids, sometimes sweeping away the long familiar places where the buoys that long marked the channels of our lives were located.

In other words, "We need to do our sociology as well as our theology," as my former colleague at Wesley Theological Seminary, Dr. James Maynard Shopshire, would always remind our faculty. Indeed he is right! People don't just come to church desperately anxious to know what happened to the Jebusites, and where Pamphylia and Phrygia are located, and what the water temperature at the Pool of Bethabara was, where John the Baptist baptized new believers. Rather, they want to know: "Preacher, pastor, is there any word from the Lord today? What is that word that speaks to my conditions, my hurts, my problems, my conflicting soul and spirit, our world and all of its desperate needs, the ethical decisions with which I and those around

---

1. Niles, "Just One Beggar."

2. Barth scholars seem unable to locate this precise quote. However, Barth did remember that he once recommended to preachers "to take your Bible and take your newspaper, and read both. But interpret newspapers from your Bible." (*Time* magazine, May 31, 1963). See the discussion of the history and meaning of this saying at the Center for Barth Studies: "The Bible in One Hand and the Newspaper in the Other."

me are struggling to make?" They want to know, "Can the gospel that you preach help me find purpose in a seemingly purposeless world?"

GOING BEYOND THE TEMPTATION TO ACCOMMODATE

There is the temptation in such disorderly and frightening times to simply accommodate the people who want their answers clear, clean, and easy. But it is not the task of the preacher to simply offer easy answers and glib shibboleths, not just simplistic answers that represent a rearrangement of the facts of life which will inevitably lead to disenchantment. I remember an old wise scholar used to say to his students, "Answers that begin by explaining all too much, end always by explaining all too little."

Our great teacher and friend the late Fred Craddock, the master of inductive preaching, has probably done as much as anybody in homiletics to change our approach to the sermon in the last 40 to 50 years. Craddock conceives of the sermon as an on-going conversation between the listeners and the Scriptures.[3] By drawing on the deep resonances from both the Bible and the memory of the congregation, the adept preacher is able to see some wisdom in the folk wisdom that "the heart, and not the mind or the will, is the shortest and surest way to God." My old professor at Boston University, Howard Thurman, would have insisted on "the mind *and* the heart."[4] But anyone who preaches and expects only the mind to be changed and does not make an effort to appeal to touching and transforming hearts is probably going to fail in most situations.

To ask the question "What is the matter with preaching today?" would not be a new endeavor. Clyde Fant pointed this out in several of his important works, first in his book *Preaching for Today*,[5] that every age has found it easy to romanticize the preceding ages as the golden years of preaching and have asked that same question.

In the nineteenth century with such greats as Henry Ward Beecher, Phillips Brooks, John Jaspers, Adam Clayton Powell, Sr., and Theodore Parker, articles were being published with titles such as "Dull Sermons." Harry Emerson Fosdick of Union Theological Seminary and Riverside Church of New York asked that question in his classic article in *Harper's Review* almost 100 years ago. In his 1928 article when people were flocking to Riverside in droves to hear him every Sunday, lining up early on Sunday

---

3. E.g., Craddock, in Duiduit interview, "From Class to Pulpit."
4. Thurman, *With Head and Heart*.
5. Fant, *Preaching for Today*, 21–29.

morning to get a seat in that famous church, his article was entitled: "What is the Matter with Preaching?"[6] His conclusion then was that good preachers are still hard to find and are few and far between.

The question was revived a few years ago by Mike Graves of St. Paul School of Theology in Kansas City, who edited a volume bearing a similar title.[7] It features chapters by noted scholars of preaching, such as Craddock, Barbara Brown Taylor, Ernest Campbell, Cleophus Larue and others. In various and sundry ways, all of the contributors call for change. Perhaps Barbara Brown Taylor's two questions go to the heart of the matter for all of us. She asks two fundamental questions: (1) What, if anything, makes a Christian different from anyone else? (2) How are Christians called to live with everyone else, including those who may wish them dead?[8]

I say to my homiletics students that there is a good reason why the church provides pastors with a place to do their preparation for preaching. It is called a "study." Every preacher who is going to serve the people well must make use of that place called a "study!"

Whether the study is in the church building, the parsonage, manse, rented place, or a home provided by a housing allowance, every preacher needs a place to study, pray, and compose their sermons. Although every preacher is not going to be a great preacher, and probably not even outstanding, every preacher can be excited about the task, enthusiastic about the needs of the people, passionate about the call to preach, and demonstrate from the pulpit that he or she has made a concerted effort to prepare to bring a fresh word from the Lord. The preachers can "be diligent to present themselves as workers who need not to be ashamed, rightly dividing the word of truth," as the writer of 2 Timothy reminded us [2 Tim 2:15, KJV].

EVERY PREACHER IS NOT A PROPHET

Not every preacher or pastor will be a prophet. People need priests to stand with them as much as they need prophets to stand over against them. In addition to prophets, they need priests who will be the ecclesiastical caretakers to ensure that the place of worship is always ready and the order of worship designed to usher the people of God into the presence of the living God. They need pastors to nourish their souls and help heal their hurts as well as prophets to speak truth to power to an establishment that cares not about its children and the poor and the "strangers within our gates." Our challenge is

6. Fosdick, "What Is the Matter with Preaching?"
7. Graves, *What Is the Matter with Preaching Today?*
8. Taylor, "Weekly Wrestling Match."

to develop a generation of priests who preach like prophets, and a generation of prophets who serve like priests.[9]

When Martin Luther was asked in Leipzig, "Brother Martin, where will you be when church, state, princes, and people turn against you?" he answered, "Why, then as now, in the hands of Almighty God."[10] That is at least the witness every preacher can make.

A humble servant of the Word, D. T. Niles closes his book *Preaching the Gospel of the Resurrection* with these words: "That is what I am. I am a sinner for whom Jesus died. I am just one of those who has been loved by God in Jesus at the cross. That is the central truth about me. All of the rest is peripheral."[11]

CHURCHES CAN TRIVIALIZE THE GOSPEL

The sad and startling fact of so many mainline churches is not that we have abandoned the gospel, it is that too often we have trivialized the gospel and felt that it no longer has transforming and saving power. We have scuttled any talk of God's rule on earth. Jesus, the Christ, whom the faith handed down to us and maintains was God getting *to* us by getting *with* us, becomes little more than a character in a long ago, once-upon-a-time almost fairytale-like story that we read from the Book. The vision of hope for repentance and change has been exchanged for cynicism and despair, and the salvation of society has been left to those churches on the margin or on the side streets where the vendors of cheap grace and the merchants of escapism dispense a right-wing religion that is not religion at all, but rather political ideology that only serves and promotes themselves and their causes, lining the pockets of the rich and the well-to-do.

I do not know that the U.S. Senate and the House of Representatives need to call for an investigation of popular prosperity preachers and their lavish lifestyles while ignoring their incredible abuse of domestic and international tax laws, and filling their coffers with profits gleaned from oil interests and unnecessary wars. But I do know that "the time has come for judgment to begin with the household of faith!" (1 Peter 4:17) What I do know is that the gospel is a two-edged sword and not some "fake news." What I do know is that the Christian faith requires that truth and good news be declared. If not, the rocks will cry out that God is on the move.

---

9. I owe this idea to Hicks, "Some Challenges," 8–9.
10. Quoted by Coffin, *Credo*, 150.
11. Niles, *Preaching the Gospel*, 93.

The late David Buttrick used to tell of a little parish in Waverly, Tennessee, that had a sign outside of their little church that read, "Come see the Realm [Kingdom] of God!" He said that if you drove into the church complex you found a peculiar little building with a few members. The sign was a bit of an overstatement; the little church could not convey the full glory of God's realm. But insofar as the members heard the word truthfully, faithfully preached, believed, and broke bread sacramentally, the Spirit of God was with them, and they became a living symbol of God's promised future. Buttrick further comments in his book, *Preaching the New and the Now,* "If a handful of members organize themselves in praise and care compassionately for common vulnerabilities, they may be a 'disclosure symbol'" for God's promised future, a living metaphor of the realm.[12] They may have exaggerated slightly, but they still believed in the power of the gospel to transform the world.

PROPHETIC PREACHING IS NECESSARY FOR THE CHURCH TO BE THE CHURCH

For the church to be the church and to exist as God's people, there must be prophetic preaching—and prophetic worship and prophetic action—lest it be co-opted and pressed into service of the culture as a conforming institution, serving the social conventions of existing powers. There must be prophets willing to speak truth to power, to insist that justice must "roll down like water, and righteousness like an everflowing stream" (Amos 5:24).

The renewal or survival of the 21st century church is not a foregone conclusion. At this crucial time and critical moment in the history of the church, the decisions we make can move toward and enable our renewal or we can become the pallbearers of an institution that died an ignoble death—having ignored and turned away from opportunities to respond courageously to the challenges of our time, having bargained away and compromised our values among theologians committed to market values and political ideology in the name of religion, surrendering the social imperatives of the gospel along with its demands to transform society—but, rather, willing to bargain away and make a "deal" with the market square theologians and their political ideology they call religion, thereby surrendering the social hermeneutics of the gospel and the demands for transforming society.

Far too many of our churches have succumbed to focusing on issues of personal morality like abortion, homosexuality,and same gender marriages while divorcing our preaching and worship from the more fundamental

12. Buttrick, *Preaching the New*, 18.

ethical imperatives of ending poverty, repairing and correcting our crumbling public school system, healing a broken planet, welcoming the strangers within our gates, and seeking peaceful and non-violent solutions to conflicts around the world. We have witnessed a stunning reversal of the timeless emphases of the Bible on social justice, peace, care for the poor, orphans, widows and little children. Fear, fundamentalism and Fox Broadcasting Company must not be allowed to set the agenda for the Church of Jesus Christ and the gospel it proclaims, the good news it declares.

Our nation and its churches in the present age must ponder their role and responsibility at a time when some use religion to provide the foundation for social values that are contrary to the gospel of Jesus Christ. We do not need to look further than our own country to see what happens when the church is drawn into the role of supporting political ideologies. With human lives at stake, we have often compromised the gospel for the sake of upholding values that run contrary to God's just and loving intentions for all people.

Even now in the 21st century the United States is still recovering from the debilitating and devastating consequences of the Christian Church's support for slavery, its capitulation to the market square, slave block theologians, and the Magnolia Missions.

In the nineteenth century, many denomination split over different positions regarding slavery (e.g., Baptists, Lutherans, Methodists, Presbyterians) before the nation did. Had the church heeded its own prophets as well as the gospel and biblical teachings about justice, our sad racial and social history could have been different. We had broken churches before we had a broken nation. And the nation was re-united long before most churches were re-united—and some have yet to re-unite. Today also we need prophetic preaching to remind the church that to be at peace with the world is to be in conflict with the Lord and that position is a very dangerous place to be.

Peter Storey, the remarkable white Methodist preacher, freedom fighter, former President of the South African Council of Churches in the heat of the battle against apartheid in South Africa, who more than once risked his life to make a prophetic Christian stand against that heinous evil, wrote a book entitled, *With God in the Crucible: Preaching Costly Discipleship*. In the Preface to that book, he looks back at what he has seen:

> The miracle South African Christians have to proclaim is not the story of faithfulness; it is the wonder of a God who could use such a feeble witness so powerfully. And the question must

arise: What if the witness had been stronger? What could God not do with a truly faithful church willing to take on the world?[13]

Where have all the prophets gone who will call for a church who will work with God to take on the world? Will we teach students who dare to be prophets? Can we join with them to help create and preach to such a church in the 21st century? Our future may very well depend upon it!

---

13. Storey, *With God in the Crucible*, 6.

15

Building Bridges Week by Week

MARY ALICE MULLIGAN

OUR SURROUNDING SOCIETY INFLUENCES who we are. We might say society shapes us.[1] We are formed by how we are treated in our families, by what we are told in school, by the news reports that blare seemingly everywhere, and by how we are treated even by strangers around us. But more and more, people in our society are being shaped by the number of mind-numbing hours of screen-time we focus on each day. As we watch the backstabbing intrigue of "reality" shows or movies where killing others is legitimized if there is a "good" reason, those lessons are being absorbed into our being. Day after day we are told: our own success is what matters; alliances should be made with those from whom we can benefit; weak people are dispensable; society would be better off without those who drain resources. Through the years, we hardly notice how completely we accept these ideas.

What chance does the church have to counteract such powerful forces? Those who step into the pulpit week after week often realize that the forces of our surrounding society stand opposed to the gospel we hope to communicate. How can we successfully teach something different, especially when we have so little time with the congregation each week and when we admit those social forces live in our own consciousness, too? How can we, week by week, build anything?

---

1. We are also, to a certain extent, shaping society by how we live in it, but that is a topic for a different article.

In the following pages, I explain my belief that our chances for declaring the gospel and having it heard within our congregations are excellent.[2] Additionally, I believe hearing the gospel makes a difference in the lives of listeners and in our society as a whole. We are able to build bridges between our congregations and surrounding society, even in 20 minute sessions, by intentionally constructing our sermons week by week. Football running back Walter Payton is said to have rushed with the football 9 miles in his career. The amazing accomplishment is, of course, that although he ran 9 miles, he got knocked down, on average, every 4.6 feet. Little by little, finding himself on the ground often, Mr. Payton accomplished an amazing feat. Think what preachers can do with such perseverance and the empowering presence of the Holy Spirit.

PREACHING DOES SOMETHING IN THE CONGREGATION

When Dale Andrews and about a dozen others of us were homiletics PhD students under David Buttrick's guidance at Vanderbilt University in the 1990s, we learned to trust preaching to "do something" within the listening congregation. Something happens when a congregation listens together to a sermon. From reading Walter Ong, we learned oral events have distinct traits. "Oral communication unites people into groups."[3] Whereas we are internally (thus individually) focused when we read, oral events draw us together as a hearing community. Buttrick taught us that as the sermon is preached into the congregation, a faith community is being shaped. We develop a communal consciousness. He spoke this idea frequently, but he also published it: "What preaching may do is to build in consciousness a new 'faith-world' in which we may live and love!"[4] In preaching moments, listeners are individually and socially changed.

Although there have been criticisms of Buttrick's emphasis on the specific experience of the individual sermon, with little regard for the cumulative effect of preaching to the same congregation over time, I am convinced

---

2. Due to the space restrictions of this chapter, I will leave the term "gospel" undefined except to note I mean in part that when we preach the gospel, we declare the good news of God's love and unconditional grace communicated best through the life, teachings, death, and resurrection of Jesus Christ; which is perhaps more than Ed Farley would say, since he noted: "Gospel is not a thing to be defined . . . From the hearer's perspective, preaching the gospel is a summons to faithful existence in the face of whatever happens, whatever is to come." Farley, *Practicing Gospel*, 80.

3. Ong, *Orality and Literacy*, 69.

4. Buttrick, *Homiletic*, 17.

the changes in our communal consciousness that happen week after week in the preaching event do have collective results. This consistent, weekly practice of hearing together shapes and reshapes the listening congregation. Or at least it should. In clergy gatherings, some colleagues sadly complain that their congregations are stuck in the 1960s. I often remind myself that somehow they got from the 1930s to the 1960s, so if a minister has been with the congregation for 10 years, they should at least be in the 1970s by now. Congregations do change—and often change comes because they have been stretched, invited to reach beyond what they commonly know. Dale Andrews would probably add, they have participated in building a bridge which connects what they know and where they are to a new and liberating understanding of God and faith. Preaching with intentionality, week by week, makes something happen in the congregation. As the minister presents new ideas, the congregation can be stretched to absorb these ideas into their faith life. They do not merely echo back the preacher's words; rather they take in the ideas and make them their own, fitting them into their own circumstances and the life of the congregation.

On the other hand, at least one study shows that when the preacher is not able to articulate theological ideas clearly, worshippers can likewise have trouble. In a particular congregation, people were unable to easily answer a question about what they think God is doing in the sermon. Although they responded comfortably to other questions, they were inarticulate and hesitant in speaking about God. When the interviewer asked the same question of their preacher, the response was similarly vague, confused, inconsistent, and hesitant.[5]

An even larger study found an additional troubling trait in congregations. In the mid-1990s, funded by the Lilly Endowment, Dean Hoge, Charles Zech, Patrick McNamara, and Michael Donahue undertook an extensive research project to discover what influences financial giving in the local parish. In their published findings, we find this admission: "We have been impressed repeatedly by how encapsulated church members are in their own religious worlds. For people in every denomination, their own congregation and, especially, their friends in the congregation fashion their understanding of religious reality."[6] As we consider preaching week after week, the situation of congregational isolation needs to be addressed. We need to discover ways to help our faith communities break out of their shells. If we are imprisoned in our little circles of like-minded Christians, happily holed-up with familiar friends and ideas, the preacher's task be-

---

5. Mulligan, et al., *Believing*, 165–68.
6. Hoge, et al. *Money Matters*, 161.

comes doubly important, both to help people see their confinement and to help them break out to new territories.

What the preacher offers to people matters. And what the people are willing to hear matters. When we speak from the pulpit, we make claims about God and about Jesus Christ, we model theological reasoning, we interpret scripture, and we present the gospel. If people are willing to hear our words, the congregation is being shaped; a communal faith consciousness is formed. As that experience repeats week after week, the formation continues. If the preacher is intentional and the people trust her/him, the shaping is taking the congregation somewhere.

In a 2007 conference lecture, David Buttrick reminded us that preaching must take into account the passing away of the subjective-objective interpretation of reality and the presence of interpersonal realms of consciousness. Reality, he said, is undergirded by "a web of relationship they call the interhuman."[7] Although responding to a lecture by Eugene Lowery, in the same setting, Dale Andrews used similar ideas to talk about the interworking of preaching and hearing. The preacher constructs something to communicate; the hearer prepares and participates in the preaching event.[8] The preacher and listeners are all involved in what happens during the sermon. Sermons today need to take into account our interconnectedness and the responsibilities of both speaker and listener to communicate the faith.

BUILDING BRIDGES IN THE CONGREGATION

For years, Andrews has used the metaphor of a bridge to encourage our efforts to connect seemingly disparate ideas.[9] It is quite a helpful image for thinking about the academic study of theology and the reality of local church life, which often treat each other as distant and out of touch (sometimes even as enemies). As we think about ongoing preaching in the life of congregations and the need for relating with larger (sometimes even opposed) ideas from the world, theologians, the gospel, and even as we anticipate church life in the future, the bridge metaphor continues to be helpful.[10] Congregants and preachers may decide together what areas need growth, but then they must figure out how to get from where they are to where they

---

7. Buttrick, "Homiletic Renewed," 110.
8. See Andrews, "Response," in Allen, *Re-Newed Homiletic*, 96–99.
9. See for instance, Andrews, *Practical Theology*.
10. Andrews' bridge metaphor is to be distinguished from Edward Farley's description of the bridge as paradigm for preaching (bringing "the truth" of a specific passage into the situation of the current congregation). See his *Practicing Gospel*, 72–73.

believe God is stretching them to be. I believe intentional, ongoing preaching is a most useful tool for such change.

Using a bridge image can be helpful. If we think of building a bridge from where we are to some new place, we realize a bridge helps us cross over to discover a place we have never been before, yet does not disconnect us from where we have been. And bridges allow others, previously separated, to come join us where we are. Bridges connect us to new realms. In other words, bridges make our world larger. The connection between where we are and where we are going has to be strong enough to support us or we will not make it across; yet if we spend all of our time focusing on constructing minute details of the bridge, we will never mount it, much less use it to get someplace.

There are several areas where the congregation I have been serving for over five years is intentionally building bridges. In my weekly preaching, I join with them to participate in this construction. Three specific areas are: human sexual identity, who God is, and who we are.[11] In the sections below, I demonstrate some of the techniques we are using to build bridges, with special focus on building bridges through preaching.

BUILDING BRIDGES TO DEEPER UNDERSTANDING OF HUMAN SEXUAL IDENTITY

One of the most volatile topics for many congregations to grapple with is human sexual identity. Some people are still inclined to say they are struggling with "the issue of homosexuality" (as if people are an "issue"), but actually the situation is much broader. Even if limiting the conversation to same sex relationships, the topics of biblical interpretation, nature versus nurture, and God's creative goodness enter into the discussion. To build a bridge between where we are and what we need to know about sexual identities, we have to be aware of where we are and then to learn about other Christian responses and possible positions. What are the ingredients for a fuller understanding of human sexual identity?

A preacher can begin constructing some of the scaffolding for the bridge merely by mentioning LGBTQ people from the pulpit. Just saying

---

11. This congregation, Westview Christian Church, Indianapolis, Indiana, has a very strong sense of mission and outreach, so building new bridges in these areas has not been a priority although it is not ignored. As we stretch our understanding of God, what we are discovering is that our perspective on humanity is enlarged. As we stretch our understanding of human sexual identity, our sense of mission is enriched. Our bridges seem to be connecting to each other, reminding us of the interconnectedness of all reality.

"lesbian" or "transgender man" from the pulpit disempowers the atmosphere of isolation from people of diverse sexual identities many congregants experience. Conversations within many congregations never mention anyone except heterosexuals, as if no one else exists. Of course, ministers need to articulate people's discomfort or unfamiliarity. We cannot deny where people are. For instance, in a sermon illustration, if using the term "bi-sexual," I might admit some of us are uncomfortable saying the word; it just may not come out easily. But then I might quote a statistic (how many bi-sexual people probably live in Indianapolis) or remind us of the discomfort a teen-ager might experience in admitting her own gender questions.

Another possible step in preliminary bridge construction is to pay attention to the many occasions we list different types of people in our preaching. We do not have to limit the list to wealthy or poor, child or adult, employed or not, students, retired folks. We can include: gay or straight. Our congregants hear television preachers make frequent, bold statements about sexuality (although rarely about their own). We need to be bold, too. Of course, just as bridges take time to build, so does helping the congregation get more comfortable talking and thinking about human sexual identity in more public ways. Early on, the preacher can use illustrations where the gender of people is left purposely vague. A man and his spouse go to a movie; housemates decide what to have for dinner. Or we can use gendered references for people doing things more typically done by the opposite gender: a man frustratedly searching for a changing station for his baby; a welder and her husband out to dinner. On several occasions, when talking about the importance of welcome in our congregation, I have invited people to think through the importance of being welcoming when people smell bad, or have loud children, or if four burly guys come in the door in evening dresses. These examples give people the opportunity to entertain new images of who might walk in and become part of who we are. More basically it reminds us of God's purposely diverse creation.

But eventually, the preacher needs to use illustrations of couples who are clearly same sex or someone who has transitioned. For some of us this may feel awkward or risky. We do not want to alienate anyone. Let me encourage us to be bold and try it. Some years ago, one of the first times I used an illustration of a gay couple in a sermon, a middle-age man came to me after worship and said that he had been in the church his whole life, but that was the first time he ever heard himself referred to in a sermon. Imagine never being able to identify yourself in how the gospel is being declared. How important it is to for all of us to hear illustrations using a broad range of people. We owe it to our congregants to include everyone.

Getting the congregation comfortable with new language, diverse people and illustrations is an important start. But of course, there needs to be more work done to help move people across a bridge. In October of 2014, the elders and ministers[12] were eager to allow our church members to talk openly about their thoughts and feelings following the United States Supreme Court's decision for marriage equality. We wanted people to be able to talk about marriage equality before a request came in from a couple interested in having a same sex wedding ceremony so that the conversation would not be about a specific couple. In worship, I quoted some of the elders' differing opinions. One thought we were already Open & Affirming;[13] one thought we would be better off not rocking the boat by talking about it; others wondered how we might best get our ideas out in the open. From the pulpit, I admitted that as a congregation we were not single-minded in our opinions or beliefs about sexual identity. We prayed for God's guidance, and for our own openness and understanding of each other. I wanted to make sure that in building bridges to LGBTQ persons and ideas we were not destroying bridges between church members of differing opinions. Welcoming everyone sounds simple, but we are realizing more and more that the demands of Jesus Christ are more complicated and difficult than we used to believe. We rejoice as our congregation grows more diverse but we also recognize the complexity of living in a diverse church. Conversations are going on in various settings among us that the time is ripe for our congregation to enter into the open and affirming process. I believe our intentional preaching choices assisted in building bridges between where we were as a congregation and toward acceptance of a broader understanding of human sexual identity.

BUILDING BRIDGES TO WHO GOD IS

A primary reason people come to worship is to hear something about God and to offer adoration and praise. Preaching can assist people in what one of our associate regional ministers calls an "expansive" understanding of God. But a minister can also restrict people's understanding of God and in the very setting they have entered for assistance. A clergy colleague always begins her public prayers with the address: "Loving and Eternal God." Her

---

12. During this period we had a student associate minister, whose preaching also worked to build bridges in this area.

13. The term used in the Christian Church (Disciples of Christ) indicating a congregation which has gone through the process of choosing full inclusion of people into the life of the church regardless of sexual orientation or gender identity.

opening is worshipful and respectful, but not very helpful in stretching the praying congregation's comprehension of the holy. Her start is as predictable as the abundance of Sunday morning prayers around the world which begin "Dear Heavenly Father." Although there is nothing wrong with either of these forms of address, the repetition of them becomes monotonous and borders on meaninglessness. How we begin our prayer offers people a way to consider God. The congregation benefits from addresses which invite them to consider new aspects of the divine (Generous Provider, Ever-present Comfort, Persistent Teacher). In prayers and sermons, we can actively stretch our own and our members' understanding of God. What is so terrific about building bridges in this case is that, as we extend our thinking, there is God. If God is infinite (or even, as one of our seminary professors used to argue, God is not infinite, but is "big enough"), then God is beyond our full comprehension. Our understanding, no matter how huge, will always be limited. So, we have the great experience of an expanding concept of God which invites us to cross into new territory all the time, while still having comfortable access to what we have known and felt about God for our whole lives.

Occasionally I use male language for God in preaching, usually on Father's Day or when I preach about the parable of the waiting father. Often I begin such a sermon with something like: "Today I will be using male language for God. As many of you probably notice, usually I either mix gender references, 'Heavenly Mother, Father God' or use gender neutral language, 'Ever-forgiving Parent,' but on this special occasion it makes sense to spend our time together reveling in the Father-love of God."

On Mother's Day or when preaching on the parable of the lost coin or Sophia Wisdom, I offer a reverse explanatory introduction concerning the use of female language on this special day, noting the importance of stretching our experience of God, and the biblical appropriateness of feminine imagery for God, again reminding them that I usually mix or use gender neutral language. My guess is many members of the congregation may not notice my intentional use of mixed or neutral language, so lifting up the distinction when I use gender specific language helps refine our thinking about a gendered God.

To increase the congregation's security with God language, through the years I worked on helping people become comfortable with the word "theology." Apparently some folks initially felt almost as if it were a dirty word. Theologians were considered people who dissect the faith until it lays shredded and dead on the table.[14] But we have learned together that each of

---

14. The preacher may benefit from reading Andrews, *Practical Theology*, especially

us is a theologian just because we articulate ideas about God. In sermons I can now mention a theological position about Jesus or about evil and no one panics. This particular scaffolding was constructed using what Buttrick would call "contrapuntal" help.[15] That is, for some time when I mentioned the word theology, I also gave voice to the resistance some people felt. Of course then I needed to clarify how we are all theologians and need to be able to articulate our beliefs so that we can share our ideas and learn from each other. I realized the scaffolding was holding when I discovered one of our Sunday school teachers now begins her email communications with her class: "Dear fellow theologians . . ."

Experiencing God in worship is as important as embracing ideas about God. African American sermons are known for ending with celebration.[16] Although it doesn't happen every week in the racially-mixed church I serve, I believe it is important for listeners to be swept up into the overflowing experience of God's effervescent mercy and love from time to time. When the sermon contains a section (often the final piece) which catches the entire congregation in a joyous divine embrace, when almost everyone seems to experience the swirling presence of the Holy Spirit, when the unconditional mercy of the Almighty is splashing all over the sanctuary, people's understanding of God is simultaneously solidified and amazingly expanded. More than merely learning something about God which our intellects can confirm (as important as that is), the celebrative experience of God also engages our emotions, our will, and even our bodies. In these moments, our God concept expands, so that when the sermon is over, that larger understanding of who God is stays with us.

Preaching needs to present material about God that can be grasped by our intellects, our emotions, our ethical being, and our desire for connection.[17] We also need to invite people to stretch their understanding of God in all these ways. Preachers who intentionally try to include various types of material and to engage people at various places should find greater success in helping the congregation into new territory.

50–66.

15. Buttrick, *Homiletic*, 47–49.

16. See Mitchell, *Black Preaching*, 119–22; Mitchell, *Celebration and Experience*, 61–75; and Thomas, *They Like to Never Quit*. Thomas notes: "Within the tradition of celebrative design, the goal of the African American sermon is to help people experience the assurance of grace that is the gospel" (45).

17. For in-depth assistance with the various paths people use in hearing and understanding sermons, see Allen, *Hearing*.

BUILDING BRIDGES TO WHO WE ARE

The church I serve has for many years had a few members who are people of color. The congregation has a fine sense of welcome and most white members would naively claim the congregation is not racist. However, we clearly live out of a white church identity, even though our congregation is now comprised of about 20% persons of color. So over the past few years, my preaching has reinforced the importance of welcome, but also has stressed that who we are is not a "white congregation." We are a racially mixed, culturally diverse group. One of our growing edges is to help us all realize that each person brings spiritual gifts. When a new person joins the congregation, that person should not be expected to merely disappear into who we are. The new person changes who we are and just by joining helps us become something new. The obvious goal here is to help people, especially the white people, realize that it is inappropriate to expect new members (regardless of race, status, or life experiences) to assimilate into the majority culture of the current congregation.

Consider the new member I will call Desmond, who helped us learn that the time of offering can be celebrative. At a worship committee meeting, he talked about the church of his youth where his congregation danced forward each Sunday, bringing their tithes and offerings. Then using his words in talking about money in one Sunday sermon, I invited the congregation to stretch in their thinking about giving. I pointed out that who we are as a congregation includes Desmond, who believes we should have joyous music at the offering and perhaps occasionally even dance our offerings forward.

I continue to refer to different ways people's ideas enlarge who we are. In making what we might call an abbreviated reference to some of our basic theological beliefs, I often remind us that each person is precious to God. Then I might mention two or three types of marginalized folk who are often rejected or ignored by society (and could easily be shunned by us), like the woman at the next table in the restaurant who calls her child a name and slaps her, or the mumbling man walking back and forth downtown, or the teen with the boom box who dances on 38th Street, or the smelly woman we pass in the grocery store, or the president of Syria, or the crying man tied to a wheelchair in the nursing home (even though it's against the law to restrain him). And if these persons are precious to God, they need to be precious to us. These soft reminders that each person is precious, I believe, help the congregation to see every person they pass on the street or hear about on the news as a beloved child of God. No matter who walks in the door of the church, that person is precious to God and must be welcomed by us. I am also clear that as soon as a person walks in the door, they are part of "us" and I am their pastor.

These ongoing invitations to stretch our thinking about who "we" are encourage the congregation to put faces on ideas we already hold. Common Christian church lingo claims God loves everyone; Jesus loves all the colors of children. Church billboards all over the nation claim everyone is welcome. In preaching, I try to put faces on the ideas we think we already hold.

At first, it is enough to put individual faces on who we mean when we say "everyone," so the congregation sees each person as beloved. But as time goes on, examples and illustrations in preaching need to push us deeper. For instance, some years ago I served a church where we worked hard to welcome everyone, including the woman I will call Bertha, who was homeless and sometimes came into the office to talk about how she literally fought demons in the night and showed me the scratches on her arms and legs to prove it. One Sunday, a woman who was visually impaired came to worship with her service dog and sat in front of Bertha. After worship I chatted with our visitor about how she could get involved, but she confessed she could never come back, because the woman who sat behind her whispered in her ear after worship, "I'm going to kill your dog." She rightly assumed the woman was mentally unstable, but was firm she could not take a chance with the safety or well-being of her dog.

When shared as a sermon illustration, this situation provides an example of the difficulty of welcoming everyone. There are barriers in attempting to live out the simple claim of "God loves everyone, so we welcome everyone." However, such difficulties require hard and ongoing work on our part as a congregation, rather than just settling for whatever is easiest. A homogenous group of people, all of a certain age, race, socio-economic class, and theological bent, might make for a more convenient congregation, but we would less represent the realm of God. In preaching, such realities can be unpacked and investigated together, so we can consider new ways of being faithful and inclusive followers of Jesus Christ.

A couple of years ago, one of our sweetest 80-year-old women came to me upset after worship. "I've made a horrible mistake," she whimpered. "I welcomed a visitor after worship by saying, 'Excuse me sir,' and she said, 'It's ma'am, but that's okay.'" The visitor presented androgynously, with very short hair and a man's cap, so the member concluded she was male. I pointed out to the member that the important thing was she had welcomed the visitor; she apologized for assuming she was a man; and she invited her to return, which by the way, she did and eventually joined. Even such awkward encounters are building bridges to parts of our surrounding community that congregations need to be connected with.

Two years ago, we chose to focus for a calendar year on Reconciliation and Anti-Racism. Although I did not preach on race each Sunday of the year, we did construct a full schedule of events to help us come to grips with our racism and white privilege, as well as the racism in the world around us. We had a film and conversation series over the summer. A small group read and met to discuss *Pre-Post-Racial America*, by Sandhya Rani Jha.[18]

Realizing that these events would not draw the majority of members of the congregation, we organized quarterly pitch-in meals following worship which focused on our personal cultures. People were invited to bring a dish representing their heritage; individuals decorated tables with elements from their family or background; and each time we chose 3 people to talk about their upbringing. We placed conversation starter sheets on the table with questions like: How did your family celebrate Christmas? When did you first realize you were ethnically or culturally different from someone else? The point of course was to help us realize we each have a culture, everyone's racial-ethnic identity is interesting, and it isn't just "normal" to be white.

These events provided great sermon illustrations to help build bridges deepening our understanding of who we are. We saw that we are adults who remember their parents' losing the farm in the Depression. We are charter members of the church. We are immigrants who traveled at night and slept in the day for safety when trying to escape from Eritrea. Underneath these experiences, I was eager for us to realize that some of us are white people who wake up with privilege every day and some of us are people of color who wake up with certain disadvantages every day, who realize our sons are more vulnerable in this society. I remain convinced that preaching week by week builds bridges to help us enlarge our world and our understanding of God.

---

18. Jha, *Pre-Post-Racial America*.

PART 4

Learning to Preach in the Mode of Prophetic Care

16

Building Bridges
Pedagogical Reflections on a Black Lives Matter Resistance Hermeneutic for Preaching

L. SUSAN BOND

TWO YEARS AGO I started a class project that changed my approach to interpreting gospel texts. I decided to teach the very traditional "Life and Teachings of Jesus" course parallel to a theological exploration of the Black Lives Matter (BLM) movement. In part, I hoped that pairing these two areas of interest would simply increase excitement among my undergrad students at a historically black college. Our cohort of religion majors is small and we depend on attracting non-majors to meet minimum enrollment for each religion course. In addition to a simple marketing strategy, I hoped the pairing would teach students that a social justice hermeneutic would expand their own options for understanding and engaging the gospel texts. In the fall semester of 2015, I promoted the course as "Life and Teachings of Jesus-#BlackLivesMatter Version."

THE PEDAGOGICAL APPROACH

From the very first class meeting, we agreed to study the Jesus Movement as a social justice movement engaged in a kind of resistance on two fronts: The Roman Empire and the Religious Elites. We used Marcus Borg's classic,

Jesus: Uncovering the Life, Teachings, and Relevance of a Religious Revolutionary (2006) as our main text, but that was supplemented by videos, articles, and social media accounts of the BLM movement and by videos, articles, and short readings by and about black theologians and biblical scholars. Each student researched the emerging voices of the BLM movement and chose one or two to follow on Twitter and Facebook. Every week our class discussions involved material from Borg, material from Black Church studies, and updates from the BLM movement.

For example, during one of our first sessions we discussed Borg's overview of historical Jesus studies and some Christological models, a chapter from Howard Thurman's *Jesus and the Disinherited*, and profiles of various BLM founders (especially Patrisse Cullors, Opal Tometi, and Alicia Garza). When we studied the process of canonization of the New Testament, we also studied the evolution of the BLM movement from its origins in street activism and slogans to the development of the Campaign Zero organization with policy positions and written guidelines. We noted that the street activists and the policy people weren't always the same group. We also noticed that the original founding women were quickly displaced and erased as various male activists and leaders gained notoriety and cable news coverage. When we studied the healing miracles in the gospels, we also studied John Dominic Crossan's reflections on the body politic in "In the Beginning Is the Body,"[1] and viewed a video by Alicia Garza on bodies and humanizing. When we got to the class sessions devoted to the passion stories, we studied Ida B. Wells' speeches and writings about lynching in the Jim Crow era, we read excerpts from James Cone's *The Cross and the Lynching Tree*, and listened to an online sermon ("The Politics of Jesus") by Rev. Starsky Wilson about the death of Michael Brown in Ferguson.[2]

Sometimes our class sessions became so engaging and organically interactive that we would remember a phrase from a song or a speech and we would stop and find it online and listen to it. That's how we found Janelle Monáe's "Hell You Talmbout,"[3] and how we dropped everything to listen to a speech by Malcolm X about house negroes and field negroes when we were discussing the politics of respectability and unmasking the powers.[4]

Student assignments were a mix of traditional short reflection papers and non-traditional art projects. The weekly reflection papers were responses to writing prompts that attempted to bring together the multiple voices

---

1. Crossan, *Jesus*, 85–109.
2. Williams, "Politics."
3. Monáe, "Janelle Monáe Releases."
4. Malcom X, "Field Negro."

around a single question or statement. One week the writing prompt was this: "Consider Chapters 2–3 in Borg (background on the Gospels as part of a developing tradition) and the readings about the origins and development of #BlackLivesMatter. How does learning about the evolution of the early BLM movement inform your understanding of the development of the Jesus Movement and its later documents?" Another week the writing prompt was this: "Reflect on the Thurman and Kelly Brown Douglas readings for this week and the distinctions between Black Christ (Douglas) and the Jesus presented by Thurman. In the second half of your reflection, discuss your own feelings about the idea of the 'blackness of Jesus.' Be sure to include some thoughts and feelings about the assigned James Cone video."

Another week's writing prompt followed a presentation from one of my colleagues in the History department. Dr. Carleen Jackson presented a lecture/discussion on "The Dynamics of Domination and Black Resistance" featuring material about the early slave rebellions in the United States and the Caribbean as well as a heavy critique of imperialism and colonialism. Her presentation concluded with twentieth-century pan-African movements and figures like Marcus Garvey, Malcolm X, and Stokely Carmichael. The writing prompt for that week's reflection paper was this: "In her PowerPoint presentation Dr. Jackson claimed that domination and resistance are two sides of the same coin. Marcus Borg claims that there was a cycle of violence found in the social world of Jesus. Make the connections between the cycles of violence found in black resistance movements and the social world of Jesus."

Instead of a final exam, students submitted a large art piece/project suitable for public display. The rationale for this capstone graffiti project was that both the Jesus Movement and the Black Lives Matter Movement were street movements devoted to the public square. For the subject matter of their graffiti projects, each student had to select a scene or a figure from each of three categories: a Jesus scene, a Black History figure, and a BLM figure or image. The Jesus Scene options included the Baptism of Jesus, the Transfiguration, Jesus and the Moneychangers, the Stilling of the Storm, etc. In the Black History category, the options included Howard Thurman, Kelly Brown Douglas, Denmark Vesey, Ida B. Wells, Malcolm X, and others. In the third category, Black Lives Matter, students could choose protestors, militarized police, Trayvon Martin, Alicia Garza, Deray McKesson, Johnetta Elzie, etc.

For the graffiti style of their project, students learned about the tradition of Christian iconography and symbols and about the history of graffiti as resistance art, from the third-century Alexamenos Graffito to the 21st Century artist, Banksy. Students learned about graphic and stylized images, the use of words and symbols, and the prevalence of stencils. I was assisted by Professor Louis Giberson from our Art department who not only presented a slideshow, but also opened the campus art studio and all its materials to the students. I sought a small one-time grant from the administration to provide large stretched and framed canvases.

The students were required to submit a proposal that included their choice of subject matter, their graffiti elements, their process and technique, and a brief statement about the intended impact of the piece. The proposal was the basis for their final artist statement that accompanied their completed projects. The Artist Statements were displayed beside their projects in a common gathering area near the student bookstore at the end of the semester. One of the graffiti projects featured the Stilling of the Storm, the face of black Jesus, the face of Martin Luther King Jr. weeping tears into the sea, militarized police climbing into the boat, and graffiti text of the words "Jesus, MLK, BLM, Police" dominating one quadrant of the canvas. The imagery evoked not only the stilling of the storm, but also echoed imagery from the flood in Genesis and from the parting of the Red Sea. The faces of Jesus and MLK dominate the center of the canvas at exactly the point where the waters are parting.

My overall pedagogical approach was most informed by two African American scholars. I adapted my strategies in light of the work of Dr. Gregory Ellison and Dr. bell hooks' work on marginal spaces and social liminality. "Although marginality is not valorized, it is framed as a site of resistance where hope is born and change is catalyzed."[5] We do not typically speak of this in spiritual terms, but promoting a sense of hope and agency and meaning is spiritual formation in its general sense. Each instance of seeing or hearing students, even hearing or witnessing anger, is an act of recognizing their personhood. In Christian terms, each student is created in the image of God and has value simply by virtue of their personhood. "Therefore, if talking is revelatory and identity-forming, then communities who can hear the authentic, uncut stories of others non-judgmentally have the power to bolster self-esteem and aid in the gestation of hope."[6]

In her pedagogical approach to authenticity in the classroom, bell hooks argues similarly that "we all enter the struggle as subjects which means that instructors and students alike must engage in a fierce truth-telling and transparency."[7] In the future, I will add readings from the body of work produced by scholars of color since 2015, including Kelly Brown

---

5. Ellison II, *Cut Dead*, xvii.
6. Ibid., 148.
7. hooks, *Teaching to Transgress*, 46.

Douglas' *Stand Your Ground: Black Bodies and the Justice of God*,⁸ Sandhya Rani Jha's *Pre-Post-Racial America: Spiritual Stories from the Front Lines*,⁹ Tamura Lomax's *Jezebel Unhinged: Loosing the Black Female Body in Black Religion and Black Popular Culture*,¹⁰ and Leah Gunning Francis' *Ferguson. . . . and Faith: Sparking Leadership and Awakening Community*.¹¹

DISCOVERIES AND INSIGHTS

Simply put our interpretations of the life and teachings of Jesus were novel and transformative. Entertaining a resistance hermeneutic not only opened new possibilities for understanding miracles, parables, and parabolic acts, but using the hermeneutic provided interpretations that were more robust and more explanatory than traditional methods provided. The truth is they made *more* sense than traditional interpretations, even those of the contextual liberation variety.

First, the life and teachings of Jesus are not primarily about salvation and/or grace in the traditional evangelical sense. They are not even about salvation and/or grace in the psychological or existentialist sense as ways of deeper knowledge and self-understanding or even Christian identity. The more we interrogated the teachings, miracles, and parables, the more we realized that exclusively spiritual meanings about souls and soul-salvation were anachronistic. An atonement theory hermeneutic was insufficient to account for the abundance of detail in the Jesus stories.

For example, the parable of The Lost Sheep, interpreted through a resistance hermeneutic, would mean that the work of the resistance group (possibly the church) is to include the most marginal and forgotten in the efforts for restorative political and economic justice. It's not enough to say that the last and the least are saved, it's not enough to claim that the last and the least are included for church membership, it's only sufficient to claim that the marginalized are worthy of political power-sharing and access to goods and services. Only a bad shepherd would let someone (or some group) slip through the cracks. The parable of The Lost Sheep affirms the core values of the Civil Rights Movement and the Black Lives Matter movement with an additional moral mandate: it's our job to go out and look for those who are so lost as to be forgotten and to seek their political and economic equity. Seeking and rescuing are resistance goals and resistance

8. Douglas, *Stand Your Ground*.
9. Jha, *Pre-Post-Racial Americas*.
10. Lomax, *Jezebel Unhinged*.
11. Gunning Francis, *Ferguson and Faith*.

methods; they imply literal entry into dangerous and forgotten places, putting our own bodies and the bodies of the other "sheep at risk." Such is holy work. Everyone is at risk until all are rescued. Injustice anywhere is a threat to justice everywhere.

Second, and related to the first, is the claim that the primary work of Jesus is performative and public. Jesus is in the roads and in the streets, itinerant and relatively homeless. He could have followed the isolationist withdrawal from society that John the Baptist modeled, but he refused to remain in a hermit community. "His mission is marked by itinerancy, by which I mean simply that he went from place to place. He did not settle down in a permanent location and have people come to him, as he might have . . . He sought to reach as many of the peasant class in Galilee as possible."[12] John Dominic Crossan has also noted this aspect of Jesus' itinerancy and his divergence from the kind of ascetic community founded by John, writing that there is "a similar contrast between a fasting John and a feasting Jesus."[13] Crossan's argument is that Jesus' ministry intentionally sought to disrupt the processes of patronage and clientage related to geographic location and real estate. "What Jesus should have done, as any Mediterranean family knew, was settle down at his home in Nazareth and establish a healing cult. He would be its *patron* and the family would be its brokers."[14]

Jesus, however, preferred to operate in the streets and in the open air. The Jesus resistance project was, in essence, a road-show, whether in rural or urban areas. He was homeless in the sense that he did not stay where people could come to him or find him. This homelessness need not be literal as much as functional or programmatic. Jesus probably had a family home to which he could return, but he opted for a functional rejection of family ties and security. He "kept to the road, brought healing to those who needed it, and had, as it were, to start off anew every day."[15] His itinerant ministry (resistance movement) was a performative solidarity that rejected the comfort, stability, and the privilege of having a home, and that brought him into direct, unmediated, unbrokered egalitarian community. It is fascinating to me that in this time of a Trump presidency, we see experts on authoritarianism advocating for more face-to-face public encounters. In his short monograph, *On Tyranny: Twenty Lessons from the Twentieth Century*, Timothy Snyder urges citizens to increase daily face-to-face encounters in the public realm.

12. Borg, *Jesus*, 145.
13. Crossan, *Jesus*, 54.
14. Ibid., 111.
15. Ibid.

Make eye contact and small talk. This is not just polite. It is part of being a citizen and a responsible member of society. It is also a way to stay in touch with your surroundings, break down social barriers, and understand whom you should and should not trust. If we enter a culture of denunciation, you will want to know the psychological landscape of your daily life.[16]

The third discovery is that Jesus seems much more interested in bodies than in souls, with a particular emphasis on the bodies of the disenfranchised and those without access to economic and political power. At first glance this claim might seem like the same claims that scholars from marginalized groups have made for decades. Jesus has a preferential option for the poor. Jesus was (ontologically) black. Jesus was a feminist. But if we go a step further, those claims take on a kind of radicality that typically undergirds public protest movements where those "disinherited" seek public and structural (political) reform of the systems that violate their bodies. It is one thing to support women in ministry or to engage in pulpit exchanges between black churches and white churches or to sponsor a food pantry for the impoverished. Those kinds of ecclesial reform, while laudatory, are so disengaged and distant from the actual structures causing misery as to be little more than Band-Aids on hemorrhages. William Sloane Coffin reminded us: "in the Bible, it is always the rich who are a problem to the poor, never the other way around. There are poor people *because* there are rich people, a connection Oscar Romero, the martyred Roman Catholic leader of El Salvador, never failed to make by calling the many poor in his country not *los pobres* but *los aprobecitos*, 'the impoverished,' those 'made poor.'"[17] Coffin, via Romero, highlights the systemic nature of multiple forms of inequality by focusing on the structures that sustain and benefit from embodied human misery.

When Jesus heals bodies or raises dead bodies, he's doing it as a public act of resistance against the forces that caused the misery in the first place. Most of my students had been taught to interpret the healing miracles as proofs of Jesus' divinity and supernatural powers. But the more we delved into the socio-political contexts behind the healing stories, the more we recognized the links between broken bodies and unquestioned power structures. In all too many cases the dominant theologies of that era conspired to mask and minimize the viciousness of the Empire's need for human "sacrifice." In John's gospel, Jesus heals a blind man in the face of theological naysayers who simply want to blame the victim and his parents for the man's

---

16. Snyder, *On Tyranny* 81.
17. Coffin, *A Passion* 37.

blindness. Jesus' detractors want to mask evil by claiming it is divine will for the man to be blind, but Jesus reverses the theology by claiming that it is God's will for the blind to see. Literal blindness in First Century Palestine was a death sentence. It reduced people to the status of unemployment and made them beggars. Blindness was an economic category as surely as being on public assistance. We can honor both the metaphorical use of sight/blindness and the literal meaning of the term; God rejects both kinds of blindness.

This one claim alone, that Jesus cared about bodies, is sufficient to support a Black Lives Matter hermeneutic. But it also supports political resistance to policies that threaten the healthcare of women and children, to policies that restrict access to physical autonomy and self-determination, to policies that incarcerate men and women for profit, and to death penalty legislation. This incarnational theology encompasses the body politic as well as individual human bodies. Crossan argues that the human body is a microcosm of the body politic.[18] What is inscribed on our bodies reflects the socio-political world.

And finally, since individual bodies are theologically significant, gathered bodies are both theologically and politically significant in resistance movements. It is one of the main reasons that the right to assemble and the power of protest are at the heart of every historic movement. When a society attempts to erase bodies or control bodies, the visibility of bodies under their own control presents a threat, a counter-narrative, an embodiment of the unmasking and naming of the powers and principalities. No wonder we see so many crowd scenes in the Gospels! When a society depends on the fragmentation of groups, on divide-and-conquer strategies, the sheer physicality of multiple bodies gathered to subvert power is a holy force. "Practice corporeal politics," urges Timothy Snyder. "Protest can be organized through social media, but nothing is real that does not end on the streets. If tyrants feel no consequences for their actions in the three-dimensional world, nothing will change . . . We are free only when it is we ourselves who draw the line between when we are seen and when we are not seen."[19]

Our fourth insight was that the Jesus stories critique the social and political domination systems represented by the term "empire." Where traditional atonement theories and spiritualized hermeneutics operate on one dimension of meaning, those interpretations neither exhaust nor explain awkward details that endure. Walter Wink reminds us that the powers and principalities operate within human structures to dominate through various

---

18. Crossan, *Jesus*, 86.
19. Snyder, *On Tyranny*, 84–85.

mechanisms of coercion. We cannot divorce spiritual meanings from their structural manifestations in secular politics, banking, real estate, prisons, policing, and the military. Critiques of secular government abound in the Gospels if we know what to look for. These critiques may be most overt in Luke's Gospel. Scholars have noted that Luke tends to "time-stamp" certain events in the life of Jesus by informing readers who was representing Rome and who was representing the Temple during those times.

One of the most critical things we discussed in class was the impact the Roman Empire had on ordinary peasant life in ancient Palestine. One of the novelties of the Roman Empire was their innovative and devastating practice of land-grabbing. They exercised an oppressive campaign of what we would call today eminent domain, seizing family properties and offering them back to families for rent. What made this land grab and tenant farming innovation so devastating was that First Century Palestine was a bartering economy; people didn't use money. In order to pay rent and taxes, the Jewish poor had to engage in the new monetary system imposed by Rome, which featured images of Caesar on the coins. Stamped next to Caesar Augustus' image were the words "son of God." The coins symbolized not only religious blasphemy, but they also symbolized the disaster initiated by land reform and a monetized economy. People became simultaneously homeless and dependent upon a monetized economy that insulted their deepest faith.[20]

Our insight into this historical reality led us to interpret stories about money differently. Where traditional interpretations considered money to be symbols of greed, we interpreted them as stories about the oppression of the Empire.

Another dramatic social change was the inauguration of governing classes (protector classes) and a standing military to enforce what Borg calls the premodern (agrarian or preindustrial) domination system. Borg highlights four primary features of premodern domination systems. They're politically oppressive, economically exploitive, religiously legitimized, and enforced by organized violence and armed conflict.[21]

As we discussed the social world of Jesus it wasn't difficult to find the similarities between that world and the history of blacks in America, from the days of chattel slavery to the realities in Ferguson, Missouri in August 2014 and the Black Lives Matter protests that erupted after the police shooting of an unarmed black teen named Michael Brown. The movement began in 2013 after the acquittal of George Zimmerman for the murder of an

20. Borg, *Jesus*, 87–89.
21. Ibid., 81–82.

unarmed black teenager named Trayvon Martin, but it came to national attention after the Ferguson shooting.

When we studied the social world of Michael Brown in Ferguson, we saw familiar themes: a militarized and oppressive police force arrayed disproportionately against black citizens, economic exploitation of the black citizenry in the form of police fines and property seizure, and something like a modern debtor's prison system. It wasn't so difficult, in light of these similarities, to view the Palm Sunday parade as an activity protesting Roman militarized domination of a Jewish city. Borg is not alone when he characterizes the Palm Sunday processional as a prophetic act orchestrated to counter, mimic, and mock the imperial procession of Pontius Pilate on that same day or a day earlier. Pilate's procession would have been a full military display of horses, chariots, clanking armor, trumpets, and silk banners. "What Christians have often spoken of as Jesus's triumphal entry was really an anti-imperial entry. What we call Palm Sunday featured a choice of two realms, two visions of life on earth."[22] In short, it was a massive resistance action, a street protest, a critique of the secular powers.

Finally, the life and ministry of Jesus offer critiques of religious power and the abuse of religious authority. We have to tread carefully with this interpretation, making sure we don't attribute anti-Judaism to Jesus and the resistance. It's clear that Jesus was a Jewish reformer who critiqued the role of Temple authorities for their assistance to the Roman Empire. Temple authorities and regular religious leaders maintained their authority at the pleasure of the Empire. To the extent that they supported law and order, to the extent that they tolerated or assisted in land reform and tax collection, they could continue to enjoy their religious authority over the ordinary Jewish citizenry. "Thus, early in Jesus's life, the high priest and temple authorities became the mediators of imperial rule, responsible for collecting and paying tribute to Rome and for maintaining domestic order. Jerusalem and the temple, the sacred center of the Jewish world, had become the center of native collaboration with an imperial domination system."[23]

Against this backdrop, it's easy to see "the cleansing of the Temple" during Holy Week as "the indictment of the Temple."[24] Because Rome had monetized the economy and required people to use the Roman coin of the realm, religious pilgrims had to "sell" their offerings prior to entering the Temple and convert their commodities to the proper coinage. When Jesus flips over the tables on the portico, he is not condemning greed (a stereotyp-

---

22. Ibid., 232.
23. Ibid., 91.
24. Ibid., 233.

ical anti-Jewish trope, by the way), but condemning the collaboration and complicity of the Temple authorities with Rome's monetized economy. He is, by extension, critiquing and condemning the abuse of religious power to uphold and legitimize oppressive domination. He's condemning the uncritical support of law and order. He's condemning all forms of respectability politics. He's condemning the collective laws of social convention he calls the "broad way" or what my students called "going along to get along."

Jesus challenges not only the religious authorities of his time, but also the religious authorities of our own time who conflate Christian faith with patriotism and good citizenship. Borg's extensive discussion of the "lords of convention" includes indictments of patriarchal family systems, family values, notions of honor and purity.[25]

When we turned to the contemporary church, my students engaged in a critique of the unwillingness of many black pastors to support Black Lives Matter and the homophobia of specific black pastors directed toward the founders of BLM. One class meeting stands out in particular, when female students deconstructed the chapel sermon from the previous day, calling it a "broad way sermon" for its policing of black female bodies and sexuality and for supporting respectability politics and sexual purity. They also debated the merits of boycotting an upcoming chapel service dedicated to observing Veterans' Day.

Our survey of the Life and Teachings of Jesus as a resistance movement produced new hermeneutical contours for interpreting the parables, miracles, prophetic acts, and teachings of Jesus. The life and teachings of Jesus offer both goals and methods for resisting all forms of institutional abuse of power, whether that power is religious, military, or legislative. Traditional hermeneutical approaches dominated by atonement theories are insufficient for exposing the abundance of meaning in the gospels; such hermeneutical approaches might in fact be complicit in masking domination systems. Therefore, claims about what it means to "preach the gospel" must be reconsidered in light of oppressive domination systems. We must also reconsider the theo-political value of performative public actions and speech. Speaking inside churches to transform the institutional life of churches for its members is a flawed and insufficient mission. Stories about human bodies and their healing are ultimately commentaries about the body politic and the erasure/control of bodies. Bodies matter. Black bodies matter. Black Lives Matter.

25. Ibid., 232–56.

17

"That Being Said"
A Pastoral Prophetic Transition for Doing Justice

TERESA L. FRY BROWN

TRANSITIONS ARE EMPLOYED IN written and oral compositions to unify a subject, assist the listener in connecting ideas and to build on a larger point. Isolated words, sounds, and recurrent statements are inserted in sermonic material to indicate shifts in thought or to move to another point, signify a rest or stop, assist the listeners in their anamnesia, reiterate a topic or to underscore an essential point. Transitions are the connective tissue of the story, lecture or sermon. Homiletics and Practical Theology Professor Dr. Dale P. Andrews literally and figuratively creatively employs the transitional phrase, "that being said," in casual conversation, in intense academic discussions, in explaining practical theology and homiletical theory, and also to relate the often volatile discussions of racial justice. Perhaps the melding of Andrews' vocations of clinical social worker, ordained clergy, pastor, author, preacher, activist, guild officer, and seminary professor provide increased pastoral sensibilities in consideration of deep emotional and political positions of the listeners when confronted with prophetic truth telling.

Andrews' oral presentations are hallmarked by steady then modified pacing, intentional eye contact, reversion to vernacular, universal examples, emphasized emotive words, insertion of substantiated facts, engaging facial expressions and the use of metonymy.

He would state his purpose and position, listen to audiences' response to determine if they agreed or disagreed with his statement and *heard* what he had said. He would then pause and interject, "that being said," before offering possibilities of transformation. The transitional phrase "that being said" both allows the listener time to begin to process the information and signals a "You knew most of this; now let's explore what we can do to resolve the issue" moment of pastoral prophetic discourse. This essay will briefly review examples of Andrews' pastoral prophetic engagement.

BUILDING THE CASE

The fulcrum point of Professor Andrews' approach is summarized in a key quote.

> Informed praxis is the result of critical awareness of dominant values, sound theological reflection, critical engagement with historical context in the human sciences, in a deliberate or strategic telelogical focus. It is able, therefore, compellingly to address contemporary issues in a way that does not ignore cultural and religious heritage, Christian traditions in Scripture, and contemporary social contexts.[1]

Andrews posits his philosophy of practical theology and social justice discourse in the co-edited volume, *Black Practical Theology*. His work utilizes African Diaspora socio-cultural imperatives as foundational to his understanding of religious and cultural concerns issues. The volume provides a nonessentialist review of multi-vocalic Black scholarship on theology. The importance of the volume is its applicability across cultural divisions and diminishing the traditional subordination of Black theological perspectives in the academy. This is a pastoral prophetic justice move.

Andrews' scholarly trajectory has been to "speak truth to power" whether preaching or lecturing about racism, sexism, classism or academic elitism. The concept of speaking truth to power originated with the Religious Society of Friends or Quakers. In the 1600s they stated that "everyone contains a spark that can be reached with prophetic voices." The American Friends Service Committee's (AFSC) most influential pamphlet *Speak Truth to Power* was published in 1955 as an antiwar pamphlet written by Milton Mayer.[2] Even those in positions of power who are not willing to listen, or who are brutal and insensitive can be convicted to change, correct behavior,

---

1. Andrews and Smith, *Black Practical Theology*, 9.
2. Document, "Speak Truth to Power."

or formulat new paradigms if one is bold enough to "Speak Truth to Power," to say a word, to tell the truth, to utter a defense of freedom, to look a wrongdoer in the face and say enough is enough. The ability to speak truth to power should never be taken for granted regardless of who seeks to silence the masses. Andrews uses his transformative voice to address difficult issues with an eye and ear to the subjective and objective minds of his readers and listeners. The transformational voice addresses the lived experiences of all the people and those people, places and things that comprise exploitation, marginalization, powerlessness and imperialism. It is the people's hopeful expectation that these conditions will be eradicated rather than deteriorate into vague promises of material gain. The transformational voice, which speaks truth to power, works to end practices that establish, maintain and perpetuate subordination, exploitation, marginalization, powerlessness, cultural imperialism, "othering," systematic violence and subjugated knowledge. It points to the fire on the outside of the cave, the light of truth, God's call on the people of faith.

Andrews follows the model of classical Black prophetic preaching as he builds his case for addressing social injustices. The late preacher par excellence, Gardner C. Taylor described the task of prophetic preaching:

> To seek and find God's movement in human affairs and to cry out passionately pointing to where that stirring is discernable though scarcely ever indisputable, is the preacher's task. To hear and to suffer deeply with the still sad music of humanity and then to offer to it the wonderful Gospel of healing and wholeness is the preacher's privilege. We are called to listen and to identify the tread of the Eternal God's sovereign purpose marching in private and public affairs of men.[3]

Taylor's contemporary Samuel Dewitt Proctor, delineated essential elements of prophetic discourse in his seminal book, *Preaching About Crisis in the Community*. Proctor wrote that all discourse must be person centered and affirm the worth and dignity of every person. It must seek to include each person in the realm of God's power and love. No one is excluded, demeaned or ignored. Christ calls us to renew our relationship with each other. Faith is not private or ornamental but is marked by discipline, discipleship and life obedience to God. Prophetic discourse attends to God's will and appropriates the power of God in love toward others in personal moral integrity through urging the speaker and listener toward a higher standard of behavior.[4] Communal and cultural teachings lend themselves to

---

3. Taylor, *How Shall They Preach*, 38.
4. Proctor, *Preaching about Crisis*, "Introduction."

a holistic communicative act that engages the spiritual, intellectual, social, psychological, and economical yearnings, needs, issues, needs, questions and issues of all God's family. Andrews' work is steeped in black practical theology, preaching and activism as evidenced in his writing, lectures and preaching.

Andrews' pastoral prophetic voice is a rich texture of his personal upbringing, teachings and lived experiences, Black church ministry, theological education, social-cultural-political engagement, and passion for social transformation. His work includes the basic elements of the genre of Black prophetic preaching or "pre-lect" (a combination lecture and sermon in the tradition that may or may not also include celebration). The elements of Black pastoral prophetic preaching include but are not limited to an effort to define the social reality as reflected in context's God questions i.e. "Lord, How come we here?" or "How long, Lord?" The preacher or speaker is to give information that seeks to restore humanity to events that threaten to harden us to God, others and self. God's forgiveness for the victim and the perpetrators of injustice is paramount. This is not the "Kumbayah" forgiveness without reconciliation effort, or a rush to "get over it," but a deep repentance, thought, and activism involving thought, word, and deed. Essential to forgiveness is a focused, well researched and supported information that attends to the heart and mind of the speaker and listener. One must avoid delineation of a hierarchy of sins as all unrighteousness is sin. Language that is truthful, although difficult, is necessary to state the case and prove the point. Manageable action at the end of the day is the goal. Mismanaged expectations and the pathology of good manners by the listener, speaker or writer will diminish the effectiveness of the message.

When Professor Andrews talks about "the convergence of American individualism and racism," he discusses the necessity of examining both the "metanarrative" or communal hermeneutic and Black prophetic voice.

> The convergence of American individualism and willful or socially systemic racism exacerbate identity conflicts within the African American community. For many, these conflicts also cause renewed interest in the dialectic between control and responsibility and between refuge ecclesiology and black theology. While a major strength of both black churches and black theology has been their emphasis on black identity, or self-esteem, fragmentation of the African-American community punctuates the displacement of black churches.
>
> Black theology has been quite progressive as a prophetic voice in white America and Western culture. It has challenged the social evils and ideology of racism rooted throughout

American public and private spheres. Black theology has held white society accountable to its own democratic principles, and exposed injustice culturally, politically, and economically.[5]

Here Andrews indicates that the Black prophetic voice is not only to address issues and concerns in Black churches and communities but also across other cultures. Black lives matter in all spheres of society, not just Black families, groups and institutions. The writings, lessons and voice of Black academicians and preachers are central to theological discourse, not an afterthought. When all voices are taken seriously and contributions acknowledged equally, social transformation is possible.

Dr. Andrews lays out a bridge building strategy in his compelling chapter "Preaching a Just Word in Privileged Pulpits Healing Affluenza":

> If we are to bring religious ethics to bear on self-interest, we will need greater insight into the dynamics of religion and culture... However, when religion and culture come into conflict, religious ethics still require social support. Even when religious institutions struggle to break free of domineering cultural values, they elicit social conformity in that actual effort. Perhaps it becomes the mission of churches to reshape culture. Yet, it is clear they cannot effectively do so until they establish new shared values or re-establish lost ones. It Is equally clear that secular culture may indeed reshape religious values.... Just preaching launches the reacquaintance of strangers and what otherwise has been called the "rehumanization" of the disenfranchised.[6]

Although the chapter attends to economic issues, it is important to consider his view of cultural values in further understanding his theology and approach to interrogating justice issues.

A BITTER PILL TO SWALLOW

Dr. Andrews does not shy away from thorny, emotionally laden subjects. He presented information with thick details and research. He attended to the temperature of the room yet understood the prophetic call to identify an unhealthy body, diagnose causative factors, slowly open the wounds, allow the venom to be exposed and name the disease. He would then transition to a "that being said" moment and propose the ongoing treatment. As the perennial biblical question, "Do you want to be made whole?," rang in the

---

5. Andrews, *Practical Theology*, 81–84.
6. Resner, *Just Preaching*, 176–77..

room, Andrews proceeded to "speak the truth in love." He carefully included himself as a patient in search of healing.

Dr. Andrews presented "Preaching Anti-Racism Amid the Backlash and Resistance of White Moral Injury?" for the Whiteside Lecture at Candler School of Theology, Emory University, on September 21, 2016.[7] It was a brilliant engagement of social, cultural and political realities of the landscape of America. The lecture encouraged an extensive and stimulating discussion with faculty, administration, students, community leaders and local pastors focused on Andrews' use of antiracism, moral injury and whiteness. The project's intention was to examine responsibilities of black and white churches and seminaries in establishing and maintaining dialogue, remediation, reconciliation and education around issues of moral injury and how the resultant backlash was critical to the post-election theological scholarship and education. He had previously presented a variation of the lecture at the Old Stone Church (First Presbyterian) in downtown Cleveland, Ohio, on February 7, 2016, entitled "Prophetic Praxis: Wrestling with the Moral Injury of Anti-Racism."[8] Andrews began his lecture talking about his personal encounter with racism through his work with the Justice Resource Forum in Louisville, Kentucky. He was part of an ongoing protest over a two-year period for a just resolution concerning the death of seven Black men murdered in five years yet there was no action or prosecution on the cases. After the judge muted court observers, the judge stated the verdict. It was here that Andrews began to muse about racism and backlash. This underscored the reality that there was a difference in preaching about injustice and being a part of the events that cause or are the result of injustice.

Andrews equated the injustices in the legal system with that of the theological academy with parallel instances of resistance backlash, debates on justice, morals and freedom. The lecture began with a series of rhetorical questions such as "Do we still need the Black Church?", "Is the church needed in the public arena or political debates?" and "What role does Black prophetic preaching, if at all, play in the church?" He spoke of the enormous backlash, his term of "evilization" concerning the Black prophetic preacher, Dr. Jeremiah A. Wright in 2008. A sound byte of one of Wright's sermons was eviscerated and misappropriated across the political landscape and opened a wave of white moral backlash. The mirrored images of liberal and conservative groups addressing racism and barriers to justice work became the nexus of the lecture. Using PTSD—grief, rage, outrage, guilt, nihilism, powerlessness, and hopelessness—as his operating term, Andrews began to

---

7. Andrews, "Preaching Anti–Racism."
8. Ibid.

evaluate white moral injury, macroaggressions, anger based resistance, cries of reverse racism, exclusive ecclesial and academic practices and overt racial violence as the rationale for a politics of resentment. He then addressed the inherited privilege of whites.

Just when the initial body of information was settling in, Andrews employed a Black preaching trope of "calling the roll." The roll call is a cultural imperative to honor the names of heroes of the faith and those who have died. It is a linguistic libation of sorts. Andrews paused and began to articulate evidence of contemporary racism and racist policies as he carefully called the names of Eric Garner, Michael Brown, Trayvon Martin, Mayor Marissa Alexander, Rashida McBride, Jonathan Farrell, Timothy Russell and Marissa Williams. He then proposed that premature forgiveness does not overshadow the resistance, ambivalence or duplicity in our actions, privilege or power. There should be no absolution without knowledge of the power of someone's pain by an offer of false charity. He then moved to another series of rhetorical questions such as "What is the response of the church?" "Where are the moral and spiritual consequences of moral injury?" and "How does one forgive being manipulated?" Just when one felt there was no resolution to the pain of being Black in America, pathologizing of Black presence and pain, survivor's guilt, white victimization, romanticized dehumanization, white moral injury, or backlash, Andrews invoked his patented transition: *"That being said."* Manageable expectations included his call to reach out to each other, lift each other out of isolation and degradation, offer each other safe spaces, understand what violates, become allies in the suffering of others, deep listening to each other, asking profound questions of our own moral consciences, and establishing a sacred space of protest resistance. He further insisted on the need to hold together personal and collective moral integrity, accountability, and transformative privilege with truth telling. The lecture was a masterful example of pastoral prophetic voice in the discipline of Black pastoral theology.

"THAT BEING SAID"

Dr. Andrews presented a lecture entitled "We're Never Done with the Work" at the 2011 Gardner C. Taylor Lecture Series at The Divinity School at Duke University. In many ways excerpts from the lecture reinforced his methodology of teaching, lecturing and preaching about the primacy of Black practical theology and the call of social justice.

> How that translates now into my current research is this notion of a pastoral-prophetic dialectic. What we've learned from the

black church experience is how the care for the soul relates with the care for the community and what—I'm borrowing a term from a colleague—constitutes "prophetic care."

Institutional survival is a necessity. It is critically important. There was an age when the development of the black church itself—the institutional development of the black church—was a form of political resistance, when the development of the institutional black church was a form of spiritual nurture; that personal salvation or the nurture of the soul was a form of justice-making. To re-dignify—to re-humanize—the personalities who were coming to the church was a form of protest as well as a form of nurture.

> If we're going to die, if we're looking at facing death, then let us go out trying to be the church. We still work at the institutional maintenance, but if we're facing death, let us face death with faith that our death is not the end of our life. And let us go out dying by doing that justice-making out in the community, and we will be faithful in doing it and trusting in God's faithfulness to work with us. And if we die while we're being faithful, our death is not the end of life.[9]

"That being said," Dr. Andrews embodied the care and passionate concern for the life of the church, community, academy and world. His early work on Black folk religion and preaching, preaching commentaries, attention to the listener, and leadership in professional guilds, and coveted collegiality converge in his work on antiracism. He understood the undertaking is not a one-time lecture or sermon but ongoing deep work in varied settings. The risk of confronting issues of justice is rejection by the very people who need to modify behavior but hide behind privilege, rejection by those thought to be natural allies or being typecast as a "justice freak." Dale Andrews counted the cost and paid the price and understood that the prophetic call of justice is not an easy call but a God call.

The late Salvadoran Archbishop Oscar Romero reminded us of this not long before his assassination in 1980:

> A church that doesn't provoke any crisis, a gospel that doesn't unsettle, a word of God that doesn't get under anyone's skin, a word of God that doesn't touch the real sin of the society in which it is being proclaimed, what gospel is that? . . . Those preachers who avoid every thorny matter so as not to be harassed, so as

---

9. Andrews, "We're Never Done."

> not to have conflicts and difficulties, do not light up the world they live in.[10]

Dale Andrews' words and actions light up the darkness of injustice. "That being said:" we who believe in freedom are better for reading and hearing his words.

---

10. Romero, *The Violence of Love*, 64.

18

Encountering the Word
Dale Andrews' Inductive Pedagogy for Prophetic Preaching

JOHN S. MCCLURE

MUCH OF DALE ANDREWS' teaching career has been devoted to searching for a workable inductive pedagogy for theological education that would mirror many of the best aspects of the African-American mentoring tradition. Although not wanting to give up on the best of mostly white, Western, Enlightenment homiletical theories and models, Andrews has been hesitant to grant them the leading role in homiletical education. Instead, he has gone in search of a pedagogy in which such methods and models might become partners in the seminary classroom. He wrote elegantly about this search for a pedagogical method in two important articles published in the *African American Pulpit*.[1]

In those articles, he laments the fact that seminary teaching tends to focus on exegetical practices and procedures, hermeneutical approaches, and sermon construction, at the expense of students' actual experiences of the preaching event itself. In a way similar to homiletical mentoring within many Black church traditions, Andrews articulates a method whereby students might move inductively from actual experiences of their own

---

1. Andrews, "Teaching Black Preaching: Homiletic Instruction as Pre-Encounter;" and Andrews, "Teaching Black Preaching: Encounter and Re-Encounter."

preaching and the preaching of others into new processes of sermon preparation and delivery, identifying along the way the skills, tools, and methods that might be relevant for their own emerging or continuing education as preachers.

Andrews yearns for all students to have the kind of learning experience found within the apprenticeship traditions in Black churches in which a "parallel process" of learning occurs.[2] In this parallel learning process, the preaching student learns by listening to sermons by exemplars within his/her tradition, identifying along the way the kinds of things that create an "encounter" or revelatory experience of God's word during preaching. The student begins to learn to identify the ways that sermons help the community approach such encounters, which may include such things as sermon form, rhetorical styles, aspects of exegesis or delivery and so on. At the same time, the student preaches sermons experimenting with the things he/she is absorbing from listening to these sermons by others—imitating, styling on, and re-creating forms of oral speech within a tradition of preaching. On a parallel track, the mentor engages in a process of "learning the apprentice,"[3] paying attention to the ways the student talks about or analyzes favorite sermons, noting the things he/she likes, dislikes, and wants to understand. At the same time, the mentor listens to the apprentice preach, identifying the skills the student may possess, and noting areas of need. The student's own preaching provides "windows" through which homiletical methods will make sense in the learning process, and in the learner's experience and reflection on the preaching of others.[4] Over time, the student learns many tools for evaluating both his/her own sermons, and the sermons of others.

This becomes a "never-ending process"[5] in which three homiletical *experiences* are sought as learning outcomes. These experiences interact with one another in ways that are both circular and parallel in nature.

1. Encounter: the preacher's encounter with God during sermon preparation.

2. Re-encounter: the encounter with God during preaching itself. This might be an experience that occurs during the student's preaching of a sermon, or while listening to the sermon of another preacher.

---

2. Andrews, "Teaching Black Preaching: Homiletic Instruction as Pre-Encounter," 25.

3. Ibid.

4. Ibid.

5. Ibid., 26.

3. Pre-encounter. This is a self-reflective insight brought about through learning and using homiletical categories, methods, theories, models, language, and wisdom to better understand some aspect of sermonic encounter or re-encounter. The wisdom of choosing the prefix "pre-" for this temporally last experience lies in the inductive idea that as the mentor helps the student understand what he/she has just experienced, this encounter with self-knowledge becomes a new platform for further encounters and re-encounters during preaching. This circularity, at its best, is generative and supports more creativity and new forms of homiletical learning as time goes by.

Figure 2

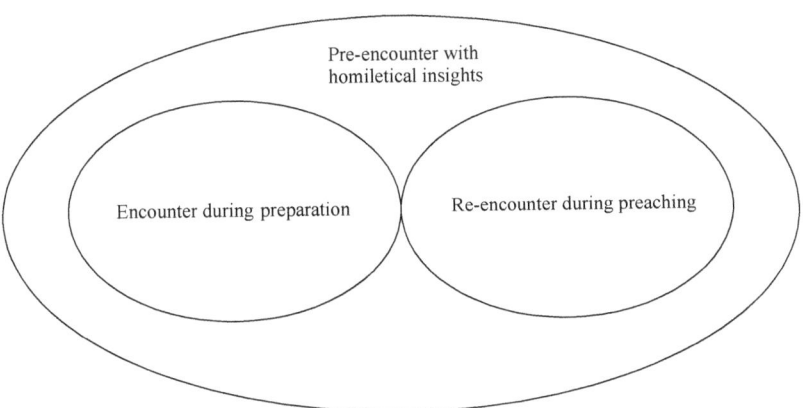

THE IDEA OF ENCOUNTER

The centrality of "encounter" within Andrews' understanding of African American homiletical pedagogy conveys a richer understanding of religious experience than many of us as children of the Enlightenment assume. Within African American traditions of preaching, experience is never merely subjective experience. It is never something identified solely with a particular individual who "has" or "creates" it. Instead, the experience of God in preaching is the result of a community of believers encountering something they know is already present—already there in their midst. It is something that is approachable from many standpoints within a gathering of those inclined toward such an encounter, and preaching constitutes one such approach.

To use John E. Smith's language, experience involves two things: (1) an *encounter* with a reality that is already and phenomenologically there, or what he calls "primary experience," and (2) an *expression* (secondary experience), or the business of "finding an adequate language" in order to both respond to that encounter and to re-approach that encounter.[6] According to Smith, "when our language proves inadequate, we return to experience, but we do so in order to criticize our language and improve it, not to force our experience into conformity with a pre-established language."[7]

In this way of understanding experience, it is crucial that primary experience (encounter) remains central and that preachers never confuse their expressive inventions, whether sermons or the theories, categories, etc. that make sense of the sermon, as the central thing for education. The entire community of faith is involved in a communal process of using the language and expressive inventions that it has, not in order to reify its own expressive life, but in order to always return to the encounter with God's revelation so that all expressions might be both criticized and improved. This is why it is so important within Andrews' pedagogy that primary experience or encounter not get lost in the teaching and learning of preaching. And it is also why the business of critiquing and renewing our categories of expression must be understood as a form of "pre-encounter," helping preachers to both critique and renew the expressive dimensions of preaching while at the same time critiquing and renewing our categories of homiletical thought and reflection. In this way secondary expressive experience is always closely tethered to encounter at every step of the process, from sermon preparation, through the preaching event, and back into reflection on those practices.

The Prophetic Dimension

It is at this juncture that Andrews' pedagogy for prophetic preaching draws life from his practical theology of prophetic ministry. In his book *Practical Theology for the Black Churches* (2002),[8] he identifies a "confluence" within the "faith identity" of Black churches between a "psychosocial refuge image and liberation ethics."[9] Using H. Richard Niebuhr's categories, he works this out carefully and cogently in terms of the Black churches' "internal history" which is built around the memory of individual and communal encounters with the God of refuge and care, which is then deeply connected to an "external history" of liberation from oppression and violence.[10]

6. Smith, *Experience and God*, 12–13.
7. Ibid., 13.
8. Andrews, *Practical Theology*.
9. Ibid., 37.
10. Ibid., 97–107.

The rhythms between these two histories inform his pedagogical model. On the one hand, as mentors learn the student and vice versa they share in the internal history of the Black churches' oral folk traditions. Many of these traditions are deeply rooted in the Black churches' communal encounters with the brush arbor God of refuge. This God, however, is also the God of the Black churches' external history of liberation, hope, and emancipation. According to Andrews, in a highly individualistic culture this external history can be easily sacrificed for a non-prophetic prosperity gospel. It is crucial, therefore, that mentors link the community's revelatory encounters with the God of refuge closely to its encounters with the God of liberation. These encounters take many thematic shapes: comfort, lamentation, healing, hope, joy, getting by, finding a way through, and so on. When these historical encounters are placed in service to prophetic preaching, they are re-created and updated in ways that will promote "re-encounter" with both the folk traditions and with the ongoing external history of radical social reform and liberation in a new historical context and situation. Prophetic homiletical encounters, therefore, are part of a shared experience of the rhythms between refuge and liberation, faith identity and prophetic practice. This means that homiletical re-encounters during actual preaching events are assessed with an ear tuned to this linkage between pastoral and prophetic rhythms. If these are missing, then it is important for the student to be shepherded into the kinds of "pre-encounters" that will nurture a more fulsome experience of both internal and external histories, and the ways in which they are linked.

COLLABORATIVE HOMILETIC PEER-COACHING

We have now identified a range of elements that Andrews considers to be important for homiletical education for prophetic preaching today. These elements became crucial in the development of the Lilly Foundation funded *David G. Buttrick Program in Homiletical Peer-Coaching* at Vanderbilt. The design of this program was meant to facilitate, as much as possible, all of these core elements.

Central to this program was the development of a particular form of *collaborative coaching* as inductive pedagogy. The spectrum of coaching models includes: 1) approaches that are highly mimetic and idiosyncratic ("do it my way"), 2) supervisory approaches in which students are evaluated according to certain clear professional standards, 3) specific skill-based learning and prompting, and 4) collaborative approaches that accentuate the kind of careful parallel listening and observation that Andrews encourages.

In collaborative coaching, the student is invited to reflect on experiences of preaching, and on experiences of being a preacher, with an eye toward places where their own encounters, re-encounters, and sense-making efforts (pre-encounters) seem to be both strong and less than satisfactory. This becomes a foray into the business of developing together a reflective homiletical language concerning preaching problems and possibilities for solutions.

If coaching is one-to-one, the coach/mentor may introduce homiletical resources (ideas, readings, sermons to listen to) that might shape a helpful "pre-encounter" for the preacher's next sermon. Facilitating a peer-coaching group, however, adds a crucial dimension to the coaching task. In a group, there is an opportunity for others to connect with whatever the preacher is concerned about, and to become involved in providing feedback that can broaden and deepen the preacher's and mentor/coach's understanding of what re-encounters are actually occurring during preaching. This clarification can go a long way toward helping the preacher discern whether his/her self-understanding of gifts or problems are, in fact, central, or peripheral to the actual gifts and issues experienced by others. In a peer-coaching group, therefore, as several preachers "learn" and mentor one another, it is possible to investigate whether the actual experience of re-encounter by listeners matches the preacher's assumptions about what is or is not being re-encountered, and why/why not. Although beginning with the preacher's own sense of disconnect between encounter and re-encounter, a peer-coaching group can begin a process that moves homiletical learning in new directions unanticipated by the preacher. In response to the range of encounter/re-encounter issues that are identified within a peer group, the group leader can identify appropriate pre-encounter resources in order to expand the larger theoretical framework in which the practice and reflection of the entire group occurs. The peer-coaching training program was designed to train leaders to facilitate this kind of inductive peer-coaching process.

A key issue in these peer-coaching groups is the business of connecting students' internal faith identities to a shared external history of liberation or justice. Most African American students in these groups tend to have a strong understanding of a shared history of justice and justice-seeking, as do some students within marginalized populations (persons with disabilities, women, GLBTQIA students, migrant farm laborers, coal miners, native Americans, persons with health "pre-conditions," the homeless, etc.). In order to broaden access to these histories, Andrews often incorporates into pre-encounter work what Rae Davis calls an "unmirroring pedagogy"[11] in which case material, works of art, readings, or events are provided in which many participants may fail to find themselves within the mirror held up by the experience, text, or event and must struggle with the presence of "distant" (marginal, vulnerable, threatened) lives that don't reflect their own sense of personal responsibility.[12] Within the context of such education many students experience "a breakdown of the mirror, as the clarity of the . . . image they expected to see illuminated fails to materialize."[13] As they go in search of their image in that picture, they have the potential to encounter basic forms of solidarity within a shared history of justice and liberation.

According to Davis, if the participant looks long and hard enough in the mirror provided during such pre-encounters it is possible that "the mirror (suddenly) emits a gaze of otherness, looking back (so to speak) in ways that alter schemes of recognition and challenge self-perceptions . . ."[14] This, then, creates a new and "often unfamiliar self-cognizance" which can involve confronting privileges, assumptions, perceptions, and self-deceptions about "normal" identity that become pathways to new forms of solidarity with those in need of justice. Within an un-mirroring pedagogy students engage readings, works of art, case materials, sermons or other artifacts that represent marginalized populations. Texts, sermons, or case materials by authors or preachers who mirror the dominant homiletic culture and the basic expectations of the class are often avoided or not introduced—at least until late in the peer-group's time together. In Andrews' language, an "external history" of justice is generated within the peer group to which students can in every instance of reflection link to their own (and their community's) internal faith identity.

This process mirrors the development of communal identity within the mentoring traditions of African American preaching in which mentors work to connect the faith identity of refuge and communal care to a specific contextual hermeneutic of liberation. The mentor is always shaping and calling to mind the pre-encounters with the African American history of slavery, emancipation, and ongoing racism that meet and intermingle with that faith identity. A history of solidarity is recalled, located in today's context, and re-imagined in the mentor-apprentice relationship. In a similar way, the facilitator of a peer-coaching group introduces pre-encounters that

---

11. Davis, "Unmirroring Pedagogies," 2.

12. Ibid., 154. According to Rae, this "distance" can be "exotic" within a still narcissistic "touristic imaginary," or it can be the distance of "having nothing in common."

13. Ibid., 150.

14. Ibid., 151.

will suggest a larger external history of solidarity-in-justice within which sermons are heard and feedback is offered. This in no way over-rides the internal histories of group members-the ways that religious piety and theological imagination are already shaped. But it asks for linkages to be made to a larger external history of justice in the ways preachers are formed, and in the ways sermons are formed.

IMPLICATIONS

There are several important implications of Andrews' pedagogy for the teaching of homiletics today.

1. Parallel learning. Homiletical education can cultivate the dynamics of parallel learning found within the mentor-apprentice relationship within African American traditions in which the learner and mentor simultaneously "learn" one another. Although hearing instructors preach regularly is seldom possible in theological education, it is important for there to be enough of a mentoring relationship for both student and instructor or for a group of peers to "learn one another." This might mean providing examples of one's sermons to students, perhaps accompanied by self-analysis using one's own homiletical categories for reflection. It will also require instructors to be forthcoming regarding the elements and aspects of homiletical theory that they deem essential. Or it might involve embedding homiletical education in a peer-coaching setting and process. At the same time, students need ways to self-disclose issues pertaining to their formation as preachers—including their sense of calling, self-image as a preacher, life experiences that are relevant to preaching, troubling experiences with preaching or public speaking, and self-assessed areas of concern or native ability. Although being a personal mentor to all students is not possible, some sort of genuine collaborative coaching role is, in fact, possible.

2. Inductive pedagogy. Homiletical education needs an inductive pedagogy in which engagement with the primary experiences of homiletical encounter is given priority over the teaching of theories, categories, and skills. There is no substitution for hearing sermons, preaching sermons, and discussing actual sermonic "encounters" in homiletical education. Many students come to theological education unformed within a tradition of preaching, or have only experienced preaching in minimal or inadequate ways. Hearing live or recorded sermons in which an encounter with God is experienced, or preaching sermons in which such an encounter is experienced and celebrated is fundamental to learning preaching. Although this may occur in field placements in congregations where preaching is central

and valued, there are many other options available—chapel preaching, field trips, conferences, and preaching and hearing sermons regularly in class or peer-groups and reflecting on what is experienced.

3. Attention to connecting internal and external histories. Homiletics teachers can create "pre-encounters" that link students' internal history of encounters with God to an external history of encounters with liberation and social reform. Classroom experiences or pre-encounters need to move in two directions: 1) toward the individual preacher situated in a particular context, nurturing their faith identity in that context, and 2) toward the public sphere as a whole, creating "unmirroring" experiences that will challenge students to connect their faith identity with the liberation of those who are suffering or oppressed.

NEW TO WHOM?

In the Fall of 2006, Dale Andrews published a short but important essay in *Homiletix*, the e-journal of the Academy of Homiletics, entitled: "New to Whom?"[15] In that essay he argued that many of the experiential and encounter-centered aspects of the "New Homiletic," focused in the works of David Randolph and Fred Craddock, have been at work in Black preaching traditions for many years, and have gone unrecognized as such. He suggests that "a major cause for this oversight is the reality that black preaching was not central to theological curricula in seminaries," while Black preaching traditions developed "apprenticeship methods of learning peaching, within our churches primarily." He goes on to argue that "the mentoring-apprenticeship process of Black preaching presses the induction movement into the pedagogical process itself," and that it is precisely this inductive pedagogy that is needed if the so-called "inductive preaching" of the New Homiletic is to be adequately taught and learned.

The pedagogy I have attempted to outline above is part of the pedagogy that, as he observes at the conclusion of this e-journal essay "consumes my current research and writing!" Dale was working on a book that will explore this pedagogy in some detail within Black preaching traditions before he became ill. In my estimation there is far more in Andrews' pedagogy than what the purveyors of the New Homiletic would typically include—most notably—the prophetic aspect, in which faith identity is constantly tethered to an external history of liberation. There is also a far less subjectivist and more communal, realistic, and historical understanding of experience and

---

15. Andrews, 'New to Whom?,' republished in Appendix A.

encounter in Andrews' work than is found in most of the literature on inductive or narrative preaching associated with the New Homiletic.

In the end, I am hesitant, therefore, to limit Andrews' understanding of homiletics and pedagogy to its potential relationship to the New Homiletic, no matter how fruitful that might be. In many respects his ideas suggest an entire re-thinking of experience-centered homiletics as a deeply relational modality of preaching from start to finish, grounded in co-experiencing and co-learning that involves God, mentor, preacher, sermon listeners, the community's internal and external histories. There is much to learn here for teaching and learning preaching in the next generation.

19

Preaching the Mystery of God's Reign

Encounter, Re-encounter, and Pre-encounter

Dawn Ottoni-Wilhelm

There is no bridge nearer yet more difficult to access than that which reaches between heaven and earth, God's realm and earthly domains. It is a bridge that Christians have prayed for throughout the centuries: "Your realm [kingdom] come. Your will be done, on earth as it is in heaven." (Matt 6:10)[1] Yet the commerce between heaven and earth appears to be slow-moving and the distance often insurmountable. To be sure, Jesus proclaimed the nearness of God's realm and embodied its presence among us (Mark 1:15). But the fullness of divine justice, mercy, and compassion for creation and its creatures has yet to be realized. Wars rage, creation groans, and hunger stabs, while political ideologies divide us, differences in gender and sexual orientation frighten us, and racism dismembers individuals and communities the world over. A pastoral ache in our hearts is met with prophetic urgency for our times as preachers stand in the chasm, longing to hear God's words and speak God's purposes anew.

Jesus was no doubt well aware of this chasm when he spoke of the mystery of God's reign (Mark 4:11). Alongside our hope for God's will to be done is our despair that it is so seldom evident among us. At the center of our longing for divine justice, love, and righteousness is a mystery

1. Here as elsewhere in this chapter, all biblical quotations are from the New Revised Standard Version.

that challenges our understanding of God's unfathomable love and mercy, namely; If God's reigndom[2] has come through Jesus Christ, why does it so often seem that Satan rules? What can we do to build bridges of justice and compassion among us? These questions are also at the heart of Dale Andrews' work as he sought to bridge the many gaps between divine justice and human injustice, between godly compassion and the hardness of our hearts. The purpose of this essay is to explore how Andrews created homiletical opportunities to engage the mystery of God's just and loving reign in preaching through his understanding of encounter, re-encounter, and pre-encounter and to do so in light of Jesus' proclamation of the mystery of God's reign in Mark 4. Through the preacher's dynamic and ongoing process of worshipful encounter with God, re-encounter experienced with others in the moment of preaching, and the work of critical and compassionate reflection in preparation for future preaching (pre-encounter), Andrews' homiletical method invites our ongoing engagement with God's mysterious presence among us.

JESUS PREACHES THE MYSTERY OF GOD'S REIGN

In one of his most enigmatic teachings, Jesus insists that the secret or mystery (Greek: μυστήριον, mystērion) of God's reign has been given to his followers "but for those outside, everything comes in parables, in order that 'they may indeed look, but not perceive, and may indeed listen, but not understand; so that they may not turn again and be forgiven.'" (Mark 4:11f, quoting Isa 6:9f) After sharing the parable of the sower and seeds in Mark 4:1–9 (including the admonition to "Listen!" both at the beginning and end of this teaching moment), Jesus' closest disciples asked him about the parables. His response was to tell them that they had already been given the mystery of the reigndom of God but for those "outside"[3] he shares his homiletical strategy for speaking in parables in order that (Gr. ἵνα) they will not perceive,

---

2. The term *reigndom* was Dale's preferred way of speaking of God's reign or rule that God seeks to establish with creation: it is a term that "preserves the sovereignty and defining authority of God in divine will for creation." Also, Dale used the term *kin–dom* "to stress God's desire for human relationships within the reign of God. Kin–dom signifies mutual relations of care, mutual thriving, living into divine will for equality, and freedom to be in relationship." He identifies these values and understandings with Black Church traditions as "the reign or kin–dom of God depicts the eschatological vision of God." See his "Black Preaching Praxis," 216.

3. It is important to note that the distinction between insider and outsider in Mark's Gospel "is not a matter of social status or role but of response to Jesus." Malbon, "Narrative Criticism," 23.

understand, or repent. After recounting several other parables of God's reign later in the same chapter, Mark explains that Jesus did indeed speak with many such parables "as they were able to hear it" and that he spoke only in parables, explaining everything privately to his disciples (4:33–34). Whereas the first allusion to Jesus' parabolic preaching in 4:11–12 addresses the hidden dimensions of parabolic speech, the latter in 4:33–34 speaks to the communicative potential of it.[4] Together, the entire chapter speaks of both the hidden and revealed nature of Jesus' proclamation-a mysterious and parabolic means of inviting listeners to engage in God's reign. In the words of Ben Witherington III, "The parables give insight to the open-minded but come as a judgment on the obdurate. Precisely because of their figurative and metaphorical character, the parables, like the poetic character of much prophecy, are intentionally multivalent, or at least can function in various ways depending on the receptivity, or lack thereof, of the audience."[5]

Two other features are significant in our consideration of Mark 4:11–12. First, a great deal may be gleaned from an appreciation of the literary and historical context of the quote Jesus recalls from Isaiah 6:9–10. It immediately follows the prophet's having been cleansed by a live coal touched to his mouth and God having called him to ministry (6:6–8). Isaiah responds robustly, "Here I am; send me!" after which God tells him to say to the people, "Hear but don't understand; see but don't perceive." In the context of Judah's imminent demise at the hands of the Assyrians (which the prophet understands to be divine judgment), Isaiah is commanded to speak an alarming message to his people that will continue to echo beyond his present context to their future downfall at the hands of the Babylonians and subsequent exile. The prophet's troublesome words appear not only to announce what is coming but to set in motion future events. However, according to Witherington, prophetic concern and compassion are also evident in the surrounding verses. Isaiah pleads with God on behalf of his people, "How long, O Lord?" (6:11) and is subsequently instructed by God to interact with King Ahaz of Judah on their behalf (ch. 7), suggesting that "The function of the hardening is not to prevent repentance but rather to make clear the need for it. The function of the obscure speech is make clear that Israel is in a state of sin, alienated from God, and desperately needs to repent."[6]

4. Hays, *Echoes of Scripture*, 99.

5. Witherington, *Isaiah Old and New*, 67.

6. Ibid., 61. Witherington's interpretation is in contrast to that of Brevard Childs who argues that the prophet's words are intended to "dull their minds, stop their ears, and plaster over their eyes, unless by seeing, hearing, and comprehending, they might actually repent and be saved" (as quoted by Witherington, 61).

Other passages in Isaiah (particularly in 1 Isaiah, chs.1–39) continue to develop these themes as the prophet speaks of the confounding nature of God's precepts (28:11–13; 29:9) and of people not seeing or hearing what God is doing and speaking (21:3b; 28:23; 30:9–10) until God's ways are revealed and accepted (29:18ff). With hopefulness, the prophet speaks of just and righteous rulers to come and a time when the people's eyes and ears will be opened at last (32:1–3; 35:5), a call that Jesus continues through his many pleas to listen and look, to see God's reign and hear the words he sows among us. In other words, Jesus, like his prophetic precursor Isaiah, draws upon figurative language and imagery to speak to the crises and challenges of his time and people. Divine judgments issued by Isaiah reverberate long after the Babylonian exile as Jesus struggles to explain the mystery of why so many seeds fail while others take root and grow (4:13–20). He also calls people to listen and look anew for signs of God's hope by engaging more deeply in the parabolic and paradoxical nature of divine hiddenness and revelation. Clearly, Jesus adapts images and ideas from Isaiah's prophesies to his listeners' situation.

Second, Jesus' way of inviting others to recognize and encourage God's reign among us in Mark 4 includes multiple expressions of homiletical engagement. According to Mark's Gospel, he speaks a parable to the crowd by the sea (vv.1–9), responds to the questions of his closest followers about the parables he preaches (vv. 10–12, drawing on images, rhetorical themes and phrases from Isaiah), then proceeds to offer a more detailed, allegorical exploration of the parable (vv. 13–20). It is tempting to see vv.13–20 as offering a simple one-to-one correlation between seeds and the activities of the soils that deny or promote their growth (and various scholars have disputed the passivity and agency of the soils in which the seeds have fallen).[7] But if we recall the fuller process at work in this chapter, Mark seems less interested in offering a definitive understanding of the various seeds and soils and more interested in addressing his listeners through a consideration of diverse layers of textual (i.e., Isaian), rhetorical (i.e., parable, wisdom-teaching, allegory), and interpersonal engagement afforded by his multi-faceted proclamation of God's reign (including the numerous other parables of God's reindom presented in Mark 4:21–32, intended for both "insider" and "outsider"). There are parallel processes at work in this chapter spanning historical epochs (pre-and post-exilic periods), the inter-

---

7. For example, Tolbert, *Sowing the Gospel*, 161–64 and 297–99, argues for the productive agency of the soil that is responsible for the seed's growth or demise, whereas Don Juel in "Encountering," 278, insists that "soil is a passive image" and "Jesus' parable includes no imperatives–except for the command to 'listen' (4:9). The parable simply describes how things are."

textual presentation of sources (Hebrew prophets and the Markan account) as well as differing modes of homiletical discourse (parable in vv.1–9, Isaian interpretive segment in vv. 10–12, allegorical interpretation in vv.13–20, alternative depictions of divine rule through other parables in vv. 21–32, and summation of Jesus' homiletical method in vv.33f). All of these reflect a homiletical texture to this passage, dynamic engagement with audiences past, present, and future, and divine confidence in our ongoing encounter with God whose presence and ways are sometimes mysterious and hidden but anticipate further opportunities for discourse and disclosure are anticipated.

ENCOUNTER, RE-ENCOUNTER, AND PRE-ENCOUNTER IN THE HOMILETIC OF DALE ANDREWS

At the heart of Dale's homiletical method is an insistence that "the preaching event occurs in the hearing and response."[8] That is, just as the preacher encounters or hears God's self-revelation during the process of sermon preparation and then responds to this in the activity of preaching, so does the sermon become both a re-encounter for the preacher and an occasion for the worshiping community to encounter some form of the original phenomenological experience that the preacher has already had with God. Together in worship, the faith community and the preacher experience in parallel fashion a divine-human encounter and re-encounter; one that is not manufactured by the preacher but engendered by God as the worshiping community participates in "a communal experience of revelation and meaning making."[9]

This dynamic, relational model of divine-human encounter and re-encounter that Andrews outlines also affords teachers of homiletics the opportunity for further reflection with their students as they consider the communicative and expressive dimensions of the sermons they have preached, what Andrews calls "pre-encounter" (i.e., in anticipation of what the preacher may do differently or similarly in future sermons).[10] Through a

---

8. Andrews, "Black Preaching Praxis," 213.

9. Ibid, 216.

10. This description of encounter, re-encounter, and pre-encounter is based on a lecture by Dale Andrews shared on 4 January 2016 at Vanderbilt University Divinity School for Colloquy 3 of the *David G. Buttrick Homiletic Peer Coaching Training*. The circles of parallel learning encompassed in this program mirror the process of critical self–reflection and peer interaction (led by trained homiletical coaches) and incorporates inductive and reflexive patterns of review, assessment, and pastoral insight into the formation of the preacher and the preacher's sermon(s).

self-reflective, inductive, and critical approach to each student's case studies and sermons within a supervised peer group, opportunities arise for greater self-awareness, theological insight, and identifying alternative modes of expression that may contribute to the preacher's continued development and the formation of future sermons. This distinctly reflexive and cyclical process invites an ongoing hearing and response between God and people, preachers and listeners, inviting opportunities for better understanding and engaging with God's mysterious presence among us. The pastoral and prophetic are also bridged through divine-human and human-human discourse: this sacred "touch" is not only evident to those who have been privileged to witness Dale's preaching and teaching but to those who have immersed themselves in this shared process of attending to the questions that arise as we critically reflect on the preacher's and participants' encounters with God, Scripture, theology, their cultural context, and others in the preaching moment. In this way, pastoral wisdom and prophetic passion are not adversaries but allies, creating a necessary dialectic in preaching that explores, invites, and encourages God's mysterious, multivalent ways in the world.

To be sure, the experience of critical review and reflection on the preacher's encounter with God and re-encounter in the sermon is not only revelatory, inspiring, and mysterious but also at times confounding. There are moments when the preacher or group does not know the way forward: just as the disciples did not always understand or receive what Jesus proclaimed and they needed more than one way to interpret and understand his words, so does Andrews' homiletical method invite opportunities for multiple layers of meaning or processes to unfold-sometimes within the preacher's own self-reflection, at other times through the observations and questions of peers and the homiletical coach, through examining a case study from the preacher's pastoral context, exploring the preacher's theological frames of reference and/or cultural codes, delving into layers of biblical exegesis, presentation of personal stories and/or public events, etc.

Andrews is clear that the roots of this pastoral-prophetic dialectic are deeply embedded in a Black hermeneutic that includes not only "call and response" but assumes the Word of God living among the people of God who hear this living word in Scripture and through their past and present experiences of oppression, resilience, and liberative hope.[11] Andrews identifies preaching in the faith community as one of four cornerstones of a Black hermeneutic,[12] with the other three encompassing the Word of God

---

11. Andrews, "Black Preaching Praxis," 211–20.
12. Ibid., 211–22.

(i.e., the Bible and its myriad ancestral faith narratives, wisdom literature, and Gospel narratives),[13] preaching as telling the story (i.e., uniting the stories of the ancestors in Scripture with the story/ies of the hearers), and the manner of interpretation (i.e., involving forms of expression, embodiment, and rhetorical strategies that seek to persuade and apply biblical narratives to everyday Black life).

In all of these, the preacher serves as divine agent: one who sows seeds and participates in Jesus' ministry of proclaiming the living words of God among us. It is a mysterious ministry, to be sure. But winding through divine presence and absence, sacred justice and human injustice, parabolic and paradoxical discourse, three inter-related facets of Andrews' homiletical method call forth our continuing encounter and re-encounter with God:

First, it is deeply dialogical and inductive. Trusting in divine-human encounters, Dale's method seeks myriad opportunities for continued dialogue and exploration. Like the parables of Jesus that "tease the mind into active thought"[14] and throw one reality alongside another (the literal meaning of the Greek word παραβολὴ, parabolē), Andrews invites us to honor our encounters with God as sacred events and to share something of that with others through the preaching moment, inviting further reflection and conversation. Further, the reflective process that follows in the model of homiletical coaching and teaching that Andrews developed is keenly inductive, never assuming what the preacher needs to hear or learn but probing carefully and faithfully toward what the preacher can and will develop in her/his future preaching. It is an approach that trusts divine agency amid human struggles, hopes, and creative endeavors, as we seek to listen and hear, speak forth and question one another in ways that prompt both preachers and listeners to more fully recognize God's purposes among us. In this way, the sermon is never the last word but a continuation of divine-human encounter that seeks further authentic encounters with others.

Second, Andrews' method of encounter, re-encounter, and pre-encounter is dynamic, ongoing, and cyclical. It reflects layers of critical reflection (both self-and group-generated), pastoral and prophetic interest, and theological-cultural-biblical-inner/interpersonal reflection.[15] Parallel pro-

---

13. Andrews further lists six biblical themes highlighted by Black preaching praxis, including: the sovereignty of God, creation, exodus from slavery, conversion, the suffering of Jesus, and reigndom or kin-dom or God. Ibid., 214–16.

14. Dodd, *Parables of the Kingdom*, 16.

15. Andrews' method was developed in conversation with his long–time colleague John S. McClure whose work on the scriptural, semantic, theosymbolic, and cultural codes in preaching greatly contributed to the range and depth of Dale's critical reflection on homiletical theory and practice. See John S. McClure, *Four Codes*. Also, Cooper

cessing arises in the classroom when small groups of students ask questions of the preacher to aid his/her insight and self-reflection (not to offer critique or suggestions) while the teacher attends to the group's questions and interests. In the case of homiletical peer coaching groups, the teacher observes the coach's leadership and direction of the peer group of preachers and queries the coach about his/her own responses and reactions to the group as well. Encompassing pastoral case studies and sermons, the process seeks continuity between the person of the preacher and the sermon preached, addressing the questions, struggles, fears, and hopes of the preacher as s/he engages in preaching. The cyclical character of this process is evident in the continuous flow of questions and observations, never content with one moment of holy-human exchange but returning to the pulpit and later to the group to consider each sermon anew, to seek and be sought by God, to listen and respond to Scripture, people, culture, and congregation. It is a process that seeks glimpses and soundings of divine presence and guidance even as preachers and group participants recognize the sometimes elusive, often mysterious and generative nature of divine-human and human-human encounters.

Third and perhaps most importantly, Andrews' method is profoundly relational. Indeed, the very word "encounter" calls to mind a meeting between two or more bodies/people. More than an "experience," the word "encounter" suggests being met by and meeting with another. It holds the potential of bringing our hearts, souls, minds, and bodies to our critical and caring conversations with others, even as we seek to attend to their words and well-being also. The value placed on the relational aspects of preaching and teaching encourages bridges to be built between us, crafted by the efforts of all participants through ongoing discourse and dialogical engagement. Andrews' model is profoundly relational in that it invites us to consider the possibilities of how preachers and listeners may hear God and one another, listening for and to each other in an ongoing conversation that develops not only better preaching but greater understanding of ourselves and others in relationships of mutual edification and understanding. In the presence of the living Christ, this encounter (as well as re-encounter and pre-encounter) is reciprocal and loving, seeking the development of ourselves and others through support and challenge, attentive listening and careful response.

There is certainly an element of mystery involved in these holy exchanges-something that the preacher, congregation, teacher, and/or peer reflection group cannot anticipate or control before, during, or after the

---

and McClure, *Claiming Theology*.

sermon. For many mainline preachers, churches, seminaries and divinity schools, these mysterious divine-human and human-human encounters are seldom explored or even recognized beyond vague references to what was "meaningful" or "moving" in the preaching moment. But Andrews has identified this mystery at the heart of preaching and integrated it into the processes involved in preparing, sharing, and reflecting upon sermons in the presence of God and others. His approach is not meant to replace the careful theological, rhetorical, and methodological approaches to homiletical theory and practice but to infuse, inform, and even transform them as the church and academy seek to form and fortify future preachers. I would add that this endeavor is at the heart of the gospel itself, akin to Jesus' innumerable efforts to convey something of God's reign and purposes among us by casting seeds of God's Word and considering their potential growth and demise, divine mystery and human hope, calling us to just and loving relationships with creation, its creatures, and Creator.

IMPLICATIONS FOR FURTHER HOMILETICAL REFLECTION AND PRACTICE

For years as a teacher of homiletics, I have led and engaged in small group reflection and feedback processes at my seminary that are largely inductive, communal, and dialogical in nature, inviting students to critically and carefully engage one another in reflecting on their sermons and what they encountered while preparing, preaching and listening to one another in the preaching moment.[16] In our current North American context and at a time when so many of my students come from diverse settings, life experiences, and theological perspectives (spanning very different political and ideological commitments, geographical areas, cultural upbringings, denominational/religious identities, spiritual-religious journeys and experiences), it has become all the more important to find ways of engaging people who may be interested in and curious about religious faith and practices but are not necessarily biblically literate and ecclesially formed (i.e., aware of and understand church teachings and re/sources). Some are keenly curious about the ideas and spiritual interests of others and a few want to learn

---

16. I am a faculty member of Bethany Theological Seminary, affiliated with the Church of the Brethren, which is of Anabaptist–Pietist heritage. As such, we emphasize the ways in which Spirit moves through community, how Jesus Christ calls us to discipleship and service, and God is active and purposeful in the church and world. See Bethany Theological Seminary, "Mission Statement." The seminary's mission and goals are in keeping with the core values of the Church of the Brethren expressed in the denominational tagline, "Continuing the work of Jesus: Peacefully, Simply, Together."

how better to express what they already know/believe. Many of my students wonder what preaching "means" in a time when fewer people attend worship and they themselves are drawn to ministries of service beyond the walls of church sanctuaries.

I hear students describe their interest in "spiritual life" which, when questioned, seems to encompass select Judeo-Christian values and rituals, spiritual journeys, questions, experiences, and/or unresolved struggles that motivate their interest and sense of calling. Near the beginning of the semester, I find it helpful to ask my students what it is they know or believe about God at this particular moment in time. Then I ask them to take a few minutes to silently reflect on how they came to know or believe this.[17] It is an exercise that often evokes intensely personal memories of divine-human, human-human, or even nature-human encounter. Those who choose to share these aloud risk disclosing something of the mystery of God's presence or absence in their lives, encounters of hope and despair, love and fear. These disclosures set the tone for subsequent sharing that bridges personal testimony and corporate trust, providing moments of divine-human and human-human encounter and re-encounter in the classroom that carry over into future conversations that invite more critical-reflective modes of theological, socio-cultural, and inner-personal analysis. Beginning where people are and remembering that divine-human encounters are not always dramatic or immediately apparent (i.e., we sometimes recognize God's presence or movement in retrospect), it is often helpful to recall the ways that God has "spoken" to or addressed us through Scripture, crises, family and friends, neighbors and enemies, nature, work, etc.

In the coming year, I will be teaching a joint classroom of students from the U.S. and our sister-church Ekklesiyar Yan'uwa a Nigeria (EYN), connecting a technological classroom in my home seminary in Richmond, Indiana with a similar technology classroom recently constructed in Jos, Nigeria. With many of our Nigerian brothers and sisters having suffered the destruction of their churches, the murder of their pastors, the abduction and rape of dozens of their members at the hands of Boko Haram, my U.S. colleagues and I are humbled at the prospect of joining with members of EYN to listen and learn together what it means to share the gospel of Jesus Christ in our churches and communities. God knows, I wish my brother and colleague Dale was around to talk with me about how best to proceed in this endeavor. But I bring with me his lively commitment to listen carefully

---

17. This activity represents a modified version of a much fuller exercise developed and described by Frank A. Thomas, including time for students to share their thoughts aloud in response to the question, How did you come to know what you believe most deeply about the character of God? See Thomas, *Introduction to the Practice* 123.

to the ways each student and preacher encounters God, how they and others encounter and re-counter God in preaching, and what we will call forth from one another as we seek to listen for God's vision and voice among us. My suspicion is that the dialogical, inductive, dynamic and relational model of homiletical reflection developed by Dale will provide a helpful grounding in whatever modes of critical reflection on Scripture, theology, culture and inter-personal dynamics we may develop. We will trust in the mystery of God's presence and purposes among us, building bridges that span our efforts to listen and learn from God and one another.

20

"The Thursday After"
The Crisis of Formation in the Post-Election Theological Classroom

SHELLY RAMBO

As MINISTERIAL WAVES RIPPLED over social media the Sunday after the presidential election in November 2016, asking "What do we preach?" theological educators were wrestling with a similar question, "What do we teach?" Both held expectations that theology had something to say, that it could speak meaning/meaningfully to the moment. But the Thursday after the election in the "Feminist and Womanist Theologies" course I taught, wounds surfaced. There was a surfacing of mistrust within this theological community, a palpable sense that the rift between the theological worlds of white students and students of color was irreparable. It was as if someone ripped off a bandage, only to reveal a cut, still alive and active. Tensions surfaced, revealing dynamics that often remain below the surface of institutional life. On that Thursday after the election, a space opened up, and several students begin to speak raw unfiltered words. The class appeared more divisive this Thursday. But the wounds were already there.[1] They were undeniably present on that day.

---

1. Willie Jennings writes: "The deep wound of our racial history has never passed—no one in America lives without it." Jennings, "What Does It Mean?"

We turned to the feminist and womanist discourse—the course material itself—to provide a container of ideas for what was happening. Students reached for insights from the authors whom we studied. Analysis of systemic racism was part of our study. Our academic foremothers offered cogent and impassioned descriptions and diagnoses. With their help, it was not difficult for us to analyze the ways in which predominantly white theological institutions operate. And yet something was still missing. Our faith in theological institutions to move theology effectively to contend with racial histories was thin. As a theological educator, I replayed the theological moves most familiar to progressive Protestants. But these moves did not make sense in this room—not in this moment.

I came to recognize this missing piece as a gap in *theological formation*. This moment in American life, this surfacing of wounds and the manipulation of wounded histories, signals a long-overdue inquiry into unattended aspects of institutional life. It brings me to my pedagogical limits and presses for a new orientation to the work of theology more broadly. Bringing together insights from the contemporary study of trauma and black theology in this essay, I suggest that this missing link of formation may be best forged by what Dale P. Andrews proposes in the developing methodologies within black practical theology.[2]

TRAUMA AND RACE

"The wound is in me, as complex and deep in my flesh as blood and nerves."[3]
—WENDELL BERRY

Contemporary studies in trauma help us diagnose the present climate of public life in the United States, a climate in which theological institutions are situated. When trauma studies expanded into an interdisciplinary venture in the 1990s, the diagnostic frame became a jumping point for insights about how overwhelming violence impacts persons and communities and transmits across generations. The altered temporality and the distortions of memory narrated in traumatic experiences press us to rethink how histories of oppression function.

History haunts the present. The effects of violence do not *simply* go away. Instead, they live on in ways that are not readily visible to the eye. The wounds, nonetheless, remain and reside below the surface of the nation's collective skin. This diagnostics of how trauma works in individual bodies

---

2. Andrews and Smith, *Black Practical Theology*.
3. Berry, *Hidden Wound*, 4.

and collective bodies, even the national body, expanded to take into account the insidious dimensions of systemic racism in America. Moving beyond analysis of single-event trauma, scholars began to reflect on the ongoing effects of racialized violence, stemming from histories of violence continuously covered over by those who perpetrated the harm. Beloved, the ghost in Toni Morrison's novel, figures the ongoing presence of the wounds of racial histories.[4] Although the wounds are not visible, they nonetheless live below the surface of the nation's collective skin. Beloved returns, haunting the present, signaling the work of reckoning, white America for the harms done and black America for the effects of harm they carry forward in the present.[5]

Racism is like a collective wound that is not always evidenced on the surface of everyday life but nonetheless operates to shape it. Small gestures, slight turns of phrase, side-glances are symptoms of this untended wound. It provides a way of accounting for America's failure to come to terms with histories of violence enacted on enslaved black peoples. The intentional forgetting on the part of white America and the erasure of memories enacted in modes of black survival attests to the temporality of trauma. It also resonates with the insight in trauma that what is not integrated returns. The unintegrated past returns in a different context, which makes it difficult to address harms done.

Neurobiological insights reveal that traumatic experiences are registered in the fight/flight part of our brain. A shutdown in the high-order cognitive arena challenges cognitively oriented therapies and the assumption that persons can provide words and narratives for the experience. You cannot simply talk out trauma. Trauma lives in the body. This somatic turn in clinical treatment also shifts the epistemological locus for other disciplines. What does it mean to *know*, or, more fittingly, to *not know*? Cognition, and even intention, will not touch the trauma that lives inside of bodies. What is required to receive or register those histories lies outside of the grasp of the intellect. Trauma studies turns attention to body knowledge and summons us to conceive of bodies as sites of truth and truth-telling.

The concept of witness and what it means to witness these histories turns us to bodily witness, to register movements and track affect. If one is attuned to trauma, one will be attuned to what is unsaid, to fragmented language, and to the somatic and sensory register of life. Although the dimension of witness describes self-witness (witness of one's own experience and survival), the need for a reconnecting presence, for external witnesses,

---

4. Morrison, *Beloved*.
5. This resonates with Cone's observations in his *Cross and Lynching Tree*.

is critical. To work through these wounds will take a different set of skills. To access them requires careful and attentive work. Those who intentionally take up the task of witness need to be retooled and formed differently. They must be positioned differently. This requires the cultivation of ways of seeing and of practices for acknowledging memories that remain lodged in bodies.

On this "Thursday after," wounds surfaced. For some students in the class, the election made visible longstanding dynamics operating within predominantly white institutions. For them, there was a palpable sense of relief that the curtain was pulled back and the mechanics of white privilege and power were exposed. It is a privilege *not to see*. This surfacing of the wounded and distorted architecture was a welcomed confrontation. White America has to stare into the mirror and see herself for the wounding that she has enacted. For white students, and for me, there was immobility at the limits of "liberal" good intentions and a shedding of a cognitive righteousness that we held in place to distinguish us from "less-illuminated" peers. As a white professor, it turned me away from the question, "What will I say?" and, instead, to the question, "How do I witness the complexities of what is taking place, as a theologian responsible to the theological enterprise within the United States?" Theological schools claim formation as an essential ingredient of theological education, and yet discussions of formation rarely reach below the surface of things.[6] If we take into account the impact of histories of violence in the doing of theology, it will require skills and capacities that come about through reconfigured processes of formation.

CHRISTIAN THEOLOGY'S FORMATION PROBLEM

"I have watched with a sense of melancholy the formation process of Christian intellectuals."[7]
—WILLIE JAMES JENNINGS

---

6. The major accrediting body for theological schools in North America is The Association of Theological Schools. Their guidelines for the Master of Divinity Degree include formation: "A.2.4–Personal and spiritual formation: The program shall provide opportunities through which the student may grow in personal faith, emotional maturity, moral integrity, and public witness. Ministerial preparation includes concern with the development of capacities—intellectual and affective, individual and corporate, ecclesial and public—that are requisite to a life of pastoral leadership." Association of Theological Schools, "The Commission on Accrediting."

7. Jennings, *Christian Imagination* 7.

Black theologians offer critiques and re-workings of Christian theological claims and methods. However, more recently, theologians offer sharp expositions of the *formational* enterprise of Christian theology that speak directly to this "Thursday after" gap. They reflect a post-traumatic sensibility in their appeals to other modes of knowing and attention to unexamined dynamics within the everyday operations of theological institutions. They provide a compelling diagnosis of the impasse of theologies to come to terms with the theological enterprise as raced. Coming to terms will require a change of heart and body, not merely a shift in intellect.

In *The Cross and the Lynching Tree*, James Cone describes the limitations of theologian Reinhold Niebuhr with respect to race.[8] He notes that while Niebuhr's logic of the cross was compelling—even brilliant—Niebuhr remained unable to connect his analysis to the realities of black suffering. There was something lacking in his posture. Why, Cone asks, did Niebuhr not see?[9] Cone identifies this failure on the level of feeling and affect. Niebuhr's logic of divine suffering did not move him to see the suffering around him. The problem was not a problem of cognition but, rather, an inability to *feel* the suffering, to be moved by it. Niebuhr, he writes, "missed an opportunity to move into the river of the black experience."[10] The exercises of theologizing as they were carried out did not facilitate a posture of responsiveness. This posture would require a process of personal and institutional examination about what constitutes theological knowledge. Cone suggests that logic alone does not facilitate the connection. It does not move the white theologian to respond. Cone concludes that the limitation was a limitation of the imagination, what Cone describes as a combination of aesthetics and affect. One needs to cultivate a "theological imagination" capable of witnessing suffering; this imagination is a way of seeing that can hold together tragedy and beauty.[11] It is a logic, according to Cone, but it is a paradoxical logic achieved only by wedding heart and head.[12]

Willie James Jennings opens *The Christian Imagination* with stories of disjunctions similar to the one that Cone narrates of Niebuhr. Inviting

---

8. Cone, *Cross and the Lynching Tree*, 30–64.

9. Cone writes: "Why did Niebuhr fail to connect Jesus' cross to the most obvious cross bearers in American society?" Ibid., 38.

10. Ibid., 47.

11. Ibid., 48.

12. Cone fluctuates between saying that imagination is something that someone possesses and something that must be cultivated. This distinction is important, I think, because the cultivation suggests a process of formation that all, if attentive to it, can develop. When he discusses certain figures, such as Martin Luther King Jr., he suggests that King possesses this imagination. Cone turns away from cultivation language.

readers into two autobiographical moments, Jennings asks the chilling question, "Why did they not know me?"[13] White Christian performances conveyed a lack of awareness about how the words landed, reflecting unexamined ways of being and thinking. Jennings insists on staying with the strangeness of the encounters, with the dissonance he experienced, a young black Christian and later theology student, when men within the dominant ministerial and educational culture assumed knowledge of him. They assumed knowledge without authentic recognition, by folding him into their knowledge worlds. This folding occurred by way of small and subtle practices, brief conversations and clips that represented a deeper problem difficult to detect. Jennings attempts to interpret these moments and the subtlety in these encounters in order to get at their root. Jennings' diagnosis is that western Christianity operates within a "diseased social imagination."[14] He attempts to trace the history of Christian theology as rooted in the soil of colonial operations of modernity, drawing out the contradictions in word and practice. Jennings is trying to unearth and surface "the constellation of generative forces that have rendered people's social performances of the Christian life collectively anemic."[15] The container for these forces is the realm of the imaginary. Whereas words and professions convey one thing, gestures convey another. The imaginary accounts for the combination of words, expressions, wishes, and desires. If we consider this broader network of formation, we will be able to diagnose how academic cultures function and facilitate an inability to recognize its practices of insidious racism.

The everyday practices of not seeing and not knowing, exercised by white theologians, creates identities that remain unquestioned. Evaluative weight is placed on particular performances of the intellect, those that hover above the soil of history.[16] What Jennings describes is an intentional forgetting of place that Christian theology performs. The erasure of the particular in the quest for the universal, the practical in quest of the theoretical, is not just a division of disciplines within the theological school. It is laced with dreams of racial hierarchy. What is recognized as the normative fabric of theological life is constituted by a forgetting. Without mechanisms to regis-

13. Jennings, *Christian Imagination* 4.
14. Ibid., 6.
15. Ibid.
16. Jennings provides the image of theological production as one being done from the "commanding heights," as positioned above the soil of history, as if to map realities without having to acknowledge the situatedness of its own inquiry. Theology, in its modern manifestations, operates as if it is divorced from its own history, as a discourse located in a particular time and place. The product of this inquiry is thus assumed to be ahistorical and universal. *Christian Imagination*, 7.

ter what lies below the surface of the institutional skin, academic life persists in its anemic state. According to Jennings, as long as Christian theology fails to come to terms with its colonialist roots, it will operate with the blindspots and disjunctions that do damage over time. On the surface, all looks well. But the wounds remain, always below the surface of theology's skin.

Phillis Sheppard sounds her call for womanist-lesbian pastoral ethics from the post-election classroom.[17] Reflecting on the "Thursday after" classroom, Sheppard exposes the limitations of present pedagogical strategies within theological institutions. Adeptly revealing her own pedagogical inadequacies to interpret all of the dynamics in play on that day, she analyzes the ruptures taking place during the post-election classroom discussion. The discussion was "more akin to an unplanned, un-sacramental ritual" and the "dialogue was subject to the pull of disintegration."[18] Sheppard's work is distinctive for its acknowledgment of the psychic impact of insidious trauma.[19] Eyes wide open to the ways in which "political forces take up residence in systemic structures," she is attuned, as a womanist, to the impact on black women.[20] And yet she expands womanist discourse by placing particular emphasis on how the psyche is impacted by these forces. With emphasis on the external conditions and the status of black women in society, Sheppard notes that womanist reflections can ignore the ways in which black women internalize the views of dominant cultures. She calls for an ethics that also accounts for the ways in which "the psyche is assaulted."[21] She sheds light on the toll of such performances, particularly for students of color. And yet Sheppard's eye is on the larger task of theological education. Her attention to these psychic operations helps us understand how much is going on in the post-election classroom and how cursory analysis must expand into an ethical positioning if the wounds are to be touched and potentially transformed.

Each theologian points to the limitations of Christian theological education, contributing to the diagnosis of the situation we found ourselves in on post-election Thursday. If theological schools are going to have transformative dialogue about privilege and race in this volatile period of history, theological ideas alone will not carry us forward. In fact, they may, in many cases, be getting in the way of important formative work. They point to the arenas of what is unsaid, to what cannot be spoken, and to modes of

---

17. Sheppard, "Womanist-Lesbian Pastoral Ethics," 152–70.
18. Ibid., 157.
19. Sheppard, *Self, Culture, and Others*.
20. Ibid., 161.
21. Ibid.

observation that require reading below the surface of things. They think long-term about the cultivation of habits that prepare us for disruptive moments and point to practices and processes that cultivate certain habits of mind *and* heart. In short, they identify the problem as one of *formation*. The vocabulary shifts to terms familiar to the study of trauma. What are the conditions in which theological education is occurring? What do the spaces of education look like, smell like, and feel like? How are bodies moving in the hallways? Who takes up space and who retreats? The questions seem incidental, but, in fact, these theologians suggest that by discounting these, "intellectual and pedagogical performances" remain unexamined.[22]

BLACK PRACTICAL THEOLOGY

While these theologians diagnose the formational limitations of theological institutions, an alternative formational process may come about through the developing methodologies of black practical theology. In his early scholarly work, Dale P. Andrews identifies a chasm between black theology and black churches, between the liberative project of black theologians and the black ministerial project of grounding identity and faith. In *Practical Theology for Black Churches,* he traces the relationship between the two, as a kind of sibling relationship in which both will the thriving of black communities and yet rival for ways of bringing that about. Gaining status within the academy, black theology forged a "prophetic national and international voice."[23] This prophetic call, however, was more complicated to live out within black church settings. Black churches provided a home for black communities who were seeking identity and refuge. Black theology's work was perceived as "explicitly disruptive" by many black churches and appeared to threaten the project of grounding black faith; thus, an "adversarial dialectic" emerged.[24] It has resulted in inaccurate representations and a lack of generosity, with misunderstanding on both sides.[25] The language of misunderstanding, pain, tension, and a potential break in relationship is of concern to Andrews, who does not dismiss the tensions but, instead, works with them.

Andrews' practical theology is adept "in-house" work—deeply relational work—to draw out the best of both black churches and black theology and to facilitate understanding and appreciation between them. Both have not adequately recognized the impact of American cultural forces shaping

---

22. Jennings, *Christian Imagination*, 7.
23. Andrews, *Practical Theology*, 84.
24. Ibid.
25. Ibid.

black churches, Andrews notes.[26] There are factors at work that, if understood, would facilitate understanding. While they seem at odds, Andrews claims that the chasm between black churches and black theology, as it is carried out in the academy, can be bridged. He proposes a bridging between the pastoral and the prophetic, the postures of refuge and liberation, by remodeling ecclesiology.

Andrews carries forward this work by developing a bridging methodology in collaboration with Robert London Smith Jr. and multiple dialogical partners.[27] While the focus of Andrews' work has been on black ecclesiology, his proposal transfers to diagnosing the relational dynamics within the predominantly white theological institutions in which students of color find themselves. Andrews situates the work *within* the academy so that this future set of academicians will simply repeat the problems that he outlines in his first work. These students will read the critiques of liberation theologians, but they will default to preexisting methodologies and modes of intellectual thinking. Unless a different mode of inquiry and practice is developed, the infrastructure of theological education in its "pedagogical performances" will continue to fold matters of race into existing approaches.[28] And present modes and patterns will not move us in this post-election room.[29]

The theological institution is a site for practical theological analysis. The combination of the prophetic and the pastoral that Andrews proposes is a cultivated skill-set. Andrews' operationalized black practical theology—his institutional presence—positioned him close to the surface of institutional skin. He carried out his work attuned to the invisible wounds of epistemological racism that function below the surface of white theological education. His work recognizes the thin, almost imperceptible, needles that thread the fabric of white institutions and keeps in view what often recedes from view through thick analysis of the locations and movements of academics. Andrews carried out his work attuned to the architecture and workings of theological institutions by investing time in observing deliberations in faculty meetings, in advising meetings with doctoral students,

26. Ibid., 11.
27. Andrews and Smith, eds., *Black Practical Theology*.
28. Jennings, *Christian Imagination*, 7.
29. In my book, *Resurrecting Wounds*, I interpret the Upper Room scene in John 20 in light of the current U.S. dynamics of race and racial wounding. Dale Andrews was instrumental, in the early drafting stage, in helping me confront some of my assumptions about how the contemporary "Upper Room" is constituted in terms of white privilege. As a homiletician, he challenged me to think about how I would preach the Upper Room passage today.

in tenure decisions, etc. The pastoral and prophetic combination is about staying in the work and refusing to hover above the surface of everyday institutional operations.

But this is not an individual skill-set. It is a developing methodology for practical theology. It is dialogical, reflexive, and attentive to formation. In their longitudinal studies of spiritual development, Ian Todd Williamson and Steven J. Sandage claim that theological education is carried out through processes of "spiritual dwelling and spiritual seeking."[30] Within the seminary context, students engage in practices that both ground them in particular religious traditions and also challenge prior understandings of the sacred and encourage questioning.[31] When students enter theological institutions, they undergo a process of formation. The interplay between dwelling and questing leads to growth. But the process is not smooth. Growth occurs through the dialectic, but it often surfaces by way of tensions and disruptions. Theological educators can tend to locate and organize their teaching around *one*, while neglecting the importance of the other. These two poles, one of grounding (dwelling) and the other of risk (questing), resonates with the dynamic that Andrews speaks about as the combination of the pastoral and prophetic within black churches. The importance of linking Williamson/Sandage and Andrews is that spiritual growth and development is often interpreted as separate from the work of racial justice within seminaries, and it can even be distributed to particular areas of the curriculum. These scholars refuse this separation. The "dialectics of relational spirituality" and the methodology of black practical theology may signal ways forward for interpreting the "Thursday after" classrooms differently—as sites for spiritual growth.[32]

THEOLOGICAL POST-ELECTION BRIDGING

If we expect something productive to happen in theological classrooms, something beyond the present social performances, it will not come about by anything that we "say" in the moment. It will come about through deliberate attention to, and invocation of, processes and practices of learning

---

30. Williamson and Sandage, "Longitudinal Analysis" 788. This language was developed earlier in Schultz and Sandage, *Transforming Spirituality*.

31. Williamson and Sandage, "Longtitudinal Analysis:" "Seminaries represent an interesting context for studying relational spirituality because the seminary context can potentiate both spiritual dwelling and seeking in a highly religious context" (789). Cf. Sandage et. al. "Relational Spirituality," 182—201; Sandage and Jensen, "Relational Spiritual Formation."

32. Williamson and Sandage, "Longitudinal Analysis," 797.

communities. Andrews invites us to move away from thinking about how we respond in a given moment and turns us to the "reflexive ecology" of theological education.[33] By positioning the work of black practical theology on the surface of fragile institutional skin, Andrews does not underestimate the spiritual fortitude necessary to witness wounds as they break the surface. If theological institutions dare to do this work, bandages of intellectual thought applied to the surface must be removed.

"White people, do your work," was the message from one student who spoke up that Thursday. The implication was that white people should go away, retreat, huddle together, and contend with our histories. We nodded. It made sense to us. Why, after all, did students and faculty of color have to guide predominantly white institutions in this work? The work of guiding, as I was hearing it from the students, was exhausting. It took a toll on their psychic lives and their spiritual well-being. And yet this proposed retreat for white scholars did not seem right. I feared that with this retreat, the guiding methodologies of Andrews and Sheppard would be relegated to methodologies applicable only to academics of color. These methodologies operate dialogically, to potentially disrupt the familiar moves of white theologians and educators. They "hold instructive capacities" for transforming "Thursday after" classrooms.[34] If the sources of black theology and of black religious life are read, engaged, and methodologically mobilized within classrooms and theological institutions, what could happen? Until that happens, white theologians find ourselves at the site of the wound, performing familiar moves that continue to render the collective life anemic.

The realities of trauma tell us that there is no going back to life as it was before. Often in response to events of trauma, the calendar date becomes a marker for a departure into the unknown, into a new way of constructing life beyond that event. 9–11 for the turn to the new century. 11–9 for our moment. This insight that some things are irrecoverable is difficult news. But it may be the news that releases us from familiar postures in a room that generates only stale air. How do we change the postures? In Andrews' work, the bridging metaphor becomes a bridging methodology. His bridging metaphor, when carried superficially into this space, could be gravely misunderstood. But do not be fooled. It is not about accommodation. Instead, it is about transforming theological analysis altogether.

Start with reading the sources. Do not turn away from Delores Williams, he told me. Think *with* her. Honor her methodology. If we follow

---

33. Andrews and Smith, eds., *Black Practical Theology*, 4. "Firstly, we take 'praxis' to denote a kind of reflexive ecology encompassing religious practices and theology that is informed by theory and guided by values and ultimate purpose(s)" (4).

34. Andrews, "African American Practical Theology" 28.

Andrews closely, his eye never leaves the black community. He took the academy seriously as a primary site for the work, but this was first rooted in his love for black religious communities and the life-blood that he drew from them. A formidable institutional mentor, Andrews understood that his isolated bits of wisdom about how to disrupt dominant epistemologies and how to speak truth to the liberal Protestant elite could not, in the end, be tied to him as a solo figure. The insistence on developing a methodology worked against what Eddie Glaube describes as the "discourse of the hero" that is often a part of the culture of black leadership.[35] If that is released, perhaps, he speculates, it could lead to a politics of a collective, a coalition of witnesses that dedicate themselves to "tending wounds."[36] This was Ella Baker's way. Follow her, Andrews whispers.

---

35. See Glaude, "The Heroic," in the W.E.B. Du Bois Lecture Series, for his critique of the exemplary leader/solo hero in black religious thought.

36. Ibid.

PART 5

Prophetic Care: Particular Topics

21

The Importance of the Pastoral and the Prophetic

For Preaching among the Traumatized

TERESA LOCKHART EISENLOHR

> How does someone overcome the negative impact and internalization of abusive or traumatic experiences, images, and shame? Preaching, as well as pastoral counseling, presents opportunities for healing by helping persons to reframe, or "re-plot," their unfolding stories. This healing creates future possibilities and strengths for developing wholeness.[1]

"WHY IS IT THAT when my life took a tragic turn," a middle-class white main-line Protestant asks, "that I had to stumble half-dead into a African American church to find God?" When pressed for details, this woman, whom we'll call Sarah, went on to recount that during the time after her nineteen-year-old died from a drug overdose and her marriage of twenty-five years subsequently fell apart, she felt too ashamed to go to her predominately white Anglo-American church. "But I needed the church," Sarah said with tears in her eyes. So, upon invitation from a friend at work, she went to an AME Zion church ... and kept going. There, she could just sit in the back and cry. "It was ok to need God there," she said. "I mean, really, desperately,

---

1. Andrews, *Practical Theology* 29, citing Wimberly, *Moving from Shame*, 17–18.

need God." The music and the preaching ministered to her in a way that her own tradition did not during that time.

When asked specifically about what was different about the preaching of the two churches, Sarah thoughtfully compared and contrasted. Both were biblical, but they ultimately took different aims. Sermons in her white main-line church usually ended with a focus on what individuals, as part of the church, can do to make the world a better place in their day-to-day lives. Too often, she lamented, what it felt like she was called to do in order to be a good disciple of Christ was attend a church meeting on something tangentially related to God. But Sarah didn't have anything to give to anyone, and she wasn't getting anything from her church to give, either. So the last thing she needed was one more thing she couldn't get done on her to-do list for some inarticulate, supposedly divine, reason. Going to church made her feel worse, not better. On the other hand, the AME Zion church's preaching spoke to Sarah in such a way that she felt loved by God who empathized with her suffering and was there with her in it to bring about something new that would be good—not just for her, but for all people who are broken and sinful. That care in the midst of brokenness, along with a vision of eschatological hope, enabled her to see a better day coming and gave her the strength to not despair and stay sober without succumbing to her alcoholism that she feared had contributed to her son's death.

While we may suspect that the AME Zion church was playing the idealized role of Mammy during the time of this white woman's need, reality is more complicated and rich.[2] To dismiss the spiritual succor that the black church can offer to a fellow human being today because of a historically problematic socially-constructed unjust relationship would be to deny the transformative power of God at work in the world through the gifts of the African American church. Indeed, it is the uniqueness of the African American church's preaching traditions that offers us strategies for preaching among the traumatized, strategies that are both pastoral and prophetic, transcending all problematic human categories with a divine vision of God's compassion.

TO WHOM ARE WE PREACHING?

The first insightful gift that African American homiletics offers us involves the preacher's consideration of the presumed rhetorical audience. Whether consciously or not, one of the first things a speaker does in composing any public address is construct a presumed rhetorical audience based upon

---

2. Williams, *Sisters in the Wilderness*.

knowledge of specific persons and upon some universal notion of who will be in the audience.[3] Thus, homileticians require preaching students to know their audience through research and pastoral visits. This involves more than mere demographic labels. Instead, working like ethnographers, preachers probe into the values of people to ask questions like, "What does it mean that Aunt Mabel just drove up in a new matador-red Lexus wearing her beat-up Sunday hat?" While this may seem like an elementary exercise, it is exceedingly complex. A good pastor who knows Aunt Mabel will know that she bought the car used with proceeds from an unexpected inheritance. Otherwise, she'd have continued to drive her practical blue Chevy Impala until it died an agonizing death. Of course, the pastor who knows Aunt Mabel may not be given access to this information, either. A preacher who doesn't know Aunt Mable may presume that she is a rich, perhaps snobbish, woman just because she drives a Lexus. Because it's red and not a more conservative color, the same preacher might assume that she has a little sass in her when, in fact, it was the only color option available; Aunt Mabel is, by all accounts of mythical proportion, quite dour. This one protracted example is but a miniscule slice of the specific presumptions a preacher constructs not only for individual parishioners, but for an entire congregation. (And we never even got to her hat!) What's more, congregants are also shaped by a larger, more universal cultural world with varying degrees of shared values. In the church, the most universal construction of our rhetorical audience consists of an awareness of the communion of saints whose values we share as fellow citizens of God's Realm. All of this is to illustrate that, whether we are aware of it or not, preachers construct a presumed rhetorical audience for our sermons based on our knowledge (and lack thereof) and our prejudices.[4] In order for the gospel to gain a hearing, the preacher must know and respect the rhetorical audience gathered in the room while also working within the larger culture outside the sanctuary in order to point us to the largess of the world of God's grace that holds all within the firm tenderness of divine compassion.

Too often in white mainline Protestant churches, our presumed rhetorical audience is based on surface demographic knowledge without mining the deeper soul of a congregation. Historically, white mainline

---

3. Perelman and Olbrechts-Tyteca discuss the difficulties of this in *New Rhetoric*. See also Gross and Dearin, "A Theory of the Rhetorical Audience," 31–42.

4. Prejudice is being used here as Hans Georg Gadamer uses it in *Truth and Method*, as a set of assumptions by which we navigate our world based on past experiences. It is not necessarily a pejorative term, just a set of a priori assumptions that are often tacit. For more on preachers working as ethnographers, see Tisdale, *Preaching as Local Theology*.

Protestants have been the pillars of their communities. They look like they are the ones who have rock-solid lives. Consequently, the presumed rhetorical audience for the white main-line church is often constructed as a group of can-do people who have it all together. However, any pastor who listens to the people knows what a fallacy this is. Scratch the surface of most saintly parishioners' lives with a listening heart and what you find is brokenness, confusion, and a longing for a wholeness that eludes despite the external trappings of success by the world's standards.

So to whom are we really preaching? The African American church knows what the white church is only beginning to learn: we are preaching to a people shaped by various degrees of trauma. Even good suburban white church folks who've been ghettoed off in peculiar post-liberal communities are finding themselves in trauma. Trauma, here, is being defined as the aftermath of a world-shattering event. Ecclesially, the white mainline Protestant church is suffering from the trauma of no longer being who they once were—respected leaders who exercised their power in the shaping of our communities. The rather rapid decline of these churches, fueled by nasty theological infighting over issues of sexuality, has decimated these denominations and left them reeling and wrestling with who they are now—similar to what happens to individuals when they suffer a trauma.

On a personal level, trauma occurs when something you have depended upon for stability disappears so that it feels like you're trying to build a life during an earthquake with the ground beneath you roiling. Sometimes, however, it is not one earth-shattering experience that traumatizes. It could be a captivity in an unstable or abusive situation or even series of tragic events that just keep coming one after another without any time for healing in between, that leave one in trauma.[5] Trauma not only reshapes the external circumstances of our lives; it also changes our bodies. During a tragic event, the body's sympathetic nervous system prepares for fight or flight so that it can survive an imminent threat. Adrenaline comingles with fear and anxiety in a toxic cocktail that hinders rational thought as, on some level, you register how fragile life is and how vulnerable you are. For some, the somatic switch that gets turned on during times of trauma gets stuck in the open-throttle position and continues to wreak havoc long after the initial trauma has passed so that the nightmare of post-traumatic stress disorder becomes normative reality.

It is impossible now for even privileged white folks to ignore that we live in a culture shaped by trauma. Gun violence stalks our streets. Domestic violence shatters notions of having a safe haven. Rape has its own culture.

---

5. Herman, *Trauma*.

Tribal war lords terrorize while ISIS continues to gather adherents. Natural disasters are on the rise. And loved ones still die before their time. Veterans and sexual abuse survivors live with PTSD, an acronym we no longer have to spell out, often spiraling down into ever-widening vicious circles of hell. Even if we are privileged enough not to have experienced any of these directly—yet—we cannot escape the fact that trauma shapes our world and that, in a global village, to say nothing of the communion of saints, we are all touched by its effects. The truth is that very few people will leave this life without some trauma. Yet too many white mainline pulpits treat trauma as something unmentionable even though the heart of the Christian gospel is in the shape of a cross and empty tomb.

It is no wonder, then, that a white mainline Protestant in trauma would find a haven in an African-American church where the presumed rhetorical audience is one constructed out of the history of traumas faced by African-Americans. Indeed, the black church was a deliberately constructed refuge for those traumatized by the atrocities of slavery, and it has remained as such for the continuing traumas that stalk black lives in America.

ANCIENT WISDOM OFFERED BY THE BLACK CHURCH

However, at its best,[6] the black church also has a way of dealing with personal trauma by offering a comprehensive theological hermeneutic that incorporates both the pastoral and the prophetic within a broader view of the Christian tradition to give people the hope, courage, and strength it takes to act in life-giving ways in the face of evil. The best of African American preaching resists offering thin therapeutic sermons shaped out of an individualistic self-help American society.[7] Instead, it offers the larger church the brilliance of a holistic homiletic approach to the depths of the human condition in the way that it construes the Bible's narratives for preaching to a broken people about the wholeness of God's compassionate and just

---

6. L. Susan Bond's work, *Contemporary African American Preaching*, notices many different kinds of black churches with many different kinds of sermons that run the gamut from astonishing to appalling. Overgeneralizing runs the risk of painting with such a broad brush that hard truths may be whitewashed (in all senses of that word). Perhaps we would do better to talk about the preaching of specific preachers like Gardner Taylor, James Forbes, Prathia Hall, Jeremiah Wright, and any others, like Dale Andrews, who offer solace from out of the divine compassion that simultaneously judges and loves all equally. We will continue to use African American or black preaching as a short-hand way of designating this kind of preaching, aware of the shortcomings.

7. As David Buttrick describes it, therapeutic preaching in our "me-first" culture has become a "narrow personalism" that reduces God to "a reflection of our personal needs." See Buttrick, "Preaching in an *Un*Brave," 12.

Reign. While the white mainline denominations have all but split along personal piety vs. social justice lines, the black church has generally held these two together, though not without the tensions conferred by the rise of American individualism that threatens to undo this tradition's holistic brilliance when it comes to dealing with the trauma its people have suffered, as Dale Andrews' explicates in *Practical Theology for Black Churches*.

In addition to his acknowledgment that trauma is a part of the African American preacher's presumed rhetorical audience, Andrews lauds the black church's historic engagement in a robust practical theology that works out of a unique hermeneutic consisting of a dynamic interplay of biblical exegesis, theology, spiritual nurture, and social analysis. As Andrews expounds, this hermeneutic orientation is actually a faith identity shaped by the grand themes of the Bible understood in a particular way. These motifs are at once biblical and theological, transmitting a faith identity that is both individual and communal in nature. These grand themes include the following: (1) God created everything that is and called it good. Created in God's image, all humans are also created equal. As Creator, God is sovereign with a design for the end of creation and history, which includes a liberation from all that enslaves and oppresses. (2) God is at work in the world on behalf of those oppressed by sin, which is both corporate and individual, to bring about freedom and wholeness. (3) Jesus Christ is the incarnate divine, suffering with humanity and proving that God works for redemption even in the midst of the worst of evil. Through Christ and being converted to his resurrection reality, we can experience a victory over the destructive forces that are at work in the world seeking to devour us. (4) Jesus' resurrection gives us our eschatological hope that one day, under his rule, creation will fulfill the divine intention of wholeness and flourishing with liberty and justice for all. We experience now, in part, what one day will be complete—justice, peace, harmony, healing, wholeness—i.e. shalom. Until then, we live, as much as possible, within and out of that divine reality. Indeed, it is this vision of that Day that is surely coming that gives hope's strength to persevere in the face of this world's crucifying traumas.[8]

White mainline churches are more hesitant to name their construal of a biblical theological meta-narrative, although Graeme Goldsworthy demonstrates that every preacher works from some notion of the grand scope of the Bible's overarching story of God-with-us, even those who assiduously seek to preach "nothing but the Bible."[9] African American theologians lay their hermeneutic theological commitments bare in a way that many white

---

8. Andrews, *Practical Theology*, 40–49.
9. Goldsworthy, *Preaching the Whole Bible*.

preachers do not. However, all of us would do well to name our conceptions of the grand narrative of the Bible that shapes what we conceive to be the good news of its gospel that we are called to preach. In this way, we can examine the richness of our heritage and critique theologically threadbare sermons that send people fleeing.

Besides, working out of a larger narrative of how God is at work in the world enables the pastor to comment on how God is at work in similar ways here and now, placing each person within a story larger than their own personal biography. An African American theological hermeneutic emphasizes that our lives matter to the Holy One who created and loves us and wants only the best for us as beloved individuals. However, it also renders us as part of a beloved community. Escaping the individualistic self-help preaching that dominates televangelism and pressures pastors to preach like Joel Osteen or Joyce Meyer, black preachers can more easily address individuals in need without pandering a profiteering gospel that is ultimately not good news. Instead, with a larger vision of where the whole story of God and humanity is headed, they can show how individuals' lives fit into the divine work as one who is no more, nor any less, special than anyone else whom God so loves. Individuals can thus be addressed in their fullness as the social individuals they are—created in a Trinitarian *imago Dei* as part of a community. Black preaching renders an anthropology that depicts human beings as a complicated complexity of multiple identifications: we are a strange conglomeration of sinners and saints all comingling in one body, and we're talking about an individual here, not to mention a congregation. The best sermons in the black church thus address the whole person—sinner, saint, head, heart, soul, warts and all. Working from a more comprehensive vision of the complex reality of Emmanuel's presence in the myriad details of our lives, preachers in African American churches cast sermons that are truly therapeutic in the sense that they are "healing" because they re-place the whole person within the "service" and "worship" of the Almighty, which are the other ways the word *therapeuo* can be translated. What is truly healing, it seems, is being re-stored within a larger vision of who we are within God's dynamic activity of blessing and redeeming all of creation.

This larger, more comprehensive ecclesial vision is what enables Andrews to challenge a reductionistic academic theology, captive to the assumptions of an Anglo-American university culture, that misdiagnoses ecclesial church traditions. Subsequently, he renders an account of the best of the black church tradition that cares for those in need of refuge at the same time that it offers a prophetic summons for social justice. Preaching that simply cares for hurting individuals under the rubrics of evangelical piety ends up in the same "narrow personalism" that panders to perceived needs without questioning the structures that keep us bound in sin, whether these be corporate injustices or a fatalistic dependency upon our next spiritual fix proffered by a pusher-preacher. However, neglecting the care-of-souls dimension of preaching in favor of summoning the church to a social justice agenda is also a perversion of the gospel, Andrews argues.

Faith identity is therefore the proper starting place for both the church and the theological academy, for it is what gives them both their purposeful marching orders. This identity begins and ends with the startling good news that through Christ we are included in covenant relationship with the Holy One who wants to be in communion with us and all of creation, as seen through the narrative construction of the main biblical motifs.[10] This good news, though, cannot be reduced to a formulaic sermonic statement, for, in reality, it is comprised of the "dynamic interplay between traditional narratives [of the Bible], narratives of the local community, and individual narratives of experiences." Precisely because it is narrative in character, Andrews contends, African American pastoral care is inherently communal. We cannot understand our story apart from the stories of our people, which, in the Christian tradition, includes the whole communion of saints, as well as our more contemporary peers and ancestors.[11] The very notion of participating as one among the whole communion of saints, though, opens up the vista of our lives into God's eschatological future.

The process of our lives' histories opening toward God's eschatological future results in the formation of the "alternative consciousness" of an ecclesial faith identity. This is also known as conversion. However, this is not just an individual's pietistic conversion, though it often includes this dimension. This new consciousness "envisions alternative realities for the deceptions of the dominating culture" that enslaves and oppresses.[12] Following Heschel and Brueggemann, Andrews demonstrates that both personal conversion and the church's social justice agenda emerge out of relationship within the sovereign rule of divine compassion.[13] It is within the covenantal relationship that our personal devotion to God and just relationships with other human beings are executed. Without this relationship with the Holy, personal piety and social action are just human activities that use God as rhetorical prop in our own narratives.

What is surprising about Andrews' work, though, is that it ends with biblical covenantal theology with a focus on the prophetic tradition.

---

10. Andrews, *Practical Theolog*, 107ff.
11. Ibid., 25.
12. Ibid., 109.
13. Ibid., 110.

The Importance of the Pastoral and the Prophetic   225

It is lamentable that he is virtually silent about Christ and eschatology at this point, though the seeds have been sown. Perhaps he wishes to avoid problematic notions of Jesus' redemptive suffering. But here is where we can harvest the trajectory of Andrews' work on behalf of those caught in trauma. As he did to African American slaves, the suffering Christ speaks to those who have been heinously abused by the sins of others in a way that no pristine God can. In the crucified Christ we see the love of a God who goes to the depths of hell with and for us in order to show us how beloved we are. The Christology here is not one of substitutionary atonement. Jesus did not die in order to pay the penalty of our sin. Rather, he steps in to act in our stead when we are being killed by sin. He dies, and we are saved. The relational dynamic thereafter is similar to the one known by those who have had someone die in a violent intervention on their behalf: the one who is saved feels that s/he must live well for the one who died so that they could live. Indeed, many speak of living the savior's life for her/him. Subsequently, those who were saved lead a life of grateful obligation. This is the spiritual source of Christian morality and ethics: our Lord stepped in to take the blows of sin's destruction so that we could live free, not just for ourselves, but on behalf of all others being oppressed by sin. In the savior's name, we have an obligation to also challenge the powers-that-be, just as he did for us. To do so honors his name and keeps his memory alive. Anyone caught within the abuse of sin, whether by her own patterns of self-destruction that prevent the divine desire for our full flourishing or by the oppressions of a society that enslaves its members in death-dealing ways that are contrary to God's Way of Life, needs Jesus Christ as Savior.

But in order to be redemptive, Christ's suffering must occur within and out of a larger vision of God-with-us. The metanarrative of the African American hermeneutic functions as this, but in Andrews' work it stumbles at a full-fledged eschatological vision at the finishing line of the good. Perhaps this, too, is due to the historical problems of reducing the grand scope of eschatology to a pie-in-the-sky in the sweet by-and-by after we die otherworldliness that shackled resistance against the oppressive systems in this world. Andrews argues, however, that in the face of death, reduction of the Bible's eschatological hope to heaven in the after life was an interim strategy aimed at simply keeping people alive in an abusive situation. Resistance was kept alive in other ways that kept people alive to fight another day. Today, however, the shackles have been unlocked, even though they are often still dragging behind. What people undergoing trauma require, especially those stuck in patterns of victimization that have become a normative worldview, is the trauma of resurrection that shatters their sin-soaked world with a vision of possibility beyond imagining. This is what an eschatology based on the biblical image of God's *basileia* can provide.

The *basileia* of God is usually translated as the "Kingdom of God," but this translation falls short. *Basileia* properly refers to the reigning activity of God, not a place, as the word "kingdom" denotes. *Basileia* is best understood as God's sovereign work in the world, which is often gently, if not invisibly, powerful, like yeast in bread dough. This divine work can be recognized by its markers of love, justice, egalitarianism, peace, creativity, providence, blessing, and compassion. The motif of God's sovereign work in the world runs like a golden thread throughout the Bible, uniting its various books' perspectives, for God is always mucking about in human affairs. In the beginning, God walks and talks with Adam and Eve in the garden. God's reign is face-to-face, paradisiacal. After the fall, God withdraws, turning the divine face from us. Nonetheless, the Holy One continues to act on behalf of the blessing and redemption of creation, seeking again and again to have it return to right relationship, as it was at the beginning. When the people of God are enslaved in Egypt, God works to liberate, educate, and raise up a people who will live under the divine sovereign rule. When they choose to have a monarch like all the other nations have instead, God continues to reign nevertheless, working hard to woo a people who are as wayward as Hosea's adulterous wife by sending prophet after prophet to urge the apostate to return to their Maker who is crazy in love with them. Then Jesus comes preaching, "God's *basileia* is at hand." He trains disciples in the Way/Torah.[14] Just as God speaks and it is so (Gen 1), when Jesus preaches the *basileia*, it starts to happen: people are healed, the demonic are cast down, the hungry fed, and destructive powers are disturbed. Hence, Jesus is killed by an empire that would be Lord over God. But God's *basileia* continues to work, making a way out of no way, rolling back the crushing stone of death's seal to bring about resurrection new life—the ultimate apocalyptic sign of the anticipated Day of the Lord when God will judge evil and establish shalom. With Christ's resurrection and ascension, the Rule of God has begun, and we've been given the abiding presence of the Holy Spirit to strengthen and comfort us.

God's *basileia* continues even in the midst of this world's sin, growing stronger through, with, and in the risen Christ until someday the vision

---

14. Torah is often translated as law, but it could just as easily be translated as Way, for it is less about the execution of legalities and more about a way of living. As Schiffman argues in *From Text to Tradition*, the ancient Pharisaical understanding of Torah that became the rabbinic tradition, which Jesus worked out of, saw Torah as the way of being in covenant with God and one another. It included the law of Moses written in the Pentateuch as well as the oral interpretative traditions of Torah.

of Paradise, life as it was intended to be, will be the Way life is under the Rule of God. Now, we only see glimpses of the reality of God's work in the world. Someday, that vision will become reality. As various Old and New Testament prophets describe it in metaphorical language, on that Day we will once again eat and drink with God who will dance and sing over us (Zeph 3:17). No one will hurt or destroy another (Isa 11:1–9). There will be no wars, no tears, no untimely deaths (Isa 2:4; 65:19–20). We will live in harmony with one another and creation. There will be plenty for all without an unjust economic system (Isa 65:21–22). We will all serve one another as God's servants, with no one lording it over us but the Lord (Joel 2:28–29). Love, peace, joy, harmony, health, justice, wholeness will form our social structures. Someday, fully. But now, only in part.

This is the eschatological vision that can comfort and strengthen all in facing the death-dealing ways of this world's sin that seeks only to destroy. Though that day may tarry, it is surely coming (Hab 2:3). In Christ's death and resurrection, the victory has already been secured. We just have to stand fast.

People in trauma need the vision of another way, one that invites us into the fullness of life and helps us take the next step toward its life. This has been the strength of the church at its best in any culture down through the ages. We are the people who embody the eschatological vision of God's *basileia*. We make banquets in the face of death. We weep with those who weep, sing and pray with those who are in prison, feed those who are sick, build hospitals, and demand to know why people are getting sick from our tainted water, earth, and sky and how our prisons can best rehabilitate. We quietly hold the hand of the anxious, and hold our divine vision for how life is to be ordered before our leaders and demand that they act accordingly. When they won't, we will go to any lengths in protest, even unto death. This is who we are because this is whose life we live as Christ's own, holy and beloved. Out of this faith identity we thus preach in word and deed, both prophetically and with pastoral care. In the process, we create bridges for those who long to embrace the dawning of God's new day coming and walk in its Way toward life re-stored.

22

Tending the Methodist Roots of Preaching and Pastoral Care

G. Lee Ramsey, Jr.

It was my good fortune to land in 1994 at Vanderbilt University to enter into PhD studies just one year after Dale Andrews. Dale quickly became a genuine friend, a colleague, a fellow minister, teacher, and scholar. It was even greater luck to be focused within the doctoral program upon the same areas of concentration as Dale: homiletics and religion and personality. To go through 4 years of coursework, comprehensive exams, and dissertation writing with Dale, and with overlapping research and ecclesial interests, was a gift that I cannot begin to measure. His personal care for all, his wit, his scholarly drive and precision, his ability to work collaboratively with others, the gift for mentoring new scholars, his leadership in church and academy, and his excellence in pulpit and classroom was humbling and inspiring. Dale's mark is lasting upon me and all who knew him, upon the congregations that he served, and upon the Academy, especially in the fields of practical theology, preaching, and pastoral care.

In many ways, Dale and I plowed similar ground in our work. For a couple of years, we literally worked side by side on our laptops in the basement of Vanderbilt Divinity School's fellows' study room, often stopping to ask (or interrupt!) each other with questions related to the progress of our work or whether it was time for lunch. Both of us studied with principal instruction from Professors David Buttrick and Liston Mills. Most significantly, we both pursued in our dissertations the foundational question of the relationship between preaching, pastoral care, and practical theology, though with different interests and contextual concerns.[1] Furthermore, for several years Dale and I collaborated with a larger group of teachers, preachers, and scholars on a professionally rewarding project focused on sermon listening. With other colleagues we continued to nurture one another's thoughts and direction for teaching and ministry.[2]

Considering our common interests, what I did not spot until recently is the largely untapped resource that Methodism offers to the linking of preaching and pastoral care, or what Andrews calls prophetic care and pastoral care.[3] It is surprising to me that neither Dale, an ordained African Methodist Episcopal Zion pastor and practical theologian, nor I, a lifelong United Methodist, have spent much effort mining the resources of our own ecclesial traditions as they inform the theology and practice of pastoral care and preaching. This may be partly due to the ecumenical nature of our training and teaching and partly due to unexamined assumptions about the denominational sources of our own thinking and belief. Andrews notes the significance of Wesley for preaching and pastoral care in a few places in his work but does not, to my knowledge, explore the theme widely.[4] Only recently have I begun to pursue it. In particular, the Wesleyan roots of both traditions (AME Zion and UMC, as well as Pan-Methodism more broadly)—in history, practice, and theology—suggest important directions for consideration as we study the relationship between preaching and pastoral care.

While space does not allow for a full exploration of the contributions that Methodism can make to the linking of preaching and pastoral care, I will suggest here several promising directions for further inquiry that could build upon Andrews' remarkable body of work, drawing in a general way from both AME Zion and UMC history, theology, and practice.

First, at the level of basic church history and practice, widely known among students of early Methodism, John Wesley's preaching in eighteenth-century England was largely among the poor, the working class, and the

---

1. Andrews, *A Covenant Model*. This became the foundation for Andrews' important work, *Practical Theology*, and it set the course for his continuing commitment to practical theology in and for the Black Church and the academy. See Andrews and Smith, *Black Practical Theology*. My initial interest in the way preaching shapes pastoral community started with G. Lee Ramsey, Jr., *Preaching and the Rhetoric of Care*.

2. McClure et. al., *Listening to Listeners*.

3. Andrews, "We're Never Done." See also Andrews' discussion of prophetic practical theology in *Practical Theology*, 122–28.

4. McClure et. al., *Listening to Listeners*, 60–70.

slowly emerging middle class. This was equally true in early North American Methodism among both African Americans and Whites.[5] Wesley's preaching, teaching, and writing demonstrated a pronounced concern to elevate the spirits and economic circumstances of those caught in poverty and to challenge the prosperity and growing consumerism of the prosperous. Indeed, Wesley feared that over time the economic improvement of Methodists who practiced discipline, modesty, and fairness in financial matters would potentially be the undoing of the movement. His sermons, "On the Danger of Riches" and "Causes of the Inefficacy of Christianity" are more than cautionary words to the faithful. They are clear challenges to those who turned from neighbor love to self-satisfaction and from zeal for the gospel to complacency born of economic security. Wesley had no trouble denouncing superfluous attention to dress, self-indulgence in consumption, and unnecessary accumulation of wealth among the Methodists.[6] He was in his own life committed to simplicity of means, and he readily shared his own financial resources with those in need. Prophetic care wove all the way through his preaching as well as his own life.

The key, though, for Wesley, was that such "prophetic" preaching was neither simply for communicating the justifying grace of God to the listener nor for excoriating the rich or self-absorbed. Rather, Wesley intended for his preaching to bring the believers and the converted into a society of Methodists—rich, poor, and middle class—where together members could "watch over one another in love."[7] These earliest Methodist societies, especially in the classes within the societies, strove to imitate the early church of Acts 2 in mutual care, regular worship and fellowship, and the sharing of earthly possessions. While the texts of Wesley's sermons are didactic and doctrinaire, the intent of much of his preaching was to bind believers into the rapidly expanding Methodist societies in order to edify them for growth in grace. Indeed, Wesley preached the preponderance of his sermons not to non-believers but among professing members of Methodist societies.[8] Preaching gave rise to pastoral care within communities—e.g. societies, classes, and bands—where in mutual love and accountability, the members helped one another grow together in grace, in love of God and neighbor.

Thus, even at his most "prophetic" moments over a lifetime of preaching, Wesley's pastoral guiding, healing, sustaining, and reconciling of persons

5. See Jennings, *Good News*; Wigger, *Taking Heaven*, chaps. 1, 2, 6.

6. Wesley, "Danger of Riches," "Causes of the Inefficacy of Christianity."

7. The phrase "to watch over one another in love" comes from John Wesley, "Nature, Design, and General Rules," in *The Methodist Societies*, 9:69.

8. Heitzenrater, "John Wesley's Principles and Practice of Preaching," *Methodist History*, 93.

and communities in times of joy or distress was readily evident.[9] Wesley simply saw no good reason for preaching unless persons influenced by the sermons—either first time converts or lifelong believers—were brought into covenantal relationship with one another as members of the Body of Christ. Covenantal life was most powerfully experienced in small, mutually caring communities.[10] In these societies, classes, and bands, members could hold one another accountable to their own ethical commitments, commitments that entailed values such as sharing with one another in need, opposition to slavery, overcoming financial indebtedness, fair business practices, and social action on behalf of the hungry, the imprisoned, and the sick.[11] The caring church that emerged from those early days of Methodism was not so much a refuge as it was a crucible for growth in grace (sanctification) and Christian action on behalf of others in and beyond the walls of the church.[12] As Methodism spread to North America, these commitments to mutual care in Methodist classes, called together through enthusiastic preaching, were firmly established in both African American and White Methodist congregations.[13] As Andrews comments in *Listening to Listeners* upon the impact of John Wesley's preaching, "While John Wesley urged that the church is continually formed by a living faith that emerges from pure preaching of

---

9. The pastoral care categories of "guiding, healing, and sustaining, and reconciling" are fully developed by Clebsch and Jaekle, *Pastoral Care* but the first three were originally used by Seward Hiltner in *Preface to Pastoral Theology*, 89–172.

10. Wesley states in his published *Journal*, writing on August 25, 1763: "I was more convinced than ever that the preaching like an apostle, without joining together those that are awakened and training them up in the ways of God, is only begetting children for the murderer. How much preaching has there been for these twenty years all over Pembrokeshire! But no *regular societies*, no discipline, no order or connection. And the consequence is that nine in ten of the once awakened are now faster asleep than ever." Wesley, *Journal and Diaries IV*, 21: 424 (August 25, 1763). For Wesley's explanation of the Methodist Societies, Classes, and Bands, see his *A Plain Account of the People Called Methodists*, 9:254. For a contemporary interpretation of the contribution that Methodist classes could make to the church see, Lowes Watson, *Covenant Discipleship*, and for an interpretation of the historical practices of the societies, classes, and bands, see Lowes Watson, *Early Methodist*.

11. Heitzenrater, *Wesley and the People Called Methodists*, 129–41; Jennings, *Good News*, chaps. 3–5.

12. Andrews develops a sustained discussion and proposed revision of the Black Church as "refuge" in *Practical Theology*. It seems to me that the covenantal ecclesiology that Andrews calls for to hold together Black Theology and the Black Church can find additional support in the Wesleyan tradition's theology and practice of the societies and classes.

13. Melton, *Will to Choose* 45; Wigger, *Taking Heaven*, 127–29. For the ongoing importance of the Methodist classes within contemporary AME Zion tradition, see Starnes, "Leadership Seminar."

the Word and in continuity with the sacraments.... The church takes shape in the fellowship, communion, accountability, and work of believers and seekers ... [who are] therefore held together in the unity of shared mission and mutual nurture."[14] While Methodism has lost much of this initial zeal for transformative preaching and pastoral care, these qualities remain latent and therefore potentially influential upon current church practices. Further fruit could be gleaned from deeper exploration of this tie between distinctive Wesleyan forms of preaching and pastoral care.

A second root within the Methodist tradition that could bring further coherence to the linking of preaching and pastoral care is Wesley's understanding of the means of grace. Many scholars in the field of homiletics explore preaching as a means of grace. Indeed, traditional homiletics, Protestant and Catholic, affirms preaching as the Word of God that communicates or offers, reveals or confronts the hearer with the present reality of God's grace. As Paul says to the leaders of the church in Ephesus, "This is nothing other than the ministry I received from the Lord Jesus: to testify about the good news of God's grace" (Acts 20: 24, CEB). Wesley and later Methodist preachers, as most preachers throughout church history, have proclaimed the gospel of God's grace into the lives of Christian believers and congregations.

What has been less pronounced, however, is a concomitant understanding of pastoral care as a means of grace. Rarely in contemporary pastoral care and theology do we encounter extensive studies of pastoral care as a means of giving and receiving God's grace. The claim is present but underdeveloped in Protestant theologies of pastoral care.[15] More often pastoral care is understood theologically as representing or re-membering the loving presence or guidance of God that sustains the believer as he or she moves through experiences of need, crisis, or change.[16] The caregiver may help individuals, families, or communities interpret their situations in light of the Christian story,[17] or the pastor may help the individual or community move toward wholeness, toward greater realization of the fullness of life under God's creation, including those who have been personally or systemically oppressed, marginalized, or abused.[18] Pastoral care has rightfully taken up advocacy concerns to correct economic, racial, gender, and environmental

---

14. McClure, et. al., *Listening to Listeners*, 68.

15. Exceptions to this include Underwood, *Pastoral Care*; and Ramshaw, *Ritual and Pastoral Care*.

16. For example, Patton, *Pastoral Care*.

17. See Gerkin, *An Introduction*.

18. See Wimberly, *African American Pastoral Care*; Kornfeld, *Cultivating Wholenesss*; Leslie, *When Violence*.

injustice in church and culture, helpfully blurring the lines between pastoral care and mission in the practice and theology of ministry.[19] While a concern for grace within pastoral care is not altogether absent from these contemporary approaches to pastoral care, it is not central.

Yet for John Wesley and generations of Methodist followers, pastoral care, broadly conceived, has been a practice for sharing the means of grace. This is particularly evident in two arenas. First, grace resides at the center of Wesley's understanding of Christian *conferencing*. When believers gather for honest conversation and for mutual accountability for one another's faith and discipleship, grace abounds.[20] Wesley particularly understood the class meetings among Methodists as the locus for Christian conferencing. Believers neglect this form of Christian community to the diminishment of the experience of God's grace in their lives. While this may seem obvious to Methodist and non-Methodists alike, contemporary pastoral care rarely points toward Christian conferencing as a means of grace. The ordinary, regular moments of talking together in honesty and humility, confessing and offering forgiveness are the ways in which grace is transmitted from one to another by the power of the Holy Spirit. Thus preaching and pastoral care are theologically and practically twin avenues of mediating God's grace among individuals and the gathered congregation. One does so from the pulpit or the lectern and the other while sitting together with a small group of believers.

Second, Wesley had a deep awareness of how the traditional practices of pastoral care such as visiting the sick and suffering and consoling the bereaved are opportunities for the giving and receiving of God's grace. He understood such actions as prudential means of grace alongside the instituted means of grace (prayer, reading and interpreting the scripture, holy communion, fasting). Visiting the sick can be a profound experience of grace for both the caregiver and the recipient of care. Tending to the needs of the poor can be an encounter with the grace of God. As Wesley instructed the minister regarding visitation, "Surely there are works of mercy, as well as works of piety, which are real means of grace."[21] In such encounters,

19. Couture, *Blessed Are the Poor*; Kujawa-Holbrook and Montagno, *Injustice*; Ellison, *Cut Dead but Still Alive*.

20 Wesley, *Works: The Bicentennial Edition* 10: 856–857. For a brief discussion on Christian *conferencing* in the Methodist tradition, see Frank, *Polity, Practice, and the Mission* 46–47, 102.

21. Wesley, "On Visiting the Sick," *Sermons*, 3:385 ff. See also Wesley's "Letter to Miss March," in which he guides the laywoman, Miss March, to attend to the poor in her midst, saying to her, "The blessing which follows this labour of love will more than balance the cross," *The Letters of the Rev. John Wesley* 6: 208–9. See Maddox, "Visit the Poor," 59–81.

mutuality of grace can emerge. Grace stands at the center of Wesleyan theology—prevenient, justifying, and sanctifying grace—and it is equally present within pastoral care and preaching. As Andrews reflects upon one of the interviews he conducted for the *Listening to Listeners* project, "In both Wesleyan and African American church traditions, praying and conferring between co-worshippers [is also a sharing] in the means of grace."[22] A Wesleyan perspective on pastoral care and preaching would further open up the means of grace as a fruitful avenue for further study.

Finally, preaching and pastoral care within the Methodist tradition (including AME Zion, AME, CME, and UMC) has been markedly "practical." To our contemporary ears, Wesley's sermons and those of earlier preachers in American Methodism—both black and white—seem unnecessarily laden with doctrine and tedious biblical exposition. Part of the problem here is that we have few actual accounts of the preached, oral sermons of Wesley and the earlier Methodists. What we have are the written documents that Wesley intended for doctrinal instruction, but these are not the actual sermons that he delivered. Wesley's approach to preaching as to theology in general was a practical one. He preached for practical results amid the congregation, aiming for a transformation of heart and mind. But Wesley also wanted to shape the living faith practices of those who heard and responded to his preaching.[23] Once Methodism took root in the North American context, preachers quickly figured out how to connect with the poor and working class hearers both in cities and rural areas through use of the vernacular that often spilled over into religious enthusiasm that allowed the worshippers the opportunity to experience the transformative power of God and to develop intimate bonds of connection with one another. On the pragmatic level, such "popular" preaching among the Methodists fostered remarkable church growth throughout the early republic and pre-Civil War periods of North America, so much so that by 1850, Methodism was the largest of all the Christian denominations among blacks and whites.[24]

Yet it is true that while *some* of Wesley's pastoral guidance in his sermons may translate into the contemporary situation, and maybe more of it should—particularly his guidance concerning riches in our society sickened by affluenza—most attempts to uncritically drag Wesley's specific pastoral advice from any given sermon of the eighteenth century into the twentieth-century pastoral situation would most likely provide comical,

22. Andrews in McClure, et. al., *Listening to Listeners*, 69, citing Langford, *Practical Divinity*, 43–45, and Williams, *John Wesley's Theology Today*, 132–35.

23. See Langford, *Practical Divinity*, 42; Maddox, *Responsible Grace*; and Outler, "Pastoral Care," 4–11.

24. Wigger, *Taking Heaven*, 3.

if not disastrous results, and be dismissed as hopelessly irrelevant. What contemporary mother or father, for example, with genuine concern for her or his children, would find helpful Wesley's advice to "Break their will, that you may save their soul?"[25] Or who among us, let's be honest, would submit ourselves or expect our congregational members to submit themselves to Wesley's advice regarding dress, to "lay aside all needless ornaments . . . to be patterns of plainness to all that are around you . . . As plain as Quakers (so called) or Moravians. [For if you do not] you declare hereby to all the world that you will not obey them that are over you in the Lord?"[26] It is not in the specifics of practical moral guidance that we find the best links to contemporary pastoral care in the Wesleyan tradition.

Rather, to clearly view pastoral care and preaching within the Wesleyan tradition we will need to look for the underlying pastoral and practical theological orientation of Wesley's preaching as it helped establish and maintain social networks of believers who shared responsibility for Christian care within the Church and among those within general society. As O.C. Edwards claims, the relationship between pastoral care and preaching is properly understood as the work of formation of Christian community. The purpose of pastoral preaching is to help the Christian community understand itself as community in its "relationships to God, to one another, and to those outside the church."[27] Careful attention to Wesley's joining of evangelical preaching with the formation of communities of Christian care will guide us as we mark the shared ground between preaching and pastoral care in the Wesleyan tradition.

On the practical level, pastoral care occurs through preaching in the Wesleyan tradition insofar as one of the primary aims and effects of pastoral preaching is to form the congregation as a community of Christian care. As preachers, we want to be certain that our preaching communicates to the congregation that they, empowered by the Holy Spirit, are pastors one for the other. They have all the gifts and graces needed to communicate God's guiding, healing, sustaining, and reconciling love to one another, even as the designated clergy leader and preacher continues to direct the edification of the Body and to offer by word and example his or her own gifts of pastoral care.[28]

---

25. Wesley, "On Obedience to Parents," *Sermons*, 3:367.
26. Ibid., 382.
27. Edwards, "Preaching and Pastoral Care," 155.
28. Ramsey, *Care-full Preaching*.

These pastoral communities are characterized by mutuality, hospitality, and compassion as well as other identifying traits.[29] These traits may boil down to the one extolled in the familiar hymn, "They will know we are Christians by our love, by our love . . . ." But I think naming them with some specificity provides actual pastoral content rather than simply subsuming all Christian virtues under the one category of "love."

Mutuality of care, between members and between the pastoral leader and members, should mark the contemporary Christian community every bit as much as it did in the early Methodist movement. We want to be wary of our own needs and tendencies to "hog the hermeneutic" of pastoral care,[30] just as Wesley was concerned, for example, in Norwich on Oct. 16, 1764, that the society there was too reliant upon his own teaching and preaching. He says, "If I could stay here a month, I think there would be a society little inferior to that at Bristol. But it must not be: they who will bear sound doctrine *only from me* must still believe a lie."[31] We know that the whole movement of Methodism grew and flourished because Wesley, though a strong leader, understood the need and discovered the methods to identify, train, and nurture other such leaders. In this way, the societies flourished as multiple communities of care within the larger Church of England, where, as Wesley puts it in *A Plain Account of the People Called Methodists*, "The thing proposed in their associating themselves together was obvious to everyone. They wanted to 'flee from the wrath to come' and to assist each other in so doing. They therefore united themselves 'in order to pray together, to receive the word of exhortation, and to watch over one another in love, that they might help each other to 'work out their salvation.'"[32] In other words, to use the language of contemporary pastoral care—to guide, heal, sustain, and reconcile one another to God and each other. This would not be possible nor would it make any theological sense without the regular preaching of God's word that justifies and sanctifies the people of God. If the Methodist societies of eighteenth-century England and the Methodist congregations of twentieth-century North America are some of the places where Christians ideally watch over one another in love, then preaching is one the means provided by God to form and sustain such communities.

Next, hospitality as an expression of pastoral care seems particularly important within the Methodist tradition, given Wesley's concern for those who lived outside or just on the margins of English respectability, those

---

29. Ibid., chap. 2.
30. Taylor, *When God Is Silent*, 114.
31. Wesley, Oct. 16, 1764, in *Journals and Diaries IV*, 21:493.
32 Wesley, "A Plain Account," 256.

who were either poor, destitute, overworked, underpaid, or simply beneath the dignity of the establishment class of British society. Wesley frequently shared his own dwelling and food with those who needed them. To these Wesley directed his preaching and among these Wesley formed the societies, whose members he admonished to welcome the stranger home.

Thirdly, Wesley's preaching sought to expand the circle of compassion. Love of God and one another within the Methodist societies was not enough. Pastoral care included active love of neighbors, especially the poor, sick, the naked, the hungry, the imprisoned (Matt 25). Wesley could become downright zealous in preaching about responsibility and compassion for these members of God's family. As he challenges in "The Causes of the Inefficacy of Christianity:" "See that poor member of Christ pinched with hunger, shivering with cold, half naked! Meantime you have plenty of this world's goods, of meat, drink, and apparel. In the name of God, what are you doing? Do you neither fear God, nor regard man? . . . Can any servant 'afford' to lay out his master's money any other wise than his master appoints him? So far from it that whoever does this ought to be excluded from Christian society."[33] For Wesley, compassion is not optional in the pastoral community. And at our best, our compassion for each other, our "suffering with," as Wesley says in his instructions for visiting the sick, becomes a means of grace for both giver and receiver. As Chuck Gerkin says in *Prophetic Pastoral Practice*,

> It is not a vocation that can be found within the secluded privacy of that community's own life, though that life should seek to become an exemplar of what it means to be a people of the covenant. Rather, the Christian community's vocation will be realized and God's call to God's people will find appropriate response, as ways are found to provide a leavening presence in all the places where human beings are together.[34]

The preached word shapes each of these pastoral attributes of the community if we believe that the Word of God preached and the sacraments duly administered give voice and flesh to the Church. While Wesley did not use the specific terms of mutuality, hospitality, and compassion for the pastoral community that is shaped through preaching, I think they are within the spirit of what Wesley wanted and believed was possible for the Methodist societies to accomplish. Hence, he was diligent in pastoral preaching, both in oral and written forms, published and unpublished, to guide, heal, sustain, and reconcile the people called Methodists.

33. Wesley, "Causes of the Inefficacy of Christianity," in *John Wesley's Sermons*, 553.
34. Gerkin, *Prophetic Pastoral Practice*, 161.

Finally, it is important when we think about Wesleyan contributions to preaching and pastoral care to consider the role of language in both. That Wesley was "focused" upon the use of language and the self of the preacher in preaching is an understatement. In his Journal of 1757, he comments "I do indeed *live* by preaching." And in a letter of October 10, 1735, addressed to John Burton, he says, "My tongue is a devoted thing."[35] While we know that the bulk of Wesley's preaching was oral rather than written, and much of it extemporaneous, we have a remarkable record of 151 sermons, preached many times in many locations that bear witness to a preacher who was rhetorically attuned. He understood classical rhetoric and the power of sacred speech, and he used every rhetorical device available to sharpen and hone his sermons until they became "Plain truth for plain people," whether written, spoken, or both.

It isn't much of a stretch to see that Wesley's attention to the subject matter of the sermon, scriptural interpretation, doctrinal formulation, linguistic style, length of sermons, vocabulary and learning of the preachers, and the delivery itself was almost an anticipation of the twentieth century's interest in philosophies of language. Philosophers, theologians, and preachers began to recognize how performative language shapes communities.[36] We are speaking creatures born of a speaking, loquacious God. Speech matters. Language shapes being and community.[37]

Why this matters in terms of pastoral preaching, and in consideration of Wesley's high emphasis upon preaching as a form of rhetoric, albeit sacred rhetoric, is that if we want our preaching to shape pastoral communities, then we have to pay attention to the very building blocks of the language that we use. Language works like water dripping upon stones to slowly mold and shape the world around it.[38] For example, if our sermons are full of examples and analogies in which the pastor or some other designated leaders are the heroes of pastoral care, then should we be surprised that the people take little care of each other? If we preach to the individual consciousness of the listener rather than to the social consciousness of the congregation, then should we be surprised that the people understand themselves as a collection of individuals rather than a corporate body of believers?[39] If we preach a Jesus Christ who fulfills our every private and personal need but forget to preach that Jesus directs us toward love of God and neighbor, then

---

35. Cited by Heitzenrater, "Preface" to *John Wesley's Sermons*, 9.
36. Austin, *How To Do Things*.
37. "With words we name the world." Buttrick, *Homiletic*, 9.
38. Ramsey, *Care-full Preaching*, chap. 3.
39. Buttrick, *Homiletic*, 296–97.

should we be surprised that the congregation is half-hearted about sharing God's compassion among the least of these? Wesley's nitty gritty attention to language, his careful attention to structure, composition, and the right word, while sometimes seeming a bit precious to our ears, or a bit dry or rational, is a word of invitation for us to think about the use of language in preaching. About whether our language from the pulpit is actually developed to form the people as a pastoral community or to unintentionally reinforce the self-understanding provided by other, competing language games that tell us that we are isolated, individual competitors who live to consume, amuse ourselves to death, steal from the earth and our grandkids, and then die alone.[40]

Wesley's sermons, in language, doctrine, and delivery, painted a very different world populated by a very different people—people who are saved by the prevenient, justifying, and sanctifying grace of God and who seek to live in complete love of God and neighbor. In short, a pastoral people, a shepherding community, where each is bound together by the love of God, and each together seek to serve God through care for the neighbor. This pastoral community may be an ideal beyond our realization in this life, but those who practice pastoral care and preaching within the Wesleyan tradition must surely have a goal, a hope toward which to live as we move along the path of salvation, a hope that finally rests in God.

Dale Andrews, in his life, witness, teaching, and to my way of thinking very Methodist approach to pastoral care and preaching, embodied that hope. His work points us toward both liberation and reconciliation for all people. His words and actions engender here and there living expressions of covenantal, pastoral communities whose members look not only to their own interests but the interests and needs of others. In his preaching and extending pastoral care, we experienced in Andrews' ways and words the greater hope of the gospel of Jesus Christ. The very same hope that John Wesley expressed in his final words, "The best of all is, God is with us."[41]

---

40. Postman, *Amusing Ourselves*.
41. *The Works of the Rev. John Wesley*, 5:547.

23

"The Wrath of God's Love"
Ethical Tension in Social Justice Preaching

AMY E. STEELE

IN HIS COMMENTARY FOR Martin Luther King, Jr. Day (January 15), homiletician and practical theologian Dale P. Andrews writes these words,

> Frankly, the wrath of God's love demands justice for the other, righteousness demands care for the other, to seek their thriving, to seek out the other in desert wandering from years of neglect, to seek out the other wandering from generations of withholding, to seek out the other wandering out from the desert.[1]

The wrath of God's love is the kind of complex gospel Andrews preached and lived. Justice, according to Andrews, does not require a divine wrath apart from a divine love. To the contrary, "God's wrath does not destroy relationship; in fact, divine wrath grieves how we have forsaken relationship." His essay in the *Preaching God's Transforming Justice* commentary is not only instructive for understanding a particular lectionary reading, Amos 5:18–24, but also for understanding a core ethos in social justice preaching. For Andrews, social justice preaching necessitates an unrelenting love for the other at its core, a core that is always reaching and seeking the other.

---

1. Andrews, "Martin Luther King, Jr. Day," 69.

In this brief essay I explore Andrews' characterization of the "wrath of God's love" and the incapacity of rationality alone to inspire justice. Rationality is dependent upon the experience of what I call maladjusted ambition and transformative engagement to spark the kind of unremitting love at the heart of an ethic of social justice preaching.

Firstly, in characterizing "the wrath of God's love" Andrews calls particular distortions into question, "distortions of divine wrath, our vainglorious fear of God and one another, the rules of human engagement with enemies, and our twisted disciplines of justice."[2] These distortions misrepresent the divine activity of God and justify our deepest fears about the other. Some of these national distortions are played out by the powerful in the favor of national interests that support hegemonic prejudices rather than inspire "expansive community." Some of the distortions are personal, neglecting folks in our care, leaving them to the wilderness of lack and negligence. Wrangling a just characterization of the "wrath of God's love" is important in sorting out what the preacher says about God in social justice preaching. Andrews' very delineation of the term "wrath of God's love" suggests that God's love and God's wrath are constitutive tensions that get resolved within a covenantal relationship with God's people.

Rufus Burrow Jr.'s helpful essay, "The Love, Justice, and Wrath of God," asks, "is it possible to reconcile the love and wrath of God?"[3] In Burrow's discussion of Abraham Heschel's conception of God, "The Great Companion," in *God in Search of Man*, Burrows surmises that Heschel's God, "is not concerned about abstractions, but about all that happens in the affairs of persons in the world...This means that God is always concerned about human relations and is angered by social injustice and other community disruptive acts whenever they occur."[4] That there is divine concern for human affairs further exposes a false dichotomy that God is either full of wrath or full of love. While to some God's wrath is a difficult and almost abusive notion, for those who suffer oppression, God's love is void of responsibility without it.[5] What Andrews seems to claim is that social justice preaching is just that: preaching that proclaims a gospel of radical concern and mercy, love and justice. It is preaching that disrupts political systems of injustice and demands a return to a covenantal spirituality and just exchange. In Andrews' own words, "The joy of the wrath of God's love is that justice ferrets

2. Ibid., 68.
3. Burrow, "Love, Justice, and Wrath of God," 3.
4. Ibid., 15
5. Ibid., 25.

out justice. . . . [6] While a mystery, the "wrath of God's love" depicts God's concern, God's anger, and God's retribution for failure in upholding the covenant or the divine imperatives for just relationship.

Preaching God's love and justice is dependent upon rationality, but also understands that reason alone will not produce a moral society.[7] Preaching is a particular kind of public discourse offered within a community whose character is largely determined by its local cultures and its most primal beliefs about people. Reinhold Niebuhr provides a helpful caution to the advocate of social justice, in this case the preacher, that humanity's "social impulses are more deeply rooted than his rational life." In the context of the United States of America these social impulses are dangerously attached to myths associated with the making of country, the settling of lands, and the protection of property and the contestations of its citizens to gain and protect their supposed "God-given" rights. Preachers recognize that these social impulses and the hegemonic machinations that buttress them are rooted in the very fabric of the idea of the American and a localized dream of prosperity. Mere rational homiletical challenges to the myths of country and countrymen, founding documents and core claims are insufficient and powerless resources. What the preacher wrestles with is how these transcendent claims are abridged by local customs, folkways, histories, policies, codes, and prohibitions.[8] Ultimately, according to Niebuhr, we are not only incapable of forming national community because of competing individual interests, but the very idea of nation supersedes our rational capacities for cooperation. For Niebuhr religious resources are even limited. At least religion makes humanity conscious of sin; at best it inspires social justice, leavening the idea of justice with the idea of love averting an ideal from becoming purely political, but even so, religion is threatened by its own will to adjust "its faith to the spirit of modern culture," which is given to "romantic overestimates of human virtue" and sentimentality.[9] The prophetic act preachers are engaged in by preaching "the wrath of God's love" is detrimental—no less than to inspire communal and possibly national understandings of the responsibility of love. Social justice preaching calls forth the love of God, a love driven by a fierce passion to create, to sustain, to give

6. Andrews "Martin Luther King, Jr. Day," 70.

7. Niebuhr, *Moral Man* 6, 26.

8. See Tisdale in *Preaching as Local Theology*, 130–31. Tisdale writes, "Theological terms like 'grace' and 'righteous anger' take root in local soil when the pastor reminds the parishioners of times when, in their own subcultural worlds, they have encountered underserved grace in a personal or professional relationship, or have witnessed anger that was genuinely righteous in nature" (131).

9. Niebuhr, *Moral Man*, 7.

"The Wrath of God's Love" 243

without compulsion, to redeem, and to demand responsibility in making and caring for the world.

Social justice preaching calls the church again and again to awaken and to detach itself from policies and systems that threaten a biologically diverse human existence. King historian Lewis V. Baldwin reminds us that King's "model of prophetic witness was not the gospel of megachurch preachers or "entrepreneurial spirituality."[10] Baldwin claims,

> As the church explores new paradigms for effective witness as the body of Christ . . . it would do well to reclaim King's model of the prophetic church, because that model can indeed be a vital vehicle in creating and sustaining a consistent ethic and culture of life, a culture of openness and enlargement, a culture of radical democracy, a culture of peace and nonviolence, a culture of sacrificial servanthood, and a culture of self-criticism.[11]

What Baldwin suggests is a church actively engaged in the service of freedom, liberative spirituality, hospitality, justice and hope, which bears the marks of a preached gospel inclusive for all. King's model of the prophetic church is at the heart of Andrews understanding of social justice preaching. It is no accident that Andrews was the Martin Luther King Jr. Professor of Homiletics and Pastoral Theology at Boston University School of Theology before joining the faculty at Vanderbilt as the Distinguished Professor of Homiletics, Social Justice, and Practical Theology. Andrews' homiletical concerns bridge theory and practice, which affords him the kind of serious reflection on praxis in churches and an ethos of just preaching. In his own words, his work emerges "from a foundation in prophetic consciousness,"[12] a consciousness tutored by the eighth-century prophets and those, like King, who continued this legacy in the twentieth century.

If appeals to rationality alone are insufficient for social justice preaching then the preacher has at least two other considerations (amongst many related to the art of preaching and the call for justice): maladjusted ambition and transformative engagement. At a speech given at Western Michigan University in December 1963, King charged the campus to be as maladjusted as Abraham Lincoln and Jesus of Nazareth. King writes,

> There are certain technical words within every academic discipline that soon become stereotypes and clichés. Modern psychology has a word that is probably used more than any other

---

10. Baldwin. "Who Is Their God?" 133.
11. Ibid.
12. Andrews and Smith, eds., *Black Practical Theology* 5.

word in modern psychology. It is the word "maladjusted." This word is the ringing cry to modern child psychology. Certainly, we all want to avoid the maladjusted life. In order to have real adjustment within our personalities, we all want the well-adjusted life in order to avoid neurosis, schizophrenic personalities.

But I say to you, my friends, as I move to my conclusion, there are certain things in our nation and in the world, which I am proud to be maladjusted and which I hope all men of good-will will be maladjusted until the good societies realize. I say very honestly that I never intend to become adjusted to segregation and discrimination. I never intend to become adjusted to religious bigotry. I never intend to adjust myself to economic conditions that will take necessities from the many to give luxuries to the few. I never intend to adjust myself to the madness of militarism, to self-defeating effects of physical violence.[13]

King's call to maladjustment is a reversal of an idea that warns against troubled formation of children. Rather than the warning being against the threat of maladjustment and the barriers to a good life, he transposes the warning and challenges people to understand and to experience the discomfort of social impulses which flow against hegemonic powers that support practices that undermine human freedom. King calls for a re-imagining and re-calibrating of these impulses from a tolerance of suffering toward an alleviation of suffering. Dale Andrews reminds us in the lectionary commentary mentioned earlier to remember King in this way: "King stood with moral and spiritual courage, calling us to be 'maladjusted' in joining with him to live the Word of God to the people of God and to a nation" "Let justice roll down like waters, and righteousness like an ever-flowing stream."[14] In other words, King's address is no less a call to reorient our personal and social allegiances to a gospel that stands in the gap with the poor, disenfranchised, and vulnerable. The gospel mantle Andrews dares to carry is a cloak woven with the threads of human dignity and a divine valuation of universal human worth and integrity—it is the demand for liberation from oppression, and an aspiration to wholeness and fulfillment. Furthermore, Andrews would claim we are held accountable by "the wrath of God's love," a wrath of "divine love driving justice and righteousness," a "love [that] rages against the gates of self-contentment. a love which thrust forth against the idolatry

---

13. Western Michigan University Archives and Regional History Collections and University Libraries. Wmich.edu/sites/default/files/attachments/MLK.pdf. 1963.

14. Andrews, "Martin Luther King Jr. Day," 68.

of craven self-images, a love that will not abate."[15] The good news compels maladjusted ambition, which reason alone cannot explain or inspire. Where reason may fail, experience and proximity to suffering may succeed.

John Dewey's discussion of adjustment sheds light on a philosophical description of the felt quality of maladjusted ambition. Though Dewey's intent is to characterize what constitutes religion vs. the religious, I find his discussion helpful in describing how social justice preaching might ascribe a sense of maladjusted ambition. I quote Dewey at length,

> The actual religious quality in the experience described is the effect produced, the better adjustment in life and its conditions, not the manner and cause of its production. The way in which the experience operated, its function, determines its religious value. If the reorientation actually occurs, it and the sense of security and stability accompanying it, are forces on their own account. It takes place in different persons in a multitude of ways. It is sometimes brought about by devotion to a cause; sometimes by a passage of poetry that opens a new perspective; sometimes as was the case of Spinoza—deemed an atheist in his day—through philosophical reflection.[16]

In a sense, social justice preaching is an act of reorienting hearers to more covenantal purposes, a reversal of ambitions. If this kind of preaching can occur within an incubator of security and a community of stability the experience might just produce the effects that Dewey describes as a "better adjustment in life and its conditions." Said differently by ethicist emilie m. townes, "Calling others and ourselves into *human* behavior is exhausting. However, I believe that is what embodied scholarship can and must address."[17] Reorienting preaching to the truth-bearing realities about the embodied oppressions of our world is paramount. Approximating suffering through personal story, biblical witness, poetry, testimony, or through ministry to and with the very local lives it serves are all examples of the multiplicity of ways transformation happens.

Transformative engagement with suffering represents the proximity in which Jesus located his ministry and his message near personal suffering and social illness. One biblical example is the story of the call of Matthew. As Jesus was walking along, the Gospel records, he saw a man named Matthew at work sitting in his local tax office counting his returns and filing his paperwork (Matt 9:9). The business was good that year, and while he stayed

15. Ibid.
16. Dewey. *Common Faith*, 14.
17. townes, "Walking on the Rimbones," 218–19 (emphasis in the original).

faithful to his profession, Matthew had heard about Jesus. When Jesus called Matthew, he immediately followed him. And the rest, as they say, is history. The religious leaders criticize Jesus for his proximity to these social and moral outcasts, subjects of the empire and enemies of the community, who manipulate taxes for exorbitant gain. What strikes me about this passage is Jesus' proximity to the issue *and* the canonical placement of the story. On the one hand, it is significant as the call story of Matthew, but this narrative is also a healing story couched between several healing stories that testify to the power of proximity, the recovery of personal relationship, and the restoration of community. The good news is that Jesus preached social justice and not merely by appealing to rationality but in becoming proximate to issues, he participated in transformative engagement with the very folk who needed the sermon the most.

I had the distinct honor of witnessing Dale's social justice preaching on many occasions, in word and deed, and witnessed it in committee meetings, in the classroom when I co-taught with him, in worship services where he preached, read scripture, and offered benedictions. I have seen it in his home. The joy in which he served family, academy, and church was self-evident. For Dale, social preaching starts first in personal relationships where he pushes for a kind of maladjustment to the status quo of our lives. Since Jesus came for Matthew, the other disciples and crowds, I would join Dale in proclaiming that social justice begins at home and in close proximity to the people we work with everyday.

Dale's notion of the wrath of God's love exposes an ethical tension in social justice preaching. The purpose of this brief essay was not to resolve that tension, as if that were possible, but to characterize its necessity for just relationship. The notion of the wrath of God calls our distortions into question—those that justify our fears about the other and those that justify the balance of power in a society that favors wealth and honors the privilege of hegemony. Preaching God's love and justice is necessary in bringing about global transformation. And though humanity is more constituted by social impulse than by rationality, the preacher is the purveyor of prophetic consciousness and called upon to engage in the mysterious work of reversing our ambitions to the divine work of justice. May we never become adjusted to the oppression of poverty, bigotry, militarism, or war.

24

Restoration and Resistance
Restorative Justice and Black Practical Theology

Scott C. Williamson

Restorative Justice (RJ) aims to repair the harm of wrongdoing and put things right between victims and offenders. The social movement models an alternative to the Western emphasis on retribution in criminal justice. RJ aims to put things right for crime victims through a mediated dialogue with offenders. This model of "encounter and dialogue" proceeds from peacebuilding principles and practices in which the needs of victims, accountability of wrongdoers, and even the participation of the broader community are instrumental in putting things right.[1] At the core of a restorative approach is the conviction that crime is primarily a violation of persons and relationships, as opposed to a violation of law and state authority. This violation obligates offenders to repair the harm that they have caused, as best they can.[2]

The concept and core principles of restorative justice originated in the US and Canada in the 1970's and 80's. A philosophy of restorative justice developed in association with the criminal justice reform practice called the Victim Offender Reconciliation Program.[3] Since its inception, the restorative

---

1. Zehr, *Little Book,* 56.
2. Ibid., 28.
3. Ibid., 53.

justice movement has grown into a global phenomenon.[4] Restorative practices are now found around the world in schools, businesses, hospitals, civic organizations, and local government. Even nations like South Africa have attempted a restorative approach to transitional justice. Curiously, restorative justice and the War on Drugs took root in the same US soil. President Ronald Reagan announced the drug war in 1982 and within 30 years the US penal population grew from approximately 30,000 to more than 2 million.[5] More troubling, African American men bore the brunt of this growth. In some states African American men were imprisoned on nonviolent drug charges at rates "twenty to fifty times greater than those of white men."[6] These widely disparate rates of incarceration belie the fact that "people of all colors use and sell illegal drugs at remarkably similar rates."[7]

RESTORATIVE JUSTICE AND THE NEW JIM CROW

Alexander's searing critique of the justice system and its blatantly racist hyper-incarceration of black males raises important questions about the social politics of racism in the US. Aversive racism refers to the contemporary phenomenon of "colorblind" racism. Egalitarian whites who uphold antidiscrimination principles can fail to appreciate their complicity with systems that uphold white privilege and preserve neocolonialist domination. Further, they fail to recognize that whiteness is the normative standard by which public policy decisions are made. Consider that in the mid-1980s, as the War on Drugs was ramping up survey data revealed that 9 in 10 whites thought black and white children should attend public schools together; 7 in 10 whites thought that whites did not have a right to keep blacks out of their neighborhoods.[8] The upshot is that whites failed to identify the moral incongruity of holding an "antidiscrimination principle" while voting into office public servants who engineered a racially discriminatory criminal justice system.[9]

Black male criminality is the lie that justified a colorblind assault against black people waged under the auspices of a War on Drugs. Liberals and conservatives alike found common cause in a public discourse that branded black males as dangerous thugs, drug dealers, gangbangers, and

---

4. See Johnstone and Van Ness, *Handbook*.
5. Alexander, *New Jim Crow*, 6.
6. Ibid., 7.
7. Ibid.
8. Ibid., 100.
9. Ibid.

super-predators. The political, economic, and social beneficiaries of this lie never questioned the hyper-incarceration of black males as indicative of a white pathology. Indeed, the racist ideology of black male criminality obscured the pathology of white segregation.[10] In an excellent chapter entitled "White Complicity in US Hyper-Incarceration," self-described "white Catholic theologian" Alex Mikulich, identifies the cause of this pathology in white culture. Quoting moral theologian Bryan N. Massingale, Mikulich writes that white culture features a:

> . . . presumption of dominance and entitlement in which white culture does not acknowledge its structured advantage. Further, white culture does not see its particular standpoint at the top of the racial hierarchy within society and does not name whiteness as the norm that judges everything.[11]

Mikulich makes a compelling case. His reflection on the racial pathology that emanates from the soul of white culture is profound as it is prophetic. "We white Americans need to see our complicity in the deadly symbiosis between prisons and marginalized urban communities. There we will look into a mirror into our own souls."[12] What part does restorative justice play in this deadly symbiosis? In the context of white privilege, aversive racism, and the hyper-incarceration of black males, how does RJ put things right? Or, has RJ integrated itself so thoroughly in the US racial hierarchy that it poses little resistance to actual racism? Absent culturally-sensitive and contextualized strategies of resistance in service to restoration, RJ lacks a much needed corrective against aversive racism.

Though work still needs to be done, Howard Zehr asks the right questions on behalf of restorative justice. In a revised and updated edition of *The Little Book of Restorative Justice*, Zehr reflects on Michelle Alexander's *The New Jim Crow* and asks two questions that are central to my work in this chapter. "Have we adequately considered the possibility of built-in biases and assumptions in the way we articulate and practice restorative justice? Have we encouraged and listened to diverse voices about what restorative justice should involve?"[13]

Kathleen Daly and Julie Stubbs ask another important question. To what extent do restorative practices function as an "adjunct rather than

---

10. Mikulich et al., *Scandal of White Complicity*, 67.
11. Ibid., 66.
12. Ibid., 67.
13. Zehr, *Little Book,* 12.

an alternative" to the justice system?[14] Finally, what are the implications of aversive racism for restorative justice?

I have two hopes. First, I hope that black theologians, practical theologians, pastors, and congregants will join with other respondents and say what restorative justice should require. People on the margins who claim a liberation ethic, for example, might find benefit in restorative practices that are contextualized to fit their needs. Further, marginalized people might identify built-in biases that prevent restorative justice from becoming a more helpful ally in the fight for liberation. Second, I hope that RJ theorists will recast a vision of cooperation with social justice, in dialogue with Black Church partners. I do not intend to make restorative justice into social justice. But I confess that I want to nudge it in that direction.

CLARIFYING QUESTIONS AND THESES

In his chapter, "Race and Racism," Dale P. Andrews investigates the social politics of race in religious thinking. Andrews is interested in the ways that racist ideologies and religious conscience mutually inform religious thinking. Religion has supported ideas that justify racialized violence, even as it has developed the moral conscience to resist those ideologies. In short, one finds that the "the justification for and resistance to racism abound in church praxis."[15] This ambiguous reality leads Andrews to ask three clarifying questions. First, who or what is responsible for the mutating survival of racism? At stake is whether individuals or society is primarily responsible for racism.

Second, how do we restore public life without perpetuating the passive violence that avoids the exigencies or costs of restoration? If racial privilege is not named and resisted, then it will re-engage with aversive racism and prevent the restoration of public life. Third, what roles, then, should repentance, reparations, and forgiveness play in overcoming the injustice of racism?[16] Strategies that resist the US racial hierarchy should be employed to disrupt the constant re-engagement of racial privilege and political power with aversive racism. Among these resistance strategies, Andrews includes federal apology and just reparations. But, more significantly, he commends the practical theological methods employed by demonstrators during the US civil rights campaign in the 1950s and 1960s. Martin Luther King, Jr. developed a method of nonviolent direct action around four steps:

14. Johnstone and Van Ness, *Handbook*, 161.
15. Andrews, "Race and Racism," 401.
16. Ibid., 401–3.

exposing structural injustice, negotiation with one's oppressor, continual self-purification so that the demand for justice does not become conflated with a desire for retribution, and direct political action in the public square. Absent these resistance strategies, Andrews warns that political power and racial privilege will continue to do "blunt damage" to marginalized communities, and privileged penitents will continue to use their power to avoid the costs of their penance.[17]

Let's turn to RJ theory. In his chapter, "Restorative Justice and Social Justice, "John Braithwaite, develops three competing theses that clarify the connection between restorative justice and social justice.[18] Given that both forms of justice include a core commitment to non-domination, Braithwaite accepts a formal or theoretical connection between the two. At issue is whether a more substantial relationship holds them together. Braithwaite's first thesis holds that restorative justice is unimportant to social justice.[19] One can depict restorative justice and social justice as concentric circles in which the smaller circle, criminal justice reform, is only a tiny part of the larger structural realignment work of social justice.

Braithwaite's second thesis holds that restorative justice risks the "worsening of social injustice."[20] RJ can become an instrument of social injustice when it privileges neocolonialist narratives and culturally univocal meanings of justice.[21] I share Braithwaite's concern. Social privilege and political domination authorize the control of meaning-making systems. In turn, the exercise of neocolonialist power inhibits marginalized people from claiming the *say-so*, the authority, to do restorative justice outside the superintendence of its cultural keepers. Braithwaite's third thesis and the option he favors holds that restorative justice can be a major strategy for advancing social justice.[22] RJ can improve social justice insofar as it promotes foundational values such as respect, honesty, empathy, and inclusive dialogue. Braithwaite might add the "empowerment" of disadvantaged persons in the criminal justice system to this list. Restorative justice can also improve social justice by "reducing the impact of imprisonment as a cause of the unequal burdens of unemployment, debt, and suicide," for example.[23]

17. Ibid., 403.
18. Braithewaite, 157.
19. Ibid., 157–58.
20. Ibid.
21. Ibid., 158.
22. Ibid., 160–61.
23. Ibid., 161.

THE CASE OF SOUTH AFRICA

South Africa's experiment with restorative justice provides a test case for Braithwaite's theses. In 1995 the South African Truth and Reconciliation Commission (TRC) was established by the Government of National Unity to facilitate national healing in the aftermath of apartheid. The hearings, which began in April 1996, took an approach to restorative dialogue that combined elements of a legal process with elements of a restorative process. Public testimony before the commission gave the hearings the feel of a legal process. Yet the hearings were grounded in the restorative values of respect for victims, full participation, and truth-telling. Even though the model adopted by the TRC had restorative elements, it was less than fully restorative for several reasons: it granted amnesty to offenders in exchange for their truthful testimony; it disallowed victims from naming what they needed to put things right; and it required no accountability from offenders who testified. In place of offender accountability, victims who testified received a one-off monetary settlement of approximately $4000, plus other social benefits. The lack of accountability for racist violence disempowered the victims, and reinforced apartheid.

In one of the many poignant personal narratives told before the Truth and Reconciliation Commission, Ms. Beatrice Sethwale told how her son, a black police officer, was murdered by black people who identified police officers as agents of the apartheid system. I quote at length.

> On the 13th November 1985, it was a Wednesday morning. My son was driven out of the house by a crowd of people who were stoning the house. We were in the house . . . He was driven out of the home and shortly afterward he was killed and burnt . . . I feel I am already dead and that this process will be a very long and time-consuming one. It will take a lot of effort to make me entirely normal again because I have become quite used to my pain and place where I find myself currently. I don't bear any grudges against anybody. But if you lose your confidence and your faith in other people, it is very hard to restore. My faith in my fellow human being has been shattered, but I don't bear anybody any grudge'[24]

I do not expect that any system of justice can fully restore persons, like Ms. Sethwale, who have been shattered and become accustomed to their pain and place. But I think that restorative justice can do more than it

---

24. Public testimony of Ms. Beatrice Sethwale. Individuals murdered Officer Sethwale, but his murder was occasioned by the socially sanctioned violence of a historically racist political system.

accomplished in South Africa. My concern is that the RJ approach used by the TRC became an adjunct to apartheid instead of a transitional alternative. In the context of a historically racist state dominated by whites, black victims, like Beatrice Sethwale, had no say in how restorative justice might be proactively used.[25] Further, power brokers in the old system did not have to identify how they would work with black communities to restore public life "without perpetuating the passive violence that avoids the exigencies or costs of restoration."[26]

One can critique the TRC for employing a less than fully restorative process, given the absence of both offender accountability and appropriate reparations. But accountability for individual acts of wrongdoing in an apartheid state or a Jim Crow state is insufficient to disrupt racialized violence without massive structural dislocation and reallocation of resources. When the faith of marginalized people shatters because they have lived too long with the multiple effects of white privilege and the oppressive race culture that protects it, then what exactly does restorative justice fix for people under siege? Whose good does it ultimately serve?

In a 2014 article on the current state of restorative justice in South Africa, authors Nadine F. Bowers du Toit and Grace Nkomo make the case that restitution and reparations are essential as a means of restorative justice in South Africa.[27] They cite a 2010 report by economist Murray Leibbrandt *et al.* to argue that the policies of apartheid have prevented both the dismantling of white privilege and a broad scale socio-economic transformation. Leibbrandt states: "In addition to high poverty levels, South Africa's inequality levels are among the highest in the world. Furthermore, levels of poverty and inequality continue to bear a persistent racial undertone."[28]

This social, economic reality, reflective of the unfinished nature of restorative justice in South Africa, prompted Archbishop Emeritus Desmond Tutu to call for a one-off "wealth tax" on wealthy white South Africans in 2011. Archbishop Tutu recognized that government *after* President Nelson Mandela was not interested in following the recommendations of the TRC, which included a proposal for meaningful reparations. The one-time transfer of wealth from haves to have-nots was intended to generate not only healing but also the equity necessary to national healing. Tutu called the wealth tax "a vehicle for those who had benefitted from the past to

---

25. Zehr, *Little Book*, 12.
26. Andrews, "Race and Racism," 401–2.
27. Du Toit and Nkomo, "Ongoing Challenge."
28. Ibid., 2.

contribute to the future."²⁹ Instead of achieving the values of healing and restored community, the case of RJ in South Africa underscores what Dale Andrews calls "the passive violence that avoids the costs of restoration."³⁰ And for this reason, one might conclude contra Braithwaite that restorative justice risks the worsening of social justice.

RESTORATIVE JUSTICE POLARITIES AND FAULTLINES

Twenty years after the first gathering of the Truth and Reconciliation Commission on Reconciliation Day in 1995, the soul of apartheid South Africa survives in the inequitable distribution of wealth and social services based on a great measure of racial privilege and the political power that privilege and wealth can buy. South Africans were once united around a common cause to hear the stories of past injustice, but they are not united around a common cause to make right an unequal society.

Should restorative justice attempt to transform structures as well as persons? Is it even possible to change unjust structures? Donald Shriver identifies the tension at the heart of these questions as an underlying theme in restorative justice discourse. "Personal initiative and institutional influence," is one of six polarities that Shriver identifies in restorative justice.³¹ Shriver surmises that we are vulnerable to repeating wrongdoing if we do not change "our relation to some past."³² Instead of being a source for change, South African institutions, and especially government, undermined the work and recommendations of the TRC. For example, judges who refused to challenge racist apartheid laws were not summoned to testify and did not seek amnesty; higher-ranking officials in the apartheid system did not confess to wrongdoing or ask pardon. Further, perpetrators who refused the offer of amnesty in exchange for their story were not prosecuted. Instead, the offenders who took the amnesty deal were lower-ranking local agents who policed or managed systems designed by the powerful.³³

Shriver's thematic polarities are ethical concerns that point to fundamental conceptual conflicts in restorative justice. Theo Gavrielides, founder and Director of the IARS Institute identifies six faultlines of conceptual confusion. The faultlines are topics of debate in restorative discourse that

29. Tutu, "Unfinished Business."
30. Andrews, "Race and Racism," 402.
31. Shriver, "Repairing the Past," 214–17.
32. Ibid., 210.
33. Ibid., 214.

illuminate either a lack of consensus or a general ambiguity about core matters. The first two faultlines identify stress in reconciling the relationship of RJ to the criminal justice system. Gavrielides asks: (1) whether RJ functions independently of the criminal justice system or in connection to it and (2) whether restorative practices should work outside or within the criminal justice system. The next two faultlines consider the model itself regarding its purpose and participants: (3) Is RJ a unique decision-making process or a process designed to produce good outcomes? And (4) should RJ practices include the participation of a smaller number or larger number of stakeholders? The fifth fault-line marks division concerning punishment. Gavrielides asks (5) whether RJ is an alternative punishment or an alternative to punishment. Finally, Gavrielides asks (6) whether RJ principles should be more or less flexible. Conceptual ambiguities and the ethical polarities they occasion are factors in "the mutating survival of racism."[34]

THE CASE FOR RESISTANCE IN SERVICE TO RESTORATION

But there is a bigger problem, and liberation theologian Enrique Dussel names it:

> The problem, of course, is that once the system of the world has asserted itself as the foundation or law, morality will depend precisely on the actualization of the scheme. An act will be *morally* good if it is "adequate to," if it complies with, the ends of the prevailing system. If I pay taxes, the minimum wage, and so on, as required by law, I shall be a "just" person, a "good" person. The law itself may be unjust. The taxes may be insufficient, and the wages may be starvation wages. But all of that lies *outside* any possible moral consideration.[35]

The problem with restorative justice is that it adapts its practices to unjust systems. In the US, for example, the restorative justice movement does not resist the racial discrimination of the criminal justice system. Rather, RJ practitioners labor in earnest to mitigate the effects of incarceration on communities that bear the brunt of structural discrimination and aversive racism. In the gap between restorative justice and social justice, restorative practices reengage aversive racism.

---

34. Gavrielides, *Restorative Justice*.
35. Dussel, *Ethics and Community*, 32 (emphasis original).

Hope and worry emanate from these in-between spaces, most notably the space between restorative theory and practice, and the space between restorative justice and social justice. One hopes that the actualization of corrective values into just practices can make a seismic shift in how communities approach wrongdoing and peacebuilding. Yet one worries that aversive racism also dwells in those gaps between the principles we profess and the practices we employ.

Let's take a closer look at these in-between spaces. Kathleen Daly maps an in-between place in her paper, "Mind the Gap: Restorative Justice in Theory and Practice." Using data collected from the South Australia Juvenile Justice (SAJJ) project on conferencing in the late 1990s, Daly identifies gaps in the meeting process, outcome, and effects. To "mind the gap," in a theoretical sense, means to identify, question, and negotiate the spaces between the ideal restorative justice conference and the outcomes experienced by victims and youth offenders.[36] Among the results, Daly reports that gaps tend to arise due to "organizational, cultural, and individual" factors that participants bring into the conference room.[37] These factors limit the success of conferences. Regarding organization, Daly reports that "organizational routines and professional interests can supersede the justice ideal for the conference."[38] The volume of cases, difficulties in scheduling, and preparation of coordinators are factors that can create an organizational culture in which the appropriate handling of cases becomes a more pressing matter than the repair of harm. The behavior of the coordinator determines the proper process. Conference facilitators must establish appropriate ground rules for the meeting, be polite, listen attentively, and show respect for victims and offenders. Conference fairness takes precedence over restorativeness in some cases because being fair is easier to achieve than doing justice.[39] More than this, fairness speaks directly to the professionalism and good name of the organization as it interfaces with participants.

Beyond organizational factors, restorativeness also depends on individual and cultural factors. Individuals have differing abilities to be empathic, to express remorse for wrongdoing, to take accountability for their actions, or to comprehend wrongdoing as a violation of persons. Aversive racism affects conference outcomes even when victim and offender reach an agreement. Racism undermines the efficacy of consensus arrangements to build an equitable and just community. Racial bias can also influence

36. Daly, "Mind the Gap," 1–2.
37. Ibid., 14.
38. Ibid., 15.
39. Ibid., 17.

whether victims trust the sincerity of an offender's remorse, or whether wrongdoers care more about their own social standing than the harm that victims experience. Conference coordinators expose racial bias when they mistake discrete cultural expressions for disrespect or a failure to take accountability for wrongdoing. Though Daly does not consider aversive racism in this paper, one wonders if racial bias presents itself in some of the data that she reports. For example, Daly says "while most YPs [young people who have committed an offense] stated that they apologized because they were genuinely sorry, most victims did not think the young people's apologies were genuine."[40] I do not claim that racial bias is the default explanation for every gap in restorative justice. Nor do I think that racism is the unmoved mover of all disagreement. Rather, I contend that racial bias is present in restorative practices, a factor for which restorative justice theorists have an insufficient causal explanation.

Given the organizational, cultural and individual factors that influence the conference process and outcomes, Daly advises readers to mind the gap between the "nirvana story" of restorative justice and what is practically achievable. Daly writes:

> The Nirvana story assumes that people are ready and able to resolve disputes, to repair harms, to feel contrite, and perhaps to forgive others when they may not be willing and able to do any of these things at all. It holds out the promise that these things *should happen most of the time* when research suggests that these things can occur *some of the time.*[41]

The concept of nirvana is an apt metaphor to describe the high ideals that predispose us to hope for a measure of justice that exceeds our best efforts. Religious thought provides an insightful source for reflection about the gaps between our beliefs and practices. Theologian Amy Plantinga Pauw attends to the continual "slippage and compromise" that occurs between faith and practice.[42] The coherence of belief and practice is insightful for RJ practitioners who question the in-between places in restorative justice. This integration is also insightful for religious communities that contextualize restorative practices for particular ministries.

In her chapter, "Attending to the Gaps between Beliefs and Practices," Pauw names fundamental Christian beliefs that orient disciples to the troubling space in-between belief and practice. I think three lessons in particular hold significance for understanding the gap in restorative justice

40. Ibid.
41. Ibid., 18 (emphasis original).
42. Volf, and Bass. *Practicing Theology,* 33.

between theory and practice. First, Christians believe that no human life "entirely escapes disfigurement."[43] Our beliefs, desires, and practices, no matter how vibrant or virtuous, are not good enough to avoid the disfigurement that comes from our engagement with culturally biased norms. Cultures reengage particular biases so thoroughly that the effects are evident in the automatic and implicit associations we make about ourselves and others who are not like us in some relevant respect. Second, beliefs are not reducible to particular practices.[44] There is no straight line from conviction to the action that replicates it, and no straight line between a body of beliefs and a set of practices. Finally, deep-seated "desires and dispositions" play a vital role in linking beliefs and practices.[45] Right views do not yield good practices without sincere desire.

With respect to restorative justice, Dussel, for example, describes an ethical disfigurement when practices are adequate to unjust prevailing systems, thereby becoming instruments of injustice. Restorative justice needs a strategy to identify and resist the ethical disfigurement of its practices. Second, one can make a compelling case for a straight line between fundamental restorative principles and core practices. It makes sense, for example, that violations of persons and relationships are put right by methods in which offenders take responsibility for the abuse they caused and restore equity through restitution, apology, or an expression of shame for their behavior. The practice fits well with the principle in many contexts.

Now consider the context of "a race culture that refuses accountability for generations of inherited racial privilege."[46] Racial privilege and the domination necessary to preserve it foster a system of "racialized social control."[47] The primary instrument of power over black people in this culture is the structure of mass incarceration and the abrogation of citizenship rights in its aftermath. The structure worked so well that by 2006 "1 in every 14 black men was behind bars compared with 1 in every 106 white men."[48] A 2007 study sponsored by the US Justice Department found that "African American youth account for 16 percent of all youth, 28 percent of all juvenile arrests, 35 percent of the youth waived to adult criminal court and 58 percent of youth admitted to state adult prison."[49] In this system,

---

43. Plantinga Pauw, "Attending to the Gaps," 34.
44. Ibid., 37.
45. Ibid., 34.
46. Andrews, "Race and Racism," 403.
47. Alexander, *New Jim Crow*, 58.
48. Ibid., 100.
49. Ibid., 118.

most felons are not in prison or jail, but under "community correctional supervision," better known as probation or parole.[50] During this period of corrective oversight, the felon's jurisdiction enforces legal mandates that bar them from public housing and discriminate against them in obtaining safe housing. But this is only the beginning of the reentry nightmare. Having a criminal record makes felons ineligible for food stamps, forces them to indicate a felony conviction on employment applications. Alexander writes that formerly incarcerated people "find themselves locked out of the mainstream society and economy—permanently."[51] Given this reality, what does restoration entail? In the context of racial privilege and political power, terms like restoration, accountability, equity, putting things right, participation, respect, and community-building underscore very different realities for privileged communities and marginalized ones.

Resistance against white privilege and the deconstruction of racial hierarchy are necessary for this context. Political resistance is needed not only in search of social justice politics but also in pursuit of entirely restorative practices. If privilege, domination, and disinterest have maintained social structures that reduce community to a warehouse for disposable people, what, then, is the virtue for disposable people in community-building dialogue? If healing generational trauma is beyond the scope of the justice that restores, then what is the merit in holding traumatized people accountable for healing trauma? The double-standard where race is concerned betrays the universality of the moral principle ("accountability," in this case), and reveals the principle to be an instrument for the normalization of racialized control. Pathologies of segregation have worked this way in the US. During slavery, Jim Crow segregation, and mass incarceration, whites portrayed blacks as being preternaturally violent, and established systems of control. And nothing short of a "major social movement" will heal these pathologies. Michelle Alexander writes: "Meaningful reforms can be achieved without such a movement, but unless the public consensus supporting the current system is completely overturned, the basic structure of the new caste system will remain intact."[52]

Herein lies the danger for restorative justice. The RJ movement can achieve significant reforms and still perpetuate the new caste system. Kathleen Daly and Julie Stubbs get it right. Restorative justice is "a white justice model," and therefore it "cannot be prescribed, nor adopted formulaically."[53]

50. Ibid.
51. Ibid.
52. Ibid., 80.
53. In Johnstone and Van Ness, *Handbook*, 162.

I worry that restorative justice is colorblind to the collective impact of its conceptual ambiguities, ethical polarities, and gaps in-between theory and practice. Given these concerns, restorative justice has to reconceptualize resistance before it can be fully restorative in the context of aversive racism. If it fails to do this work then RJ becomes an intramural sport in regard to the needs of marginalized people. Further, given that RJ is a white justice model, the black church has to contextualize a restorative approach for it to function as a source of liberation in contemporary black church praxis.

I propose below a model developed by Dale Andrews and Robert Smith that addresses both tasks. In *Black Practical Theology*, Andrews and Smith construct a model that functions as an intermediary between restorative justice and Michelle Alexander. The scholarship of Dale Andrews in particular shows how both stakeholders are part of the same public conversation.

PRAXIS AND CRITICISM IN THE BLACK RELIGIOUS STORY

Systematic theologian James H. Evans contends that praxis is at the heart of black religion.[54] That is to say, black religion provides normative guidance that takes seriously the uniqueness of an African American worldview, ethical principles developed in the crucible of horrific violence, and the rich interplay of black cultural and religious expressions. (21) Moral behavior in the black religious tradition mirrors an ethos of shared doctrinal and cultural beliefs, faithful witness, theological interpretation, inherited religious practices, and stories of what it means to be a community.[55] The task for religious adherents is to determine what it means to be a community of faith in their discrete social historical setting. Take for example the praxis of African slaves. Evans tells us their beliefs about God always correlated closely with their actions. Slaveholding Christians preached a racist gospel of black subservience and obedience that African Christians rejected as a violation of God's righteousness.[56] Instead, religious belief and cultural self-understanding generated an ethics of liberation, with practices that were unique to their contexts.

Evans argues that praxis in black religion is accompanied by "the search for truth."[57] This search occasions a "critical consciousness" that complements and informs religious practices. (22) The search for truth in-

---

54. Evans, *We Have Been*, 21.
55. Ibid., 22–26.
56. Ibid., 21.
57. Ibid., 22.

dicates a cognitive value to praxis. As Evans puts it, "what one knows as the truth is very much conditioned by the reality in which one participates."[58] For black people that reality has been largely shaped by the deliberate misrepresentations of themselves as being an inferior people. Distinguishing between the reality of oppression and the reality of God's creation is a chief hermeneutical task of black religion. In its hermeneutical function, black religion asks why things are the way they are and how do we experience God in our lives.[59] Moreover, black religion promotes an essential knowledge of who black people are in the eyes of God and this knowledge informs faithful practices.

The dynamic interplay of praxis and the meaning-making processes of black faith communities are central to the model proposed by Andrews and Smith.[60] Praxis entails an ability to see oneself as a self in relation, a reflexive self. Reflexivity, in the words of Archie Smith, is "the key to understanding the capacity of the self to bring a critical perspective to bear in the present light of the whole."[61] The self in relation can gain insight, for example, about embedded biases and power arrangements that contribute to the mutating survival of racism. Reflexivity is a core component of praxis along with inherited theological traditions and devotional practices, culture, history, social sciences, and moral agency.[62]

There are lessons here about praxis for restorative justice. Let me name a few of them. First, praxis requires a meta-analysis of the society in which restorative justice is done as well as the places that RJ holds in that society. A meta-analysis can inform not only restorative practices but also restorative principles and questions. Guiding questions (such as, "Who has been harmed?" and "What are their needs?") are the essence of restorative justice, but these questions alone fail to expose the terrifying reality that Michelle Alexander describes so vividly in *The New Jim Crow*. What sort of guiding question for restorative justice practitioners might orient them to pay attention to such realities before they ever meet with stakeholders in restorative practices? Should antiracism training become a regular practice for all conference facilitators? How can restorative justice utilize qualitative and quantitative analysis to evaluate how racial bias is experienced in restorative practices by RJ practitioners and stakeholders?

58. Ibid.
59. Ibid., 22–23.
60. Andrews and Smith, *Black Practical Theology*, 22–23.
61. Andrews, *Black Practical Theology*, 14.
62. Andrews and Smith, *Black Practical Theology*, 4.

A second lesson for RJ pertains to restorative outcomes. RJ needs a way to evaluate the extent to which it functions as an alternative to a racially biased justice system and as an adjunct to this system. RJ might ask its stakeholders and local communities, What are we really restoring here? The question indicates a meaning-making process that is essential to having a critical consciousness, and that sheds light on how well restorative justice is functioning in African American communities.

Lastly, RJ can learn a lesson from black practical theology about the significance of reflexivity for praxis and meaning-meaning processes. This insight can help RJ to become a more robust and dynamic dialogue partner for African American faith communities. RJ might consider how to engage and be present with these communities as they resist the historic wrongdoing by a nation that has no intention to put things right. If a restorative approach extends no further than conferencing with African Americans when they are about to be sentenced, paroled, or expelled from school, then RJ will miss an opportunity to model a new practice of reflexive engagement with black people. Reflexivity, in the search for truth, is a key conceptual insight to develop a type of resistance that promotes restoration.

In addition to lessons about praxis, the praxiological response criticism proposed by Andrews and Smith can also instruct RJ about the meaning-making processes of black faith communities. Andrews contributes a proposal for hearer-response criticism to black practical theology. As a practical theological method, response criticism attends to the meaning-making activities of faith communities in response to inherited sacred texts, religious doctrines, and an awareness of current social realities in the community of faith.

Andrews' hearer response criticism, indebted to reader response criticism, is well-suited to the three distinct encounter and dialogue models at the heart of restorative justice. A central insight of reader response criticism is that "the reader is a producer rather than a consumer of meaning."[63] Not only the reader but the hearer too participates in meaning-making activities. In Andrews' proposal, the hearer engages with the faith community in a particular social context, church leaders, sacred texts, scholars and scholar-pastors, inherited belief systems, and traditional practices. A reflexive ecology includes all of these sources to make meaning and to do justice. No one source owns the copyright to meaning. Making meaning is a dialogical process.

Beyond its commitment to the production of meaning, praxiological response criticism is also committed to justice and to the "future flourishing

---

63. "Reader Response," in *Glossary of Literary Theory*.

of dispossessed peoples." Andrews and Smith envision that the collaboration of scholars and scholar-pastors will yield "a fresh, creative approach to articulating black liberation." (4) In this regard, it advocates for a social and political liberation no less than a spiritual one. The work of liberation is the work of transformation. Hearer-response criticism sets a theoretical foundation for the transformation of theological traditions, black theological worldviews, and religious practices.

One insight for RJ is the idea that hearers produce meaning. This is no doubt a controversial idea in restorative theory. Restorative justice has by design a rather straight-line approach from principles to practices. Stakeholders are encouraged to participate freely in restorative practices, but the practices are part of an immovable system. As a result, restorative principles are inflexible. If the criticism is correct that RJ is a white system of justice, then the normativity of whiteness is preserved in principles and practices that can only be consumed by stakeholders but not produced. How much flexibility do practitioners and stakeholders have in reconceiving restorative norms? My interest is not to remove restorative sacred texts or scholarship as sources of meaning, but to promote the involvement of an enlarged circle of truth-seekers. A second lesson for RJ concerns the role of criticism in resistance. In hearer response criticism, as in feminist criticism, the first task is to resist false narratives, stereotypes and biased assumptions. Writing about feminist criticism, Judith Fetterley makes the point that, "Feminist criticism is a political act whose aim is not simply to interpret the world but to change it by changing the consciousness of those who read and their relation to what they read."[64] Hearers, no less than readers, participate in the transformation of their consciousness by resisting the hegemonic perspective of whiteness and its normative authority. One last lesson for RJ from black practical theology concerns advocacy. Restorative justice advocates for reform. Black practical theology advocates for liberation. RJ advocates for a process that addresses the "future intentions" of offenders. Black practical theology advocates for the "future flourishing of dispossessed people."

The two models of justice are by no means mutually exclusive. On the contrary, they are part of the same justice conversation. My proposal is that restorative justice can learn from black practical theology how to rethink the interrelatedness of principles and practices in a way that resists aversive racism. In short, RJ can learn to have respect for black people. I use the term *respect* deliberately. Howard Zehr writes, "If I had to put restorative justice into one word, I would choose respect."[65]

64. *Glossary of Literary Theory.*
65. Zehr, Little Book, 47.

In conclusion, praxiological response criticism can help restorative justice to name biases, expose hypocrisy, disrupt complicity, and resist other features of aversive racism that can hide in conceptual ambiguities and ethical polarities. The model also welcomes dialogue that is committed to seeking truth and that occasions justice and human flourishing. Perhaps respect requires RJ practitioners to ask two questions in tandem: Who or what is responsible for the mutating survival of racism? And have we adequately considered the possibility of built-in biases and assumptions in the way we articulate and practice restorative justice? If this work is possible, then perhaps the scholarship of Dale Andrews can provide a way for black churches, practical theology, and restorative justice to "help society celebrate the successes over racism without contributing to its survival."[66]

AFTERWORD

I became interested in restorative justice a few years ago. Interestingly, my study of African American theological ethics and social justice did not bring RJ to my attention. Rather, I was introduced to restorative concepts and practices through my volunteer work in the Louisville Metro community where I trained to facilitate family group conferences that function as a diversionary program of the Department of Juvenile Justice. I have participated in enough conferences to have high hopes and significant worries about restorative justice.

The bulk of my cases involve black boys who have been charged with assault or criminal mischief. The offenders I met are mostly black. The victims I met are mostly white, or represent white institutions. The facilitators I worked with have all been white. My goal as a conference facilitator is to guide the participants through a carefully designed process of engagement and dialogue that leads to an agreement between victim and offender. The agreements I recorded detail what victims need from offenders, within reason, in order to feel that the offenders have demonstrated sufficient accountability for their wrongdoing. The agreements also carry the hope of the broader community that the young offenders will not commit more crimes in the future.

I witnessed what I can describe only as minor miracles when white victims requested that black offenders participate in an educational enrichment experience in lieu of repaying monetary damages. I witnessed empathy take over a cold room where I feared vengeance would erupt. I leave these conferences nevertheless feeling tired, grateful, and conflicted.

66. Andrews, "Race and Racism," 409.

I am grateful that I had a hand in keeping a black boy out of the juvenile justice system. I leave feeling conflicted, however, because I know that I can facilitate these conferences indefinitely without moving the needle toward social justice in my community. I tried to content myself with the idea that RJ is not designed to resist aversive racism, but to no avail. My enthusiasm for restorative justice has been tempered by my concern that it is not doing enough to restore the at-risk children I meet.

I lamented that the restorative justice conversation and the social justice conversation were hopelessly estranged from each other. I changed my mind, however, in reading the scholarship of Dale Andrews. I found in Dale's scholarship a model of prophetic practical theology that provides a bridge between restorative justice and Michelle Alexander. More than this, the model provides a way for me to engage restorative justice and recommend resources for addressing conceptual ambiguities as well as gaps between theory and practice. Dale's hope that practical theology can help society to celebrate successes over racism without contributing to its survival is the inspiration for my hope that restorative justice can resist aversive racism. The work of contextualizing restorative justice for transformed modes of black church praxis remains for me to do.

25

A Three-Fold Homiletic Lesson from Dr. King's Pastoral and Prophetic Preaching on Violence

SUNGGU YANG

IN 1992 WHEN WALTER Wink stated in his *Engaging the Powers*, "Violence is the ethos of our times. It is the spirituality of the modern world," he was more than right.[1] Nowadays, we experience violence everywhere we breathe, walk, and look, even though not every violent case is visible or directly felt. In his statement, Wink was referring specifically to two aspects of violence that make us particularly uncomfortable or sad living in the twenty-first-century North American context.

First, he made the statement in 1992, twenty-four years after Martin Luther King was assassinated in 1968. A great deal had changed over those two decades, yet violence itself had not changed all that much! Violence still remains violence. Though when Wink discusses the violent ethos of the modern world, he does not have the Civil Rights Movement foremost in mind (yet still, he mentions King several times in his writing), his critical observation that our time and place is more permeated with violence is valid and helpful.

The second thing that makes us sad is that Wink observes that human violence has become a more acceptable *spirituality* of the modern world. That is, with violence being a *real* part of our souls and lives, now we not

1. Wink, *Engaging the Powers*, 13.

only accept violence as a *natural* part of our life, but also in many cases *approve* the use of violence. Of course, in the twentieth century, including King's era, violence in various forms was sanctioned in many ways, but now we see this tendency more elevated in everyday life.

Indeed, the most dreadful thing about violence is that once we start accepting and approving violence as a natural or inevitable part of our lives, there is no remedy for violence except for more violent actions against another act of violence. Given the circumstances, we must ask: In a culture with such a violence-saturated ethos, where do we find hope and what message should be proclaimed? Specifically, what hope or message do we preachers have and will we proclaim it? When these urgent questions come to visit our troubled hearts, gratefully we may find King's homiletic practice or his pastoral and prophetic message still applicable today for many a great benefit. I see at least three benefits or lessons from King that we can adopt in formulating the message of hope, justice, and reconciliation for our context.

A THREEFOLD THEOLOGICAL AND HOMILETIC LESSON FROM KING

Before delving into a detailed discussion of King's homiletic practice or message on violence, we need to realize that when King was fighting against the violent culture of his own era, he was not only struggling with the racial issue (which was immediately related to black people's lives), but was also trying to deconstruct all kinds of violence in the modern world. He realized that many kinds of violence had permeated North America, such as economic injustice, socio-political inequity, and immigrants' perils caused by the oppressive social and political powers. For instance, one of his biggest concerns regarding the violence of his era was the Vietnam War in which the U.S. was taking a significant part. He furiously and publicly opposed the Vietnam War because of its unjust causes and the misjudgment of the U.S. citizens about that war. Many citizens were excited about and supported the war, which made King both severely depressed and irritated. He could not accept U.S. citizens' unjust minds and violent actions in the Vietnam War. Hence, King preached:

> I am convinced that it is one of the most unjust wars that has ever been fought in the history of world. Our involvement in the war in Vietnam has torn up the Geneva Accord. It has strengthened the military industrial complex; it has strengthened the forces of reaction in our nation. It has put us against the self-determination of a vast majority of the Vietnamese people, and

put us in the position of protecting a corrupt regime that is stacked against the poor.[2]

Sadly enough, unjust social matters, political inequity, and other types of violence of King's era continue to exist in ours. In everyday life, we often witness the economic injustice between Hispanic immigrants and their employers; we hear of plans to destroy black churches; we watch cruel killings and other violence on T.V. reality shows and dramas; we witness how unjustly children and women are treated in our society; we read in the morning newspapers about the increasing death toll of and by U.S. soldiers dispatched to other countries; and we hear the news of violent rapes and killings happening every hour in Darfur, Sudan and around the globe. De facto, we continue to live in the era of violence in which King once lived, which eventually led to his assassination. There is, therefore, no cultural difference between his time and ours regarding violence, at least in terms of its level of cruelty and pervasiveness.

This is why I invite us to revisit preacher King's reconciliatory theology and his preaching messages. His theology and messages still have much to teach us in the 21st century. In at least three ways his preaching theology and messages can help us to cope with our own issues of violence.

UNVEIL AND DENY THE CULTURAL ETHOS OF VIOLENCE

First, King guides us to unveil the current cultural ethos of violence and its denial. Whereas King mourned in his time, so too nowadays we tend to accept and, even worse, approve the violent cultural ethos of our society, which in turn engenders a great deal of injustice. In other words, we accept and approve violence without reflecting on it critically. How sad is that! We tend to think that violence is a natural and inescapable thing. We believe it is the way in which humans and society are created to live. "The survival of the fittest" has become a daily mantra. For instance, we tend to accept as natural that a very few people have abundance while most people struggle to get by, or that nations invade other nations to get more land, resources, and power. By our actions or our inaction, ultimately we accept that people with economic and socio-political privileges monopolize their powers. We have come to believe that this is the natural way to live! Rather than contest the inequality, we accept it, or worse, we actually endorse it. Yet that very kind of thinking regarding social, economic, and political violence King opposed.

---

2. Carson and Holloran, *Knock at Midnight*, 219.

For him, there is nothing natural about humans being violent toward each other. Indeed, it is a corruption of original human nature created in *imago Dei*. According to the Holy Scriptures, specifically the book of Genesis, humans were never created to live in that violent way. Rather, we were created to live in harmony and peace with each other as well as with God. On that basis, God created the whole universe. The God of universal love and justice created the world for humanity to live in peace, love, and justice with all others, King believed. It is no secret that we are far from living in the way God intended. We fallen humans have corrupted the original Garden of peace and love and generated unnatural violence. To have any chance at recapturing the original nature of this world and our society, thought King, we first have to condemn and deny that corruption and violence.

PARTICIPATE IN GOD'S TRANSFORMING WORK IN HISTORY

Second, whether Christian or not, we are all invited to participate in God's transforming work in history through everyday life situations. Such partnership and collaboration is crucial. For God does not exist "over there," beyond the mess of the human world, nor is God an abstract projection of human's spiritual ideal. Rather, God is *here and now*, working with the oppressed and afflicted for the historical transformation of the unjust human world. Indeed, this is both (1) a strong counter-cultural statement against the broad societal atheistic notion of God today, which tends to make us regard the God of real historical liberation and reconciliation as a God of creative human invention for an imaginary mythic world, and (2) it is an adamant denial of the current church's supernatural eschatology or so-called "after-death eschatology." Already common capitalist society has lost any notion of divine judgment upon the historical world. As regards justice, capitalist society knows only its own laws, customs, and regulations. So, when its laws, customs, and regulations justify its ideals of life and social actions, there can be no higher judgment upon it, even though its ideals and actions may be unjust in the light of basic human nature or from any fine religious perspective. In such a society, there is no such thing as the God who acts against its unjust causes. Unfortunately, nowadays many Christian churches have also abandoned the notion of divine judgment upon human history. The churches seem to be satisfied with after death eschatology or Last Day eschatology, as Jürgen Moltmann lamented decades ago.[3] With this type of eschatology, the churches are unable to think about and act

---

3. Moltmann, *Theology of Hope*, 15–16.

for God's historical transformation of oppressive life circumstances. Many churches no longer talk about justice and transformation on the earth in the here and now, but project it to some far off date or far off heavenly place. In so doing, churches do not recognize their own redemptive and transformative capacity, a capacity planted in them long ago and demonstrated in Christ's life, death, and resurrection.

Facing these two misguided social and ecclesial notions of divine judgment and transformation, King cannot be more unyielding in asserting God's historical judgment upon the violent reality (or the oppressors) and God's historical restoration of the afflicted. Judgement is not the final phase, however. Ultimately, God works toward the reconciliation first between God and people and second between the afflicted and the violent oppressors or systems. King is more than convinced that God is working with the afflicted for the transformation of the unjust causes in concrete history. So King reiterates over and over again that God is present now, for and with God's people. King realized that in history there had been a number of vivid examples of God at work in such people and events as Thomas Jefferson, Abraham Lincoln, Sojourner Truth, the Emancipation Proclamation, and the Civil Rights Act of 1964. To his mind, such instances of God's redemptive, transformative, and reconciling work in people's everyday lives is the best example churches today can give of God's participation in the lives of the afflicted, the poor, and the abandoned here and now.

THE PREACHER'S PASTORAL AND PROPHETIC MESSAGE

Third, King realized that when the churches awaken to the violent causes of society, preachers can play a significant role in that transforming and liberating work by preaching pastoral and prophetic messages on the Word of Christ. Indeed, King came to acknowledge this reality by his own experiences in Montgomery. When one third of the black population of the city gathered together to listen to the Reverend King, and when he experienced that his voice was a most powerful instrument for black people's non-violent liberation movement, King instantly knew that the preacher could play a key role in the liberation of afflicted black people. As his life shows, King himself played that key role as a prophetic mediator for reconciliation between God and humans and between afflicted persons and oppressive systems. By being a prophetic mediator for transformation and reconciliation, King created his own pastoral and prophetic message for Christians and all of society. Doubtless, his message was both pastoral and prophetic. Pastorally, he pursued peace, love, and reconciliation of all people; prophetically, he actively invested himself in social transformation.

King's witness provides a huge challenge to preachers today. Confronting social injustice and all kinds of violence, we preachers are encouraged and challenged to preach pastorally and prophetically for all people's reconciliation and social transformation. Of course, we preachers are not expected to deliver a pastoral *and* prophetic message all the time. At times, genuinely pastoral preaching is required, as in a case of a beloved elder's peaceful funeral service in a local church, while for some occasions justice-seeking prophetic preaching is mandatory, as in the case of a Women's Rights March. Yet in the final analysis King himself showed, and Dale Andrews has taught us as well, that combining the Christian message of agape-oriented human care with adamant social prophecy is the best mode of any preaching for the sake of the suffering violent world.

Thankfully, preacher King is still alive among us. We can refer to him and his many sermons and speeches as we shape our own pastoral and prophetic messages for transformation and reconciliation in the present violent world. Thus, we are called *here and now*, just as King was, to work for transformation of social violence, for peace and love between conflicting parties, for healing and restoration of the afflicted, and for harmonious life among all nations. To this transformational yearning and continuing pursuit of reconciliation, King seems to have his own theological and homiletic answer to violence that he shares with us preachers today: that is, for us to trust, preach, and act in the same compassionate God who works for and within us for liberation, peace, justice, and reconciliation of the afflicted in our particular historical contexts today.

THE KING LEGACY CONTINUES

In January 2009, Bishop Woodie W. White, the Bishop in Residence at Candler School of Theology in Emory University then, wrote his 33rd annual letter to King as follows:

> Those days of marches and protests were aimed at simple but important goals: to eat at a lunch counter, to try on a garment before you purchased it, to attend a school in the neighborhood where you lived, to be hired for a job for which you were qualified, and yes, to exercise the most fundamental right of citizenship, to vote . . . We sought to be accepted, and to be treated as a person and a full citizen in our own nation . . . That said, it would be naïve to conclude that racism and bigotry in America

are dead. *They are very much alive. Racism dies hard.* But its grip in the minds and hearts of Americans, Martin, is not as deep or as broad as you experienced . . . We need to still challenge every expression of injustice, bigotry and racism in individuals and institutions. Mr. Obama's election should encourage us to continue rather than end these efforts! . . . In so many ways, Martin, we are a better nation, a better people than you left. Not perfect, but better. And in some ways, the nation is moving beyond The Dream! Thank you and happy birthday, Martin. We are overcoming![4]

What Bishop White is telling us through his letter to King is straightforward: King's legacy of the pastoral and prophetic message has continued ever since he left America by his tragic assassination. And we are the inheritors and practitioners of King's legacy and challenged to continue King's work and King's dream. In fact, this is what would best serve as the conclusion to my essay. Vis-à-vis the ever-daunting violent reality, King looked up to God, who has been proclaimed through the universe and who has also participated in human history to overturn the perils of the afflicted toward a Beloved Community of peace, justice, and harmony. Especially, King found and experienced this God represented in many historical instances and preached that God in his own present—physical and historical—moment. He was a preacher who *re-represented* this God of peace, care, and justice through his own words. It was one of King's dreams that every person who experienced the same God that King preached would be able to come together to make the world more peaceful, just, and harmonious. For then "every valley shall be exalted, and every mountain will be made low; the rough places would be made plain, and the crooked places straight; and the glory of the Lord shall be revealed, and all flesh shall see it together."[5] In Bishop White's letter to King, we find that ambitious dream of King being achieved through the people who listened to his words and adopted King's dream as their own. Among the many reasons why this has been possible is this: the God that King found is a real participant in human history. This God is a loving Friend of the afflicted and an all-embracing Reconciler between the oppressed and the oppressors. King knew that this God would be a sincere Companion of the oppressed, the poor, and the abandoned until the day when the Beloved Community is achieved in human history. Until then, people's struggle for the salvation of human history and liberation of the afflicted from violence will continue. Until then, the preacher's pastoral

---

4. White, "A Letter to Martin Luther King, Jr." (my emphasis).
5. Carson, *Knock at Midnight*, 112–13.

and prophetic message will not cease. Preachers will preach the message of reconciliation and justice until God's universal love fills the whole human land, until God's justice rolls down like waters on the earth, and until righteousness like an ever-flowing stream courses through all human hearts. King's homiletic dream still breathes among us.

PART 6

Sermons that Embody Prophetic Care

26

A Biblical Apprenticeship in Bridge-Building Ministry

A Two-Part Series

LUKE A. POWERY

A BRIDGE PERSON

THE REV. DR. DALE Andrews was a "bridge" individual in his scholarship, ministry, and life, as a professor, pastor, and person. Throughout his ecclesial and academic career, he bridged the theological fields of preaching and pastoral care as well as the academy and the church. In particular, he bridged the prophetic and pastoral voices in preaching and refused to silo any of these expressions; rather, he suggested that we "lift every voice and sing."[1] Beyond the halls of academia or the naves of the church, he took this bridging approach in interactions with a wide spectrum of people as he worked toward God's justice and reconciliation. He refused to separate justice and reconciliation and recognized the essential presence of each for the work of God in the world. Thus, in personal, professional, pastoral, and public domains, he embodied the gospel ideal of striving for a beloved community in word and deed.

Moreover, Dr. Andrews promoted the concept of apprenticeship, so important in African American settings, as a means of teaching and

---

1. Johnson, "Lift Every Voice."

learning. In this educational approach, a novice preacher is paired with an experienced preacher/pastor to be mentored in ministry, including preaching. This goes beyond the more formalized field education offered at seminaries and divinity schools and reveals his respect for "the folk" as sages, whether they have PhDs or no "D" at all. Even in this way, Andrews bridges educational styles and different walks of life, while tapping into a fruitful model of apprenticeship that is itself a bridge toward ministry.

Because building bridges is such a key theme for Dr. Andrews, a teacher of preaching and the practices of ministry, I offer the following two sermons in his honor as a kind of biblical apprenticeship in bridge-building ministry. The hope is that this practical theo-homiletical offering would provide biblical fodder for thoughtful reflection on building bridges in contemporary ministry. Both sermons were preached at Duke University Chapel but are offered here for a wider audience as we strive to be apprentices of the Spirit.

SERMON NUMBER 1: OUR OWN NATIVE TONGUE (ACTS 2:1-21)[2]

After hearing the sound of a rushing violent wind, seeing the divided tongues like fire resting on each of them, and hearing those filled with the Spirit speak in other languages, it's no surprise that those present ask each other the question, "What does this mean?" Of course, some think they are drunk from wine served at a college frat party. Peter assures them later that they aren't drunk at all with spirits but filled with another Spirit. "What does this mean?" It's a great question. People have been interpreting this passage for centuries trying to figure out what the Day of Pentecost means.

This Acts passage holds a special place in my historical memory since I spent my childhood and adolescent years in a classical Pentecostal church, although I'm ordained a Baptist, making me a "Bapticostal!" In classical Pentecostal doctrine, Acts chapter 2 is used as a proof text to teach that the initial physical evidence of a person having received the baptism of the Holy Spirit is speaking in tongues. This experience is subsequent to conversion. I heard this doctrine my entire life. I heard and saw many things in that Miami, Florida congregation. I heard people speaking in tongues. I saw people get slain in the Spirit. I heard ecstatic music with drums, organs, guitars, and brass instruments. I saw people clapping, dancing, and shouting. I can confirm writer James Baldwin's description of his father's Pentecostal church, when he writes, "I have never seen anything to equal the fire and excitement

---

2. All biblical quotes are from the NRSV.

that sometimes, without warning, fill a church, causing it to 'rock.'"³ There weren't necessarily holy rollers but we definitely had some holy rockers.

Pentecostalism, in all its forms, has exploded all over the world and is a major force in global Christianity such that we have charismatic Catholics and charismatic Anglicans, perhaps even charismatic Duke Chapelians. The world's Christian population has shifted from "the North" to the global South and this shift has been due to the tremendous growth of Pentecostal communities worldwide—in sub-Saharan Africa, Latin America, and numerous parts of Asia. The largest Christian congregation in the world, the Yoido Full Gospel Church, is in Seoul, Korea, which claims eight hundred thousand members, making Joel Osteen's megachurch look like a mini-church.

As a PK, a preacher's kid, I've seen and experienced all kinds of things in the ecumenical church in general and in the church of my youth in particular. The rhythmic clapping and dancing were captivating at times but they weren't the only things that captivated me at a young age in that congregation because I met a little 7-year-old girl who is now my wife. Pentecost has its benefits! But what does Pentecost really mean? Or, more accurately, what are its meanings?

Liturgically, Christians celebrate Pentecost as an end of the Easter season after fifty days, linking the resurrection and ascension of Christ with the sending of the Holy Spirit. Historically, Pentecost was related to the Jewish harvest festival of Shavuot or Feast of Weeks. It commemorated the giving of the Law at Sinai but also celebrated harvesting of wheat. During this festival, people could bring their first fruits to the temple as an offering. Using this historical lens, one might then say that Pentecost is the human experience of the first fruits of the Spirit. The liturgical or historical significance of Pentecost is not unimportant because this is part of its significance.

What else does Pentecost mean? As Christians, it's vital to attempt an answer to that question because Pentecost and Pentecostalism are not disappearing; it's on the rise, even if not in actual experience, but in the collective consciousness of the global church. In the third wave of the National Congregations Study, led by Duke sociology, religion, and divinity professor, Mark Chaves, we learn that from 1998–2012, drumming, jumping, shouting, dancing, raising hands in praise, using visual projection, and speaking in tongues have increased in congregations, while singing by a choir and use of a written program have decreased. Worship has become more informal and ethnic diversity in congregations is on the rise.⁴

---

3. Baldwin, "Letter from a Region."
4. Chaves, "Final Report."

The present state of the changing church would have been more welcoming to B.B. King, the King of the Blues, who died in May 2015. In his early days, there was tension between blues music and the church. Some viewed the blues as the devil's music and believed it had no place in the church. The church was a religious gatekeeper of who's in and who's out but what Pentecost reveals is that whatever is different or foreign may actually be the gift we need. Pentecost has many meanings but at the core of its meanings is the idea of gift.

Pentecost suggests that the ground of our spiritual life is fundamentally a divine gift. "And suddenly from heaven there *came* a sound sound. . . ." (2:2). The sound came. The Spirit came by divine volition. The Spirit is God's gift to us; and one of the gifts of the Spirit is the gift of multilingual speech. "All of them were filled with the Holy Spirit and began to speak in other languages, as the Spirit gave them ability." (2:4) Some were amazed for sure. "But others sneered and said, 'They are filled with new wine.'" (2:13) People don't always understand what God is doing or what is being said or played. It's like an unknown tongue. The blues wasn't accepted in every church because it was different but it was the blues that seemed to call B.B. King and others, even though some didn't understand the music and the man.

In a 1999 public conversation with William Ferris, chairman of the National Endowment for the Humanities, B.B. King recounted how he came to sing the blues. He said,

> Growing up on the plantation there in Mississippi, I would work Monday through Saturday noon . . . I'd go to town on Saturday afternoons, sit on the street corner, and I'd sing and play. I'd have me a hat or box or something in front of me. People that would request a gospel song would always be very polite to me, and they'd say: "Son, you're mighty good. Keep it up. You're going to be great one day." But they never put anything in the hat. But people that would ask me to sing a blues song would always tip me and maybe give me a beer. They always would do something of that kind. Sometimes I'd make 50 or 60 dollars one Saturday afternoon. Now you know why I'm a blues singer.[5]

B.B. King and the church, in particular, saw themselves as incommensurable with each other; there wasn't mutual understanding but the gift of the Spirit works toward comprehension and common ground.

Another prominent gift at Pentecost is the gift of understanding. The gift of speech makes breaking news but the gift of speech is not given in order *not* to be understood. Pentecost reveals a gift of the Spirit to be hearing

---

5. King, "Conversation with B.B. King."

A Biblical Apprenticeship in Bridge-Building Ministry 281

in one's own language. When disciples are filled with the Spirit and speak in other languages as the Spirit enables them, "Jews from every nation under heaven" become bewildered and amazed because "each one heard them speaking in the native language of each." (2:5–6) "And how is it that we hear, each of us, in our own native language?" (2:8) The miracle is not the physical ability of hearing but it is the understanding of what is said, despite the different cultures of the speakers. The lens of Pentecost urges us to seek understanding, not mere hearing, and to do so across native cultures.

The Spirit engages in the work of translation by translating the word of God into each native language present so that others may learn about God. Thus, the word is not monolingual. Pentecost reveals the Spirit's embrace of cultural particularity and context and promotes "essentially worldwide proclamation."[6] Translation into each language demonstrates a divine care for diverse cultures, ethnicities, and languages. In the Spirit, diversity is not a dirty word but a beautiful one in the light of God. If one has problems with diversity, one has to take it up with the Spirit who creates diversity in the first place, as the gospel is expressed in particular contexts, cultures, languages, and bodies.

Diversity is an "enduring theme" of Duke University's 2006 strategic plan, and it states, "In a world characterized by globalization and increasing inter-cultural interaction, it is critical that our students engage other cultures and the differing perspectives they offer in their daily experiences both inside and outside the classroom."[7] The range of human differences matters at Duke and in the world. Through the theological lens of Acts 2, we might call "diversity" a "pentecostal ecology." In this ecology, the notion of gift prioritizes the work of God, yet God doesn't deny or erase human identity. Pentecost reveals that human speakers and hearers are needed for "God's deeds of power" to be known. The Spirit embraces the cultures of humanity and Pentecost suggests the flourishing of humankind, not its destruction or eradication.

To have everyone speaking English in the same manner or having certain ethnic names changed to English may be questioned in the burning light of Pentecost because Pentecost reveals that we need Parthians, Medes, Elamites, and residents of Mesopotamia, Judea and Cappadocia, Pontus and Asia, Phrygia and Pamphylia, Egypt and the parts of Libya belonging to Cyrene, and visitors from Rome, both Jews and proselytes, Cretans and Arabs, East Carolinians and West Carolinians. We shouldn't erase our names, our languages, our cultures, our skin color, our hair texture, the color of

---

6. Welker, *God the Spirit*, 230.
7. Duke University Strategic Plan.

our eyes, the shape of our bodies, our identities. We shouldn't obliterate whom and what God has created in order to suit our needs and comforts and opinions—God made all of us with our own native tongue and when we are tempted to erase that which is different, it is an affront to God and God's collective body.

Pentecost is the creation of a particular kind of human community, a God-centered community, another key gift of the Spirit. The cultural particularity of the Spirit's gift is not contrary to a universal quality. The gifts of speech and understanding reveal the common message of the Spirit: God. What the people heard in their native languages was the message about "God's deeds of power." (2:11) In whatever language, God is central, both object and subject of life in the Spirit. Pentecost privileges God as the universal content of our message through particular cultural means. The end is always God but the means is always particular, holding together the creative relationship between particularity and universality. Dietrich Bonhoeffer once preached that people were bored with the church and the cinema appeared to be more interesting than the church "because we talk too much about false, trivial human things and ideas in the church and too little about God."[8]

The Spirit will not allow us to forget about God because "Through the pouring out of the Spirit, God effects a world-encompassing, multilingual, polyindividual testimony to Godself. . . ."[9] Though there is a diverse community, there is unity around the presence of God. Pentecost is a "community-building festival"[10] but it is a distinct community in which God is the center. Cultural specificity is important but in the Spirit it is decentered. God dethrones cultural or ethnic hegemony at Pentecost. But it's also necessary to note that cultural identities are not demolished either. Cultural identities are fully present and fully inspirited while the Spirit leads the people to speak about and praise God.

We can take the Spirit seriously and not hide behind or promote God as a way to homogenize the community into one totalizing paradigm. There is no homogenous universal church. Though God-centered, Pentecost reveals the gift of a community that represents boundary-breaking, bridge-making realities across culture, ethnicity, race, and language. In the Spirit, there's no room for segregated enclaves. The Spirit breaks us out of our totalizing patterns, breaks us out of seeing and understanding God in only one

---

8. Bonhoeffer, "Ambassadors for Christ," in *Collected Sermons of Dietrich Bonhoeffer*, 91.

9. Welker, *God the Spirit*, 235.

10. Johns, "Preaching Pentecost to the 'Nones'"

way, one theology, one perspective. The Spirit leads us to different views and voices, a different way of seeing the world and God. The Spirit leads us to embrace diversity as a gift of God while the Spirit moves us toward integration, collaboration, and mutuality between different voices as a way to form community.

The formation of a global community through the in-breaking of the Spirit breaks humanity out of our proclivity toward sameness and moves us to embrace a broad, inclusive gospel for "the ends of the earth." (1:8) The Spirit breaks open our hearts to include all people, and as my Baptist brothers and sisters might say, to "open the doors of the Church" and break us out of our tendencies to be with those who are just like us in every way. The gift of God opens us up to a hospitable vision in which the Spirit is poured out on "all flesh." (2:17) Thus, no one is exempt from the blessing of the Spirit being poured out over your life, regardless of race, age, gender, or class. Any person anywhere can be a conduit of the Spirit. There's no limit to whom or where the gospel can be preached because the gospel travels and knows no bounds as the Spirit creates a diverse human community. Pentecost suggests that the Spirit opens us up to the possibility of hospitable relationships across cultures as opposed to closed off systems that restrict the full scope of the gospel of God. This means Bach and Brahms can be in the same spiritual family as B.B. King and Branford Marsalis. Hymns and Hip-Hop may actually commune with each other when the Spirit blows.

The promise of Pentecost is that even though we may not speak the same language, we serve the same God and are members of the same community built on the love of Christ. Without different tongues or languages, the fire of the Spirit might be dimmer but with one another from every tribe and nation in the unity of the Spirit, we may come to understand the light and beauty of God in a fuller way. The gift of this community is that it is "not a homogenous unity, but a differentiated one."[11] Pentecost represents the preservation and goodness of human diversity in God's community. The church is called to be unified, not uniform. We aren't the church when we are uniform; we are the church in the power of the Spirit when we are unified, a unified diversity focused on God. This is a powerful witness in a world that is so divided. Pentecost reminds us of the unmerited gift of God resting on all flesh like fire that doesn't destroy but builds, creates, and invites us to a mutual hospitality.

From the cosmopolitan church of my youth, I remember Bro. Hing, Bro. Keith, Bro. Timms, and Bro. Mack. I remember Sis. Timms, Sis. Santiche, and Sis. Bostwick. I remember the cloud of witnesses, including Sis.

---

11. Welker, *God the Spirit*, 228.

Jean. She had a big smile on her face and a bounce in her step every Sunday. We sang in the choir together when I was a teenager. I can still hear her greeting me—"Hi, Bro. Luke." She had a way of saying it—"Bro. Luke." After several years passed after high school, I went back home to Miami expecting to hear good news about the sweet elder Christian sisters from my youth. Instead, I found out that the bounce in Sis. Jean's step had been stolen. Stolen from a sickness that was decaying her body. She still went to church. She even had special seating. A couch was placed right in the front of the sanctuary near the pulpit platform. They put it there so she could still hear the hymns of faith. They put it there so she could rest when needed. Her heart still sang even though it was broken. Broken because the disease she had was AIDS, contracted from her very own husband who had been fooling around. A God-fearing, church-going woman with AIDS.

Pentecost reveals that the church is not made in our image but in the mosaic image of God. It shows us that the beauty of God is more fully revealed in the collective face of others and is distorted when particular cultures and languages are muted because they are different. The image of God at Pentecost is multilingual, multicultural, and multiethnic, not for a politically correct agenda, but because the gospel demands it. The gospel and the church are polyphonic.

In other words, your voice matters. Be yourself, not an imitation of someone else. *You* are a gift—old, young, male, female, PhD or no D at all, professor or student, northerner or southerner, healthy or sick, whether you sit in a pew, a Baldwin auditorium chair or a couch. There are gifts of the Spirit and Pentecost reveals that you are a gift of the Spirit, with your particular culture, ethnicity, voice, language, body, idiosyncrasies, interests, fields, talents, some of you with hair, and others of you without so much hair. You have something to contribute to the church and world that only you can do. Emory professor Gregory Ellison told me a long time ago, "Do you." What does Pentecost mean? It means if you don't do you, we can't really do us.

SERMON NUMBER 2: WHERE DID THEY COME FROM? (REVELATION 7:9–17)

Each week we pray, "on earth as it is in heaven" because our present doesn't yet match God's promise so we keep striving, praying, moving, pressing, working, going to church, attending Bible studies, singing hymns, taking communion, giving alms, and serving in the community. These are some signs that we desire "on earth as it is in heaven." We want God's future now, God's future present, and so many have yearned and dreamed for this moment that there are all kinds of end-of-the-world predictions throughout history.

Well before the end time imaginary predictions of the *Left Behind* book series, or the visions of Harold Camping, there was the year 1806. In that year, a domesticated hen in Leeds, England, appeared to lay eggs inscribed with the message "Christ is coming." Many people reportedly went to see this hen and began to despair of the coming Judgment Day. However, it was soon discovered that the eggs were not in fact prophetic messages of the future but the work of their owner, who had been writing on the eggs in ink and reinserting them into the poor hen's body. If it was the end of anything, it was the end of that poor hen! But well before hens or Harolds, well before any of these, there is the revelation of John, literally the "apocalypse" of John. Don't get nervous: I'm not making any predictions today and besides, John's vision is much more hopeful and joyful than the usual doomsday predictions we hear. It's much more expansive than the way we usually live or how we think.

"On earth as it is in heaven" but our present doesn't seem to match God's promise in this vision. "There was a great multitude that no one could count, from every nation, from all tribes and peoples and languages, standing before the throne and before the Lamb, robed in white, with palm branches in their hands." The palms are signs of joy and triumph. But even in what is considered to be utopia, the perfect world, God's world, God's eternal home, there's a question that arises from this encounter with diversity—every nation, all tribes, peoples, and languages. The question is, "Who are these, robed in white, and where have they come from?" Where did *they* come from? Here's someone who already knew the answer to his question. Sometimes we ask questions for which we already know the answer. Do I have to do my homework? Do I really need to make up my bed every morning? Do I need to practice piano today? Should I vote in the presidential election? Do you love me? Where did they come from? The elder who asked knew that "These are they who have come out of the great ordeal." He's referring to the persecution of Christians in Asia Minor, a time of brutality under Roman imperialism which is why Revelation is known as crisis literature. Christian martyrs, past and present, suffered and died for the faith all across the world.

Where did they come from? It's almost as if he's surprised. Like ants or spiders sneaking their way into our homes, we wonder where *they* came from. You know how we like to say "they" or "them" which is a way of saying "not us.". Not our church, not in our house, not in our social clubs and networks. Not in our graduating class at Duke. Not at our workplace or in our neighborhood. They. Moving into our neighborhoods so we quickly put up a "for sale" sign to take flight. They. Speaking a language that is not English and taking employment opportunities "away" from others. They. The way they dress. The way they practice their religion. They. Where did they come from? We (not they) may be in for the surprise of our lives when we see who is in that great multitude no one can count—from every nation, tribe, people, and language. They may not be in our circles but they have always been a part of the circle of God—they came from God, born of God, breathed into this world by God's love. God is not the problem. Look at this vision of John. No, we are the problem.

French philosopher Jacques Derrida and others are onto something when they attempt to deconstruct our binary oppositions. We love binaries. We adore either/or. White or black. Male or female. Rich or poor. Republican or Democrat. Faith or science. Them or us. Eastern Carolina barbeque or Western Carolina barbeque. Duke blue or Carolina Tarheel blue. The binary pits one thing against another with one being greater or better or more powerful. We function with an either/or mentality many times even when it comes to the Realm of God. Evangelical or mainline. But it's God's realm, not ours. Where did they come from? They aren't supposed to be here. They don't have the right ID. I never met them. God never asked me for a reference letter on their behalf. Where did they come from? When our operative theological modality is "they" we can quickly *other* someone and stick them in the object camp of non-human entity in order to control them. We adore the "or" but God is an "and" God with a wide tent, the great multitude that no one could count. Not you or you, but you *and* you. Our disjunctive or disjointed vision is why sometimes people don't know if we believe in justice or "just us." But just as suffering is non-discriminatory for this great number from every nation, all tribes, peoples, and languages, so is God's love, which will wipe every tear from every eye.

We may be an "or" people but God is a conjunctive God with a conjunctive imagination. "From every nation, from all tribes and peoples and languages." With all the talk about building walls and the treatment of immigrants and refugees ("they") and taking America back from "them," it's so critical to remember God so loved the world, not just the United States of America, because God has a conjunctive imagination. Every nation and all tribes and peoples and languages. And. This is not a vision of singularity but one of plurality. Not a "me" perspective but a "we" approach.

In 2014, the Duke alumni magazine did a special cover story on "The Changing Face of Duke." It focused on the growing and largest minority group on Duke's campus—the Asian and Asian-American student population with all of their various ethnic identities. Some come from families who lived in the U.S. for years; others are international students. As the article says, this blooming presence on campus is creating a "ripple effect of institutional change along social, cultural, and academic lines."[12] But what was telling were some of the alumni responses to this cover story through such statements like "Duke's not for me anymore." Me or We?

When Jesus enters the temple in the Gospel of Mark, he reclaims that space as a house of prayer for all nations (Mark 11:17). The day of Pentecost in Acts is a vision of the joining together of many languages and cultures and ethnicities (Acts 2). It's a surplus of God. Even God, in God's own being, is conjunctive—Father and Son and Holy Spirit, three persons in one. Our future as the people of God is to see the promise to Abraham fulfilled so that by his offspring "all the nations of the earth [will] gain blessing for themselves" (Gen 22:17–18). It may take a while for God's promises to be fulfilled but they will be fulfilled. The "and" will come to pass. Both/and, not either/or. Every nation and all tribes and peoples and languages. As a familiar song teaches us,

> He's got the whole world in His hands
> He's got the whole world in His hands
> He's got the whole world in His hands
> He's got the whole world in His hands
>
> He's got you and me sister in His hands
> He's got you and me sister in His hands
> He's got you and me sister in His hands
> He's got the whole world in His hands.[13]

You *and* me. Conjunctive. God makes room for every nation, all tribes and peoples and languages. There's always room for more in God's economy.

> Get on board, little children
> Get on board, little children
> Get on board, little children
> There's room for many-a-more.
>
> The fare is cheap.
> All can go.
> The rich and poor are there.
> No second class upon this train.
> No difference in the fare.[14]

"There's room for many-a-more." There's room for the conjunctive "and." Rich *and* poor.

12. "Changing Face of Duke."
13. "He's Got the Whole World," in *Songs of Zion*, 85.
14. "De Gospel Train," in *Songs of Zion*, 116.

A choir is not a soloist, though some diva sopranos may think they are the choir. For a choir to be a choir we need "and." Sopranos and altos and tenors and basses. And what we've seen on campus at times with various protests and sit-ins, it's important to affirm both students and administrators if we are to live into the future vision of God. Not just students or administrators in bipolar opposition. I'm an administrator as well and it's dangerous and lethal to move into "they" the students or "they" the administration whoever that may mean. Where did "they" come from? When we do that, even as Christians, we can write people out of the book of humanity, living our disjointed vision rather than the conjunctive hope of God.

A conjunctive imagination recognizes that there is a number in the throne room of God which no one can number. To function with a conjunction theology is to openly embrace the other; it is anti-closure and anti-dominance. It is the embrace of the wide community of God and the "one great fellowship of love throughout the whole wide earth."[15] We get into trouble when we want to close people out, box them in, shut them down because they don't look like us, act like us, think like us. Just because they are not like us, we think they are not God's. But John's revelation of God's future reminds us that there's a great multitude that no one could count from east and west, north and south, meeting for fellowship in Christ. The holy rollers and the frozen chosen.

We may prefer a monochrome past or present, but we have a polychromatic future—ready or not. Will we make room in our hearts and lives for God's "and"—every nation, all tribes and peoples and languages? This is not about the collapse of the world but the collapse of myopic stereotypical thinking about others and the Realm of God, while building up a deeper Christian understanding of life in the conjunctive Jesus Christ who is both divine and human.

It's always been about conjunctions for God from the beginning when God created the heavens and the earth. There was an evening and there was a morning. Waters and sky. Plants and trees. Birds and sea creatures. Male and female. Always conjunction—winter and spring and summer and fall. Jews and Gentiles. There are no built walls in the Realm of God because those walls are torn down in Christ (Ephesians 2). Immigrants and refugees and orphans and widows, all citizens in God's city.

> In Christ now meet both east and west;
> in him meet south and north.
> All Christly souls are one in him

---

15. Oxenham, "In Christ There Is no East or West," in *Presbyterian Hymnal*, 317

throughout the whole wide earth.[16]

We may want to build walls but God will eventually just tear them down and finally we'll understand. We'll see the consummation of the holy conjunction when we gather with the angels and elders and the four living creatures and the mosaic multitude from every nation, from all tribes and peoples and languages, crying out to the one seated on the throne and to the Lamb with a conjunctive celebration of never ending praise, "Blessing and glory and wisdom and thanksgiving and honor and power and might be to our God forever and ever!" On earth as it is in heaven. Let it be so, now and forever. Amen.

BRIDGING AS THE BEGINNING AND ENDING

These two sermons, in honor of the Rev. Dr. Dale Andrews, reflect on two examples of Scripture that push us toward the building of bridges between people rather than the construction of walls on existential borders. Just as I have been apprenticed by Andrews' "bridge" scholarship and life, his habitus, through the power of the Holy Spirit, I hope that these sermons have apprenticed the reader in such a manner that he/she is baptized in the bridge-building life of the Spirit, who spans the past, present, and future.

This emphasis on bridging should not be too surprising as the Bible itself is a "bridge book" in that it is made up of different cultures, languages, writers, historical periods, and genres. Though there are differences in the canon, it functions as a literary bridge, not in an attempt to make the distinctions uniform, but to provide a type of unity that speaks of God in particular ways. Because the Bible is a bridge book and provides the general context for thinking and living the faith, the theme of building bridges can be discerned in multiple places in the "good book." Even Jesus Christ was a bridge-builder (Eph 2:14). In addition, these two sermons show that from the beginning of the church on the day of Pentecost, bridges were built between diverse peoples. In the future that God intends for us, as imagined in the book of Revelation, there will be bridges that invite us all to God's beloved community. It is inescapable. It is undeniable. We were made for each other. Therefore, our preaching and other forms of ministry should build bridges and not barricades.

---

16. Ibid.

27

The Wall at the Well
A Sermon on John 4:3–30, with Reflection

ANNA CARTER FLORENCE

THOUGHTS ON THE WAY TO THE SERMON

IT IS IMPOSSIBLE TO be a part of the homiletics community and *not* know Dale Andrews. His work is on all our syllabi and his students have become our faculty colleagues and his presence filled every room he entered. I have known who Dale is since my first Academy of Homiletics meeting when my teachers introduced me to him. But I didn't really get to know Dale until a few years ago, when we were both the primary teachers and lecturers at a Danish "Festival of Homiletics" in Copenhagen.

It was an amazing few days. After years of admiring Dale's books and following his career and having the occasional brief conversation at meetings, suddenly we were eating three meals a day together, deciphering the same city map together (in other words, getting lost), and sharing a remarkable experience of Scandinavian preachers in their own context. I will never forget it, or what it was like to hear Dale's work through Danish ears and eyes. We both loved to eat, so there was a lot of that—often with the two graduate students he had brought with him, to teach and preach alongside us. And I remember a walk one evening when we spotted the words "Black Lives Matter" painted (in English) in enormous letters, on the side of a building. two blocks from our hotel. We marveled at how moving it was to see prophetic speech from our own country so carefully and artfully rendered in a city across the ocean.

When I thought about what I might contribute to a *Festschrift* for Dale Andrews, I thought about that time together in Copenhagen, and what it was like to share our work with *preachers*. Preaching to preachers is very different than preaching to students, or colleagues, or even the Church. It really is its own peculiar form of practical theology. When I am with preachers, I get to reflect, for a few moments, on the work we (they) do, and the reasons we do it, and why it is such beautiful and difficult and impossible and essential work, and what I've learned from watching them do it. That's my job, in this odd division of labor professors have, between church and academy: to watch preachers do what they do, and then to try to say some things that will help them in that work.

When Dale and I were in Copenhagen, we gave lectures to Danish preachers that were warmly received, but what we *learned* from them in our exchanges after those lectures was so much more important. It made us stop and think about how our work might and might not reverberate in another context. It gave us new ideas, new insights, new heartaches to consider about the preacher's task in the Church of Denmark. And it sent us to our evening meals in local restaurants bursting to talk over all we'd learned, which we did, over good Danish beer. That's the gift of leading a conference with a colleague: you get to immediately think through all you've witnessed of preaching in another place, to begin to wrestle and ponder and engage it out loud, before the time comes for each of you to get on a plane and return home to your own settings and routines. In short, you get to do practical theology of a very peculiar kind, in space and time that is both fleeting and liminal.

The spring after Dale died, I was in San Antonio for the Festival of Homiletics, and Dale was on my mind as I prepared this sermon. Since the festival is an annual gathering of preachers, and I would once again be lecturing and preaching to *preachers*, I thought about Copenhagen, and how Dale's work had resonated so profoundly in another context. I thought about the theme of the conference—"Preaching on the Borders"—which struck me as the sort of preaching that calls for bridge-building. I thought about the questions that are vital for Dale and tried to bring them front and center as I wrote: What is it to read and preach the Word of God for transforming justice, but also as an ongoing conversation between theology and practice, liberation and salvation, the body of the church and the body of the preacher? What is it to sit down at a well in John 4 and to enter the text as a preaching practical theologian? What might we hear then that we would miss, utterly, if we were back home in our faith communities?

The preachers who heard this sermon were mostly from North American contexts quite different from the ones Dale first wrote of and into. But an Andrewsian practical theological homiletic matters for all preachers, perhaps in ways Dale never intended but would—I hope—delight in. His work builds bridges across cultures and contexts in ways I expect we will continue to notice and appreciate, for years to come. I, for one, will be looking for them-with gratitude, reverence, and hope.

THE SERMON: THE WALL AT THE WELL[1]

I've been reading John with my students, this semester. Every week, and all the way through. Not for *fun*, although it was, surprisingly; for a class, one I teach every Spring, with a different book of scripture. This year, it was John. And the first time we met to read through it, here's what my students said, after we had twelve chapters under our belts and were still facing the Farewell Discourse: "Wow. Jesus talks a lot."

It's true. Jesus talks more in the Fourth Gospel than in any other. And *this* text, from the fourth chapter, gets the prize for his longest conversation on record.

I hadn't noticed that, until my student Caitlin pointed it out to me, and told me I could share with you, in case *you* hadn't noticed, either. Think about it. The longest conversation Jesus has in the whole New Testament is with a person he wasn't supposed to be with, talk with, spend five minutes breathing the same air with, in public or private, in his office, by appointment, day or night, nowhere, no how, that's it; end of story. He wasn't supposed to talk religion with her, or politics with her, or Supreme Court nominees, or FBI directors, or whether she watched Fox News or CNN, or if she was married or single or registered with Match.com; he wasn't supposed to ask, and he wasn't supposed to care. The longest conversation Jesus has in the Bible is an exchange that should never have happened.

And it might not have, if the Samaritan woman had just let the moment pass. If when Jesus said, "Give me a drink," she had said, "Sure, whatever," and simply handed him the bucket. Without stopping to point out to him that he had just crossed a line, and it was not appreciated: "How is it that you, a Jew, ask a drink of me, a woman of Samaria?" She could have let it pass—some days, you just don't have the energy to get into it, with yet another strange man who says something mildly offensive—but this day she didn't; she chose to engage; and I wonder if that's how Jesus' longest conversation that should never have happened began.

1. The biblical citations are from the NRSV.

This is a great text for a Festival of Homiletics on-the-borders, crossing-the-borders theme: Get yourselves to Samaria, you preachers that live in Judea and Jerusalem, and find someone you're not supposed to be with, talk with, spend five minutes breathing the same scriptural air with—and get into a long conversation that the world thinks should never happen! Isn't that what we all need, right now? Especially those of us who happen to live in the United States of America (or next door, or an ocean away), when the country has gone crazy, and respectful discourse that lasts longer than two minutes or two tweets is almost extinct. Wouldn't it be incredible if the church could step up and model what real on-the-border, crossing-the-border, long conversation looks like—if *we* could teach the world to choose a well over a wall?

That's a message I need to hear. Those are the kinds of conversations I want to have: the kind where we choose to engage, with hope, rather than lash out, with glee. And if John 4 can help me get to that border, I'll take it.

But you knew I was going to say that. It's what you would say, if you were standing here. Sisters and brothers, let's choose conversation over retaliation. Let's go out on a limb and over the border to do it. I bet it's what you're preaching to your people at home right now—I *know* you are—and God bless you for it and through it.

What you probably *aren't* preaching to your people at home (because they're not a conference full of preachers in San Antonio) is what I'd like to think about today. This is the only week of the year when we get to read texts just for us, for the life and work of the preacher; and the ache of it, and the pain of it, and the madness and impossibility and relentless pace of it—but also the joy of it that passes all understanding. This is the only week when I get to read scripture and make you the reason. Or at least the work you do and the call we live. So that's what I'm going to do: read this text as if it held the wisdom for which preachers yearn. As if we preachers were the ones John had in mind when he wrote the fourth chapter of the Fourth Gospel, about Jesus and his longest conversation on record.

To read a biblical text with a festive homiletical context in mind, is an invigorating exercise. You get to ask some questions you usually don't, such as, "If you plunk a preacher into the middle of John 4, what happens? With which character in the story will she identity most? Whose sandals will he want to stand in or try on?" The nice thing about this text is that there are only two characters to choose from—the Samaritan woman and Jesus—and since John tells us we are not worthy to untie the thong of you-know-who's sandals (let alone try them on), that makes it an easy choice, where we get to stand. An easy choice, and a best practice, since relinquishing the Son of God subject position is usually smart, for preachers. We do far better standing in the shoes of the characters that get to interact with Jesus, as the Samaritan woman does, here.

So imagine this. You, the Samaritan woman, a.k.a. Preacher, coming to the well to draw water for your sermon, because it's noon, and the sun is high in the sky, and time is running out for you to put this sermon to bed by 5:00 o'clock, when you promised you'd be home. All the other preachers came to the well early. They were there at dawn, having set their alarms and brewed their coffee and diligently opened their laptops six hours before you did, and now, their sermons are uploaded and their afternoon is free. They don't have to come back to the well in the scorching heat of midday. They don't have to lower their buckets for water that might or might not jumpstart a parched brain. They haven't had five husbands, and a man who isn't their husband, a.k.a. Needy Parishioners That Go Way Back, clamoring for their attention and bossing them around, and treating them like servants they can fire at will and wives they can dump on impulse. Because that's what *you* were doing all morning: dealing with the needs of the ones who claim you. It tends to cut into your sermon writing time. And it means that when you *do* finally sit down to prepare, it's noon, and you're tired, and all the imaginative textual insights have gone into the buckets of other preachers. Everyone will see you slinking to the well at midday, well past the industrious preachers of early morning, but you don't have any choice. So you slam down your laptop and throw it in your bag and grab your bucket—which has not a drop of sermonic fodder left in it—and head to the well to see if you can haul up a Word from the Lord. Just one bucket full of sweet, fresh water that might revive a preacher-drought.

And then, imagine this. You, the Samaritan woman, a.k.a. Preacher, arrive at the well, and someone is sitting there, waiting for you; someone you don't recognize.

> Let me say that again.
> The One we proclaim
> is there at the well
> where you and I go
> in the heat of the day
> to fill up our buckets
> to water our sermons—
> and he's there every week, right on schedule.

I love how the text underscores this. Jesus left Judea, John tells us, and started back to Galilee, but he had to go through Samaria to get there, which as Karoline Lewis reminds us, isn't strictly true; there are other routes he could have taken to avoid it.[2] Stopping at Sychar isn't geographically necessary. But it's *theologically* necessary—and homiletically, too. Jesus has big news to spread. God so loved the *world* that God gave God's only Son. So borders don't matter anymore: the *world* needs to hear this, and a Preacher needs to tell it, which is why Jesus shows up in Sychar, where the preacher lives, and sits down at noon at the well.

And the preacher of course is preoccupied. Not focused on much but her own emptiness. Not in the mood for a long conversation. The clock is ticking: time to get an idea, find a good quote, douse that lectionary passage with the water it needs to yield, fast. By noon on sermon preparation day, a preacher just wants results, and something to say that the flock can feed on. It would be great if it were a Word from the Lord, but you're not always sure that it is; last week, it was hard to tell. So you open your Bible, or Bible Gateway on your smartphone, and pull up the passage, while you let down the bucket—oh no; it's John 14, again:

> I will not leave you orphaned;
> I am coming to you;
> in a little while,
> the world will no longer see me,
> but you will see me;
> because I live,
> you also will live;
> on that day you will know
> that I am in my Father,
> and you in me,
> and I in you—

—and on and on. Jesus just never stops talking in the Farewell Discourse; the sixth Sunday of Easter, and we're still saying goodbye—

> This is the spirit of truth
> whom the world cannot receive,
> because it neither sees him nor knows him;
> you know him, because
> he abides with you, and he will be in you . . .
> he abides with you, and he will be in you. . . .

—and you look up, and there he is, the Word Incarnate, perched on the edge of your well, in your town, watching you read. And would it be remiss of you to expect that he might be there to help you with this passage, so *you* can

---

2. Lewis, *John*, 53.

help the flock? Isn't he there to give you the prophetic and pastoral word of the week?

He is, but not in a form we expect. Jesus is not a sermon database. He is a talker, a *big* talker—in conversation, in dialogue, in discourse and debate. For Jesus, conversation is a form of abiding. To stay in conversation is to be in relationship. The longer we talk, the longer we *abide* with one another's lives and experiences, and joys and sufferings, and points of view and angles of vision, and insights and blindnesses, all of which are the human condition. Talking with us is how Jesus is one of us. And I think conversation is his favorite part about being human—in John's gospel, anyway.

So now imagine this. You, the Samaritan woman, a.k.a. Preacher, looking up from your scripture passage of the week, to see Jesus sitting down at the very well you came to plumb, in the heat of the day and the pressure of the moment. And instead of offering to fill your bucket for you, like the Easter Sermon Rabbit, he asks you a question—*your* question, actually. The one you came to the well to ask, but didn't dare to say out loud: "Give me a drink."

"Give me a drink." That's a very different question from, "Give me a sermon." Which is all that came to mind, after the morning you had carefully set aside for sermon preparation exploded in a dozen pastoral directions. All the other preachers were putting the finishing flourishes on their manuscripts, and you were running around with a hose, putting out brush fires all over the church. You were worried and distracted by many things—another week of playing Martha, when you meant to be Mary, sitting at the Lord's feet and taking your time with the words. At noon, you're past that window of time. So "Give me a drink," becomes "Give me a sermon," and you know the order is off, somehow, but who has time to be thirsty when the bulletin, not to mention the sermon, must be done by 5:00?

"He abides with you, and he will be in you." . . .

At the well, Jesus knows what you need. He knows the question you need to ask. And since you cannot, he'll ask it for you, to stir a memory of living water, gushing up to eternal life. "Give me a drink."

It may catch you off guard, that question. It may strike you as impertinent, or rude, or even a little offensive, that Jesus—the way, the truth and the life—would begin this meeting at the well with a request for something you so clearly cannot provide. Not with that bucket. And you do have the option to not engage. Slop up some water and hand it to him, without a word. Put your head in your smartphone and walk away. Look to someone else to help you with that John 14 passage. Some weeks, it's what we do, as preachers: we're so steamed by the time we get to the well that we can't even engage

Jesus. Even though we know he's going to be sitting there waiting for us, just like last week, with the same jarring question on his lips: *"Give me a drink."*

We can choose to walk away. Or we can remember that Jesus' question is just a conversation starter. It's his way of getting our attention and slowing us down and reminding us to breathe . . . and let the walls of defense go . . . so we can sit down, right there at the well, for a drink and a conversation we really need to have.

That conversation is our weekly abiding practice. We never think we have time for it. We usually forget it's on our calendars. But Jesus doesn't. He keeps passing through Samaria, stopping at Sychar every week. At the hottest and worst time of the day for sermon conversations, I might add—unless you have a cool drink, first, from the well of living water, gushing up to eternal life.

And afterwards? You're ready to preach. You're ready to go announce to the whole village, "Come see a man who told me everything I've never asked! He can't be the Messiah, can he?"

Here's a thought. What if the hardest sermons to prepare are just long conversations that were always supposed to have happened, the ones that take us across a bridge and over the border and out on a limb?

I think Jesus really enjoys those. He calls it *abiding*. And I think he secretly hopes that we come to the well thirsty, and ready to settle in for what might become the longest conversation on record.

Just tell him you have to be home by 5:00.

Appendix A
New to Whom?

DALE P. ANDREWS

MOST REVIEWS OF THE "new homiletic" that I have encountered agree upon a few central figures of this mid-twentieth century phenomenon that extends into the present-day affairs of homiletics. H. Grady Davis, David James Randolph, and Fred Craddock have helped to formulate pedagogical shape to this so-called "new homiletic" in the theological academy and many mainline churches. We are indeed in their debt for identifying and calling for an expanding impact of preaching that underscores the experiences of listeners and the experience of listening to sermons.

Perhaps the beginning point of this developing new homiletic was to understand the sermon as an event in time, or rather a movement in time.[1] Understanding and experience are part of the speaking-hearing event. Davis introduces the idea of inductive continuity as one that moves through the particulars of our experiences to arrive at the central idea of the sermon.[2] Of course that central idea may come toward the end of the sermon or could be established midway, which would likely then require a shift in design.

Later, Craddock would expand upon the use of induction to emphasize the fundamental principle here is to identify with the experiences of the anticipated listeners.[3] Part of the decision-making process that goes into the sermon involves the kind of experience the preacher desires to arouse in the sermon and by the sermon. The experiences of the hearers are vital to the

---

1. H. Grady Davis, *Design for Preaching*, 161.
2. Ibid., 176–77.
3. Fred B. Craddock, *As One without Authority*, 59.

experience of God's revelation in and through the sermon. Perhaps, more dramatic to the period of his writing, Craddock stresses the hearer could then complete the sermon. The preachers no longer hold sole control of the conclusions, if ever they really did. Craddock anticipates a major challenge to induction in the fear of subjectivism or relativism run rampant. The question for him is not whether truth is subjective, but rather if we ever can know truth apart from appropriating it or experiencing it.[4]

In the middle of all this, Randolph steps forward to correlate the new hermeneutic to homiletics. The preaching event is a happening in which God and hearers enter an encounter, right along with the preacher.[5] The text and the listeners are not simply held in juxtaposition. The task is to relate the message of the sermon into the realities of the hearers' lives.[6] In his "new homiletic" Randolph seizes upon what the sermon "does" in the lives or situations of its hearers.

Even in facing great risk in oversimplifying the emergence of the "new homiletic," I cannot help but think that to characterize these observations as a new age creation for both the theological academy and churches alike only further evidences the nature of hegemony that leads cultures in dominance to define broadly human history based only in the experiences of that cultural dominance. Perhaps this question itself raises queries in the subjectivism of interpretation of human experience.

My point is much more basic, however. The "new homiletic" was not new to many traditions of oral culture and folk preaching. In particular, the "new homiletic" was never new to black preaching traditions. Whether one refers to induction, narrative preaching, story-telling, phenomenological experience, the preaching event, a happening, an encounter, a movement, hearer participation, hearer response, or the exigency of contemporary language and immediate experience, the new homiletic mirrors long established black preaching traditions, not to mention others. These traditions are not disparate or loosely held either. They form the development of African American homiletics through the eighteenth and nineteenth centuries and well into the twentieth century alongside the "new homiletic." I am somewhat surprised this observation did not become a prominent feature of this new homiletic. Randolph goes as far as to name the rise of the Civil Rights Movement with its preaching from such figures as Martin Luther King, Jr. among the central factors in "the renewal of preaching," but stops short of recognizing its heritage and development throughout African

---

4. Ibid., 70.
5. David James Randolph, *The Renewal of Preaching*, 5–6.
6. Ibid., 16.

American preaching and other cultures of black preaching. But he does not stand alone in the misnomer of the "new homiletic."

Perhaps a major cause for this oversight is the reality that black preaching was not central to theological curricula in seminaries or among the dominating denominations. Sorry to say, these conditions pervade in many ways today. Black preaching traditions, instead, have developed in mentoring methods of teaching preaching, otherwise characterized as apprenticeship methods of learning preaching, primarily within black churches. These methods gather around the encounter between constructive communication and experiential listening. As such, I maintain, the preaching encounter or event is actually a re-encounter. The preacher seeks an encounter with God's self-revealing Word in sermon preparations, but in the context of the anticipated hearer lives and actual listening experience. This encounter guides the construction of sermons, not to mention the mentoring-apprenticing process in teaching-learning preaching that emerges from the re-encounter of the preaching event.

In essence, the mentoring-apprenticing process of black preaching presses the induction movement into the pedagogical process itself of homiletics. The re-encounter of the preaching event invites the listeners to participate in shaping that event, quite potentially then reshaping the sermon event into its own encounter, building upon the preacher's anticipated re-encounter or perhaps even moving beyond it.

Much of what is commonly published in preaching is what I refer to as homiletic hermeneutics, as it is also in black preaching texts. I, along with many others teaching black preaching, are often approached by colleagues in the Academy of Homiletics in search of texts that shape pedagogy for teaching black preaching. This I believe is the task of a potential "new homiletic"—a task that translates the mentor-apprentice models of black preaching into accessible pedagogy for the theological homiletic classroom cross culturally. And so it is a task that consumes my current research and writing!

Appendix B
A Partial Bibliography of the Works of Dale P. Andrews

BOOKS

Black Practical Theology. Waco: Baylor University Press, 2015. Co-edited with Robert London Smith Jr.

Preaching God's Transforming Justice: A Lectionary Commentary, Year A. Louisville: Westminster John Knox, 2013. Co-edited with Dawn Ottoni-Wilhelm and Ronald J. Allen.

Preaching God's Transforming Justice: A Lectionary Commentary, Year C. Louisville: Westminster John Knox, 2012. Co-edited with Dawn Ottoni-Wilhelm and Ronald J. Allen.

Preaching God's Transforming Justice: A Lectionary Commentary, Year B. Louisville: Westminster John Knox, 2011. Co-edited with Dawn Ottoni-Wilhelm and Ronald J. Allen.

New Proclamation: Advent through Holy Week, Year A, 2004–2005. Minneapolis: Augsburg Fortress Press, 2004. Co-authored with Herman C. Waetjen, Jack Dean Kingsbury, Alice L. Laffey, with Harold Rast.

Listening to Listeners: Homiletical Case Studies. St. Louis: Chalice, 2004. Co-authored with John S. McClure, Ronald J. Allen, L. Susan Bond, Daniel P. Moseley, and G. Lee Ramsey, Jr.

Practical Theology for Black Churches: Bridging Black Theology and African American Folk Religion. Louisville: Westminster John Knox, 2002.

JOURNAL SPECIAL ISSUE

"Afrofuturism in Black Theology-Race, Gender, Sexuality, and the State of Black Religion in the Black Metropolis." *Black Theology: An International Journal* 14 (2016) 2–5. Special issue co-edited with Terrance Dean.

CHAPTERS IN BOOKS

"African American Practical Theology." In *Opening the Field of Practical Theology*, edited by Kathleen A. Cahalan and Gordon Mikoski, 11–30. New York: Rowman & Littlefield, 2014.

"Matthew 3:7-12, Matthew 3:13-17, Matthew 4:1-11." In *Feasting on the Gospels—Matthew*. Volume 1. Edited by Cynthia A. Jarvis and E. Elizabeth Johnson. Feasting on the Word Commentary. Louisville: Westminster John Knox, 2013.

"Race and Racism." In *The Companion to Practical Theology*, edited by Bonnie J Miller-McLemore, 401–11. Wiley-Blackwell Companions to Religion. Oxford: Wiley-Blackwell, 2012.

"A Response: Narrative Renewed." In *The Renewed Homiletic*, edited by O. Wesley Allen Jr., 96–104. Minneapolis: Fortress, 2010.

"African American Preaching and Sermonic Traditions." In *African American Religious Cultures*, edited by Anthony Pinn, 477–90. Santa Barbara: ABC-CLIO Books, 2009.

"African American Apprenticeship." In *New Interpreter's Handbook on Preaching*, edited by Paul Scott Wilson. Nashville: Abingdon, 2008.

"African American Biblical Interpretation." In *New Interpreter's Handbook on Preaching*, edited by Paul Scott Wilson. Nashville: Abingdon. 2008.

"Hebrews 10, Titus 2, Hebrews 1." In *Feasting on the Word: Preaching the Revised Common Lectionary*, edited by David Bartlett and Barbara Brown Taylor. Louisville: Westminster John Knox, 2008–2010.

"Job 42, Ruth 1, Wisdom of Solomon 3." In *Feasting on the Word: Preaching the Revised Common Lectionary*, edited by David Bartlett and Barbara Brown Taylor. Louisville: Westminster John Knox, 2008–2010.

"Black Preaching Praxis." In *Black Church Studies*, edited by Stacey Floyd Thomas et al., 203–25. Nashville: Abingdon, 2007.

"The Tower of Pulpits." In *African American Religious Life and the Story of Nimrod*, edited by Anthony B. Pinn and Allen Dwight Callahan, 193–213. New York: Palgrave MacMillan, 2007–2008.

"Foreword." In *The Everything Martin Luther King, Jr. Book*, by Jessica McElrath, xii–xiv. Cincinnati: Adams Media, F & W Publications, 2007.

"Preaching a Just Word in Privileged Pulpits: Healing Affluenza." In *Just Preaching: Prophetic Voices for Economic Justice*, edited by André Resner, Jr., 169–77. St. Louis: Chalice, 2003.

ARTICLES

"Do You Know Your Proper Place? Is There a Crisis in Black Preaching?" *Insights* 127/1. (Fall 2011) 20–24.

"Global Conflict and the Preaching Tradition of Martin Luther King, Jr." *Faith and International Affairs* 6/1 (Spring 2008) 61–63.

"The Living Legacy of Martin Luther King, Jr: Preaching What God's Care Requires." *Boston Theological Institute Bulletin* (2008).

"Back and Forward," *Family Ministry: Empowering through Faith* 20/4 (Winter 2006–Spring 2007) 94–95.

"Teaching Black Preaching: Homiletic Instruction as Pre-Encounter." *The African American Pulpit Journal* (Winter 2006–2007).

"Learning How to Care." *Family Ministry: Empowering through Faith* 20.3 (Fall 2006).

"Teaching Black Preaching: Encounter and Reencounter." *The African American Pulpit Journal* (Fall 2006).

"New to Whom?" *Homiletix E-Forum*, www.homiletics.org, Academy of Homiletics (Fall 2006).

"On Theology and Praxis." *Focus*, Boston University, School of Theology (Winter 2005–2006).

"Preaching the Lesson." *Lectionary Homiletics*, (four essays) March 6, 13, 20, and 27. 16 2. February–March 2005.

"Reaching Out Without Overtaking." *Family Ministry: Empowering through Faith* 20.1 (Spring 2006).

"Seeking Restoration." *Family Ministry: Empowering through Faith* 20.2 (Summer 2006) 59–60.

"Transforming Ministry." *Family Ministry: Empowering through Faith* 19.4 (Winter 2005) 79–80.

"The Ancestors Have Just Increased in Elegance." *Family Ministry: Empowering through Faith* 19.3 (Fall 2005).

"Losing Our Minds!" *Family Ministry Journal: Empowering through Faith*, Guest Editor 18.3 (Fall 2004).

"Encounters and Being." *Family Ministry Journal: Empowering through Faith*. Guest Editor 18.2 (Summer 2004) 6–8.

"Author's Reply." *Practical Theology for Black Churches. Conversations in Religion and Theology* (November 2003).

"Congregational Life: Results of the Third Survey of Racial-Ethnic Members of the PC(USA)." Louisville: Research Services, PC (USA). Spring 2001.

"The Lure of Cotton Candy." *Biblical Preaching Journal* (Winter 2001).

"The Boy Wonder (Luke 2:41–51)." *Biblical Preaching Journal* (Fall 1997).

"Advent 3." *Word and Witness*. Liturgical Publications (Winter 1996).

"Epiphany." *Word and Witness*. Liturgical Publications. (Winter 1995).

"Lent 2." *Word and Witness*. Liturgical Publications. (Spring 1995).

SERMONS/BOOK CONTRIBUTIONS

"Measuring Grace?" In *Family Ministry: Empowering through Faith* 19.1 (Spring 2005).

"Possibly a Porcupine Problem." In *Preaching 1 Corinthians 13*, edited by Susan K. Hedahl and Richard P. Carson. St. Louis: Chalice, 2001.

Bibliography

Alexander, Michelle. *The New Jim Crow: Mass Incarceration in the Age of Colorblindness.* New York: New Press, 2012.

Allen, Donna E. *Toward a Womanist Homiletic: Katie Cannon, Alice Walker and Emancipatory Proclamation.* Martin Luther King Jr. Memorial Studies in Religion, Culture, and Social Development. New York: Lang, 2013.

Allen, Ronald J. *Hearing the Sermon: Relationship, Content, Feeling.* St. Louis: Chalice, 2005.

———. "The Relationship of the Pastoral and the Prophetic in Preaching." *Encounter* 49 (1988) 173–89.

Allen, Ronald J., and O. Wesley, Jr. *The Sermon without End: A Conversational Approach to Preaching.* Nashville: Abingdon, 2015.

Allen, Ronald J., Dale P. Andrews, and Dawn Ottoni-Wilhelm, eds. *Preaching God's Transformative Justice: A Lectionary Commentary, Year A.* Louisville: Westminster John Knox, 2013.

Allen, O. Wesley Jr., ed. *The Renewed Homiletic.* Minneapolis: Fortress, 2010.

Andrews, Dale P. *A Covenant Model of Ecclesiology for Black Practical Theology: Spanning the Chasm Between Black Theology and African American Folk Religion.* Ann Arbor: UMI Dissertation Services, 1998.

———. "African American Practical Theology." In *Opening the Field of Practical Theology: An Introduction,* edited by Kathleen A. Cahalan and Gordon S. Mikoski, 11–30. Lanham, MD: Rowman & Littlefield: 2014.

———. *Practical Theology for Black Churches: Bridging Black Theology and African American Folk Religion.* Louisville: Westminster John Knox, 2002.

———. "Preaching Anti–Racism Amid the Backlash and Resistance of White Moral Injury?" Whiteside Lecture. Candler School of Theology, Emory University. September 21, 2016.

———. "Preaching Anti-Racism amid the Backlash and Resistance of White Moral Injury." Delivered at Old North Church, Cleveland. https://www.youtube.com/watch?v=vNfA25c5avI. February 7, 2016.

———. "Martin Luther King, Jr. Day (January 15)." In *Preaching God's Transformative Justice: A Lectionary Commentary, Year A,* edited by Ronald J. Allen, Dale P. Andrews, and Dawn Ottoni-Wilhelm, 68–71. Louisville: Westminster John Knox, 2013.

———. "Prophetic Praxis: Wrestling with the Moral Injury of Anti-Racism." Old North Church, Cleveland. https://www.youtube.com/watch?v=vNfA25c5avI February 7, 2016.

———. "Race and Racism." In *The Wiley-Blackwell Companion to Practical Theology*, edited by Bonnie J. Miller-McLemore, 402–4. Sussex, UK: Wiley-Blackwell, 2014.

———. "Teaching Black Preaching: Encounter and Re-Encounter." *The African-American Pulpit* (Fall 2008) 8–12.

———. "Teaching Black Preaching: Homiletic Instruction as Pre-Encounter." *The African American Pulpit* (Winter 2006–2007) 22–26.

———. "We're Never Done with the Work." https://www.faithandleadership.com/multimedia/dale-p-andrews-were-never-done-with-the-work.

Andrews, Dale P., and Robert London Smith, Jr., eds. *Black Practical Theology*. Waco: Baylor University Press, 2015.

Austin, J. L. *How To Do Things with Words*. Edited by J. O. Urmson and Maria Sbisa. 2nd ed. Cambridge: Harvard University Press, 1975.

Baldwin James, "Letter from a Region in My Mind." http://www.newyorker.com/magazine/1962/11/17/letter-from-a-region-in-my-mind.

Baldwin, Lewis V. "Who Is Their God? A Critique of the Church Based on the Kingian Prophetic Model." In *Ethics that Matters: African, Caribbean, and African American Sources*, edited by Marcia Y. Riggs and James Samuel Logan, 125–37. Minneapolis: Fortress, 2012.

Barber, William, II. "Speech at Democratic National Convention, July 27, 2016." http://www.dailykos.com/story/2016/7/28/1553896/-Moral-Mondays-Rev-William-Barber-IGNITES-the-DNC-Lead-With-Love.

———. "Moral Mondays: The New Fusion Politics." *UU World*, January 18, 2016. http://www.uuworld.org/articles/new-fusion-politics.

Barber, William, II, with Jonathan Wilson Hartgrove. *The Third Reconstruction: Moral Mondays, Fusion Politics and the Rise of a New Justice Movement*. Boston: Beacon, 2016.

Benhabib, Seyla. *Situating the Self: Gender, Community, and Postmodernism in Contemporary Ethics*. New York: Routledge, 1992.

Berry, Wendell. *The Hidden Wound*. Boston: Houghton Mifflin, 1970.

Bethany Theological Seminary. "Mission Statement." https://bethanyseminary.edu/about/mission-and-vision/.

Bond, Julian. "Civil Rights Memorial Dedication Speech." November 5, 1980. https://splcenter.org.memorial.

Bond, L. Susan. *Contemporary African American Preaching: Diversity in Theory and Style*. St. Louis: Chalice, 2003.

Bonhoeffer, Dietrich. *The Collected Sermons of Dietrich Bonhoeffer*. Translated by Douglas W. Stott. Edited by Isabel Best. Minneapolis: Fortress, 2012.

———. *Life Together: The Classic Exploration of Christian Community*. Translated by John W. Doberstein. New York: Harper, 1954.

The Book of Discipline of the United Methodist Church 2016. Nashville: United Methodist Publishing House, 2016.

Borg, Marcus. *Jesus: Uncovering the Life, Teachings, and Relevance of a Religious Revolutionary*. New York: HarperOne, 2006.

Brown, Teresa Fry. *God Don't Like Ugly: African American Women Handing on Spiritual Values*. Nashville: Abingdon, 2000.

Brueggemann, Walter. *Hopeful Imagination: Prophetic Voices in Exile*. Philadelphia: Fortress, 1986.
———. *The Prophetic Imagination*. Philadelphia: Fortress, 1978.
———. *The Prophetic Imagination*. 2nd ed. Minneapolis: Fortress, 2001.
Burrow, Rufus, Jr. "The Love, Justice, and Wrath of God." *Encounter* 59/3 (1988) 379–407.
Buttrick, David G. "Homiletic Renewed." In *The Renewed Homiletic*, edited by O. Wesley Allen Jr. 105–15. Minneapolis: Fortress, 2010.
———. *Homiletic: Moves and Structures*. Philadelphia: Fortress, 1987.
———. "Preaching in an *Un*Brave New World." *The Spire* 13/1 (1988) 12–13.
———. *Preaching the New and Now*. Louisville: Westminster John Knox, 1998.
———. The David G. Buttrick Certificate Program in Homiletic Coaching. https://divinity.vanderbilt.edu/programs/HomileticPeerCoaching.php.
Cahalan, Kathleen, and Gordon S. Mikoski, eds. *Opening the Field of Practical Theology: An Introduction*. Lanham, MD: Rowman & Littlefield, 2014.
Carson, Clayborne, and Peter Holloran, eds. *A Knock at Midnight: Inspiration from the Great Sermons of Reverend Martin Luther King, Jr.* New York: Intellectual Properties Management in association with Warner Books, 1998.
Center for Barth Studies. "The Bible in One Hand and the Newspaper in the Other." http://libweb.ptsem.edu/collections/barth/faq/quotes.aspx?menu=296&subText=468/.
"The Changing Face of Duke." http://dukemagazine.duke.edu/article/changing-face-duke
Chaves, Mark. "National Congregations Study." http://www.soc.duke.edu/natcong/Docs/NCSIII_report_final.pdf/.
Clebsch, William A., and Charles R. Jaekle. *Pastoral Care in Historical Perspective*. New York: Aronson, 1983.
Coates, Ta Nehisi. *Between the World and Me*. New York: Spiegel & Grau, 2015.
———. "Letter to My Son." https://www.theatlantic.com/politics/archive/2015/07/tanehisi-coates-between-the-world-and-me/397619/.
Coffin, William Sloane. *Credo*. Louisville: Westminster John Knox, 2004.
———. *A Passion for the Possible: A Message to U.S. Churches*. 2nd ed. Louisville: Westminster John Knox, 1995.
Commission on Accrediting. Association of Theological Schools. "Standards." https://www.ats.edu/uploads/accrediting/documents/degree-program-standards.pdf.
Conde-Frazier, Elizabeth. *Listen to the Children: Conversations with Immigrant Families / Escuchemos a los niños: Conversaciones con Familias Inmigrantes* (Spanish Edition). Valley Forge, PA: Judson, 2011.
Cone, James H. *The Cross and the Lynching Tree*. Maryknoll, NY: Orbis 2011.
Cooper, Burton Z., and John S. McClure. *Claiming Theology in the Pulpit*. Louisville: Westminster John Knox, 2003.
Couture, Pamela D. *Blessed Are the Poor: Women's Poverty, Family Policy, and Practical Theology*. Nashville: Abingdon, 1991.
———. *We Are not All Victims: Local Peacebuilding in the Democratic Republic of Congo*. Berlin: Lit, 2016.
Craddock, Fred B. *As One without Authority*. 1971. Reprint, St. Louis: Chalice, 2001.
———. Interview with Michael Duiduit. "From Class to Pulpit: Interviews with Fred Craddock and Walter Brueggemann," https://www.preaching.com/articles/from-classroom-to-pulpit-interviews-with-fred-craddock-walter-brueggemann/.

Crossan, John Dominic. *Jesus: A Revolutionary Biography*. New York: HarperCollins, 2009.

Daly, Kathleen. "Mind the Gap: Restorative Justice in Theory and Practice." 2002. https://www.griffith.edu.au/__data/assets/pdf_file/0016/50263/kdpaper19.pdf/.

"The David G. Buttrick Certificate Program in Homiletic Peer Coaching." http://divinity.vanderbilt.edu/programs/HomileticPeerCoaching.php/.

Davis, Dawn Rae. "Unmirroring Pedagogies: Teaching with Intersectional and Transnational Methods in the Women and Gender Studies Classroom." *Feminist Formations* 22/1 (2010) 136–62.

Davis, H. Grady. *Design for Preaching*. Philadelphia: Fortress, 1958.

Davos World Economic Forum Annual Meeting 2017. "The Great American Divide."

Dayringer, Richard. "Clergy and Depression." In *Dealing with Depression: Five Pastoral Interventions,* edited by Richard Dayringer. 107–126. New York: Routledge, 2012.

"De Gospel Train." In *Songs of Zion*, 116. Nashville: Abingdon, 1988.

Dewey, John. *A Common Faith*. Terry Lectures. New Haven: Yale University Press, 1934.

Dodd, C.H. *The Parables of the Kingdom*. London: Nisbet, 1935.

Douglas, Kelly Brown. *Stand Your Ground: Black Bodies and the Justice of God*. Maryknoll, NY: Orbis, 2015.

Dreyer, Jaco and Yolanda Dreyer, Edward Foley, and Malan Nel, eds. *Practicing Ubuntu: Practical Theological Perspectives on Injustice, Personhood and Human Dignity*. Berlin: Lit, 2017.

DuBois, W. E. B. *The Souls of Black Folk*. 1903. Reprint, New York: Dover, 1994.

"Duke University Strategic Plan." https://provost.duke.edu/wp-content/uploads/stratPlan2006-ch03.pdf/.

Dussel, Enrique. *Ethics and Community*. Translated by Robert R. Barr. Maryknoll, NY: Orbis, 1988.

Edwards, O. C. "Preaching and Pastoral Care." In *Anglican Theology and Pastoral Care*, edited by James E. Griffiss. 131–58. Wilton, CT: Morehouse-Barlow, 1985.

Edwards, O.C. Jr. *A History of Preaching*. Nashville: Abingdon, 2004.

Elliot, Charlotte. "Just As I Am, Without One Plea." In *The Chalice Hymnal*, 339. St. Louis: Chalice, 1995.

Ellison, Gregory C., II. *Cut Dead but Still Alive: Caring for African American Young Men*. Nashville: Abingdon, 2013.

Evans, Ieshia. Image. https://www.nytimes.com/2016/07/31/magazine/the-superhero-photographs-of-the-black-lives-matter-movement.html?_r=0/.

Evans, James H. Jr. *We Have Been Believers: An African-American Systematic Theology*. Minneapolis: Fortress, 1992.

Fant, Clyde. *Preaching for Today*. Nashville: Nelson, 1975.

Farley, Edward. *Practicing Gospel: Unconventional Thoughts on the Church's Ministry*. Louisville: Westminster John Knox, 2003.

Ferrise, Adam. "Cleveland officer who shot Tamir Rice had 'dismal' handgun performance." *The Plain Dealer*, December 3, 2014. http://www.cleveland.com/metro/index.ssf/2014/12/cleveland_police_officer_who_s.html.

Florence, Anna Carter. *Preaching as Testimony*. Louisville: Westminster John Knox, 2007.

Floyd-Thomas, Stacy, Juan Floyd-Thomas, Carol B. Duncan, Stephen G. Ray Jr., and Nancy Lynne Westfield, eds. *Black Church Studies: An Introduction*. Nashville: Abingdon, 2007.

Forsyth, P. T. *Positive Preaching and Modern Mind*. London: Hodder & Stoughton, 1907.
Fosdick, Harry Emerson. "What's the Matter with Preaching?" Reprinted in *What Is the Matter with Preaching Today?*, edited by Mike Graves, 7–19. Louisville: Westminster John Knox, 2004.
Francis Leah Gunning. *Ferguson and Faith: Sparking Leadership and Awakening Community*. St. Louis: Chalice, 2015.
Frank, Thomas Edward. *Polity, Practice, and the Mission of the United Methodist Church*. Nashville: Abingdon, 1997.
Frazier, E. Franklin. *The Negro Church in America*. New York: Schocken, 1973.
Frey, William H. "Mid-Decade: Big City Growth Continues." *Brookings Institute*, May 23, 2016. https://www.brookings.edu/blog/the-avenue/2016/05/23/mid-decade-big-city-growth-continues/.
Gadamer, Hans Georg. *Truth and Method*. Translated by Joel Weinsheimer and Donald G. Marshall. New York: Seabury, 1975.
Gavrielides, T. *Restorative Justice Theory and Practice: Addressing the Discrepancy*. Helsinki: Hakapaino Oy, 2007.
Gerkin, Charles V. *An Introduction to Pastoral Care*. Nashville: Abingdon, 1997.
———. *Prophetic Pastoral Practice: A Christian Vision of Life Together*. Nashville: Abingdon, 1991.
Gilbert, Kenyatta R. *A Pursued Justice: Black Preaching from the Great Migration to Civil Rights*. Waco: Baylor University Press, 2016.
Giuliano, Mark. "Don't abandon or blame the city, reclaim it." *The Plain Dealer*, June 11, 2011. http://www.cleveland.com/opinion/index.ssf/2011/06/dont_abandon_or_blame_the_city.html.
———. "From the Trenches." *The Plain Dealer*, September 4, 2014. http://www.cleveland.com/from-the-trenches/index.ssf/2013/09/from_the_trenches_r_mark_giula.html/.
Glaude, Eddie S. Jr. 2011 "The Heroic." November 20, 2011. W. E. B. Du Bois Lecture Series. Harvard University.http://aas.princeton.edu/blog/publication/pragmatic-reconstructions–the–prophetic-the-heroic-and-the-democratic/.
Goldsworthy, Graeme. *Preaching the Whole Bible as Christian Scripture: The Application of Biblical Theology to Expository Preaching*. Grand Rapids: Eerdmans, 2000.
Goodstein, Laurie. "Religious Liberals Sat Out of Politics for 40 Year. Now They Want In." https://www.nytimes.com/?action=click&contentCollection=Politics&region=TopBar&module=HomePage-Title&pgtype=article/.
Goto, Courtney. "Writing in Compliance with the Racialized 'Zoo' of Practical Theology." In *Conundrums in Practical Theology*, edited by Joyce Ann Mercer and Bonnie Miller-McLemore, 110–33. Theology in Practice 2. Leiden: Brill, 2016.
Graham, Elaine. *Between a Rock and a Hard Place: Public Theology in a Post-Secular Age*. London: SCM, 2013.
Gross, Alan G., and Ray D. Dearin. *Chaïm Perelman*. Albany: State University of New York Press, 2003.
Grundy, C. H. "Dull Sermons." *Macmillans* 34 (1876) 264–67.
Hanson, Paul D. "Prophetic and Apocalyptic Politics." In *The Last Things: Biblical and Theological Perspectives on Eschatology*, edited by Carl E. Braaten and Robert W. Jensen, 43–66. Grand Rapids: Eerdmans, 2002.
Hartshorne, Charles. "A Logic of Ultimate Contrasts." In *Creative Synthesis and Philosophic Methods*, 99–110. LaSalle, IL: Open Court, 1970.

Hays, Richard B. *Echoes of Scripture in the Gospels.* Waco: Baylor University Press, 2016.

"He's Got the Whole World in His Hands." In *Songs of Zion,* 85 Nashville: Abingdon, 1981.

Heitink, Gerben. *Practical Theology: History, Theory, Action Domains.* Translated by Reinder Bruinsma, 1993. Reprint, Grand Rapids: Eerdmans, 1999.

Heitzenrater, Richard P. "John Wesley's Principles and Practice of Preaching." *Methodist History* 37/2 (1999) 89–106.

———. *Wesley and the People Called Methodists.* 2nd ed. Nashville: Abingdon, 2013.

———. "Preface." In Albert C. Outler and Richard P. Heitzenrater, *John Wesley's Sermons: An Anthology,* 9–12. Nashville: Abingdon, 1991.

Herman, Edward S., and Noam Chomsky. *Manufacturing Consent.* New York: Pantheon, 1988.

Herman, Judith. *Trauma and Recovery: The Aftermath of Violence—from Domestic Abuse to Political Terror.* New York: Basic Books, 1997.

"Herstory of Black Lives Matter." http://blacklivesmatter.com/herstory/.

Hicks, H. Beecher. "Some Challenges and Promises of Contemporary Black Preaching." In *Shalom Papers: A Journal of Theology and Public Policy* (Washington: Church's Center for Theology and Public Policy, Wesley Theological Seminary) 2/1 (2000).

Hoge, Dean R. et al. *Money Matters: Personal Giving in American Churches.* Louisville: Westminster John Knox, 1996.

hooks, bell. *Teaching to Transgress: Education as the Practice of Freedom.* New York: Routledge, 1994.

Jacobs, Jane. *The Death and Life of Great American Cities.* New York: Random House, 1961.

Jacobsen, David Schnasa. "*Schola Prophetarum*: Prophetic Preaching toward a Public, Prophetic Church." *Homiletic* 34/1 (2009) 12–21.

Jennings, Theodore W. *Good News to the Poor: John Wesley's Evangelical Economics.* Nashville: Abingdon, 1990.

Jennings, Willie James. *The Christian Imagination: Theology and the Origins of Race.* New Haven: Yale University Press, 2011.

———. "What Does It Mean to Call 'God' a White Racist?" *Religion Dispatches* (July 17, 2013). http://religiondispatches.org/what-does-it-mean-to-call-god-a-white-racist/.

Jha, Sandhya Rani. *Pre–Post-Racial America: Spiritual Stories from the Front Lines.* St. Louis: Chalice, 2015.

Johns, Cheryl. "Preaching Pentecost to the 'Nones.'" *Journal for Preachers* (Pentecost, 2013). http://www.journalforpreachers.com/Pentecost-2013%20Johns.html.

Johnson, James Weldon. "Lift Every Voice and Sing." In *The Chalice Hymnal,* 613 St. Louis: Chalice, 1995.

Johnstone, Gerry, and Daniel W. Van Ness. *Handbook of Restorative Justice.* Portland, OR: Willan, 2007.

Juel, Don. "Encountering the Sower." *Interpretation* 56/3 (2002) 273–83.

Kaveny, M. Cathleen. *Prophecy without Contempt: Religious Discourse in the Public Square.* Cambridge: Harvard University Press, 2016.

———. "Prophetic Discourse in the Public Square." 2008 Santa Clara Lecture: Santa Clara University, November 11, 2008. https://www.scu.edu/ic/media--publications/santa-clara-lecture/prophetic-discourse-in-the-public-square.html/.

Kemmis, Daniel. "Living Next to One Another." *Parabola* 18/4 (1993) 6–11.
King, B. B. "Conversation with B. B. King." https://www.neh.gov/humanities/1999/mayjune/conversation/b-b-king-the-blues/.
King, Martin Luther, Jr. "Speech at Western Michigan University." Western Michigan University Archives and Regional History Collections and University Libraries. Wmich.edu/sites/default/files/attachments/MLK.pdf/. 1963.
"The King Philosophy." *The King Center* (2014). http://www.thekingcenter.org/king-philosophy#sub4/.
Kingwell, Mark. "Rites of Way: The Politics and Poetics of Public Space." Lecture presented at *Hope for the City*, The Old Stone Church, March 15, 2017 (published March 17, 2017). https://youtu.be/OUatfvfRDSc.
Kneebone, Elizabeth. "Urban and Suburban Poverty: The Changing Geography of Disadvantage." Penn Institute for Urban Research, February 10, 2016. http://penniur.upenn.edu/publications/urban-and-suburban-poverty-the-changing-geography-of-disadvantage.
Kornfeld, Margaret. *Cultivating Wholeness: A Guide to Care and Counseling in Faith Communities*. New York: Continuum, 1998.
Kotkin Joel, and Wendell Cox. "It Wasn't Rural 'Hicks' Who Elected Trump: The Suburbs Were—and Will Remain—the Real Battleground." *Forbes*, November 22, 2016. https://www.forbes.com/sites/joelkotkin/2016/11/22/donald-trump-clinton-rural-suburbs/#108616ea38b5/.
Kujawa-Holbrook, Sheryla A., and Karen B. Montagno, eds. *Injustice and the Care of Souls*. Minneapolis: Fortress, 2009.
Langford, Thomas A. *Practical Divinity: Theology in the Wesleyan Tradition*. Nashville: Abingdon, 1983.
Leslie, Kristen J. *When Violence Is no Stranger: Pastoral Counseling with Survivors of Acquaintance Rape*. Minneapolis: Fortress, 2003.
Lewis, Karoline. *John*. Fortress Biblical Preaching Commentaries. Minneapolis: Fortress, 2014.
Lincoln, C. Eric, *The Black Church since Frazier*. New York: Schocken, 1973.
Lischer, Richard. *The Preacher King: Martin Luther King, Jr. and the Word that Moved America*. New York: Oxford University Press, 1995.
Lomax, Tamura. *Jezebel Unhinged: Loosing the Black Female Body in Black Religion and Popular Culture*. Durham: Duke University Press, 2018.
Lowry, Joseph E. *Singing the Lord's Song in a Strange Land*. Nashville: Abingdon, 2011.
Maddox, Randy L. "Visit the Poor: John Wesley, the Poor, and the Sanctification of Believers" in *The Poor and the People Called Methodists: 1729-1799*, edited by Richard P. Heitzenrater 59–81. Nashville: Kingswood, 2002.
———. *Responsible Grace: John Wesley's Practical Theology*. Nashville: Abingdon, 1994.
Malbon, Elizabeth Struthers. "Narrative Criticism: How Does the Story Mean?" *Mark and Method: New Approaches in Biblical Studies*, edited by Janice Capel Anderson and Stephen D. Moore, 29–58. Minneapolis: Fortress, 1992.
Malcom X. "Field Negro Speech." https://www.youtube.com/watch?v=OFXXNzim1Yo.
Mayer, Milton. *Speak Truth to Power*, n.d. Archives of the American Friends Service Committee, General Administration, Information Services, Publications. Speak Truth to Power Correspondence, 1954.
McMickle, Marvin A. *Where Have All the Prophets Gone? Reclaiming Prophetic Preaching in America*. Cleveland: Pilgrim, 2006.

McClure, John S. *The Four Codes of Preaching: Rhetorical Strategies*. Minneapolis: Fortress, 1991.

———. *Preaching Words: 144 Key Terms in Homiletics*. Louisville: Westminster John Knox, 2007.

McClure, John S., Ronald J. Allen, Dale P. Andrews, L. Susan Bond, Dan P. Moseley, and G. Lee Ramsay, Jr. *Listening to Listeners: Homiletical Case Studies*. St. Louis: Chalice, 2004.

Meeks, Wayne. A., Jouette M. Bassler, Werner E. Lemke, Susan Niditch, and Eileen M. Schuller, eds. *The HarperCollins Bible Study Bible*. New York: HarperCollins, 1993.

Melton, J. Gordon. *Will to Choose: The Origins of African American Methodism*. New York: Rowman & Littlefield, 2007.

Mercer, Joyce Ann, and Bonnie J. Miller-McLemore, eds. *Conundrums in Practical Theology*. Theology in Practice 2. Leiden: Brill, 2016.

Mikulich, Alex, Laurie Cassidy, and Margaret Pfeil, eds. *The Scandal of White Complicity in US Hyper-Incarceration: A Nonviolent Spirituality of White Resistance*. New York: Palgrave Macmillan: 2013.

Miller-McLemore, Bonnie J. ed. *The Wiley-Blackwell Companion to Practical Theology*. Wiley-Blackwell Companions to Religion. Malden, MA: Wiley, 2012.

———. *In the Midst of Chaos: Caring for Children as Spiritual Practice*. San Francisco: Jossey-Bass, 2006.

———. "A Tale of Two Cities." Forthcoming.

Mitchell, Henry H. *Black Preaching: The Recovery of a Powerful Art*. Nashville: Abingdon, 1990.

Mitchell, Henry H. *Celebration and Experience in Preaching*. Nashville: Abingdon, 1990.

Moltmann, Jürgen. *Theology of Hope: On the Ground and the Implications of a Christian Eschatology*. Translated by James W. Leitch. New York: Harper & Row, 1967.

Monáe, Janelle. "Janelle Monáe Releases Visceral Protest Song, 'Hell You Talmbout.'" http://www.npr.org/sections/allsongs/2015/08/18/385202798/janelle-mon-e-releases-visceral-protest-song-hell-you-talmbout/.

Moore, Mary Elizabeth, and Almeda Wright, eds. *Children, Youth, and Spirituality in a Troubling World*. St. Louis: Chalice, 2008.

———. *Teaching from the Heart: Theology and Educational Method*. 1991. Reprint, Harrisburg, PA: Trinity, 1998.

Morgan, Cherríe Moraga, and Gloria Anzaldúa, eds. *The Bridge Called My Back: Writings by Radical Women of Color*. 4th ed. Albany: State University of New York Press, 2015.

Morrison, Toni. *Beloved*. New York: Random House, 1987.

Mulligan, Mary Alice, Dawn Ottoni-Wilhelm, Diane Turner-Sharazz, and Ronald J. Allen. *Believing in Preaching: What Listeners Hear in Sermons*. St. Louis: Chalice, 2005.

Niebuhr, Reinhold. *Moral Man Immoral Society*. New York: Scribner, 1960.

Nieman, James. "Why the Idea of Practice Matters," in *Teaching Preaching as a Christian Practice: A New Approach to Homiletical Pedagogy*, edited by Thomas G. Long and Leonora Tubbs Tisdale. 18–40. Louisville: Westminster John Knox, 2008.

Niles, Daniel Thambyrajah. "Just One Beggar Telling Another Beggar Where to Find Bread." at http://www.dictionary-quotes.com/evangelism-is-just-one-beggar-telling-another-beggar-where-to-find-bread-d-t-niles/.

———. *Preaching the Gospel of the Resurrection*. London: Lutterworth, 1953.

O'Conner, Colleen. "Blessed Aren't the Burbs." *The Denver Post.* January 31, 2006. http://www.denverpost.com/2006/01/31/blessed-arent-the-burbs/.
Ong, Walter J. *Orality and Literacy: The Technologizing of the Word.* New York: Metheun, 1982.
Outler, Albert C. "Pastoral Care in the Wesleyan Spirit." *Perkins School of Theology Journal* 25/1 (1971) 4–11.
Oxenham, John. "In Christ There Is no East or West." In *Glory to God: The Presbyterian Hymnal*, 37. Louisville: Westminster John Knox, 2013.
Parker, Evelyn L., ed. *The Sacred Selves of Adolescent Girls: Hard Stories of Race, Class, and Gender.* 2006. Reprint, Eugene, OR: Wipf & Stock, 2010.
Patton, John. *Pastoral Care: An Essential Guide.* Nashville: Abingdon, 2005.
Pauw, Amy Plantinga. "Attending to the Gaps Between Beliefs and Practices," in Miraslov Volf, and Dorothy C. Bass, eds. *Practicing Theology: Beliefs and Practices in Christian Life.* 33–50. Grand Rapids: Eerdmans, 2002.
Perelman, Chaïm, and Lucie Olbrechts-Tyteca. *The New Rhetoric: A Treatise on Argumentation*, trans. John Wilkinson and Purcell Weaver. Notre Dame: University of Notre Dame Press, 1973.
Postman, Neil. *Amusing Ourselves to Death: Public Discourse in the Age of Show Business.* 1985. Reprint, New York: Penguin, 2005.
Powery, Luke. *Dem Dry Bones: Preaching, Death, Hope.* Minneapolis: Fortress, 2012.
———. *Spirit Speech Lament and Celebration in Preaching.* Nashville: Abingdon, 2009.
Proctor, Samuel Dewitt. *Preaching about Crisis in the Community.* Philadelphia: Westminster, 1988.
Quinn, Robert. *Building the Bridge as You Walk on It.* San Francisco: Jossey-Bass, 2004.
Rab, Lisa. "Meet the Preacher Behind Moral Mondays." *Mother Jones*, April 14, 2014. http://www.motherjones.com/politics/2014/04/william-barber-moral-monday-north-carolina/.
Rambo, Shelly. *Resurrecting Wounds: Living in the Afterlife of Trauma.* Waco: Baylor University Press, 2017.
Ramsey, G. Lee, Jr., *Care-full Preaching: From Sermon to Caring Community.* St. Louis: Chalice, 2000.
———. *Preaching and the Rhetoric of Care: Forming a Pastoral Community for Care in the World.* Ann Arbor: UMI Dissertation Services, 1998.
Ramshaw, Elaine. *Ritual and Pastoral Care.* Philadelphia: Fortress, 1987.
Ransom, Reverdy Cassius. *Making the Gospel Plain: The Writings of Reverdy C. Ransom*, edited by Anthony B. Pinn. African American Religious Life and Thought. Harrisburg: Trinity, 1999.
Randolph, David James. *The Renewal of Preaching.* Philadelphia: Fortress, 1969.
Rawls, John. *Political Liberalism.* New York: Columbia University Press, 1993.
"Reader Response." *Glossary of Literary Theory.* http://www.library.utoronto.ca/utel/glossary/index.htm.
Resner, André Jr. ed. *Just Preaching: Prophetic Voices for Economic Justice.* St. Louis: Chalice, 2003.
Romero, Oscar. *The Violence of Love: The Pastoral Wisdom of Archbishop Oscar Romero.* Translated and compiled by James R. Brockmen. New York: Harper & Row, 1988.
Russell, Letty M. "The City as Battered Woman." In *Envisioning the New City: A Reader on Urban Ministry*, edited by Eleanor Scott Meyers, 152–55. Louisville: Westminster John Knox, 1992.

Sandage, Steven J., and Mary L. Jensen. "Relational Spiritual Formation." *Reflective Practice: Formation and Supervision in Ministry.* 2013. http://journals.sfu.ca/rpfs/index.php/rpfs/article/viewFile/268/267.

Sandage, Steven J., Mary L. Jensen, and Daniel Jass. "Relational Spirituality and Transformation: Risking Intimacy and Alterity." *Journal of Spiritual Formation & Soul Care* 1/2 (2008) 182–206.

Scharen, Christian B. *Fieldwork in Theology: Exploring the Social Context of God's Work in the World.* Grand Rapids: Baker Academic, 2015.

Schiffman. Lawrence. *From Text to Tradition: A History of Second Temple & Rabbinic Judaism.* Hoboken: Ktav, 1991.

Schultes, Peter. "They'll Know We Are Christians by Our Love." In *Chalice Hymnal,* 424. St. Louis: Chalice, 1995.

Schüssler Fiorenza, Elisabeth. *Wisdom Ways: Introducing Feminist Biblical Interpretation.* Maryknoll, NY: Orbis, 2001.

Seidman, Dov. Speech at the 2016 Fortune-Time Global Forum. *Fortune Magazine,* https://www.youtube.com/watch?v=B2ZqEBLk1-8/.

Sethwale, Beatrice. "Public Testimony." http://www.justice.gov.za/trc/report/finalreport/Volume5.pdf/, page 362, paragraph 28.

Sheppard, Phillis Isabella. "Womanist-Lesbian Pastoral Ethics: A Post-Election Perspective." *Journal of Pastoral Theology* 26/3 (2016) 152–70.

———. *Self, Culture, and Others in Womanist Practical Theology.* New York: Palgrave MacMillan, 2011.

Shriver, Donald W. "Repairing the Past: Polarities of Restorative Justice." *CrossCurrents* 57/2 (2007) 214–17

Shults, F. LeRon, Steven J. Sandage. *Transforming Spirituality: Integrating Theology and Psychology.* Grand Rapids: Baker Academic, 2006.

"The Great American Divide with Hamza Yusef." https://www.youtube.com/watch?v=uge3NuBHCuA/.

Singleton, George A. *The Romance of African Methodism: A Study of the African Methodist Episcopal Church.* New York: Exposition, 1952.

Smith, John Edward. *Experience and God.* Cambridge: Oxford University Press, 1974.

Smith, Robert London. *From Strength to Strength: Shaping a Black Practical Theology for the Twentieth Century.* London: Lang, 2007.

Snyder, Timothy. *On Tyranny: Twenty Lessons from the Twentieth Century.* New York: Duggan, 2017.

Speck, Jeff. *Walkable City: How Downtown Can Save America, One Step at a Time.* New York: North Point, 2012.

Starnes, Darryl B. Sr., "Leadership Seminar." Charlotte: Bureau of Evangelism, A.M.E. Zion Church, 2005. http://beamezion.org/resources/leadership/TheChurchandChristianDiscipleship.pdf/.

Storey, Peter. *With God in the Crucible: Preaching Costly Discipleship.* Nashville: Abingdon, 2002.

Storrar, William. "In the Hands of an Angry Electorate: Rhetoric in the Presidential Election." *Commonweal,* June 16, 2016, https://www.commonwealmagazine.org/hands-angry-electorate/.

Suchocki, Marjorie J. *The Fall to Violence: Original Sin in Relational Theology.* London: Bloomsbury Academic, 1995.

Swinton, John. *Becoming Friends of Time: Disability, Timefullness, and Gentle Discipleship*. Waco: Baylor University Press, 2016.

Taylor, Barbara Brown. "The Weekly Wrestling Match." In *What's the Matter with Preaching*, edited by Mike Graves, 171–85. Louisville: Westminster John Knox, 2004.

———. *When God Is Silent*. Cambridge, MA: Cowley, 1998.

Taylor, Gardner C. *How Shall They Preach*. Elgin: Progressive Baptist Publishing House, 1977.

Terrien, Samuel. *The Psalms: Strophic Structure and Theological Commentary*. Eerdmans Critical Commentary. Grand Rapids: Eerdmans, 2003.

Thomas, Frank A. *American Dream 2.0: A Christian Way Out of the Great Recession*. Nashville: Abingdon, 2012.

———. *Introduction to the Practice of African American Preaching*. Nashville: Abingdon, 2016.

———. *They Like to Never Quit Praisin' God: The Role of Celebration in Preaching*. Cleveland: Pilgrim, 1997.

Thompson, Derek. "Who Are Donald Trump's Supporters, Really?" *The Atlantic*, March 1, 2016 https://www.theatlantic.com/politics/archive/2016/03/who-are-donald-trumps-supporters-really/471714/.

Thompson, Lisa L. "In Search of Our Mothers Healing: Holistic Wellbeing, Preaching, and Black Women." *Homiletic* 41/1 (2016) 58–67.

———. *Ingenuity*. Nashville: Abingdon, forthcoming.

———. "Now That's Preaching! Disruptive and Generative Preaching Practices." *Practical Matters Journal* 8 (2015). http://practicalmattersjournal.org/2015/03/01/now-thats-preaching/.

Thurman, Howard. *With Head and Heart: The Autobiography of Howard Thurman*. New York: Harcourt, Brace, Jovanovich, 1979.

Tisdale, Nora Tubbs. *Preaching as Local Theology and Folk Art*. Fortress Resources for Preaching. Minneapolis: Augsburg, 1997.

———. *Prophetic Preaching: A Pastoral Approach*. Louisville: Westminster John Knox, 2010.

Toit, N. Bowersand du, and G. Nkomo. "The Ongoing Challenge of Restorative Justice in South Africa: How and Why Wealthy Suburban Congregations are Responding to Poverty and Inequality." *HTS Teologiese Studies / Theological Studies* 70 2 (2014). Article #2022, 8 pages. http://dx.doi.org/10.4102/hts.v70i2.2022.

Tolbert, Mary Ann. *Sowing the Gospel: Mark's World in Literary-Historical Perspective*. Minneapolis: Fortress, 1996.

townes, emilie M. "Walking on the Rimbones of Nothingness: Embodied Scholarship for Those of Us Way Down under the Sun." In *Ethics That Matters: African, Caribbean, and African American Sources*, edited by Marcia Y. Riggs and James Samuel Logan, 215–28. Minneapolis: Fortress, 2012.

Tran, Mai-Anh Le. *Reset the Heart: Unlearning Violence, Relearning Hope*. Nashville: Abingdon, 2017.

Tribble, Jeffery L., Sr. *Transformative Pastoral Leadership in the Black Church*. New York: Palgrave Macmillan, 2005.

Turpin, Katherine. *Branded: Adolescents Converting from Consumer Faith*. Cleveland: Pilgrim, 2006.

Tutu, Desmond. "Unfinished Business." https://mg.co.za/article/2014-04-24-unfinished-business-of-the-trc-healing.

Underwood, Ralph. *Pastoral Care and the Means of Grace*. Minneapolis: Fortress, 1993.

Vitello, Paul. "Taking a Break from the Lord's Work." *New York Times*, August 1, 2010. http://www.nytimes.com/2010/08/02/nyregion/02burnout.html?pagewanted=all.

Volf, Miroslav, and Dorothy C. Bass, eds. *Practicing Theology: Beliefs and Practices in Christian Life*. Grand Rapids: Eerdmans, 2002.

Washington, James M. editor. *A Testament of Hope: The Essential Writings and Speeches of Martin Luther King, Jr.*, New York: HarperCollins, 2003.

Watson, David Lowes. *Covenant Discipleship: Christian Formation Through Mutual Accountability*. Nashville: Discipleship Resources, 1991.

———. *The Early Methodist Class Meeting*. Nashville: Discipleship Resources, 1995.

Welch, Sharon. *Communities of Resistance and Solidarity: A Feminist Theology of Liberation*. Maryknoll, NY: Orbis, 1985.

Welker, Michael. *God the Spirit*. Minneapolis: Fortress, 2004.

Wesley, John. "The Danger of Riches," "Causes of the Inefficacy of Christianity." In *John Wesley's Sermons: An Anthology*. Edited by Albert C. Outler and Richard P. Heitzenrater. Nashville: Abingdon, 1991.

———. *Journal and Diaries IV*. Edited by W. Reginald Ward and Richard P. Heitzenrater. The Bicentennial Edition of the Works of John Wesley 21. Nashville: Abingdon, 1990.

———. "Letter to Miss March." *The Letters of the Rev. John Wesley*. Edited by John Telford. London: Epworth, 1931.

———. *The Methodist Societies—History, Nature and Design*. The Nature, edited by Rupert E. Davies. The Bicentennial Edition of the Works of John Wesley 9. Nashville: Abingdon, 1976.

———. "On Visiting the Sick." In *Sermons*. Vol. 3. Edited by Albert C. Outler. Nashville: Abingdon, 1984–1987.

———. *A Plain Account of the People Called Methodists*. Edited by Rupert E. Davis. Bicentennial Edition of the Works of John Wesley 9. Nashville: Abingdon, 1976.

White, Bishop Woodie W., "A Letter to Martin Luther King, Jr.," The United Methodist Church Official Web-Site, http://www.umc.org/news-and-media/in-letter-to-king-bishop-rejoices-over-election-of-nations-first-african-am.

Williams, Colin W. *John Wesley's Theology Today: A Study of the Wesleyan Tradition in Light of Current Theological Dialogue*. Nashville: Abingdon, 1960.

Williams, Starsky. "The Politics of Jesus." https://www.bing.com/videos/search?q=starsky+wilson++the+politics+of+Jesus&view=detail&mid=BF0F18ACB9AE86CBBB83BF0F18ACB9AE86CBBB83&FORM=/.

Wigger, John H. *Taking Heaven by Storm: Methodism and the Rise of Popular Christianity in America*. Urbana: University of Illinois Press, 2001.

Williams, Delores S. *Sisters in the Wilderness: The Challenge of Womanist God-Talk*. Maryknoll, NY: Orbis, 1993.

Williamson, Ian Todd, and Steven J. Sandage, "Longitudinal Analysis of Religious and Spiritual Development for Seminary Students." *Mental Health, Religion & Culture* 12/8 (December 2009) 787–801.

Wimberly, Edward P. *African American Pastoral Care*. Nashville: Abingdon, 2008.

———. *Moving from Shame to Self-Worth: Preaching and Pastoral Care*. Nashville: Abingdon, 1999.

Wink, Walter. *Engaging the Powers: Discernment and Resistance in a World of Domination*. Minneapolis: Fortress, 1992.
Witherington, Ben, III. *Isaiah Old and New: Exegesis, Intertextuality, and Hermeneutics*. Minneapolis: Fortress, 2017.
Wolfteich, Claire. *Mothering, Public Leadership, and Women's Life Writing: Explorations in Spirituality Studies and Practical Theology*. Theology in Practice 3. Leiden: Brill, 2017.
Zehr, Howard. *The Little Book of Restorative Justice*. Rev. ed. New York: Good Books, 2015.

www.ingramcontent.com/pod-product-compliance
Lightning Source LLC
Chambersburg PA
CBHW052145300426
44115CB00011B/1534